kare kano

his and her circumstances

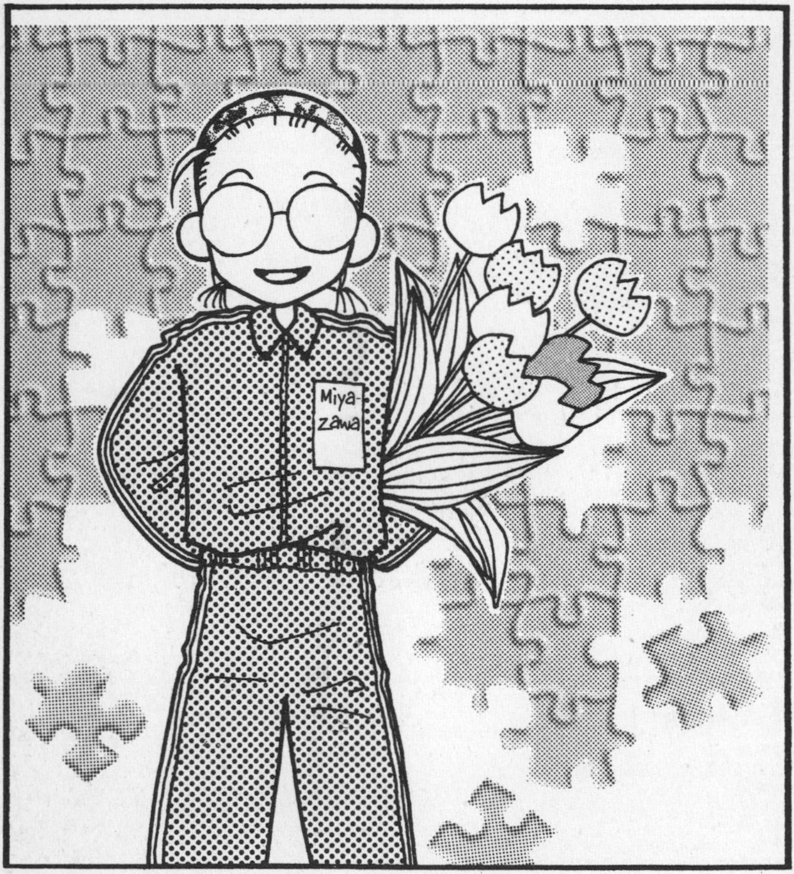
Miya-
zawa

ALSO AVAILABLE FROM 🌀 TOKYOPOP®

MANGA

.HACK//LEGEND OF THE TWILIGHT*
@LARGE (December 2003)
ANGELIC LAYER*
BABY BIRTH*
BATTLE ROYALE*
BRAIN POWERED*
BRIGADOON*
CARDCAPTOR SAKURA
CARDCAPTOR SAKURA: MASTER OF THE CLOW*
CHOBITS*
CHRONICLES OF THE CURSED SWORD
CLAMP SCHOOL DETECTIVES*
CLOVER
CONFIDENTIAL CONFESSIONS*
CORRECTOR YUI
COWBOY BEBOP*
COWBOY BEBOP: SHOOTING STAR*
CYBORG 009*
DEMON DIARY
DIGIMON*
DRAGON HUNTER
DRAGON KNIGHTS*
DUKLYON: CLAMP SCHOOL DEFENDERS*
ERICA SAKURAZAWA*
FAKE*
FLCL*
FORBIDDEN DANCE*
GATE KEEPERS*
G GUNDAM*
GRAVITATION*
GTO*
GUNDAM WING
GUNDAM WING: BATTLEFIELD OF PACIFISTS
GUNDAM WING: ENDLESS WALTZ*
GUNDAM WING: THE LAST OUTPOST*
HAPPY MANIA*
HARLEM BEAT
I.N.V.U.
INITIAL D*
ISLAND
JING: KING OF BANDITS*
JULINE
KARE KANO*
KINDAICHI CASE FILES, THE*
KING OF HELL
KODOCHA: SANA'S STAGE*
LOVE HINA*
LUPIN III*
MAGIC KNIGHT RAYEARTH*

MAGIC KNIGHT RAYEARTH II* (COMING SOON)
MAN OF MANY FACES*
MARMALADE BOY*
MARS*
MIRACLE GIRLS
MIYUKI-CHAN IN WONDERLAND*
MONSTERS, INC.
PARADISE KISS*
PARASYTE
PEACH GIRL
PEACH GIRL: CHANGE OF HEART*
PET SHOP OF HORRORS*
PLANET LADDER*
PLANETES*
PRIEST
RAGNAROK
RAVE MASTER*
REALITY CHECK
REBIRTH
REBOUND*
RISING STARS OF MANGA
SABER MARIONETTE J*
SAILOR MOON
SAINT TAIL
SAMURAI DEEPER KYO*
SAMURAI GIRL: REAL BOUT HIGH SCHOOL*
SCRYED*
SHAOLIN SISTERS*
SHIRAHIME-SYO: SNOW GODDESS TALES* (Dec. 2003)
SHUTTERBOX
SORCERER HUNTERS
THE SKULL MAN*
THE VISION OF ESCAFLOWNE*
TOKYO MEW MEW*
UNDER THE GLASS MOON
VAMPIRE GAME*
WILD ACT*
WISH*
WORLD OF HARTZ (November 2003)
X-DAY*
ZODIAC P.I. *

For more information visit www.TOKYOPOP.com

*INDICATES 100% AUTHENTIC MANGA (RIGHT-TO-LEFT FORMAT)

CINE-MANGA™

CARDCAPTORS
JACKIE CHAN ADVENTURES (November 2003)
JIMMY NEUTRON
KIM POSSIBLE
LIZZIE MCGUIRE
POWER RANGERS: NINJA STORM
SPONGEBOB SQUAREPANTS
SPY KIDS 2

NOVELS

KARMA CLUB (April 2004)
SAILOR MOON

TOKYOPOP KIDS

STRAY SHEEP

ART BOOKS

CARDCAPTOR SAKURA*
MAGIC KNIGHT RAYEARTH*

ANIME GUIDES

COWBOY BEBOP ANIME GUIDES
GUNDAM TECHNICAL MANUALS
SAILOR MOON SCOUT GUIDES

080503

kare kano

his and her circumstances

volume one

by Masami Tsuda

LOS ANGELES • TOKYO • LONDON

Translator - Jack Niida
English Adaption - Darcy Lockman
Editor - Paul Morrisey
Retouch and Lettering - Paul Tanck
Cover Artist - Gary Shum
Graphic Designer - Anna Kernbaum

Senior Editor - Julie Taylor
Managing Editor - Jill Freshney
Production Coordinator - Antonio DePietro
Production Manager - Jennifer Miller
Art Director - Matt Alford
Editorial Director - Jeremy Ross
VP of Production - Ron Klamert
President & C.O.O. - John Parker
Publisher & C.E.O. - Stuart Levy

Email: editor@TOKYOPOP.com
Come visit us online at www.TOKYOPOP.com

A **TOKYOPOP**® Manga

TOKYOPOP Inc.
5900 Wilshire Blvd. Suite 2000
Los Angeles, CA 90036

ISBN: 1-931514-79-8

First TOKYOPOP® printing: January 2003

10 9 8 7 6 5 4
Printed in the USA

kare kano

volume one

TABLE OF CONTENTS

TULIP = PASSION

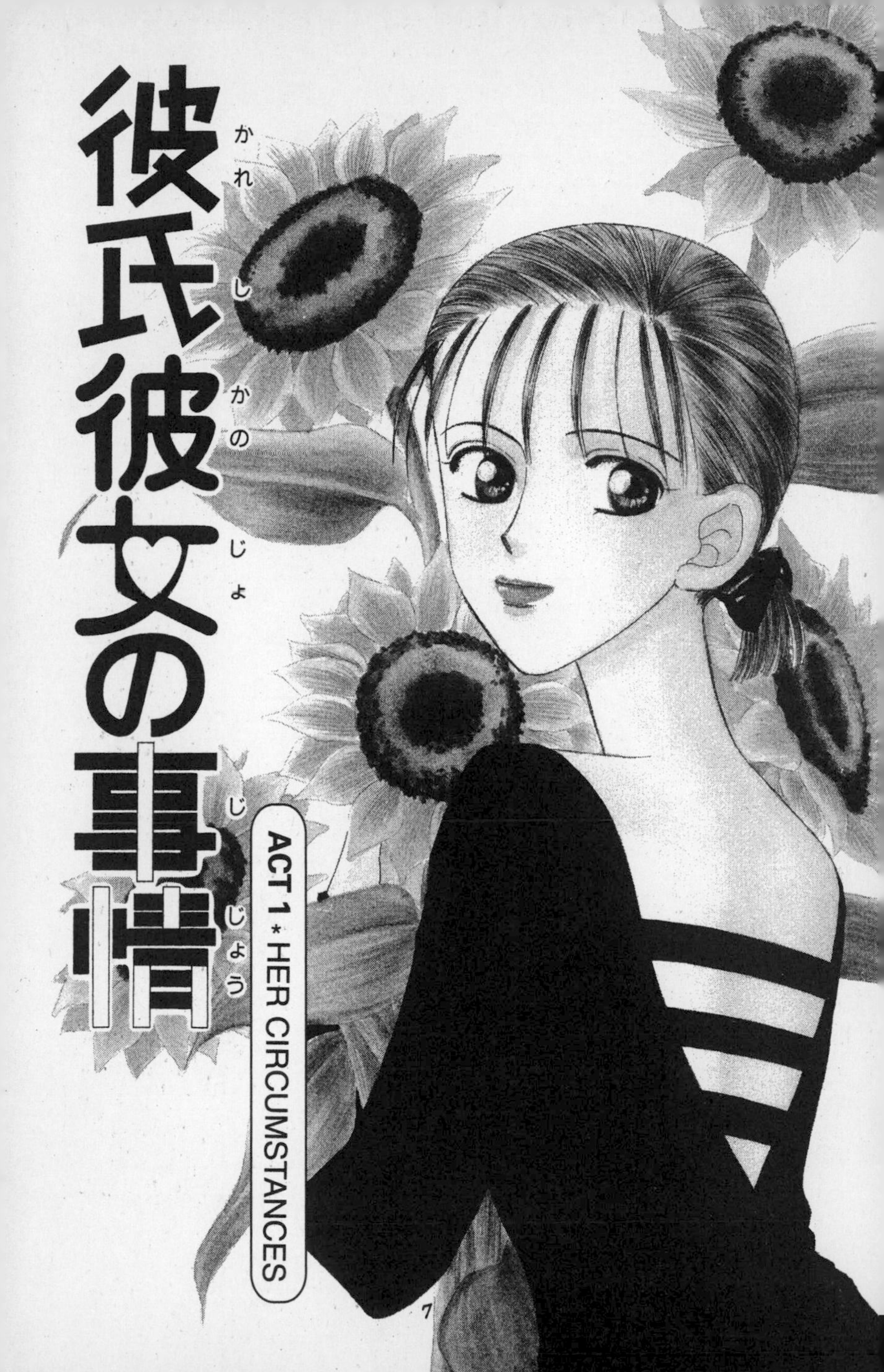

彼氏彼女の事情
ACT 1 * HER CIRCUMSTANCES

SOMETIMES, I WONDER HOW OTHER PEOPLE SEE ME.

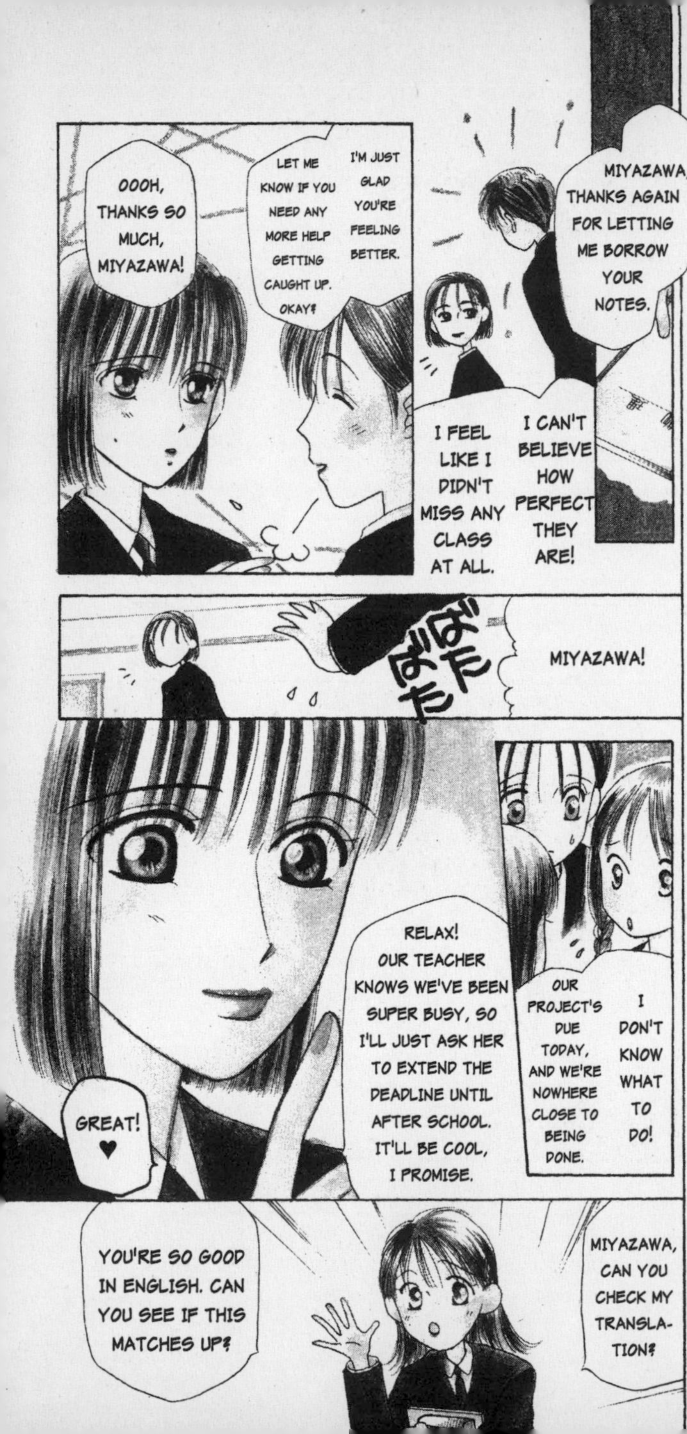
MIYAZAWA, THANKS AGAIN FOR LETTING ME BORROW YOUR NOTES.
I CAN'T BELIEVE HOW PERFECT THEY ARE!
I FEEL LIKE I DIDN'T MISS ANY CLASS AT ALL.
I'M JUST GLAD YOU'RE FEELING BETTER.
LET ME KNOW IF YOU NEED ANY MORE HELP GETTING CAUGHT UP. OKAY?
OOOH, THANKS SO MUCH, MIYAZAWA!
MIYAZAWA!
ばたばた
I DON'T KNOW WHAT TO DO!
OUR PROJECT'S DUE TODAY, AND WE'RE NOWHERE CLOSE TO BEING DONE.
RELAX! OUR TEACHER KNOWS WE'VE BEEN SUPER BUSY, SO I'LL JUST ASK HER TO EXTEND THE DEADLINE UNTIL AFTER SCHOOL. IT'LL BE COOL, I PROMISE.
GREAT! ♥
MIYAZAWA, CAN YOU CHECK MY TRANSLA-TION?
YOU'RE SO GOOD IN ENGLISH. CAN YOU SEE IF THIS MATCHES UP?

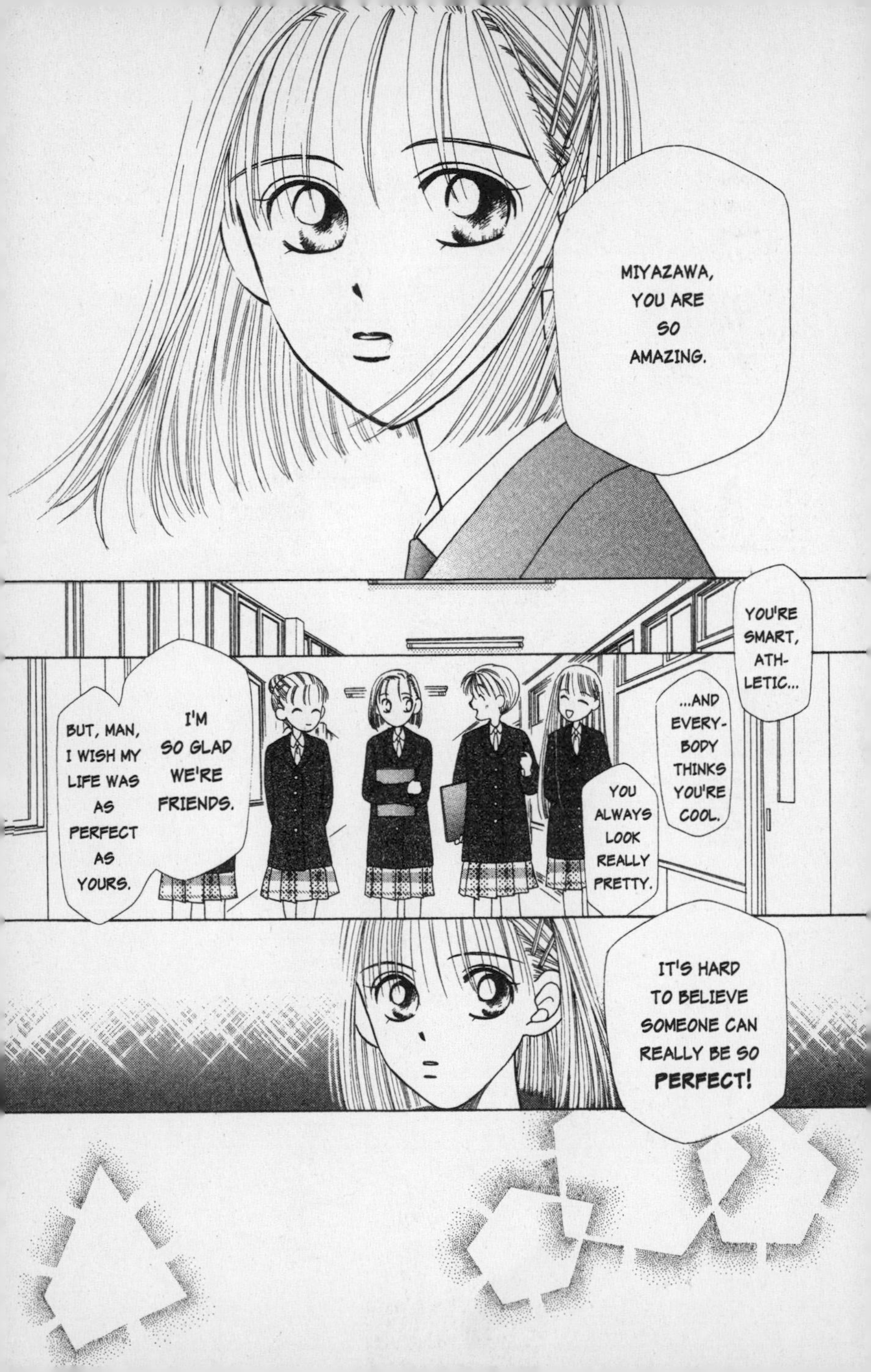
MIYAZAWA, YOU ARE SO AMAZING.
YOU'RE SMART, ATH-LETIC...
...AND EVERY-BODY THINKS YOU'RE COOL.
YOU ALWAYS LOOK REALLY PRETTY.
I'M SO GLAD WE'RE FRIENDS.
BUT, MAN, I WISH MY LIFE WAS AS PERFECT AS YOURS.
IT'S HARD TO BELIEVE SOMEONE CAN REALLY BE SO **PERFECT**!

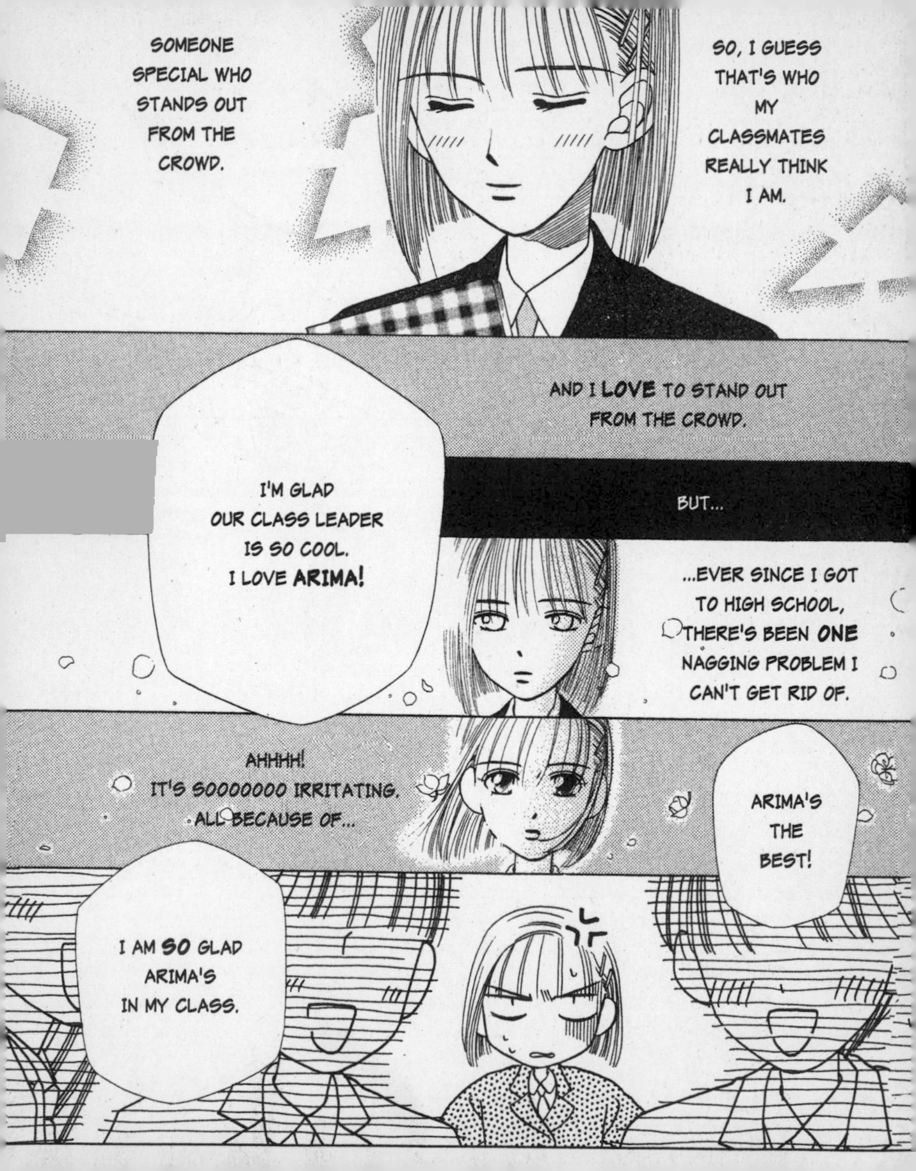
SO, I GUESS THAT'S WHO MY CLASSMATES REALLY THINK I AM.
SOMEONE SPECIAL WHO STANDS OUT FROM THE CROWD.
AND I LOVE TO STAND OUT FROM THE CROWD.
I'M GLAD OUR CLASS LEADER IS SO COOL. I LOVE ARIMA!
BUT...
...EVER SINCE I GOT TO HIGH SCHOOL, THERE'S BEEN ONE NAGGING PROBLEM I CAN'T GET RID OF.
ARIMA'S THE BEST!
AHHHH! IT'S SOOOOOOO IRRITATING. ALL BECAUSE OF...
I AM SO GLAD ARIMA'S IN MY CLASS.

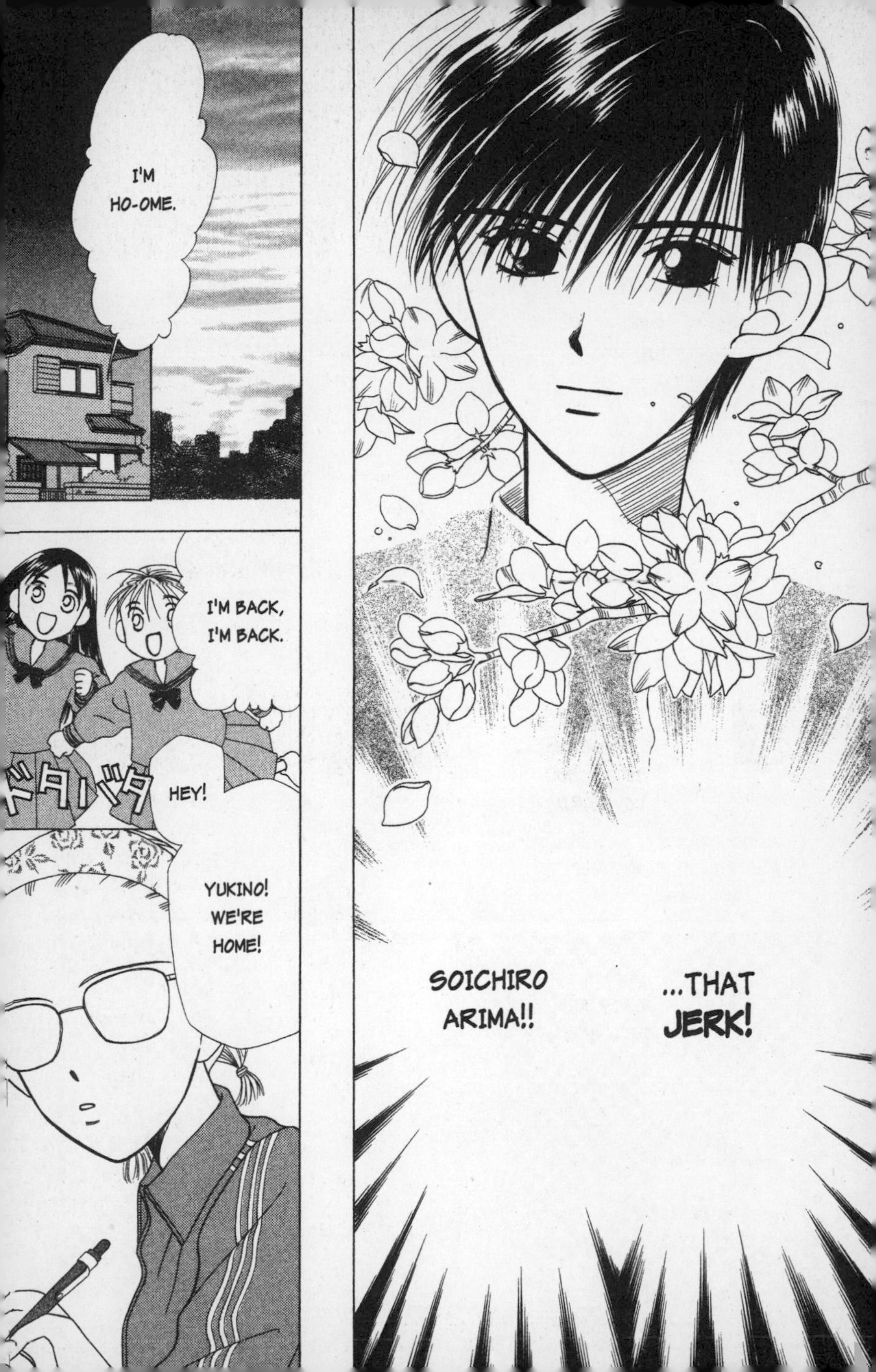
SOICHIRO ARIMA!!
...THAT JERK!
I'M HO-OME.
I'M BACK, I'M BACK.
HEY!
YUKINO! WE'RE HOME!

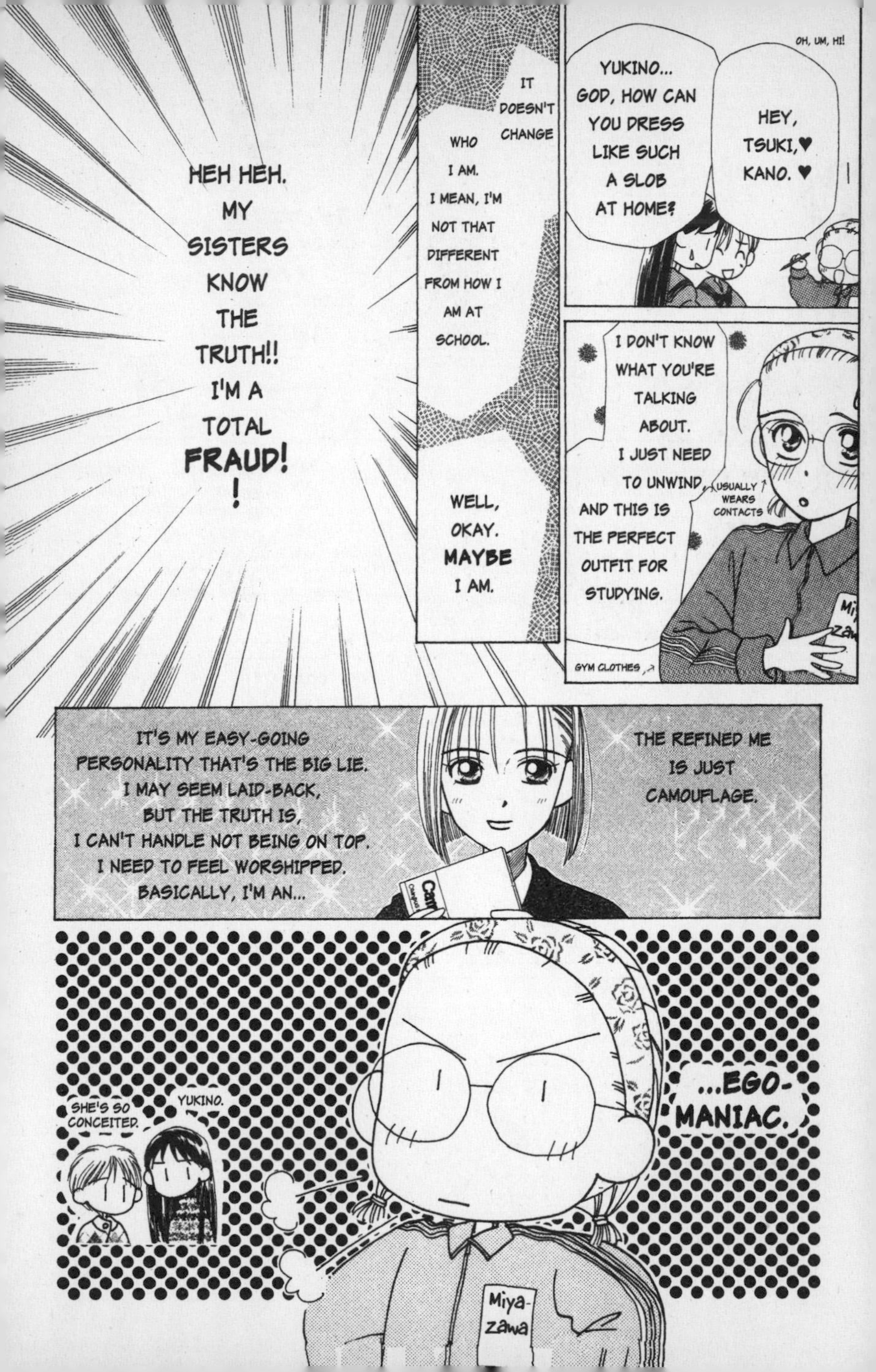
OH, UM, HI!
HEY, TSUKI,♥ KANO. ♥
YUKINO... GOD, HOW CAN YOU DRESS LIKE SUCH A SLOB AT HOME?
I DON'T KNOW WHAT YOU'RE TALKING ABOUT. I JUST NEED TO UNWIND,
USUALLY WEARS CONTACTS
AND THIS IS THE PERFECT OUTFIT FOR STUDYING.
Miya-zawa
GYM CLOTHES
IT DOESN'T CHANGE
WHO I AM. I MEAN, I'M NOT THAT DIFFERENT FROM HOW I AM AT SCHOOL.
WELL, OKAY. **MAYBE** I AM.
HEH HEH. MY SISTERS KNOW THE TRUTH!! I'M A TOTAL **FRAUD!!**
THE REFINED ME IS JUST CAMOUFLAGE.
IT'S MY EASY-GOING PERSONALITY THAT'S THE BIG LIE. I MAY SEEM LAID-BACK, BUT THE TRUTH IS, I CAN'T HANDLE NOT BEING ON TOP. I NEED TO FEEL WORSHIPPED. BASICALLY, I'M AN...
...EGO-MANIAC.
YUKINO.
SHE'S SO CONCEITED.
Miya-zawa

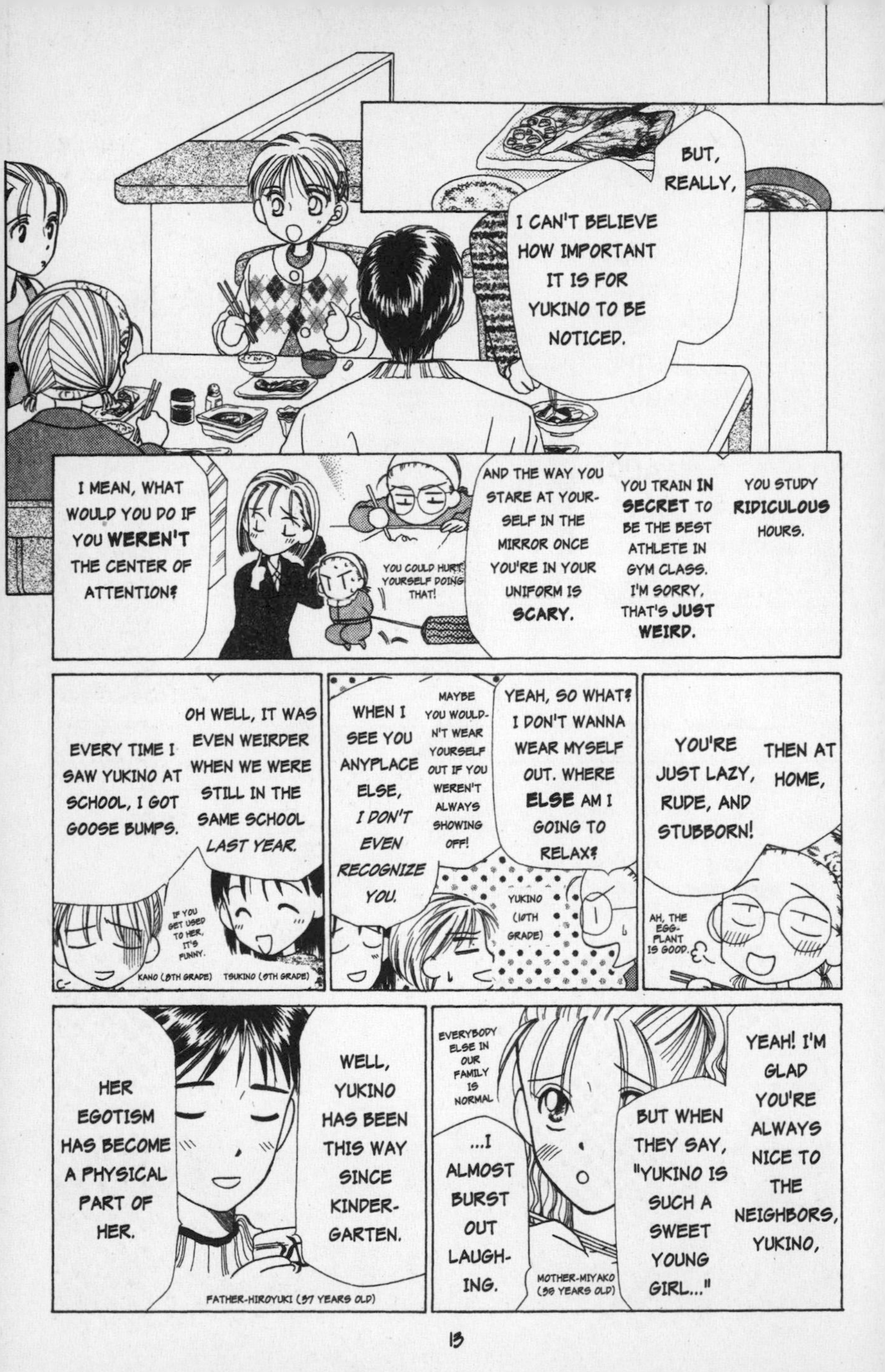
BUT, REALLY,
I CAN'T BELIEVE HOW IMPORTANT IT IS FOR YUKINO TO BE NOTICED.
YOU STUDY RIDICULOUS HOURS.
YOU TRAIN IN SECRET TO BE THE BEST ATHLETE IN GYM CLASS. I'M SORRY, THAT'S JUST WEIRD.
AND THE WAY YOU STARE AT YOURSELF IN THE MIRROR ONCE YOU'RE IN YOUR UNIFORM IS SCARY.
YOU COULD HURT YOURSELF DOING THAT!
I MEAN, WHAT WOULD YOU DO IF YOU WEREN'T THE CENTER OF ATTENTION?
THEN AT HOME,
YOU'RE JUST LAZY, RUDE, AND STUBBORN!
AH, THE EGGPLANT IS GOOD.
YEAH, SO WHAT? I DON'T WANNA WEAR MYSELF OUT. WHERE ELSE AM I GOING TO RELAX?
MAYBE YOU WOULDN'T WEAR YOURSELF OUT IF YOU WEREN'T ALWAYS SHOWING OFF!
WHEN I SEE YOU ANYPLACE ELSE, I DON'T EVEN RECOGNIZE YOU.
YUKINO (10TH GRADE)
OH WELL, IT WAS EVEN WEIRDER WHEN WE WERE STILL IN THE SAME SCHOOL LAST YEAR.
EVERY TIME I SAW YUKINO AT SCHOOL, I GOT GOOSE BUMPS.
IF YOU GET USED TO HER, IT'S FUNNY.
TSUKINO (8TH GRADE)
KANO (8TH GRADE)
YEAH! I'M GLAD YOU'RE ALWAYS NICE TO THE NEIGHBORS, YUKINO,
BUT WHEN THEY SAY, "YUKINO IS SUCH A SWEET YOUNG GIRL..."
EVERYBODY ELSE IN OUR FAMILY IS NORMAL
...I ALMOST BURST OUT LAUGHING.
MOTHER-MIYAKO (35 YEARS OLD)
WELL, YUKINO HAS BEEN THIS WAY SINCE KINDERGARTEN.
HER EGOTISM HAS BECOME A PHYSICAL PART OF HER.
FATHER-HIROYUKI (37 YEARS OLD)

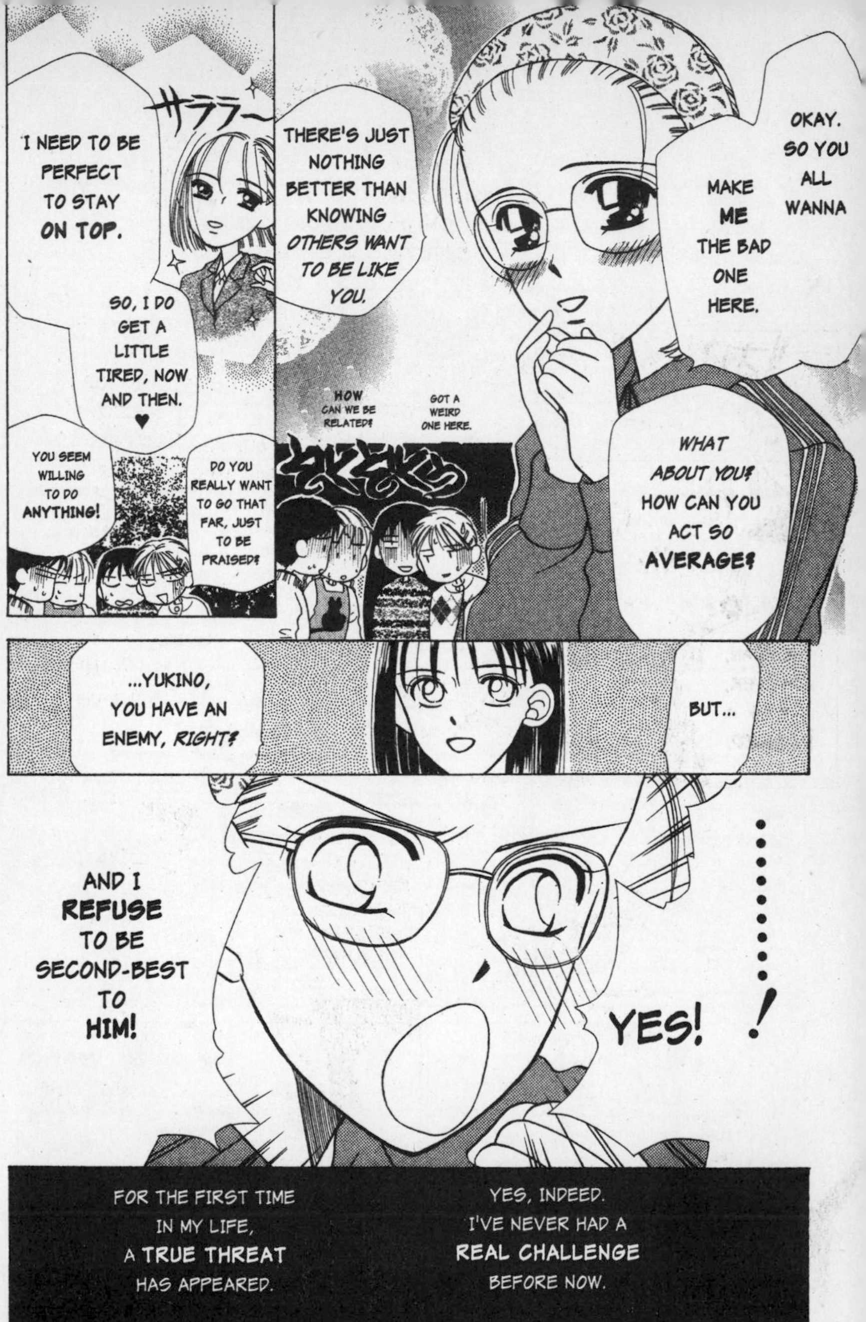
OKAY. SO YOU ALL WANNA
MAKE ME THE BAD ONE HERE.
WHAT ABOUT YOU? HOW CAN YOU ACT SO AVERAGE?
THERE'S JUST NOTHING BETTER THAN KNOWING OTHERS WANT TO BE LIKE YOU.
GOT A WEIRD ONE HERE.
HOW CAN WE BE RELATED?
サラララ~
I NEED TO BE PERFECT TO STAY ON TOP.
SO, I DO GET A LITTLE TIRED, NOW AND THEN. ♥
DO YOU REALLY WANT TO GO THAT FAR, JUST TO BE PRAISED?
YOU SEEM WILLING TO DO ANYTHING!
BUT...
...YUKINO, YOU HAVE AN ENEMY, RIGHT?
......!
YES!
AND I REFUSE TO BE SECOND-BEST TO HIM!
YES, INDEED. I'VE NEVER HAD A REAL CHALLENGE BEFORE NOW.
FOR THE FIRST TIME IN MY LIFE, A TRUE THREAT HAS APPEARED.

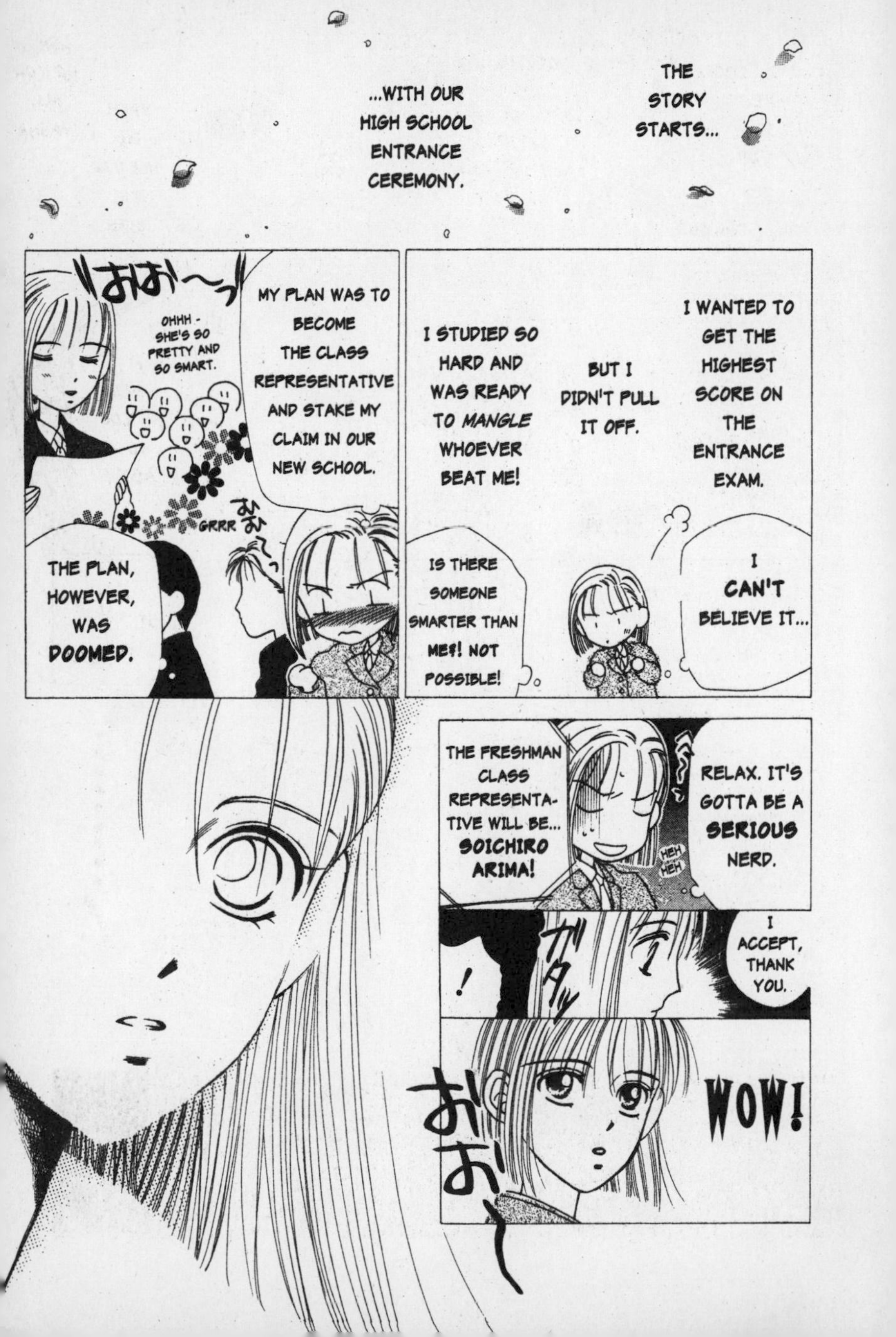
THE STORY STARTS...
...WITH OUR HIGH SCHOOL ENTRANCE CEREMONY.
I WANTED TO GET THE HIGHEST SCORE ON THE ENTRANCE EXAM.
BUT I DIDN'T PULL IT OFF.
I STUDIED SO HARD AND WAS READY TO *MANGLE* WHOEVER BEAT ME!
I **CAN'T** BELIEVE IT...
IS THERE SOMEONE SMARTER THAN ME?! NOT POSSIBLE!
MY PLAN WAS TO BECOME THE CLASS REPRESENTATIVE AND STAKE MY CLAIM IN OUR NEW SCHOOL.
おお～っ
OHHH - SHE'S SO PRETTY AND SO SMART.
GRRR
THE PLAN, HOWEVER, WAS **DOOMED.**
RELAX. IT'S GOTTA BE A **SERIOUS** NERD.
HEH HEH
THE FRESHMAN CLASS REPRESENTATIVE WILL BE... **SOICHIRO ARIMA!**
I ACCEPT, THANK YOU.
ガタッ
!
WOW!
おお～

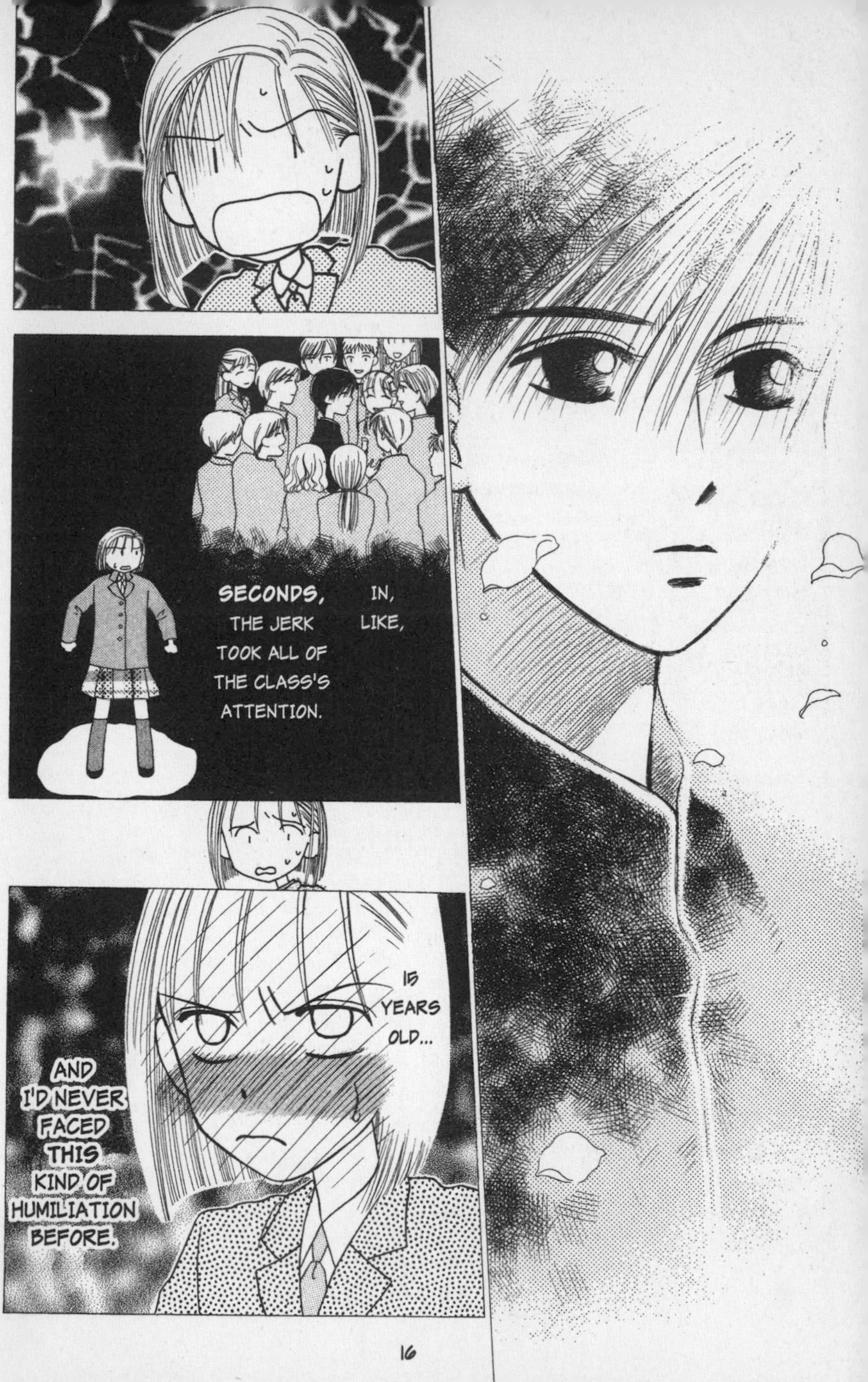
IN, LIKE,
SECONDS, THE JERK TOOK ALL OF THE CLASS'S ATTENTION.
15 YEARS OLD...
AND I'D NEVER FACED THIS KIND OF HUMILIATION BEFORE.

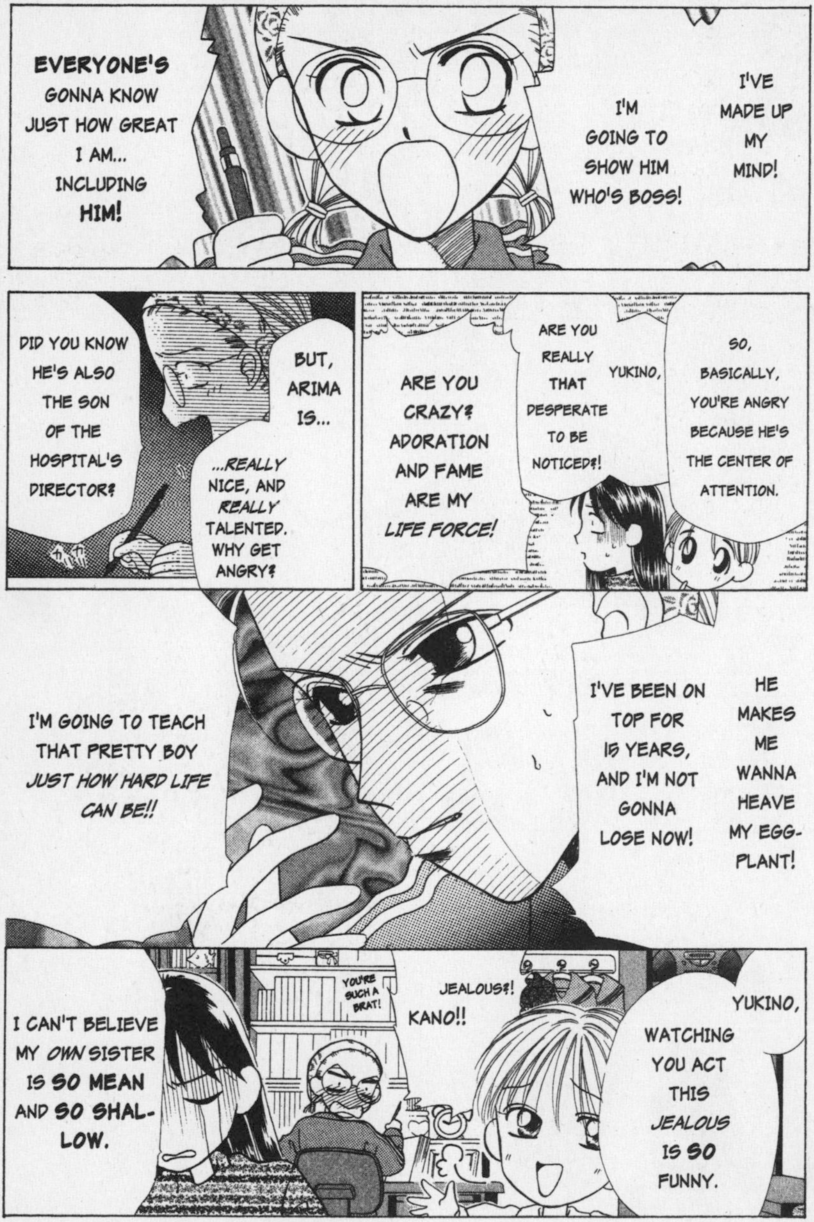
I'VE MADE UP MY MIND!
I'M GOING TO SHOW HIM WHO'S BOSS!
EVERYONE'S GONNA KNOW JUST HOW GREAT I AM... INCLUDING HIM!
SO, BASICALLY, YOU'RE ANGRY BECAUSE HE'S THE CENTER OF ATTENTION.
YUKINO,
ARE YOU REALLY THAT DESPERATE TO BE NOTICED?!
ARE YOU CRAZY? ADORATION AND FAME ARE MY LIFE FORCE!
BUT, ARIMA IS...
...REALLY NICE, AND REALLY TALENTED. WHY GET ANGRY?
DID YOU KNOW HE'S ALSO THE SON OF THE HOSPITAL'S DIRECTOR?
HE MAKES ME WANNA HEAVE MY EGG-PLANT!
I'VE BEEN ON TOP FOR 15 YEARS, AND I'M NOT GONNA LOSE NOW!
I'M GOING TO TEACH THAT PRETTY BOY JUST HOW HARD LIFE CAN BE!!
YUKINO, WATCHING YOU ACT THIS JEALOUS IS SO FUNNY.
JEALOUS?!
KANO!!
YOU'RE SUCH A BRAT!
I CAN'T BELIEVE MY OWN SISTER IS SO MEAN AND SO SHAL-LOW.

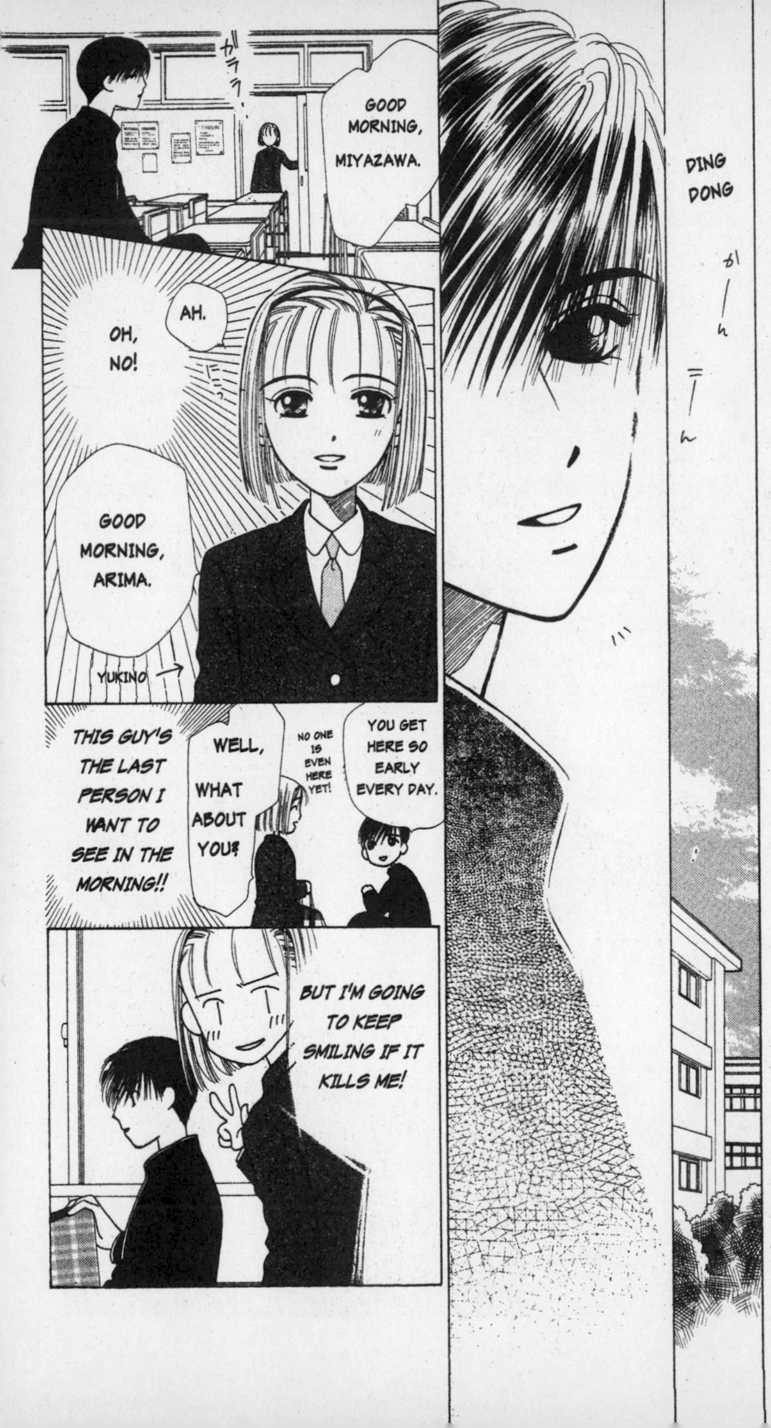
DING DONG
GOOD MORNING, MIYAZAWA.
AH.
OH, NO!
GOOD MORNING, ARIMA.
YUKINO
YOU GET HERE SO EARLY EVERY DAY.
NO ONE IS EVEN HERE YET!
WELL, WHAT ABOUT YOU?
THIS GUY'S THE LAST PERSON I WANT TO SEE IN THE MORNING!!
BUT I'M GOING TO KEEP SMILING IF IT KILLS ME!

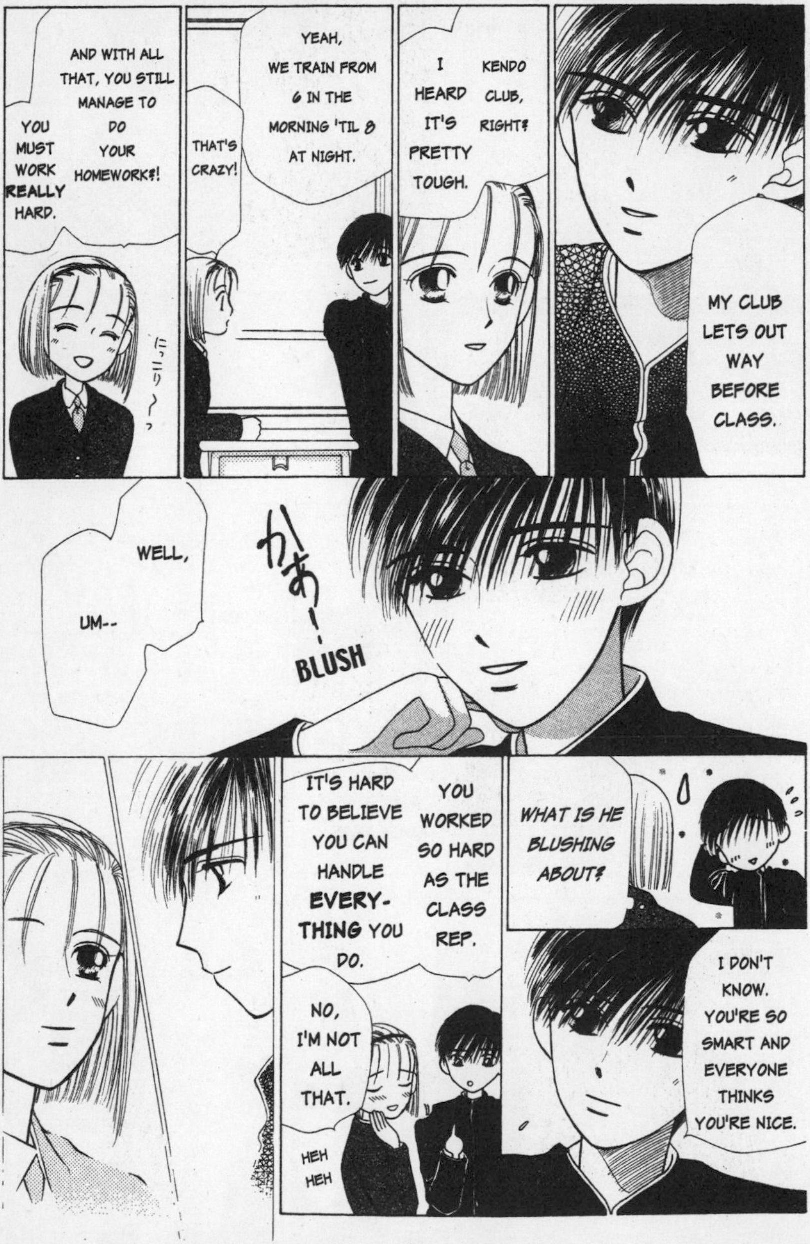
MY CLUB LETS OUT WAY BEFORE CLASS.
KENDO CLUB, RIGHT?
I HEARD IT'S PRETTY TOUGH.
YEAH, WE TRAIN FROM 6 IN THE MORNING 'TIL 8 AT NIGHT.
THAT'S CRAZY!
AND WITH ALL THAT, YOU STILL MANAGE TO DO YOUR HOMEWORK?!
YOU MUST WORK REALLY HARD.
にっこり～っ
かぁ！
BLUSH
WELL,
UM--
WHAT IS HE BLUSHING ABOUT?
I DON'T KNOW. YOU'RE SO SMART AND EVERYONE THINKS YOU'RE NICE.
YOU WORKED SO HARD AS THE CLASS REP.
IT'S HARD TO BELIEVE YOU CAN HANDLE EVERYTHING YOU DO.
NO, I'M NOT ALL THAT.
HEH HEH

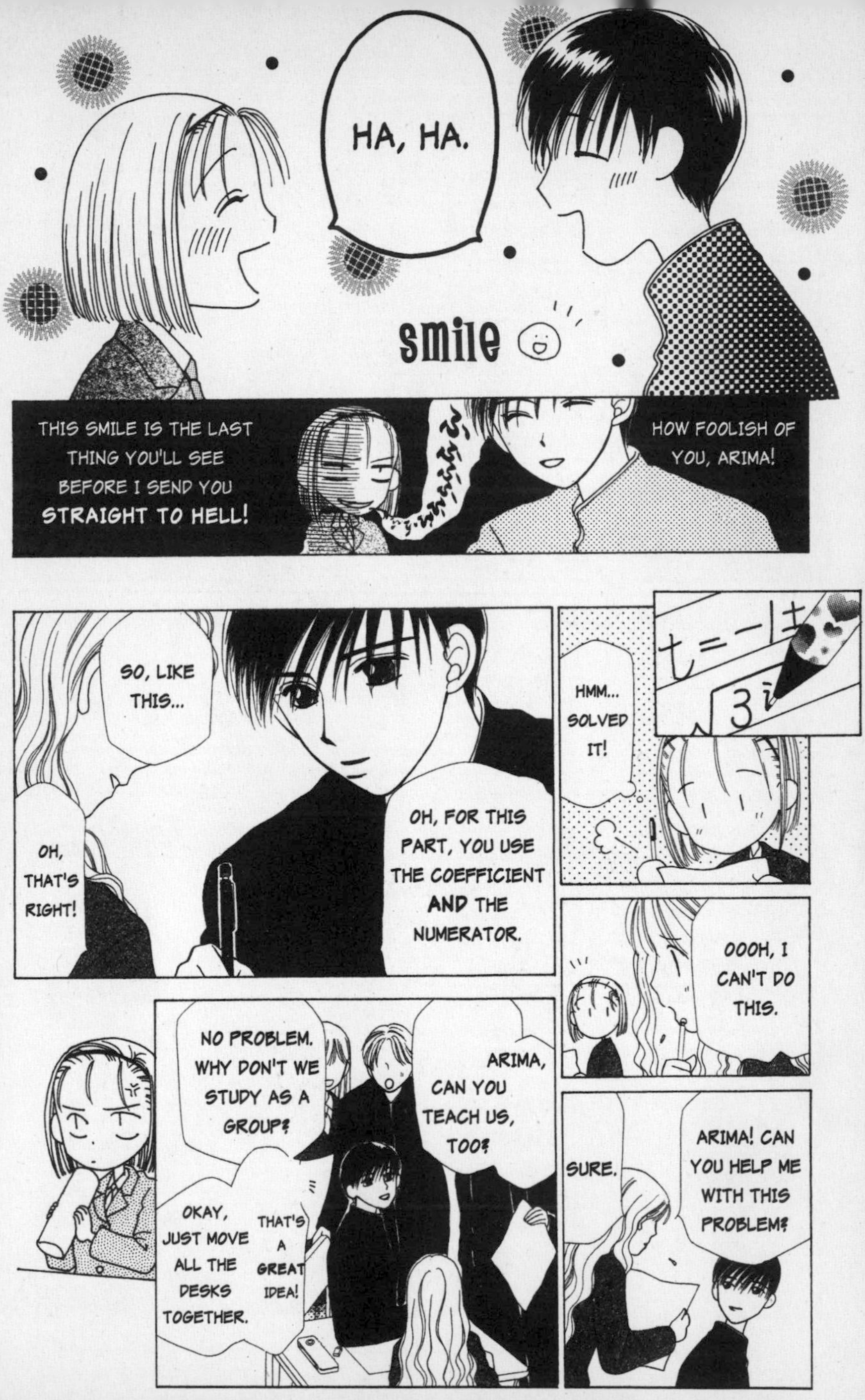
HA, HA.
smile
HOW FOOLISH OF YOU, ARIMA!
THIS SMILE IS THE LAST THING YOU'LL SEE BEFORE I SEND YOU STRAIGHT TO HELL!
HMM... SOLVED IT!
OOOH, I CAN'T DO THIS.
SO, LIKE THIS...
OH, FOR THIS PART, YOU USE THE COEFFICIENT AND THE NUMERATOR.
OH, THAT'S RIGHT!
ARIMA! CAN YOU HELP ME WITH THIS PROBLEM?
SURE.
ARIMA, CAN YOU TEACH US, TOO?
NO PROBLEM. WHY DON'T WE STUDY AS A GROUP?
THAT'S A GREAT IDEA!
OKAY, JUST MOVE ALL THE DESKS TOGETHER.

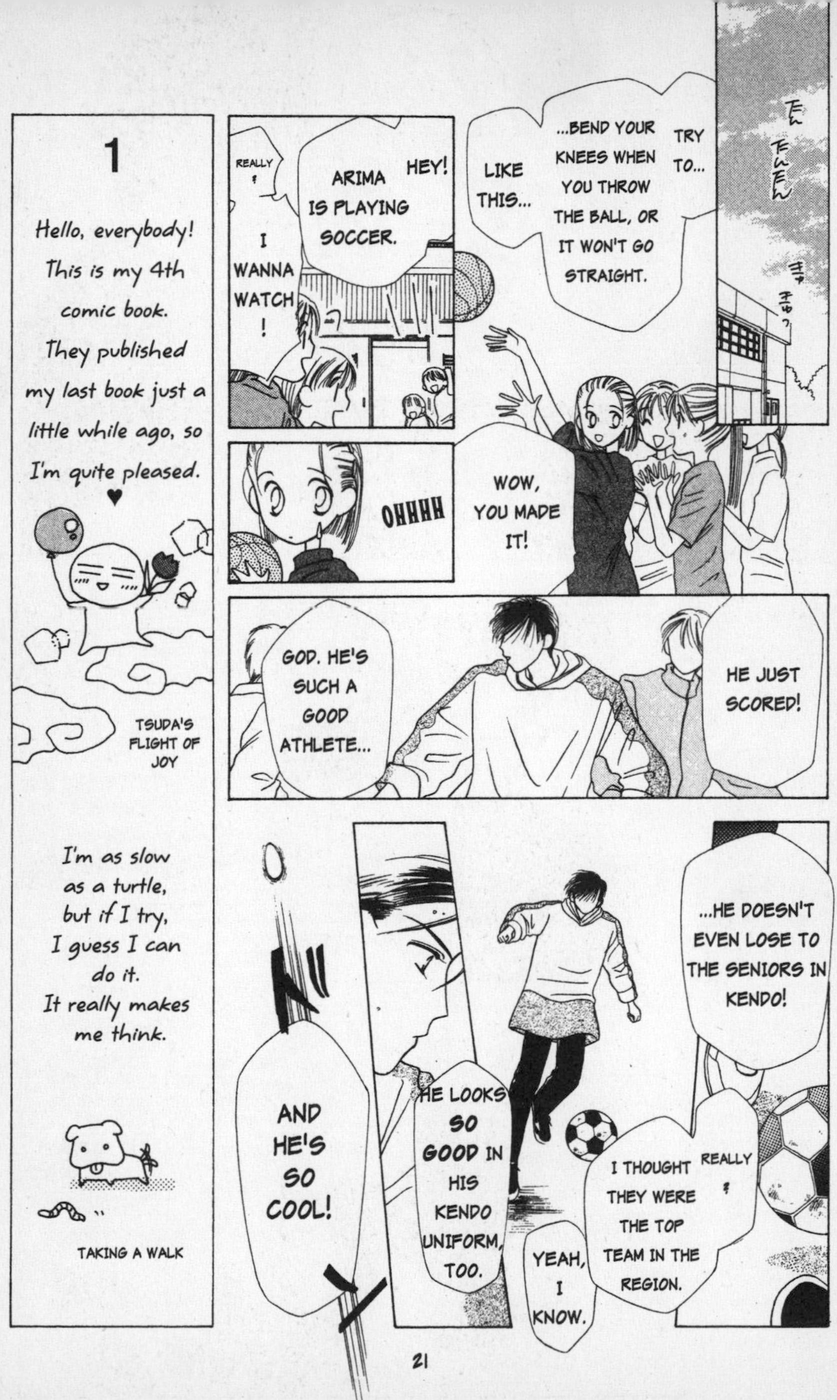
TRY TO...
...BEND YOUR KNEES WHEN YOU THROW THE BALL, OR IT WON'T GO STRAIGHT.
LIKE THIS...
HEY!
ARIMA IS PLAYING SOCCER.
REALLY?
I WANNA WATCH!
WOW, YOU MADE IT!
OHHHH
HE JUST SCORED!
GOD. HE'S SUCH A GOOD ATHLETE...
...HE DOESN'T EVEN LOSE TO THE SENIORS IN KENDO!
REALLY?
I THOUGHT THEY WERE THE TOP TEAM IN THE REGION.
YEAH, I KNOW.
HE LOOKS SO GOOD IN HIS KENDO UNIFORM, TOO.
AND HE'S SO COOL!

1

Hello, everybody! This is my 4th comic book. They published my last book just a little while ago, so I'm quite pleased. ♥

TSUDA'S FLIGHT OF JOY

I'm as slow as a turtle, but if I try, I guess I can do it. It really makes me think.

TAKING A WALK

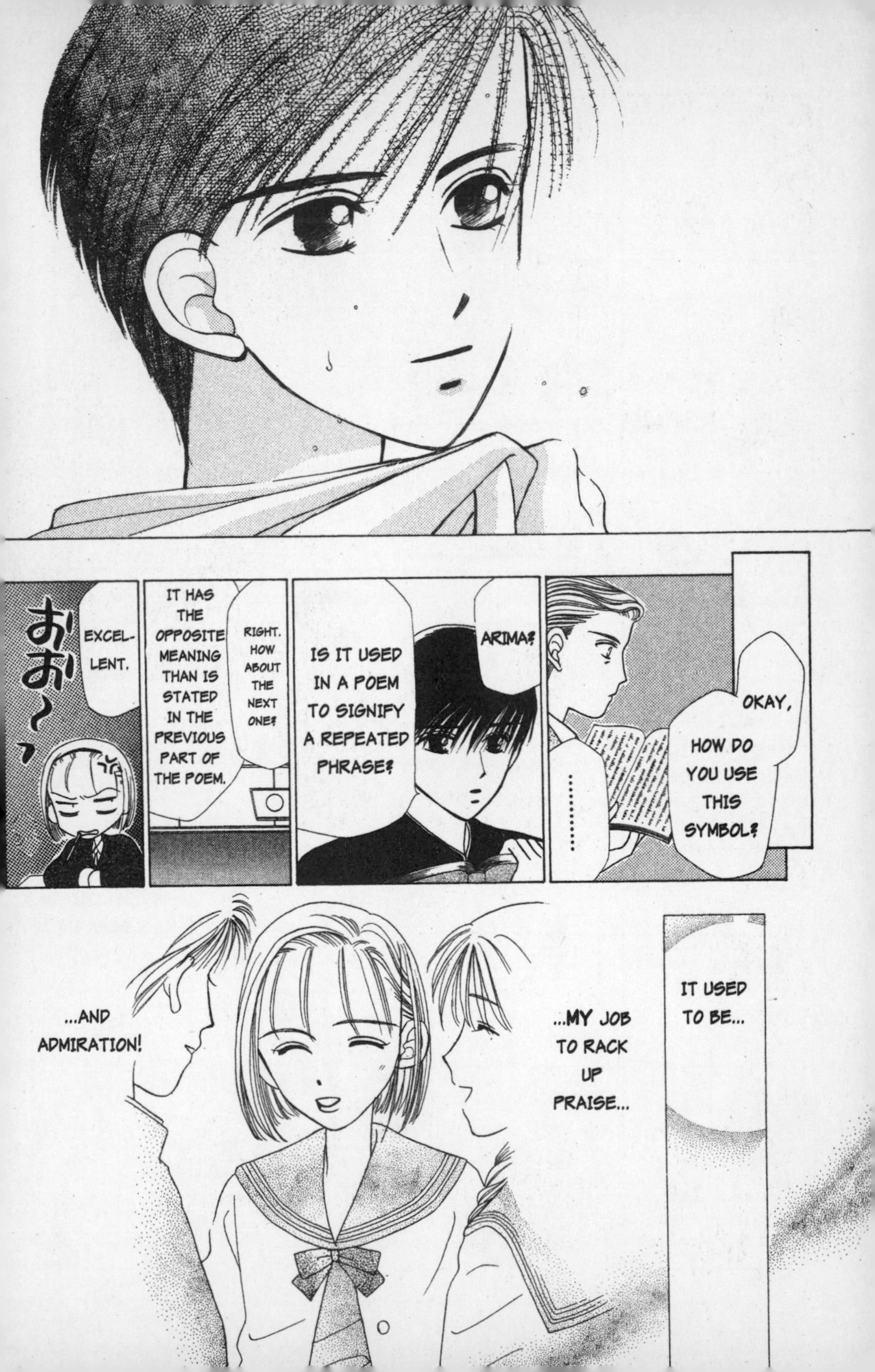
OKAY, HOW DO YOU USE THIS SYMBOL?
......
ARIMA?
IS IT USED IN A POEM TO SIGNIFY A REPEATED PHRASE?
RIGHT. HOW ABOUT THE NEXT ONE?
IT HAS THE OPPOSITE MEANING THAN IS STATED IN THE PREVIOUS PART OF THE POEM.
EXCEL-LENT.
おお～
IT USED TO BE...
...MY JOB TO RACK UP PRAISE...
...AND ADMIRATION!

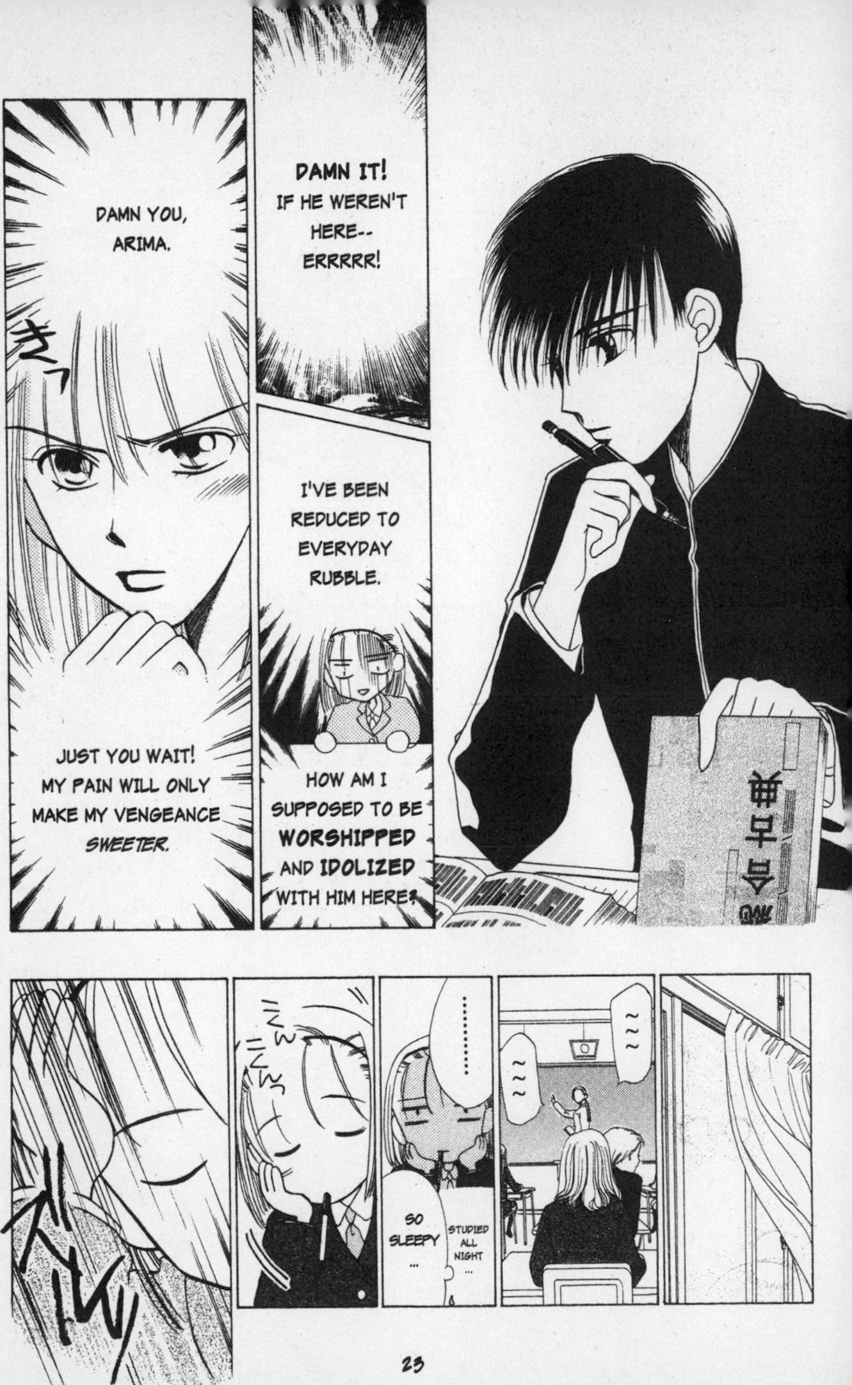
DAMN IT!
IF HE WEREN'T HERE-- ERRRRR!
I'VE BEEN REDUCED TO EVERYDAY RUBBLE.
HOW AM I SUPPOSED TO BE **WORSHIPPED** AND **IDOLIZED** WITH HIM HERE?
DAMN YOU, ARIMA.
きっ
JUST YOU WAIT! MY PAIN WILL ONLY MAKE MY VENGEANCE *SWEETER.*
~~~
~~~
....
STUDIED ALL NIGHT ...
SO SLEEPY ...

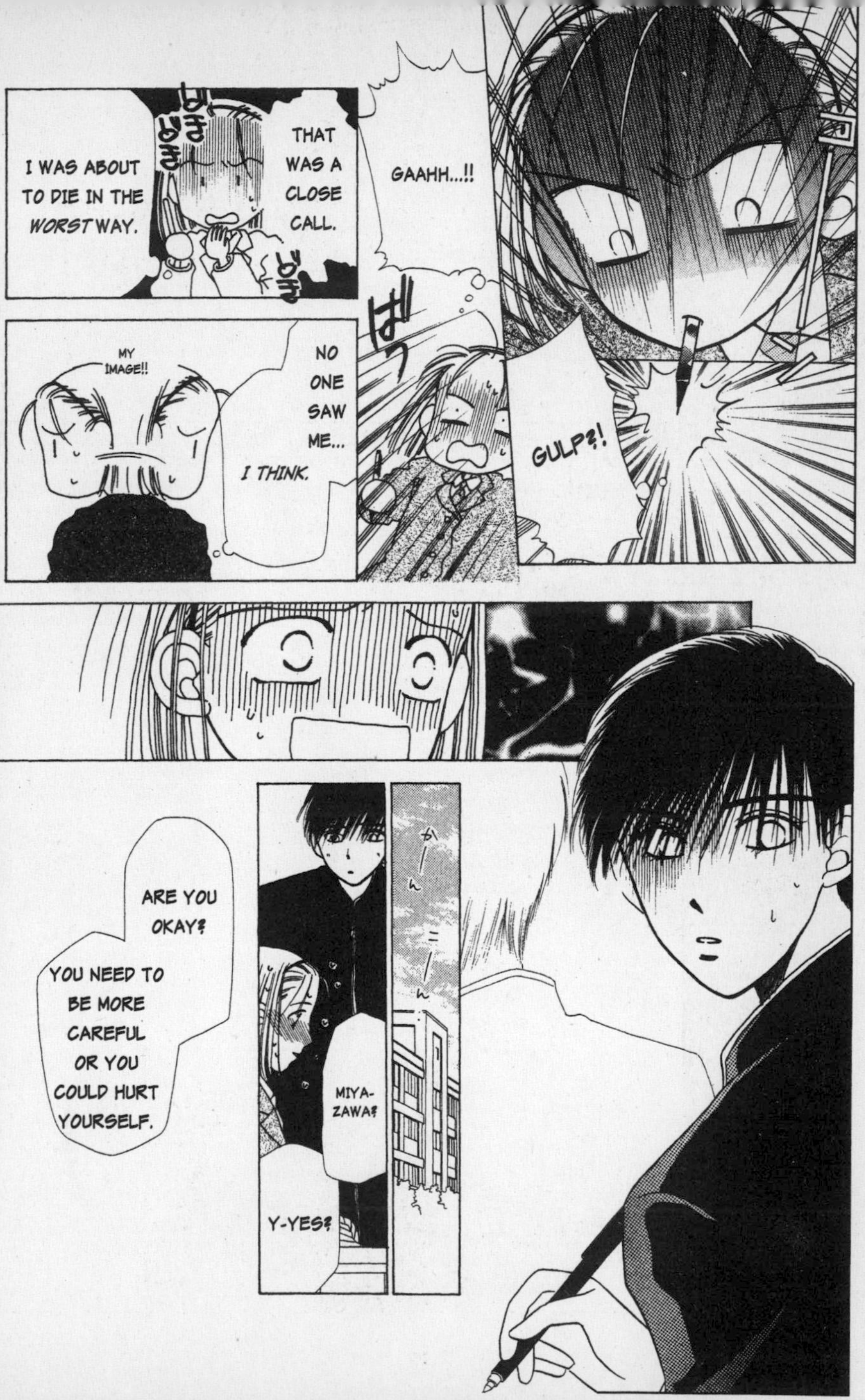
GULP?!
GAAHH...!!
THAT WAS A CLOSE CALL.
I WAS ABOUT TO DIE IN THE *WORST* WAY.
NO ONE SAW ME... I THINK.
MY IMAGE!!
MIYA-ZAWA?
Y-YES?
ARE YOU OKAY?
YOU NEED TO BE MORE CAREFUL OR YOU COULD HURT YOURSELF.

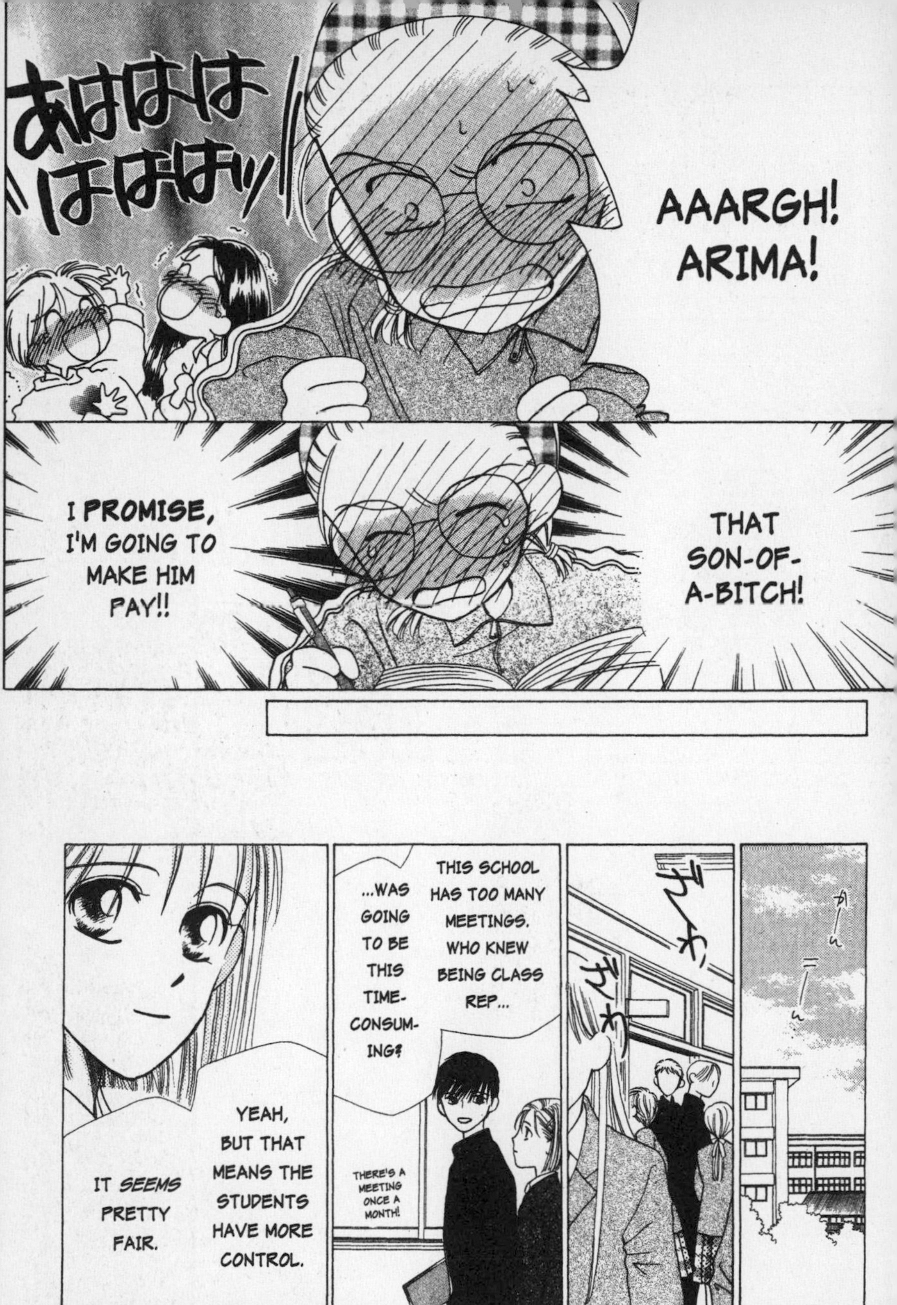
AAARGH! ARIMA!
あははーは
はははッ
THAT SON-OF-A-BITCH!
I PROMISE, I'M GOING TO MAKE HIM PAY!!
かーん
こーん
ざわ
ざわ
THIS SCHOOL HAS TOO MANY MEETINGS. WHO KNEW BEING CLASS REP...
...WAS GOING TO BE THIS TIME-CONSUMING?
THERE'S A MEETING ONCE A MONTH!
YEAH, BUT THAT MEANS THE STUDENTS HAVE MORE CONTROL.
IT SEEMS PRETTY FAIR.

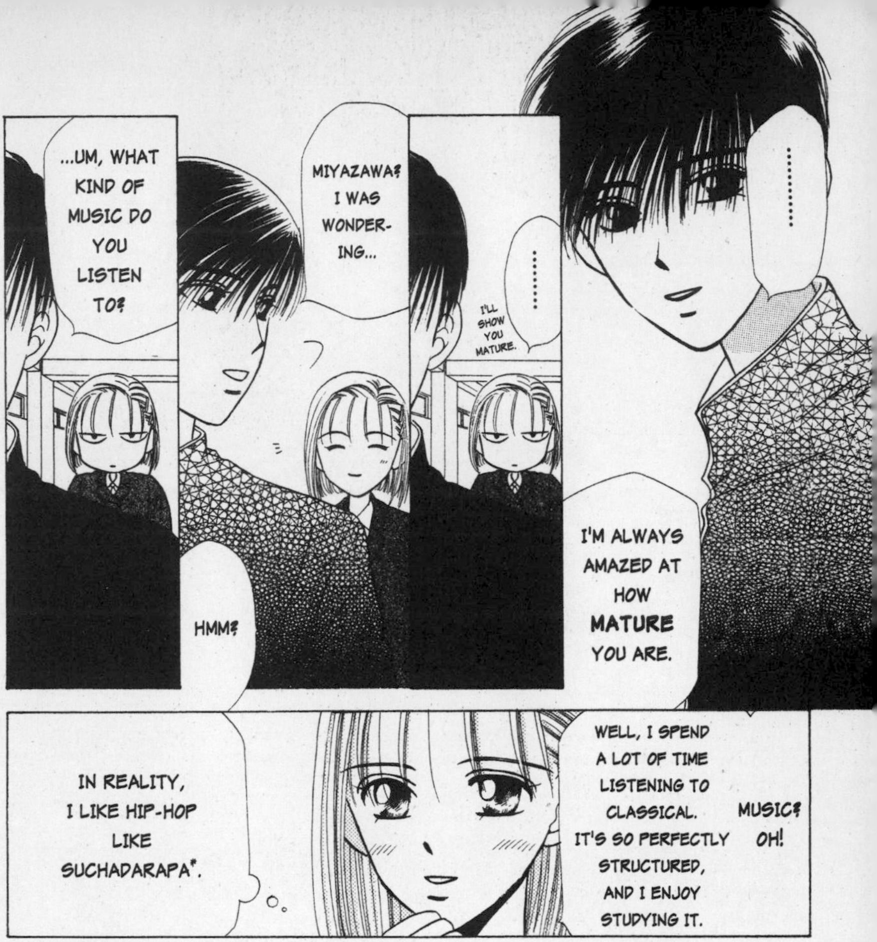
......
I'M ALWAYS AMAZED AT HOW MATURE YOU ARE.
......
I'LL SHOW YOU MATURE.
MIYAZAWA? I WAS WONDERING...
HMM?
...UM, WHAT KIND OF MUSIC DO YOU LISTEN TO?
MUSIC? OH!
WELL, I SPEND A LOT OF TIME LISTENING TO CLASSICAL. IT'S SO PERFECTLY STRUCTURED, AND I ENJOY STUDYING IT.
IN REALITY, I LIKE HIP-HOP LIKE SUCHADARAPA*.

*An underground band that's popular in Japan

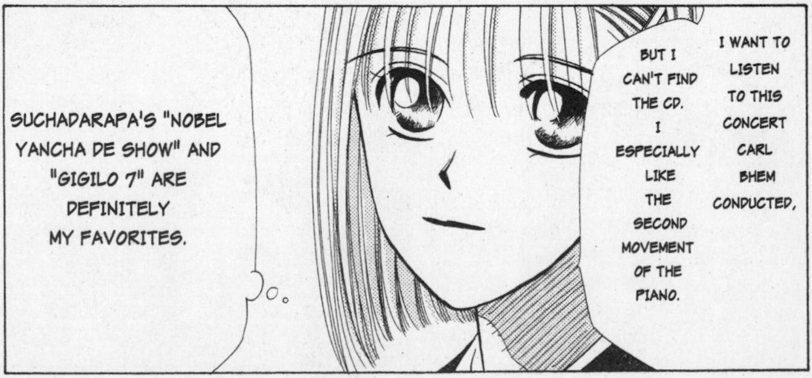
I WANT TO LISTEN TO THIS CONCERT CARL BHEM CONDUCTED,
BUT I CAN'T FIND THE CD. I ESPECIALLY LIKE THE SECOND MOVEMENT OF THE PIANO.
SUCHADARAPA'S "NOBEL YANCHA DE SHOW" AND "GIGILO 7" ARE DEFINITELY MY FAVORITES.

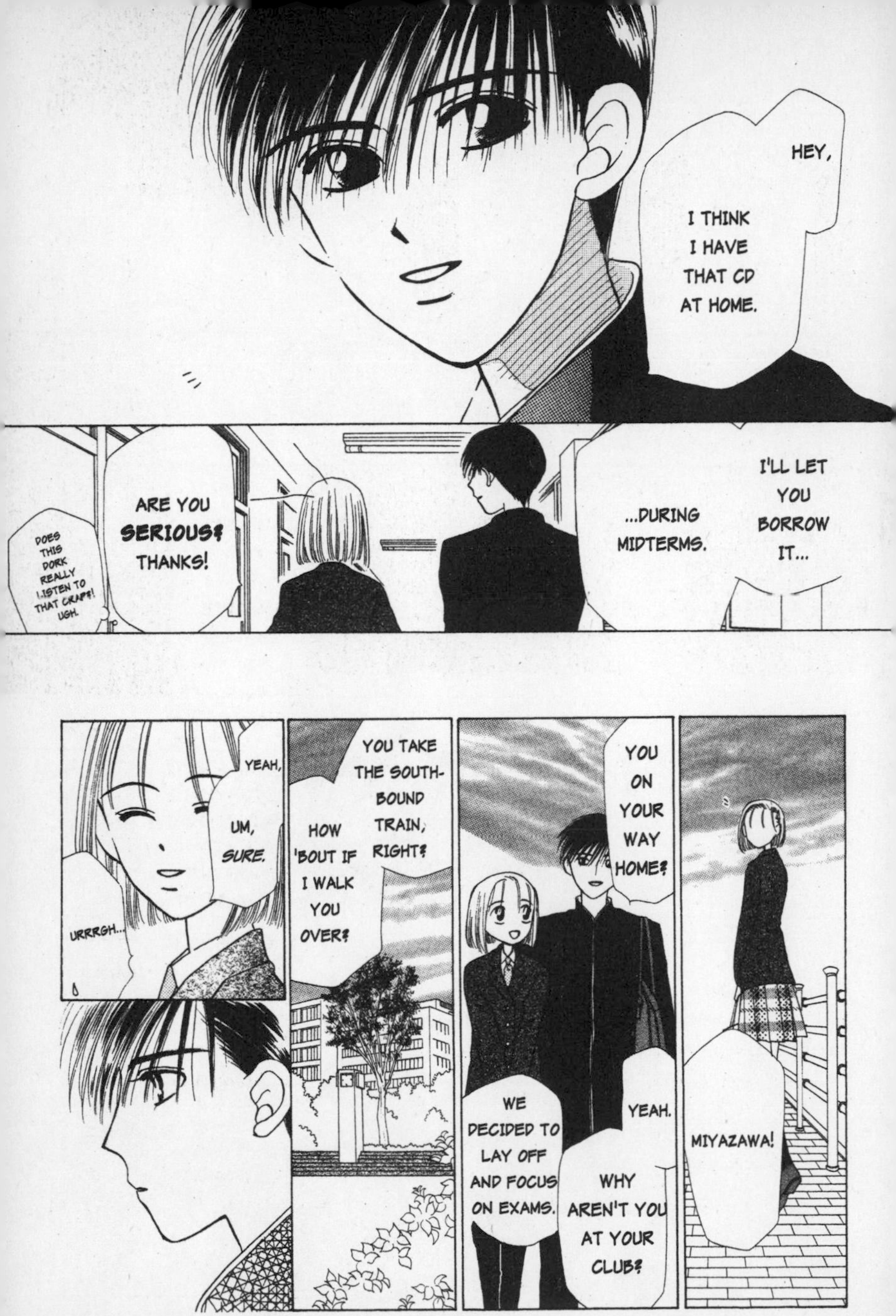
HEY,
I THINK I HAVE THAT CD AT HOME.
I'LL LET YOU BORROW IT...
...DURING MIDTERMS.
ARE YOU SERIOUS? THANKS!
DOES THIS DORK REALLY LISTEN TO THAT CRAP?! UGH.
MIYAZAWA!
YOU ON YOUR WAY HOME?
YEAH.
WHY AREN'T YOU AT YOUR CLUB?
WE DECIDED TO LAY OFF AND FOCUS ON EXAMS.
YOU TAKE THE SOUTH-BOUND TRAIN, RIGHT?
HOW 'BOUT IF I WALK YOU OVER?
YEAH,
UM, SURE.
URRRGH...

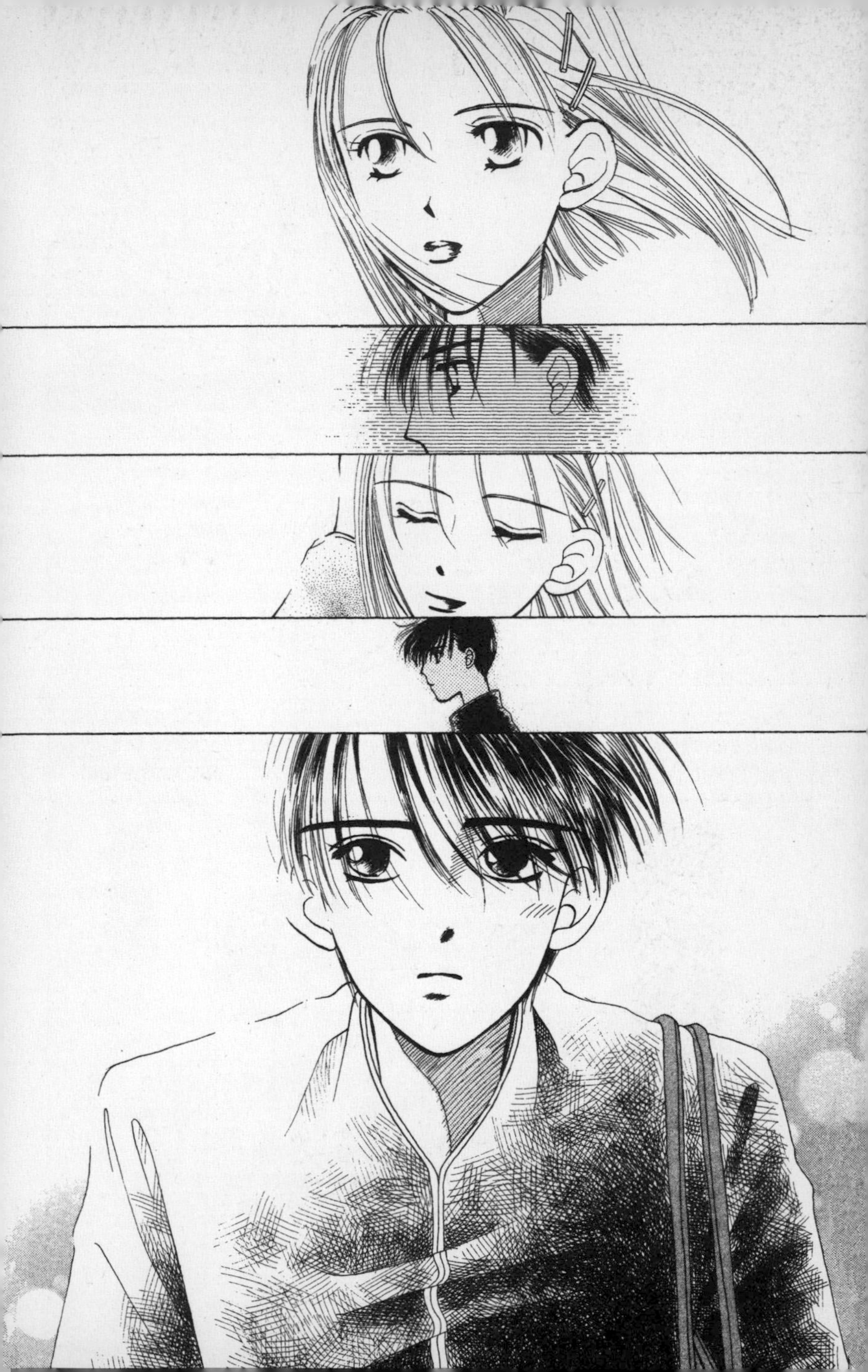

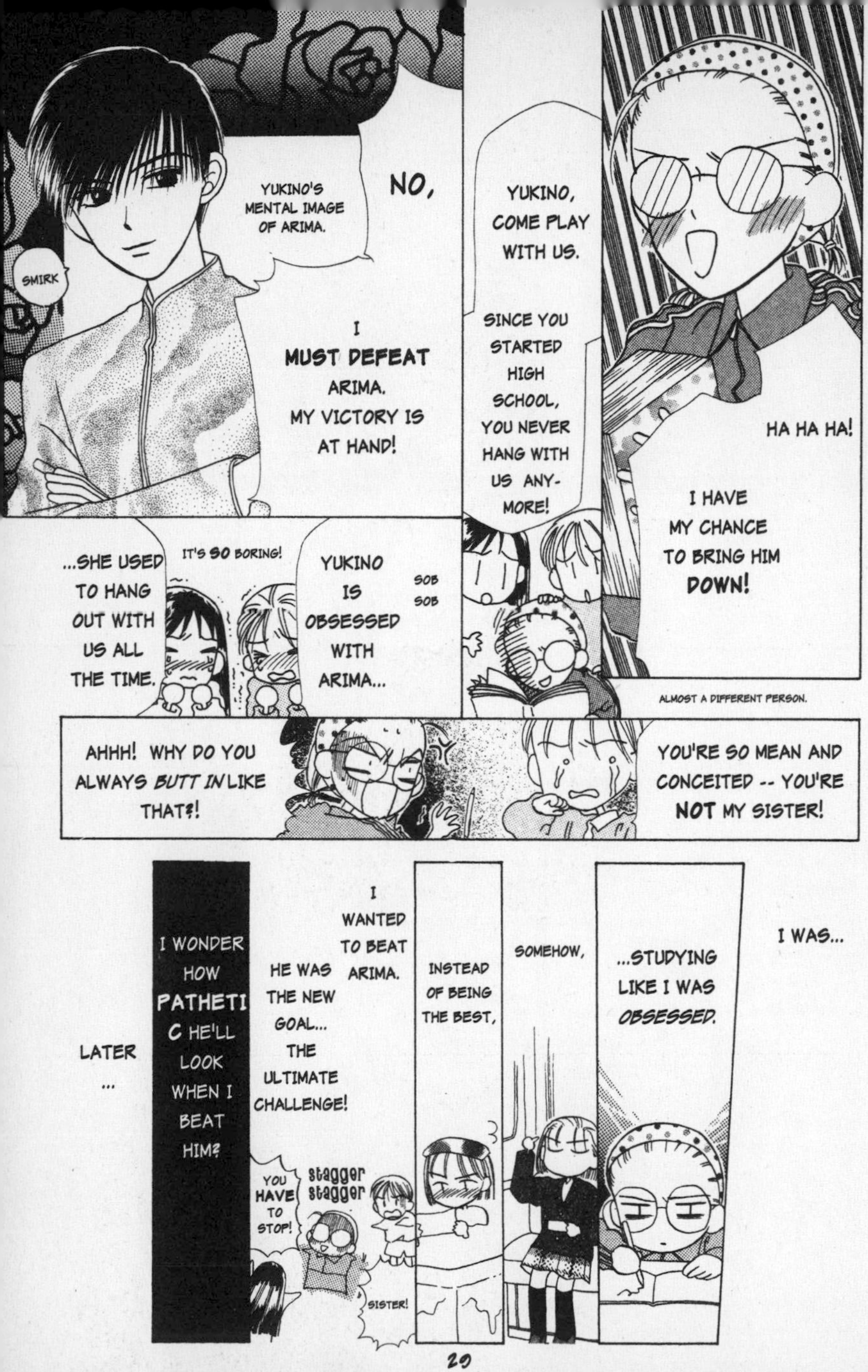
HA HA HA!
I HAVE MY CHANCE TO BRING HIM DOWN!
NO,
YUKINO'S MENTAL IMAGE OF ARIMA.
SMIRK
I MUST DEFEAT ARIMA. MY VICTORY IS AT HAND!
YUKINO, COME PLAY WITH US.
SINCE YOU STARTED HIGH SCHOOL, YOU NEVER HANG WITH US ANY-MORE!
ALMOST A DIFFERENT PERSON.
YUKINO IS OBSESSED WITH ARIMA...
SOB SOB
IT'S SO BORING!
...SHE USED TO HANG OUT WITH US ALL THE TIME.
YOU'RE SO MEAN AND CONCEITED -- YOU'RE NOT MY SISTER!
AHHH! WHY DO YOU ALWAYS BUTT IN LIKE THAT?!
I WAS...
...STUDYING LIKE I WAS OBSESSED.
SOMEHOW,
INSTEAD OF BEING THE BEST,
I WANTED TO BEAT ARIMA.
HE WAS THE NEW GOAL... THE ULTIMATE CHALLENGE!
stagger stagger
YOU HAVE TO STOP!
SISTER!
I WONDER HOW PATHETI C HE'LL LOOK WHEN I BEAT HIM?
LATER ...

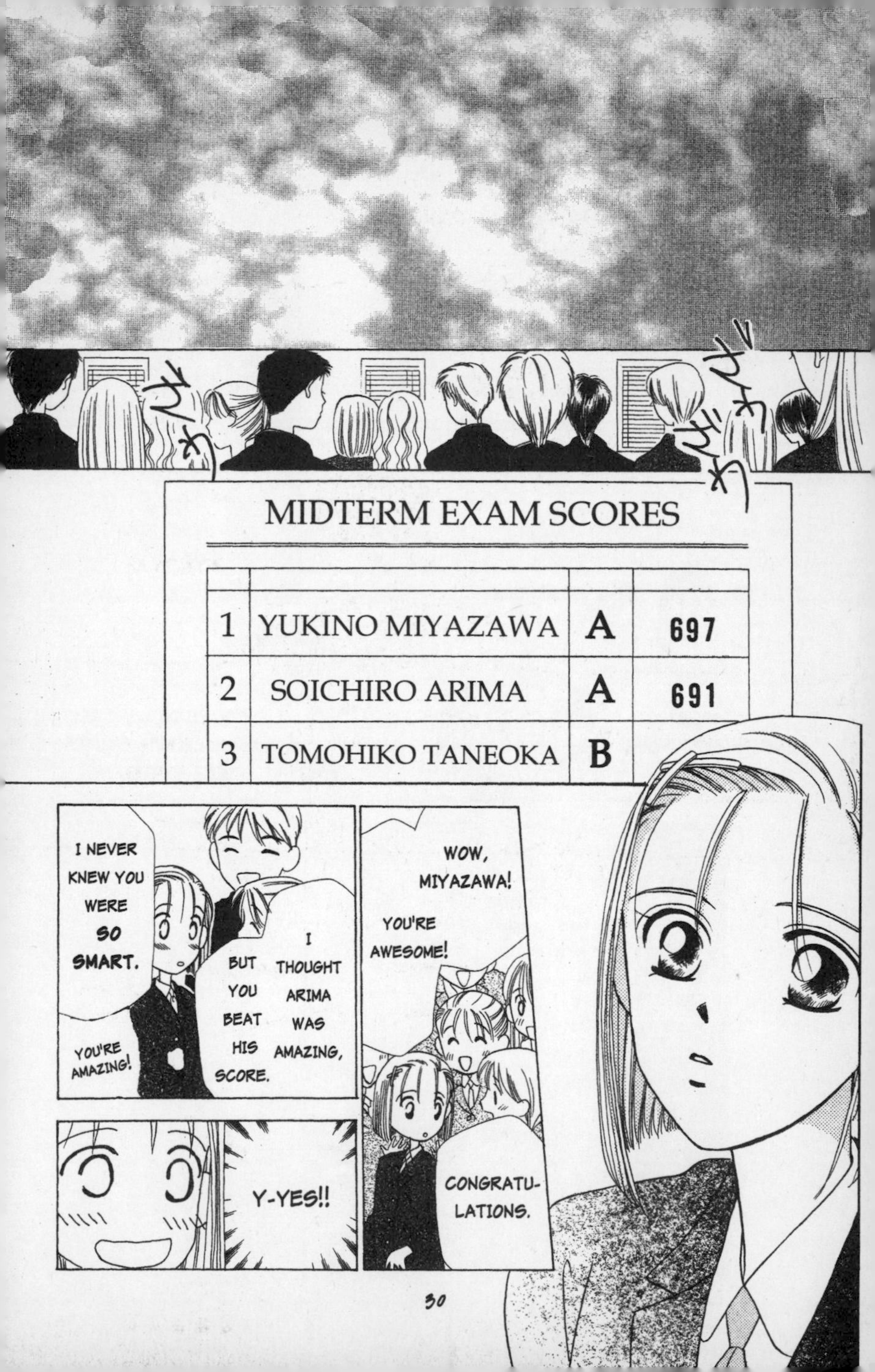
MIDTERM EXAM SCORES
1 YUKINO MIYAZAWA A 697
2 SOICHIRO ARIMA A 691
3 TOMOHIKO TANEOKA B
WOW, MIYAZAWA!
YOU'RE AWESOME!
CONGRATULATIONS.
I THOUGHT ARIMA WAS AMAZING,
BUT YOU BEAT HIS SCORE.
I NEVER KNEW YOU WERE SO SMART.
YOU'RE AMAZING!
Y-YES!!

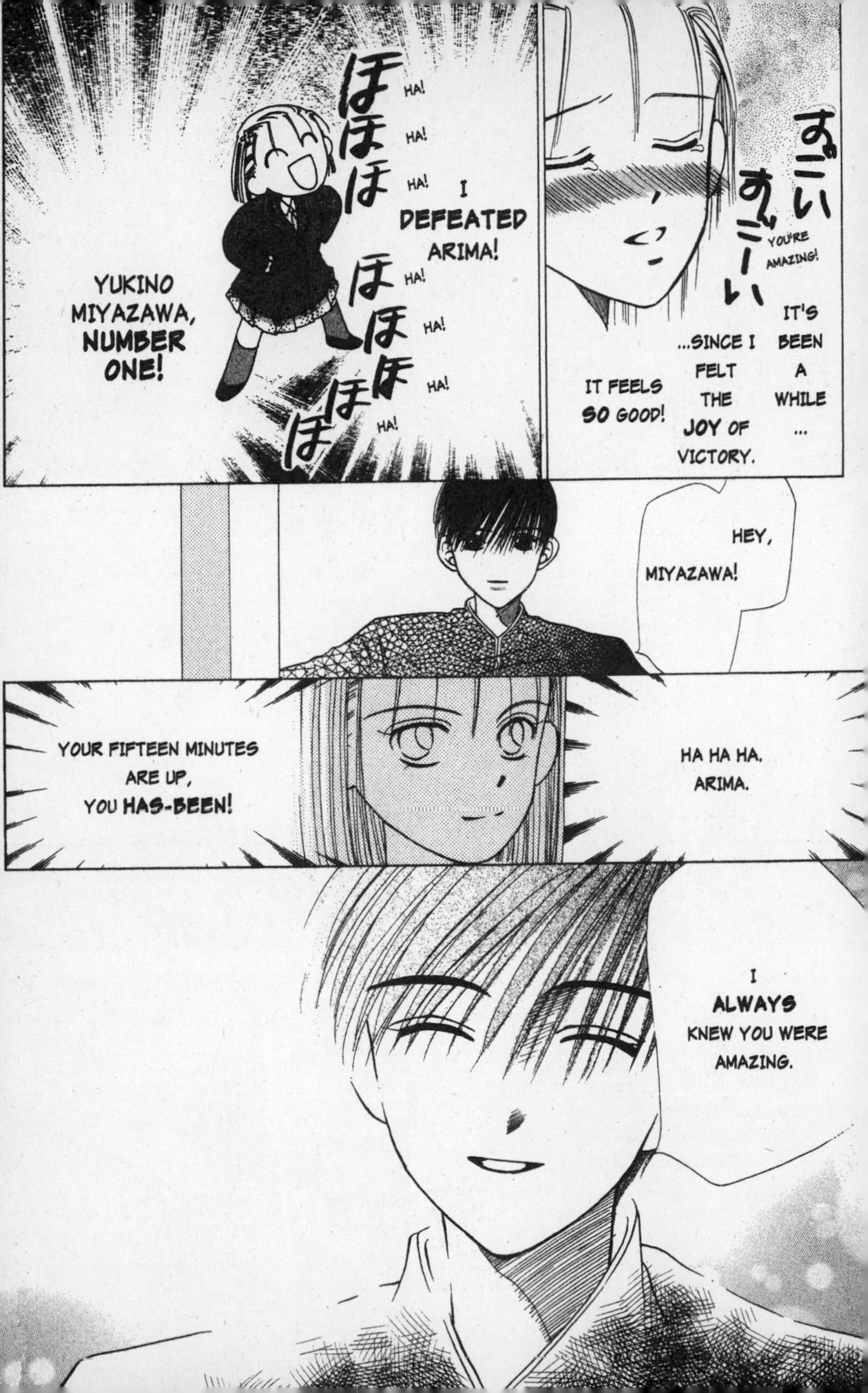
すごい すごーい
YOU'RE AMAZING!
IT'S BEEN A WHILE...
...SINCE I FELT THE JOY OF VICTORY.
IT FEELS SO GOOD!
I DEFEATED ARIMA!
ほほほほ ほほほほほ
HA! HA! HA! HA! HA! HA! HA!
YUKINO MIYAZAWA, NUMBER ONE!
HEY, MIYAZAWA!
HA HA HA. ARIMA.
YOUR FIFTEEN MINUTES ARE UP, YOU HAS-BEEN!
I ALWAYS KNEW YOU WERE AMAZING.

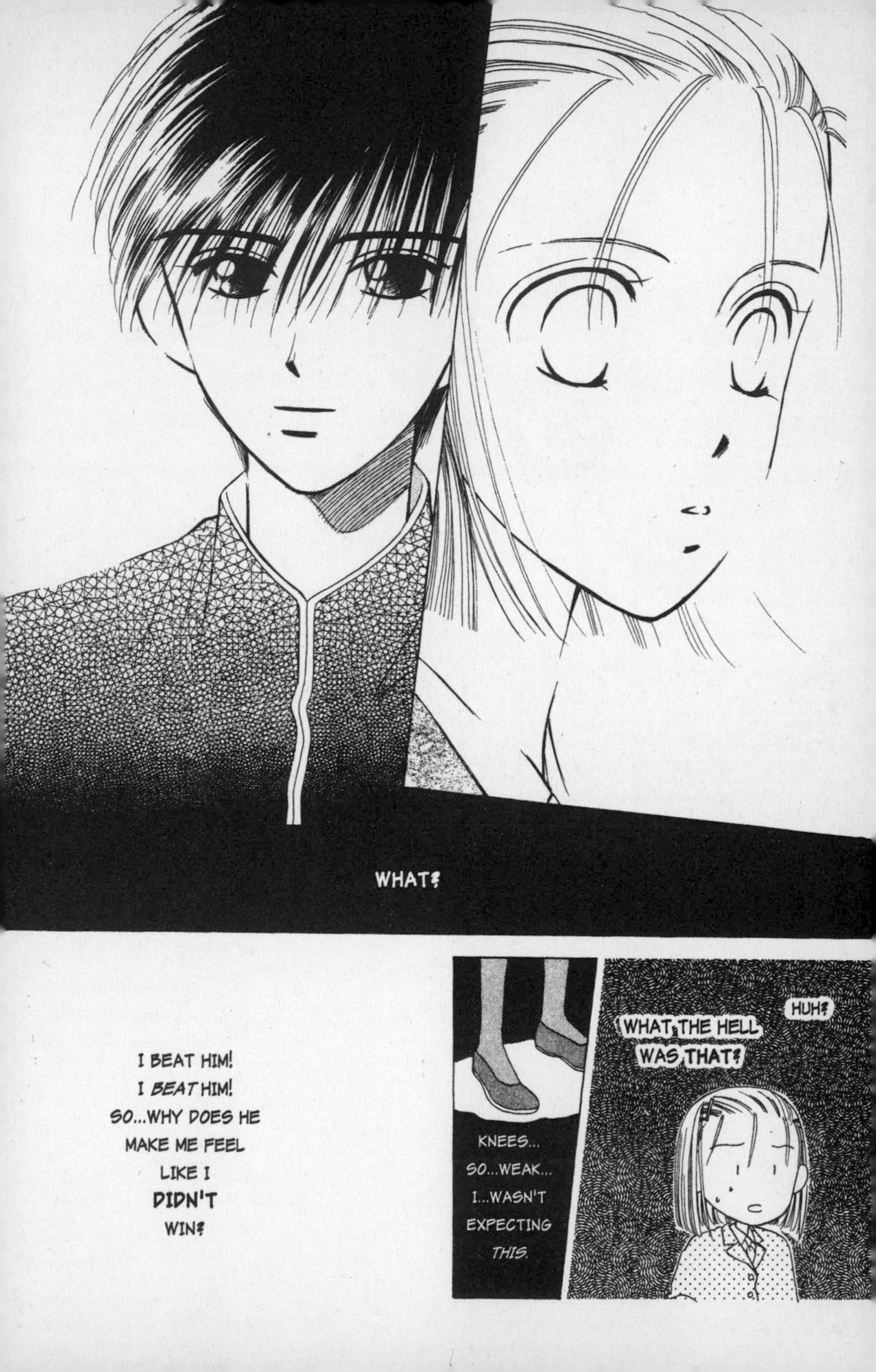
WHAT?
HUH?
WHAT THE HELL WAS THAT?
KNEES... SO...WEAK... I...WASN'T EXPECTING *THIS*.
I BEAT HIM! I *BEAT* HIM! SO...WHY DOES HE MAKE ME FEEL LIKE I **DIDN'T** WIN?

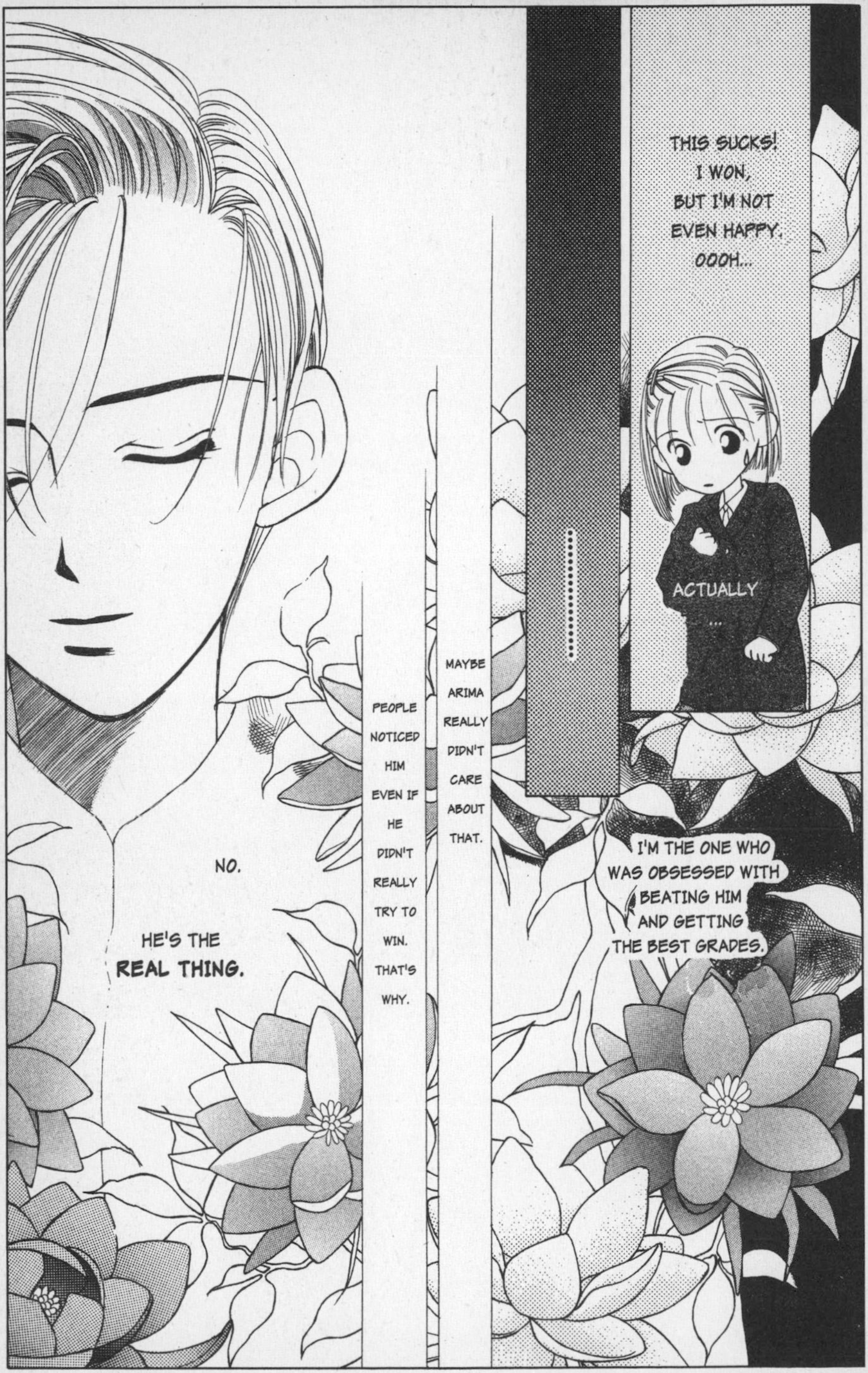
THIS SUCKS! I WON, BUT I'M NOT EVEN HAPPY. OOOH...
ACTUALLY...
I'M THE ONE WHO WAS OBSESSED WITH BEATING HIM AND GETTING THE BEST GRADES.
......
MAYBE ARIMA REALLY DIDN'T CARE ABOUT THAT.
PEOPLE NOTICED HIM EVEN IF HE DIDN'T REALLY TRY TO WIN. THAT'S WHY.
NO.
HE'S THE REAL THING.

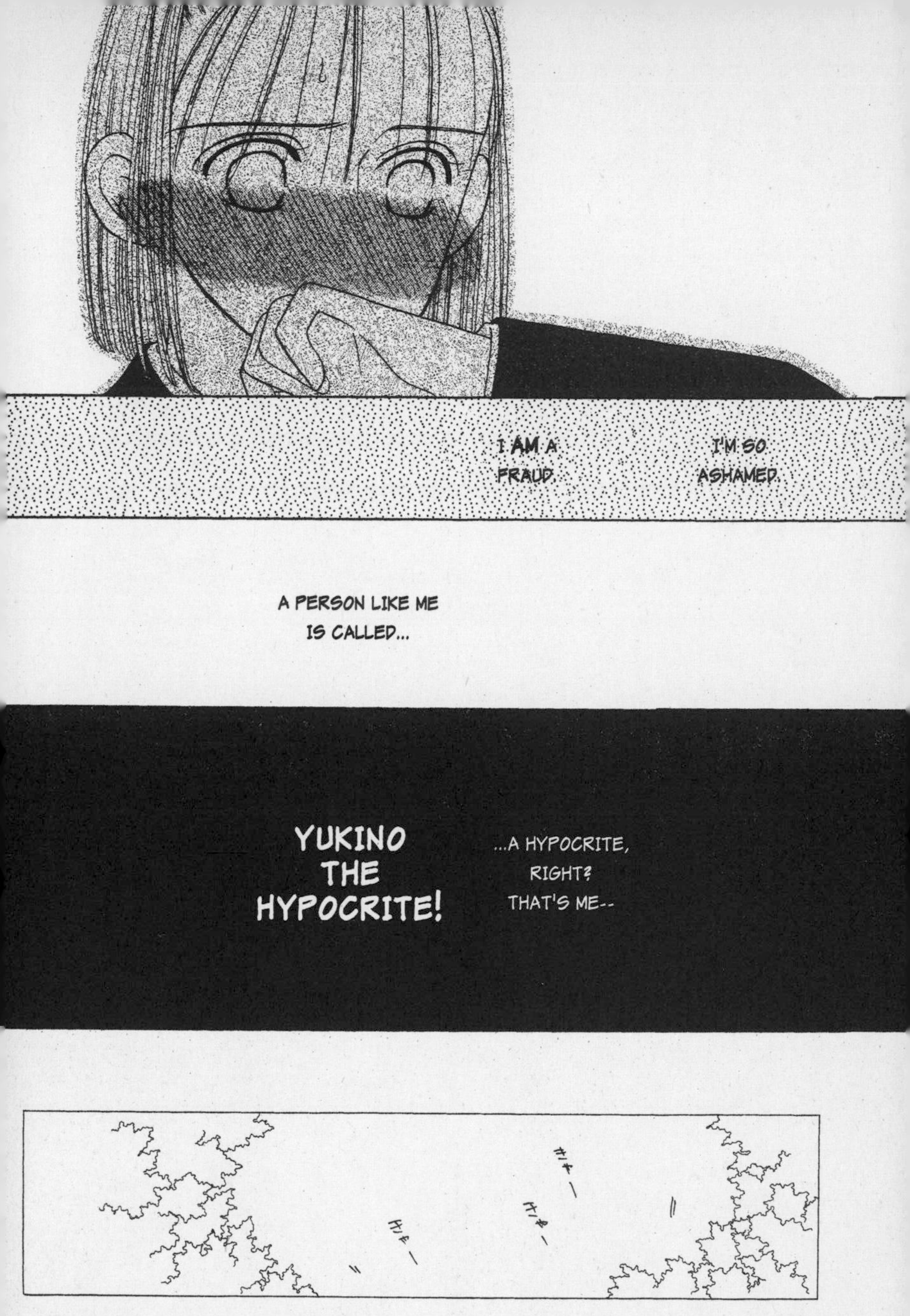

I'M SO ASHAMED.
I AM A FRAUD.
A PERSON LIKE ME IS CALLED...
...A HYPOCRITE, RIGHT? THAT'S ME--
YUKINO THE HYPOCRITE!

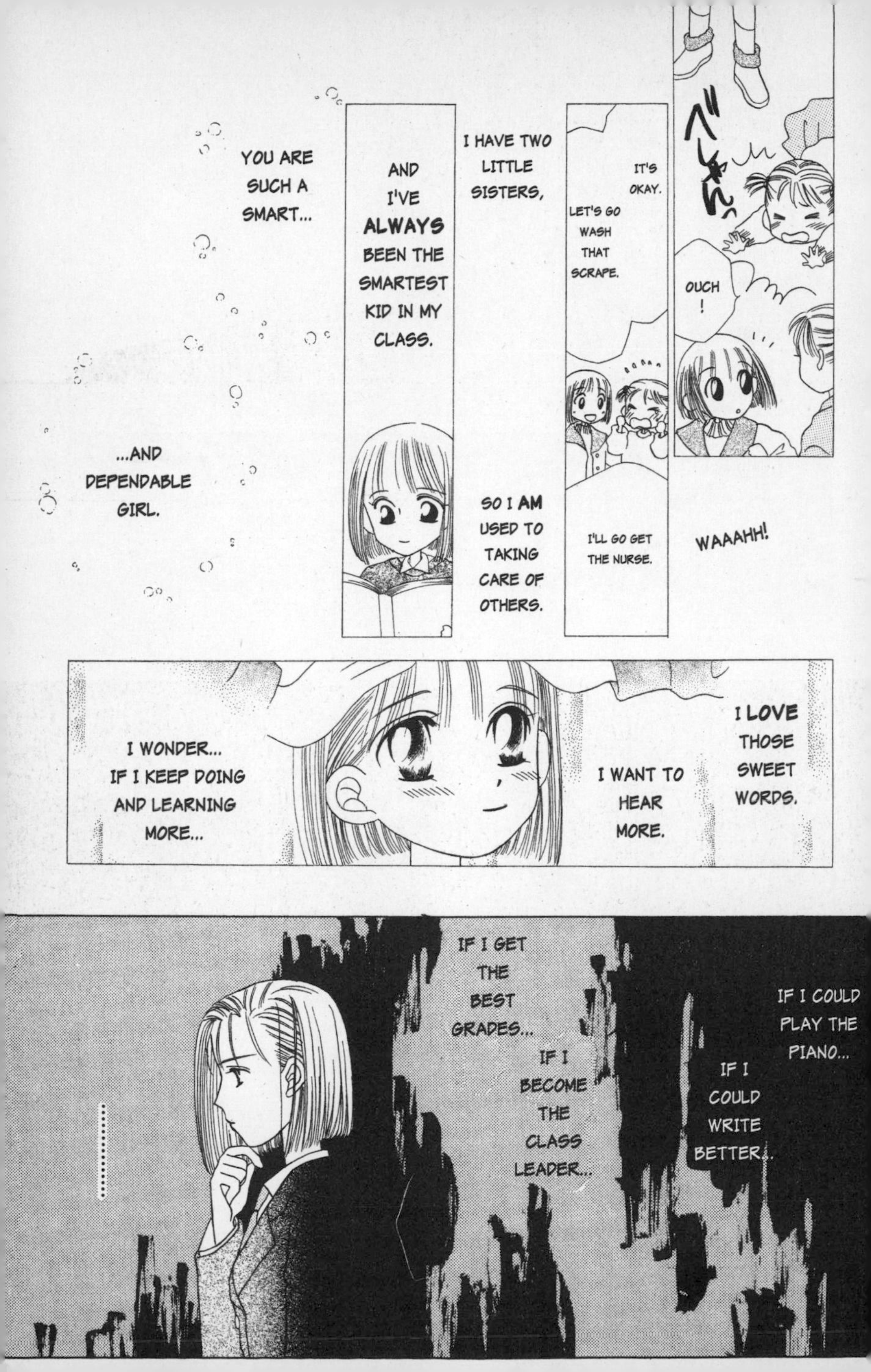
べしゃん
OUCH!
WAAAHH!
IT'S OKAY.
LET'S GO WASH THAT SCRAPE.
I'LL GO GET THE NURSE.
I HAVE TWO LITTLE SISTERS,
SO I AM USED TO TAKING CARE OF OTHERS.
AND I'VE ALWAYS BEEN THE SMARTEST KID IN MY CLASS.
YOU ARE SUCH A SMART...
...AND DEPENDABLE GIRL.
I LOVE THOSE SWEET WORDS.
I WANT TO HEAR MORE.
I WONDER... IF I KEEP DOING AND LEARNING MORE...
IF I COULD PLAY THE PIANO...
IF I COULD WRITE BETTER...
IF I GET THE BEST GRADES...
IF I BECOME THE CLASS LEADER...
......

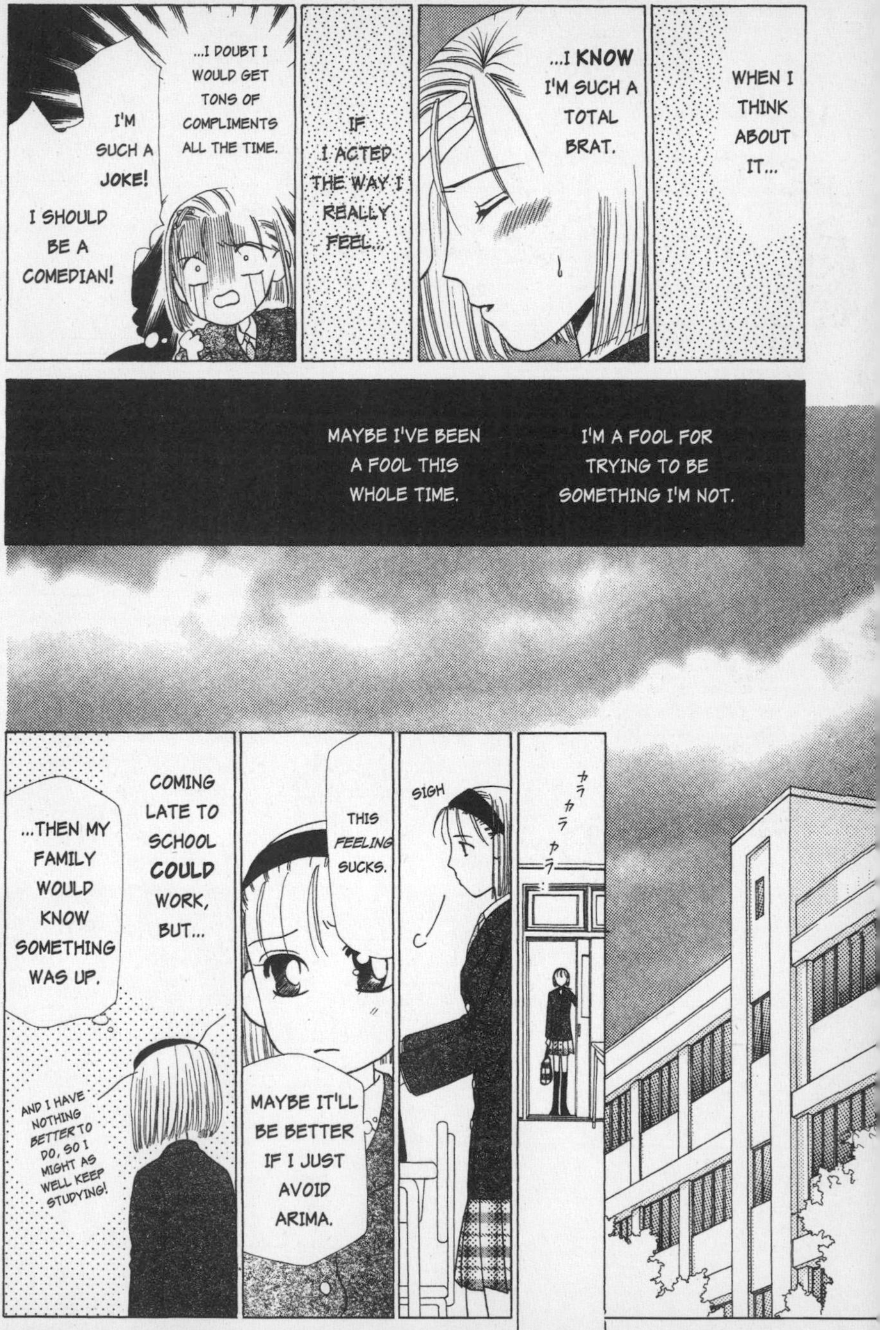
WHEN I THINK ABOUT IT...
...I KNOW I'M SUCH A TOTAL BRAT.
IF I ACTED THE WAY I REALLY FEEL...
...I DOUBT I WOULD GET TONS OF COMPLIMENTS ALL THE TIME.
I'M SUCH A JOKE!
I SHOULD BE A COMEDIAN!
I'M A FOOL FOR TRYING TO BE SOMETHING I'M NOT.
MAYBE I'VE BEEN A FOOL THIS WHOLE TIME.
カラカラカラ
SIGH
THIS FEELING SUCKS.
MAYBE IT'LL BE BETTER IF I JUST AVOID ARIMA.
COMING LATE TO SCHOOL COULD WORK, BUT...
...THEN MY FAMILY WOULD KNOW SOMETHING WAS UP.
AND I HAVE NOTHING BETTER TO DO, SO I MIGHT AS WELL KEEP STUDYING!

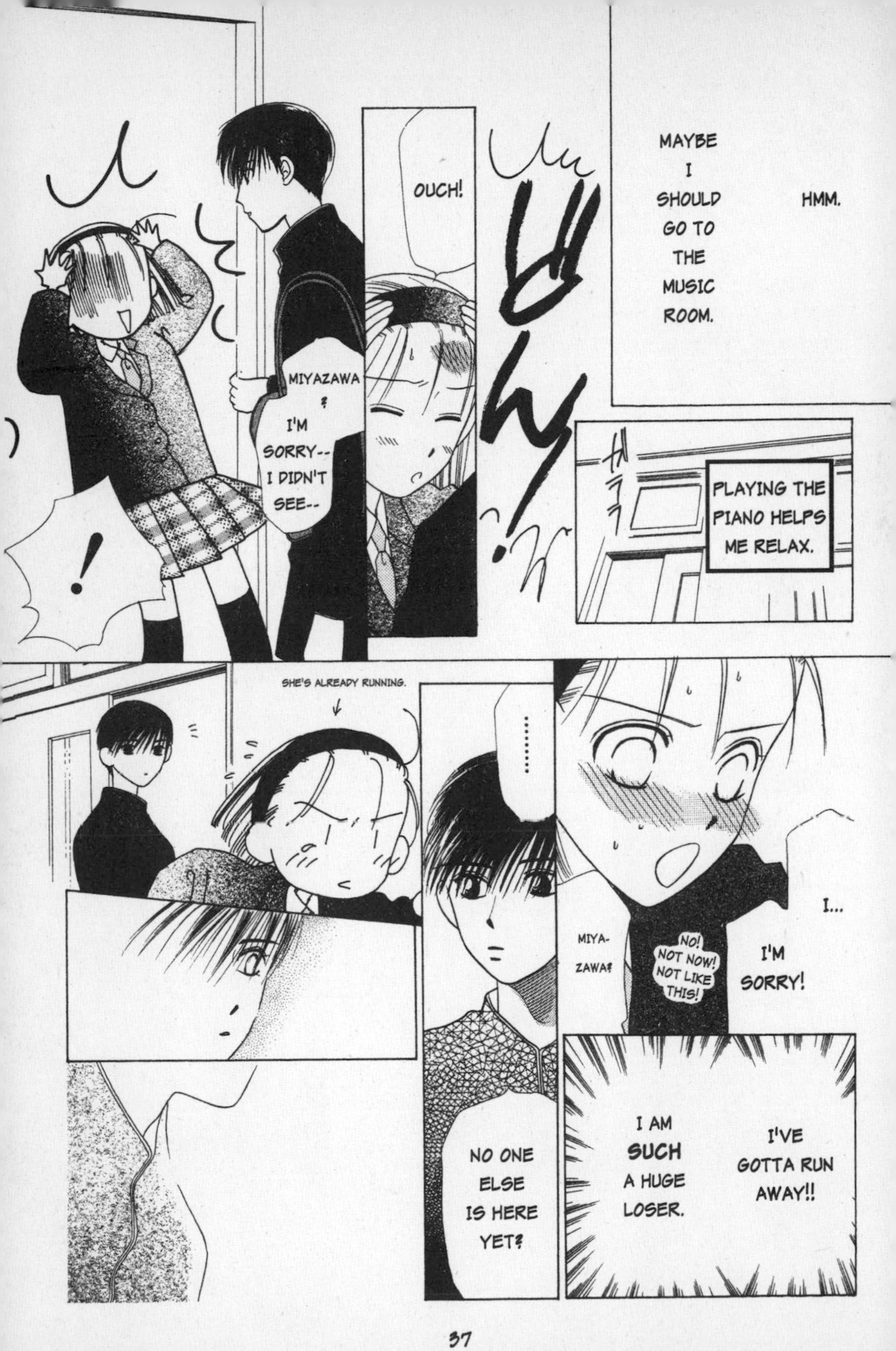
HMM.
MAYBE I SHOULD GO TO THE MUSIC ROOM.
PLAYING THE PIANO HELPS ME RELAX.
OUCH!
MIYAZAWA?
I'M SORRY-- I DIDN'T SEE--
I...
I'M SORRY!
NO! NOT NOW! NOT LIKE THIS!
MIYA-ZAWA?
I'VE GOTTA RUN AWAY!!
I AM **SUCH** A HUGE LOSER.
......
NO ONE ELSE IS HERE YET?
SHE'S ALREADY RUNNING.

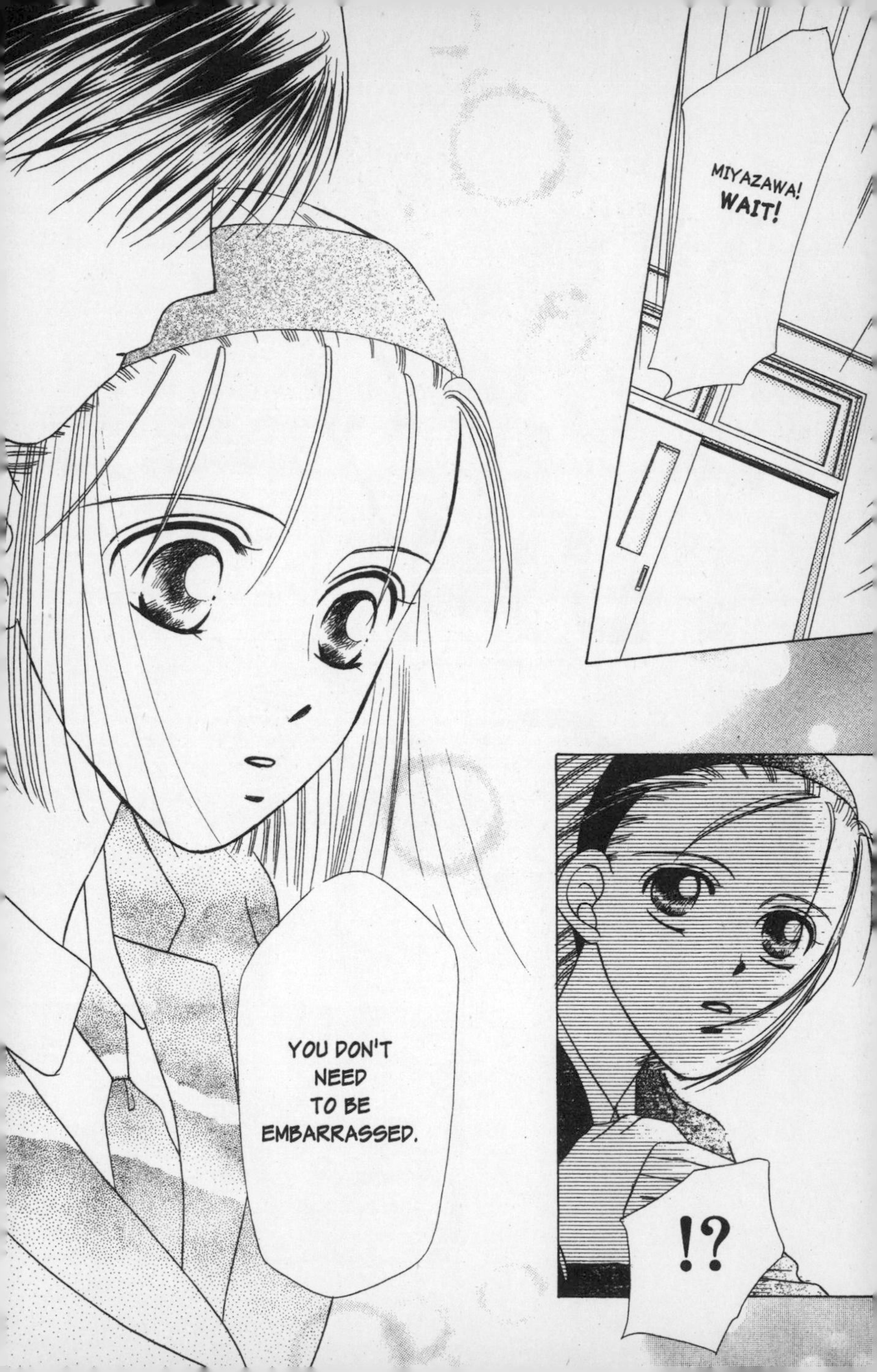
MIYAZAWA! WAIT!
!?
YOU DON'T NEED TO BE EMBARRASSED.

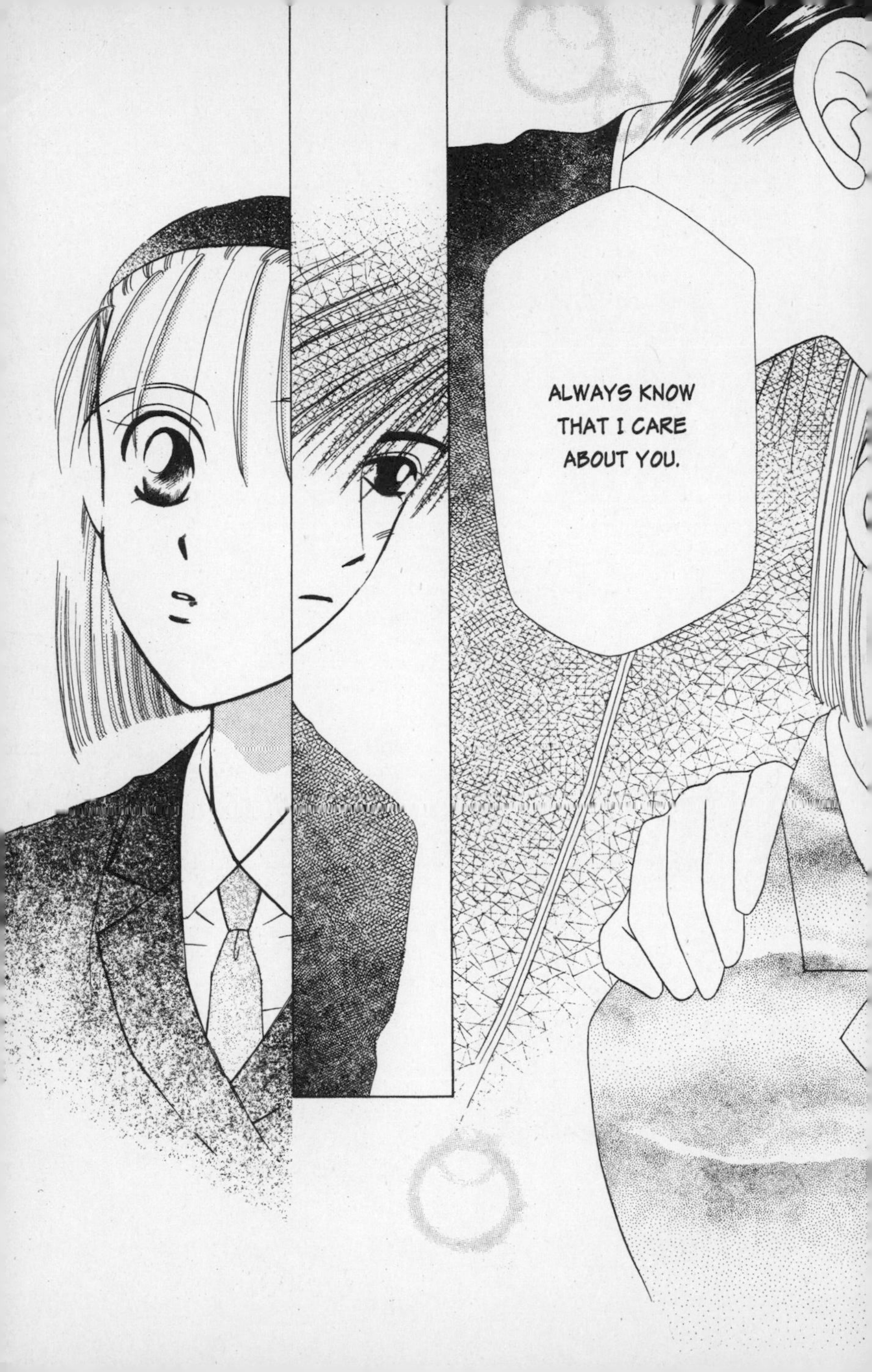
ALWAYS KNOW THAT I CARE ABOUT YOU.

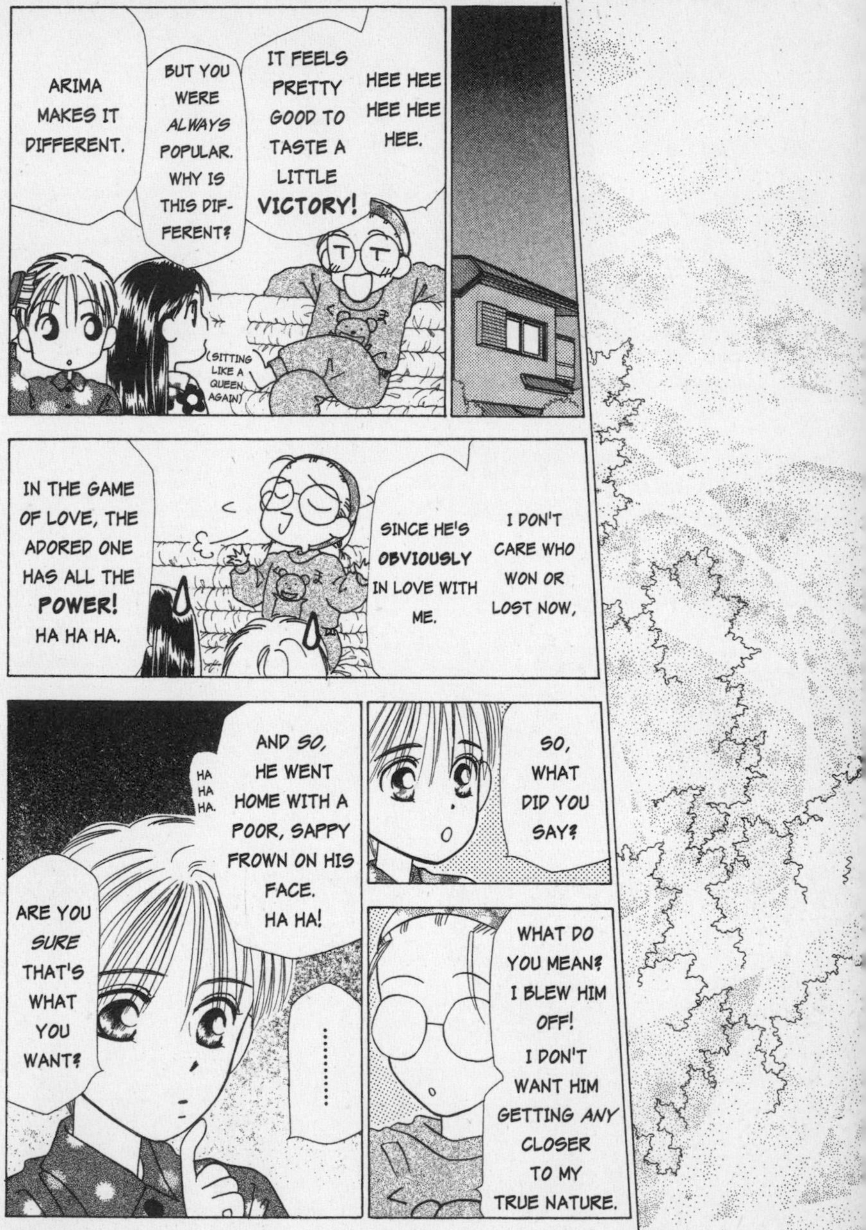
HEE HEE HEE HEE HEE.
IT FEELS PRETTY GOOD TO TASTE A LITTLE VICTORY!
BUT YOU WERE ALWAYS POPULAR. WHY IS THIS DIFFERENT?
ARIMA MAKES IT DIFFERENT.
(SITTING LIKE A QUEEN AGAIN)
I DON'T CARE WHO WON OR LOST NOW,
SINCE HE'S OBVIOUSLY IN LOVE WITH ME.
IN THE GAME OF LOVE, THE ADORED ONE HAS ALL THE POWER! HA HA HA.
SO, WHAT DID YOU SAY?
WHAT DO YOU MEAN? I BLEW HIM OFF! I DON'T WANT HIM GETTING ANY CLOSER TO MY TRUE NATURE.
AND SO, HE WENT HOME WITH A POOR, SAPPY FROWN ON HIS FACE. HA HA!
HA HA HA.
......
ARE YOU SURE THAT'S WHAT YOU WANT?

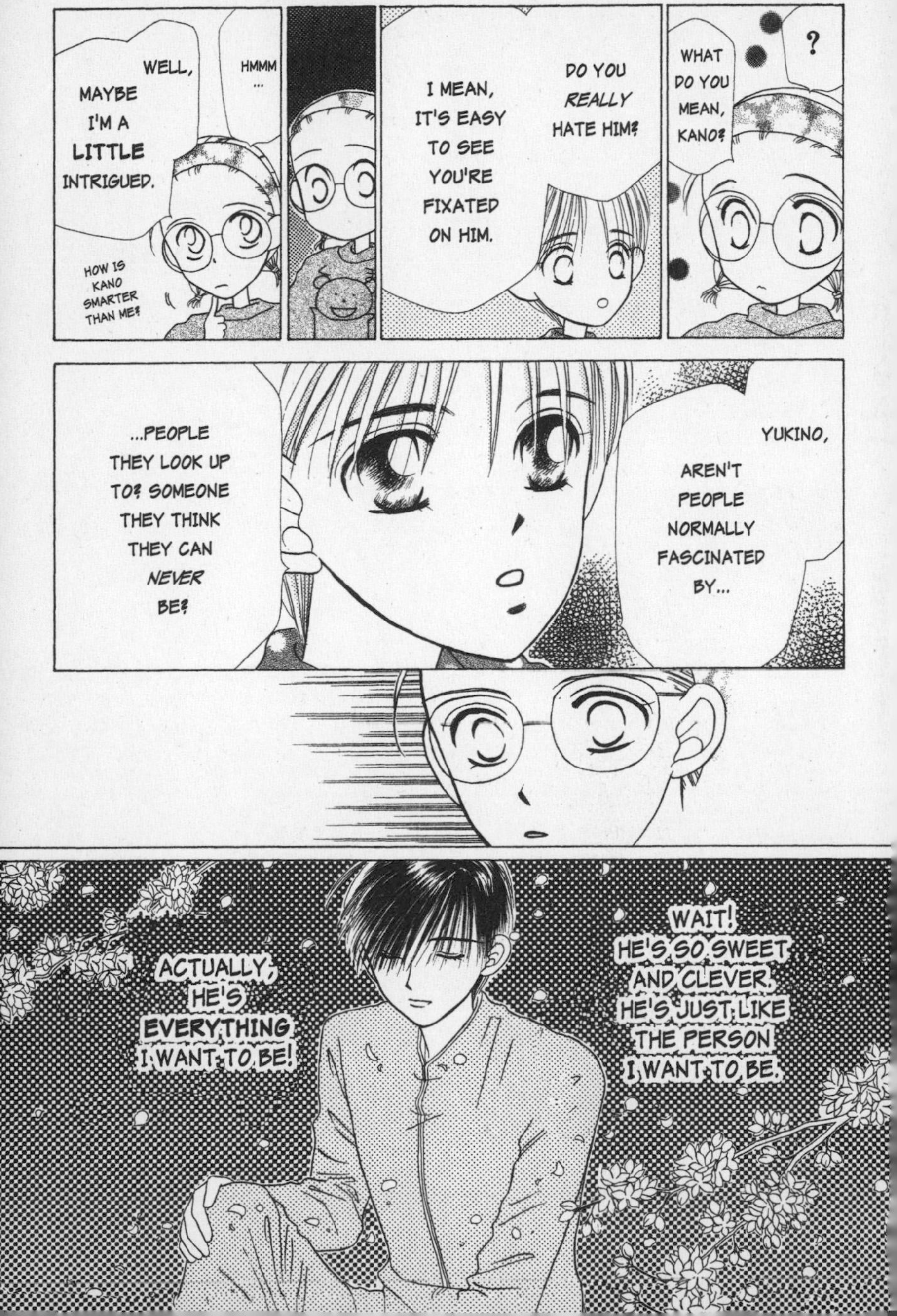
?
WHAT DO YOU MEAN, KANO?
DO YOU REALLY HATE HIM?
I MEAN, IT'S EASY TO SEE YOU'RE FIXATED ON HIM.
HMMM ...
WELL, MAYBE I'M A LITTLE INTRIGUED.
HOW IS KANO SMARTER THAN ME?
YUKINO, AREN'T PEOPLE NORMALLY FASCINATED BY...
...PEOPLE THEY LOOK UP TO? SOMEONE THEY THINK THEY CAN NEVER BE?
WAIT! HE'S SO SWEET AND CLEVER. HE'S JUST LIKE THE PERSON I WANT TO BE.
ACTUALLY, HE'S EVERYTHING I WANT TO BE!

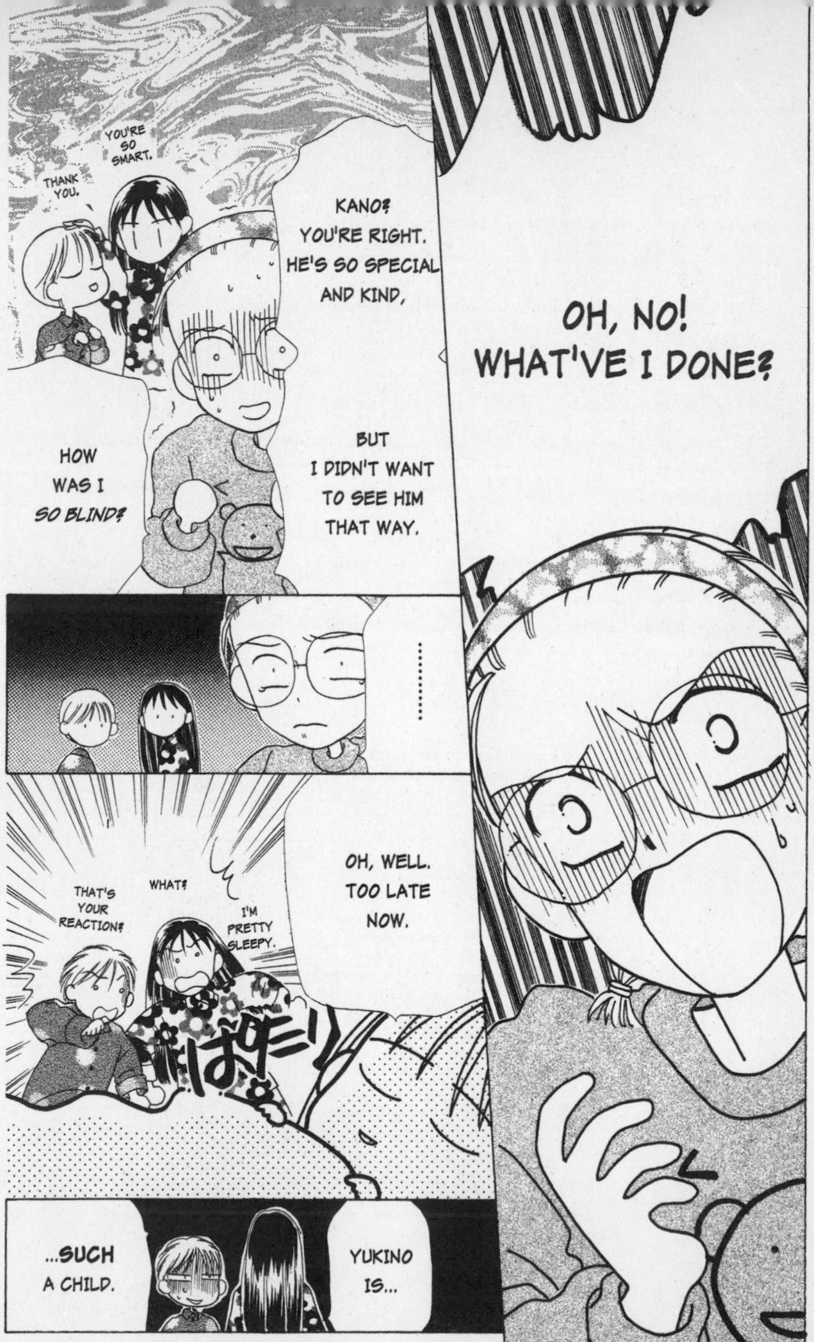
OH, NO! WHAT'VE I DONE?
KANO? YOU'RE RIGHT. HE'S SO SPECIAL AND KIND,
YOU'RE SO SMART.
THANK YOU.
BUT I DIDN'T WANT TO SEE HIM THAT WAY.
HOW WAS I SO BLIND?
....
OH, WELL. TOO LATE NOW.
I'M PRETTY SLEEPY.
WHAT?
THAT'S YOUR REACTION?
YUKINO IS...
...SUCH A CHILD.

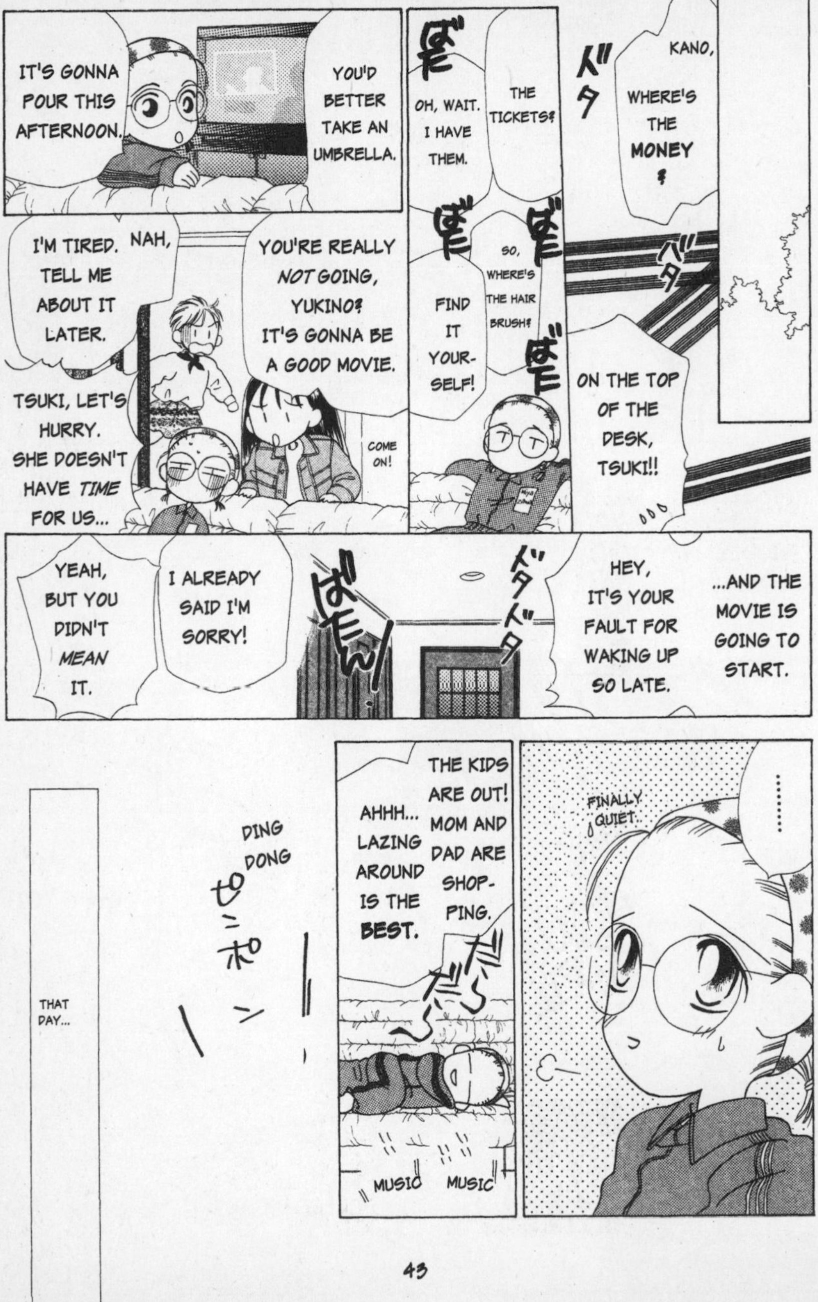
KANO, WHERE'S THE MONEY?
THE TICKETS?
OH, WAIT. I HAVE THEM.
YOU'D BETTER TAKE AN UMBRELLA.
IT'S GONNA POUR THIS AFTERNOON.
ON THE TOP OF THE DESK, TSUKI!!
SO, WHERE'S THE HAIR BRUSH?
FIND IT YOURSELF!
YOU'RE REALLY *NOT* GOING, YUKINO? IT'S GONNA BE A GOOD MOVIE.
NAH, I'M TIRED. TELL ME ABOUT IT LATER.
COME ON!
TSUKI, LET'S HURRY. SHE DOESN'T HAVE *TIME* FOR US...
...AND THE MOVIE IS GOING TO START.
HEY, IT'S YOUR FAULT FOR WAKING UP SO LATE.
I ALREADY SAID I'M SORRY!
YEAH, BUT YOU DIDN'T *MEAN* IT.
......
FINALLY QUIET.
THE KIDS ARE OUT! MOM AND DAD ARE SHOP-PING.
AHHH... LAZING AROUND IS THE BEST.
MUSIC
MUSIC
DING DONG
THAT DAY...

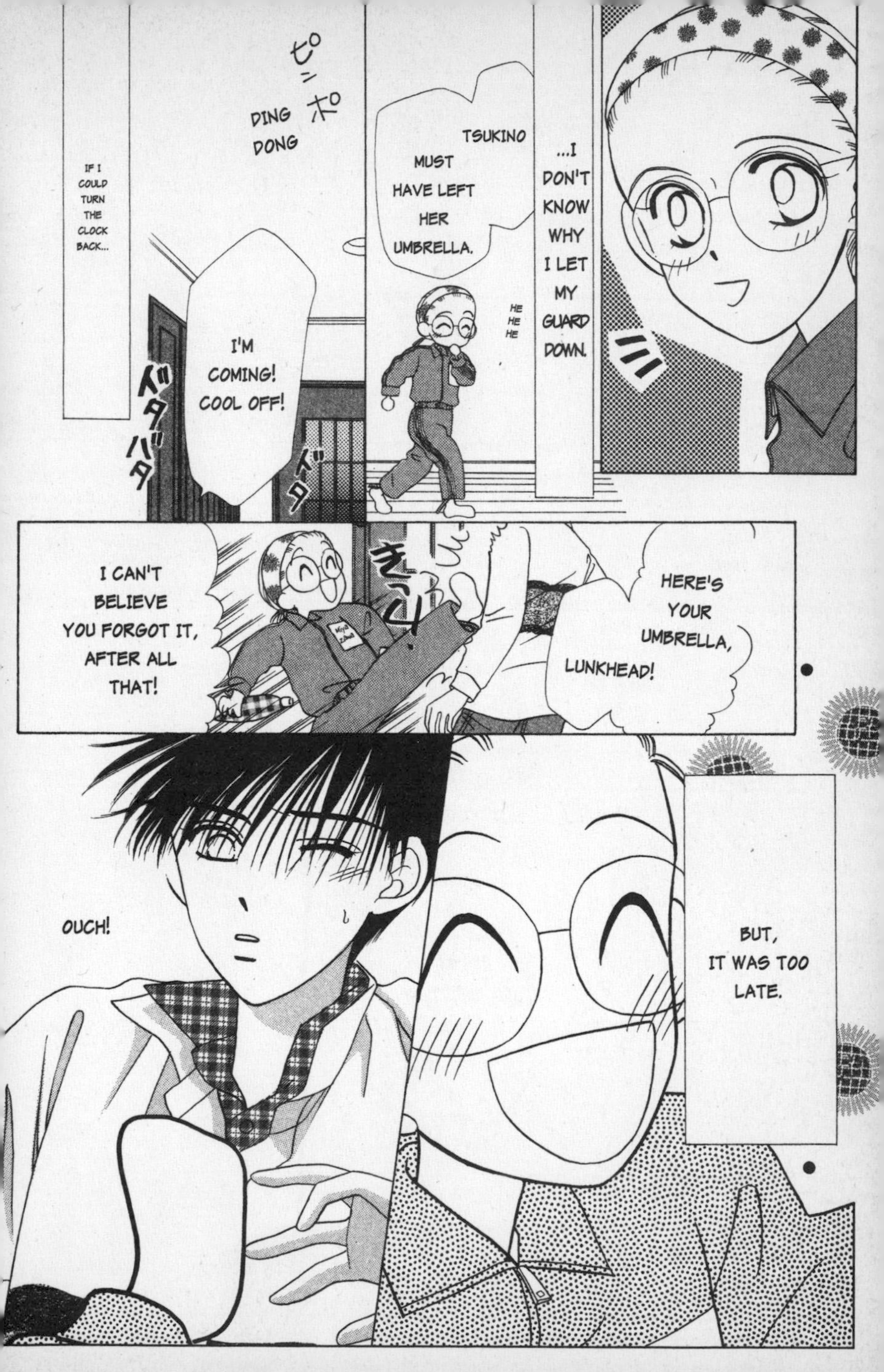
...I DON'T KNOW WHY I LET MY GUARD DOWN.
DING DONG
TSUKINO MUST HAVE LEFT HER UMBRELLA.
HE HE HE
I'M COMING! COOL OFF!
IF I COULD TURN THE CLOCK BACK...
HERE'S YOUR UMBRELLA, LUNKHEAD!
I CAN'T BELIEVE YOU FORGOT IT, AFTER ALL THAT!
BUT, IT WAS TOO LATE.
OUCH!

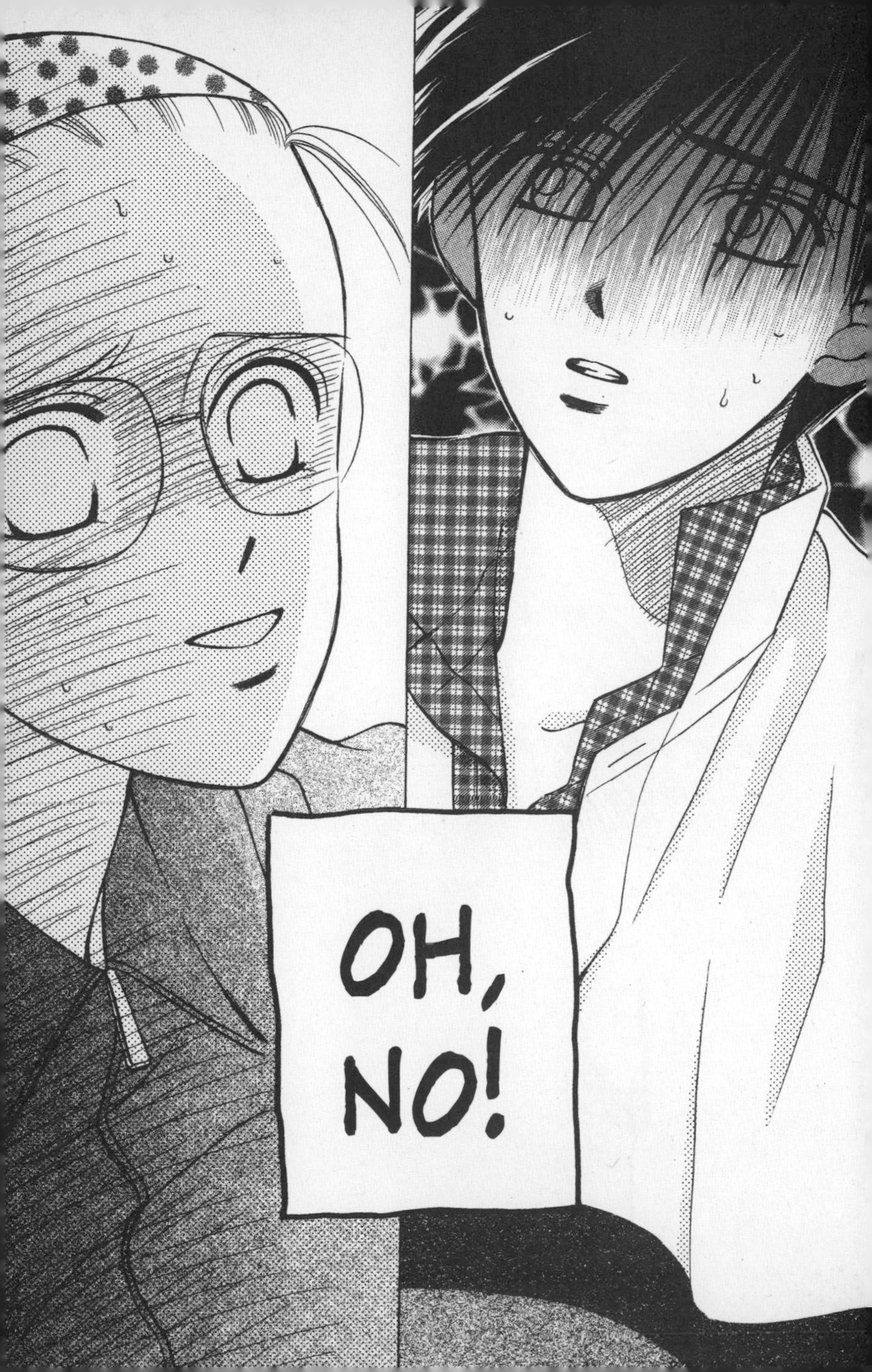
OH, NO!

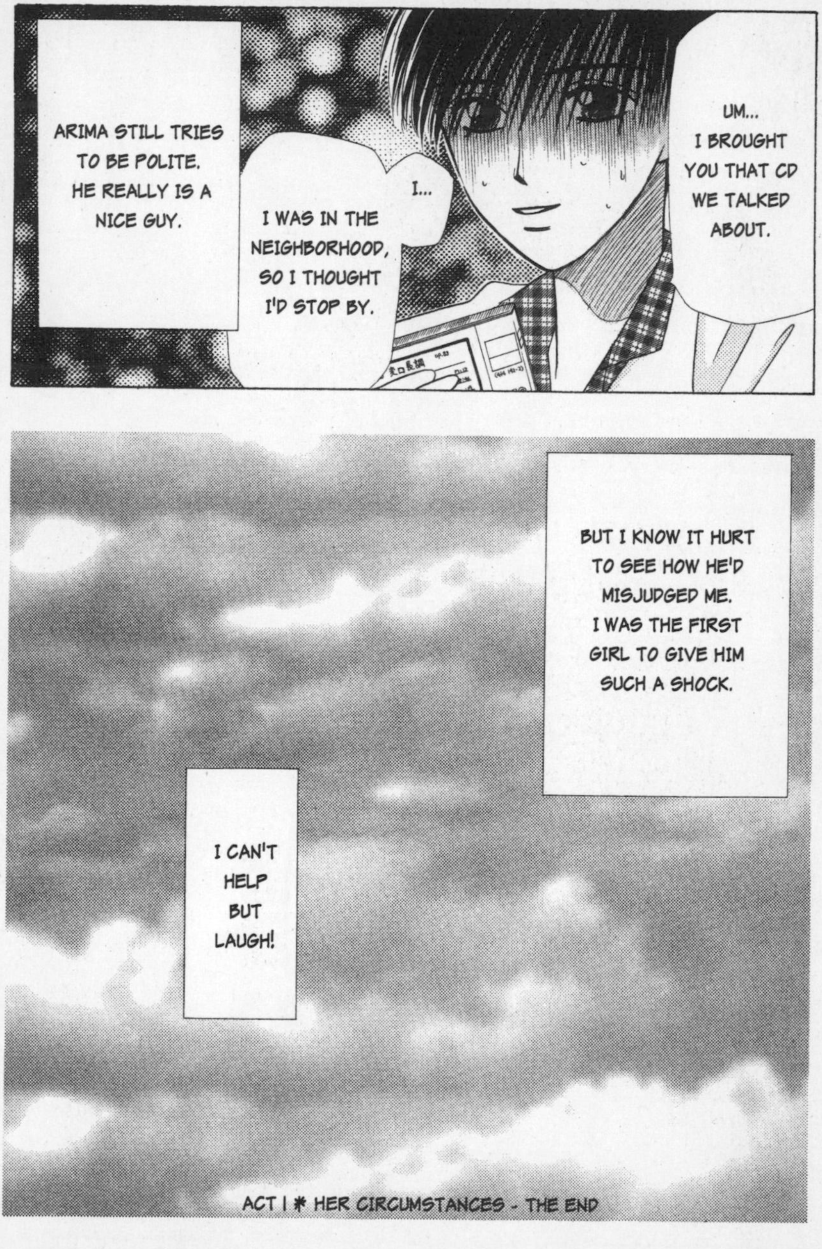
UM... I BROUGHT YOU THAT CD WE TALKED ABOUT.
I...
I WAS IN THE NEIGHBORHOOD, SO I THOUGHT I'D STOP BY.
ARIMA STILL TRIES TO BE POLITE. HE REALLY IS A NICE GUY.
BUT I KNOW IT HURT TO SEE HOW HE'D MISJUDGED ME. I WAS THE FIRST GIRL TO GIVE HIM SUCH A SHOCK.
I CAN'T HELP BUT LAUGH!
ACT 1 * HER CIRCUMSTANCES - THE END

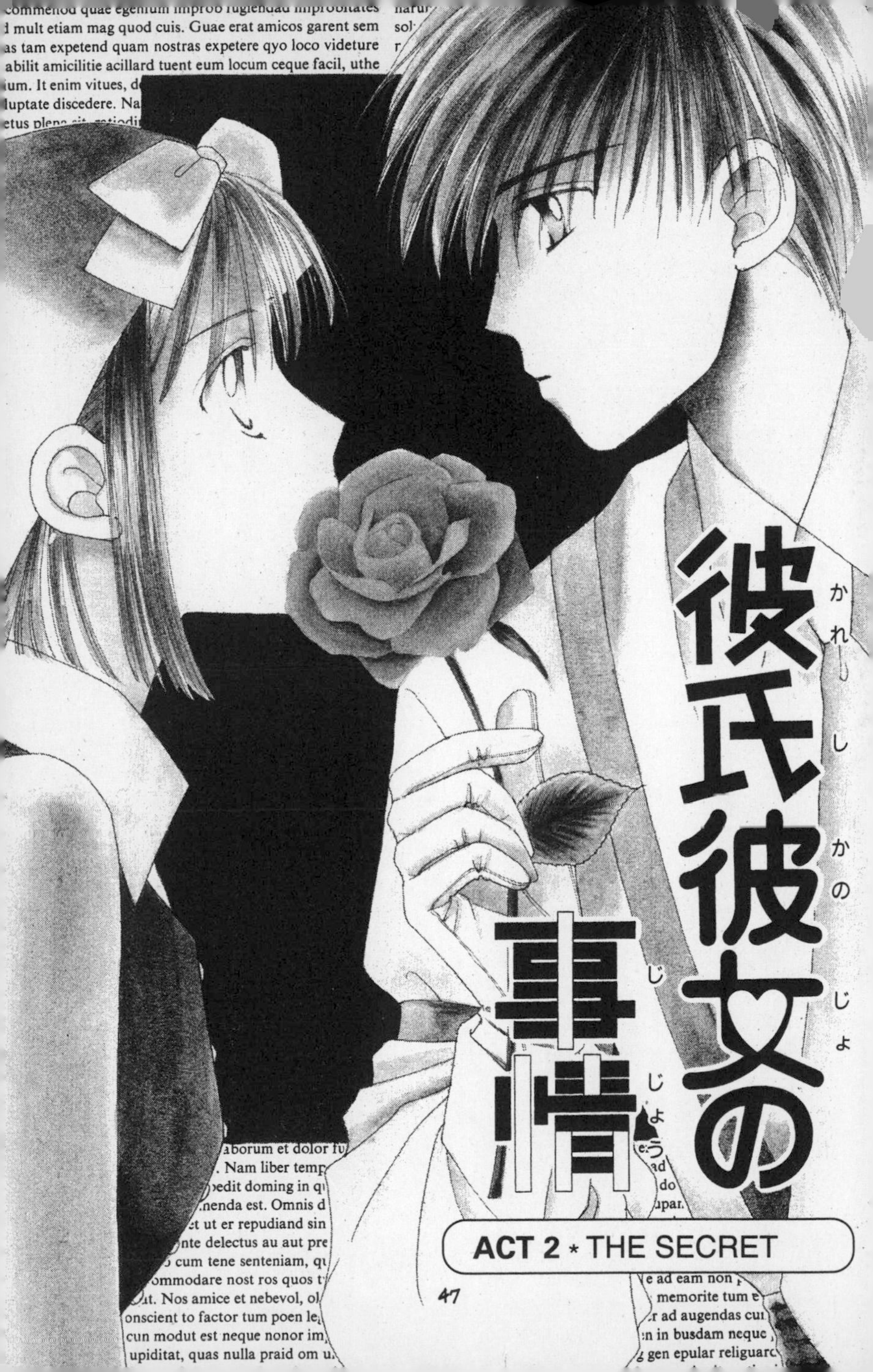
彼氏彼女の事情
かれしかのじょのじじょう
ACT 2 * THE SECRET
d mult etiam mag quod cuis. Guae erat amicos garent sem
as tam expetend quam nostras expetere qyo loco videture
abilit amicilitie acillard tuent eum locum ceque facil, uthe
ium. It enim vitues,
luptate discedere. Na
aborum et dolor fu
Nam liber temp
pedit doming in q
nenda est. Omnis d
et ut er repudiand sin
nte delectus au aut pre
o cum tene senteniam, q
ommodare nost ros quos t
it. Nos amice et nebevol, ol
onscient to factor tum poen le
cun modut est neque nonor im
upiditat, quas nulla praid om u
e ad eam non
memorite tum e
r ad augendas cu
n in busdam neque
g gen epular religuarc

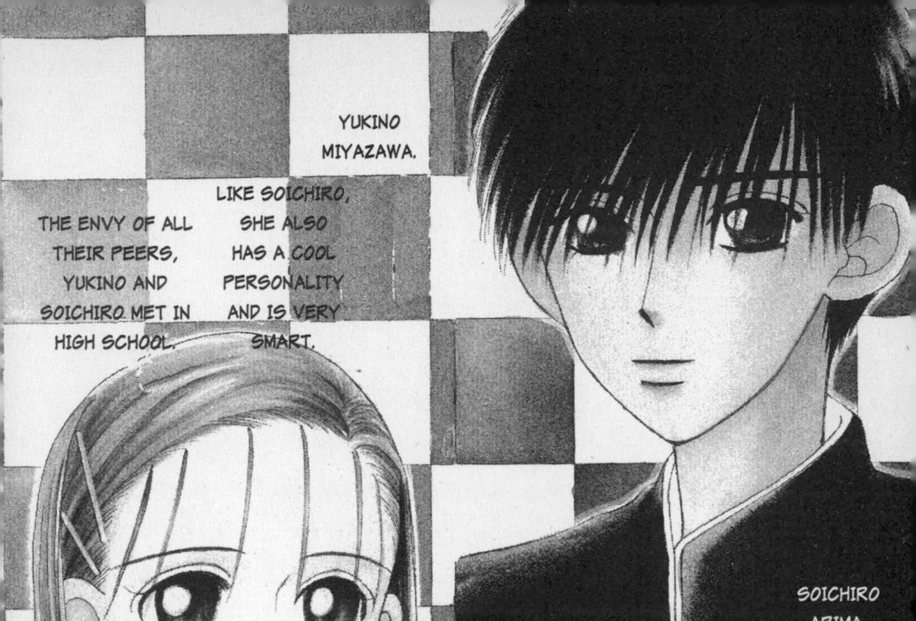
SOICHIRO ARIMA.
GOOD GRADES, GREAT ATHLETE, A TERRIFIC PERSONALITY,
AND MOST MEMBERS OF HIS FAMILY HAVE BEEN DOCTORS FOR MANY GENERATIONS.
YUKINO MIYAZAWA.
LIKE SOICHIRO, SHE ALSO HAS A COOL PERSONALITY AND IS VERY SMART.
THE ENVY OF ALL THEIR PEERS, YUKINO AND SOICHIRO MET IN HIGH SCHOOL.
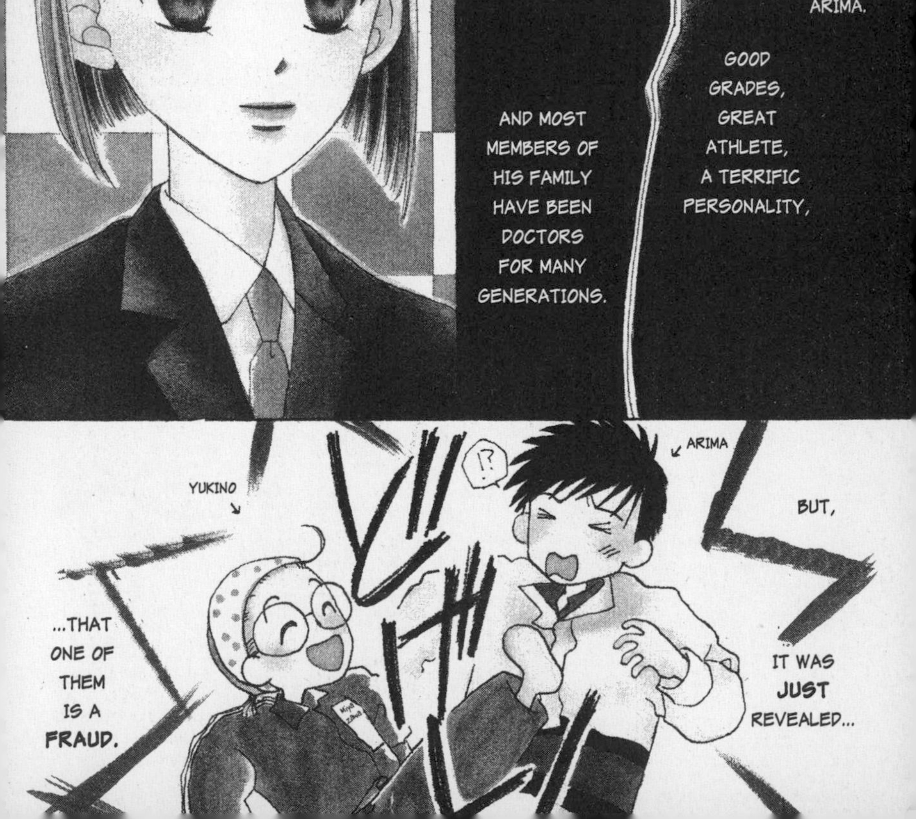
BUT,
IT WAS **JUST** REVEALED...
ARIMA
!?
YUKINO
...THAT ONE OF THEM IS A **FRAUD.**

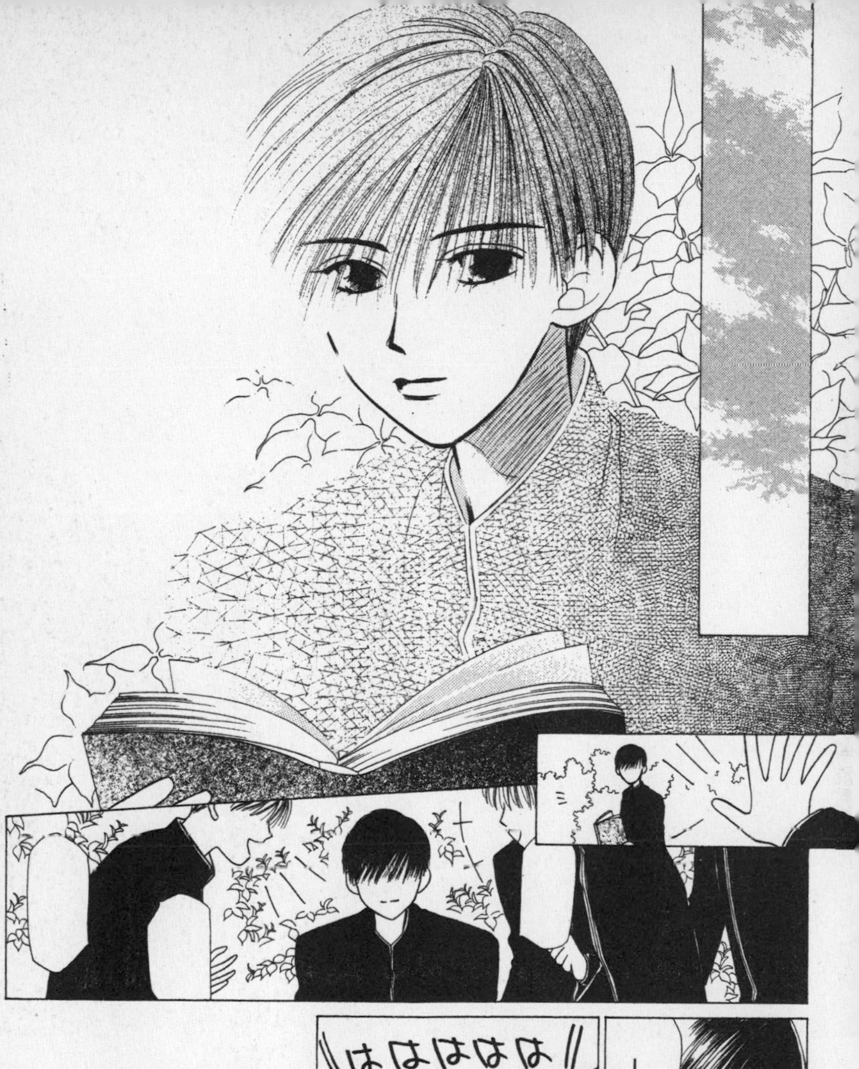

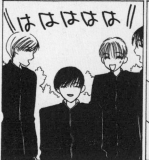

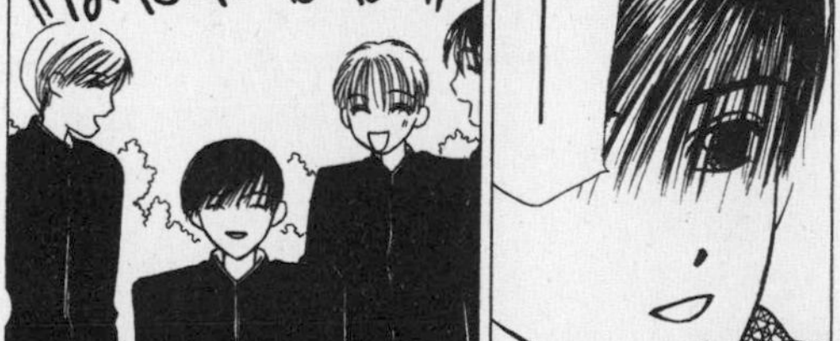
ははははは

YOU CAN TELL WHO WILL RISE ABOVE THE OTHERS WITH JUST ONE LOOK.

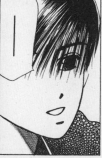

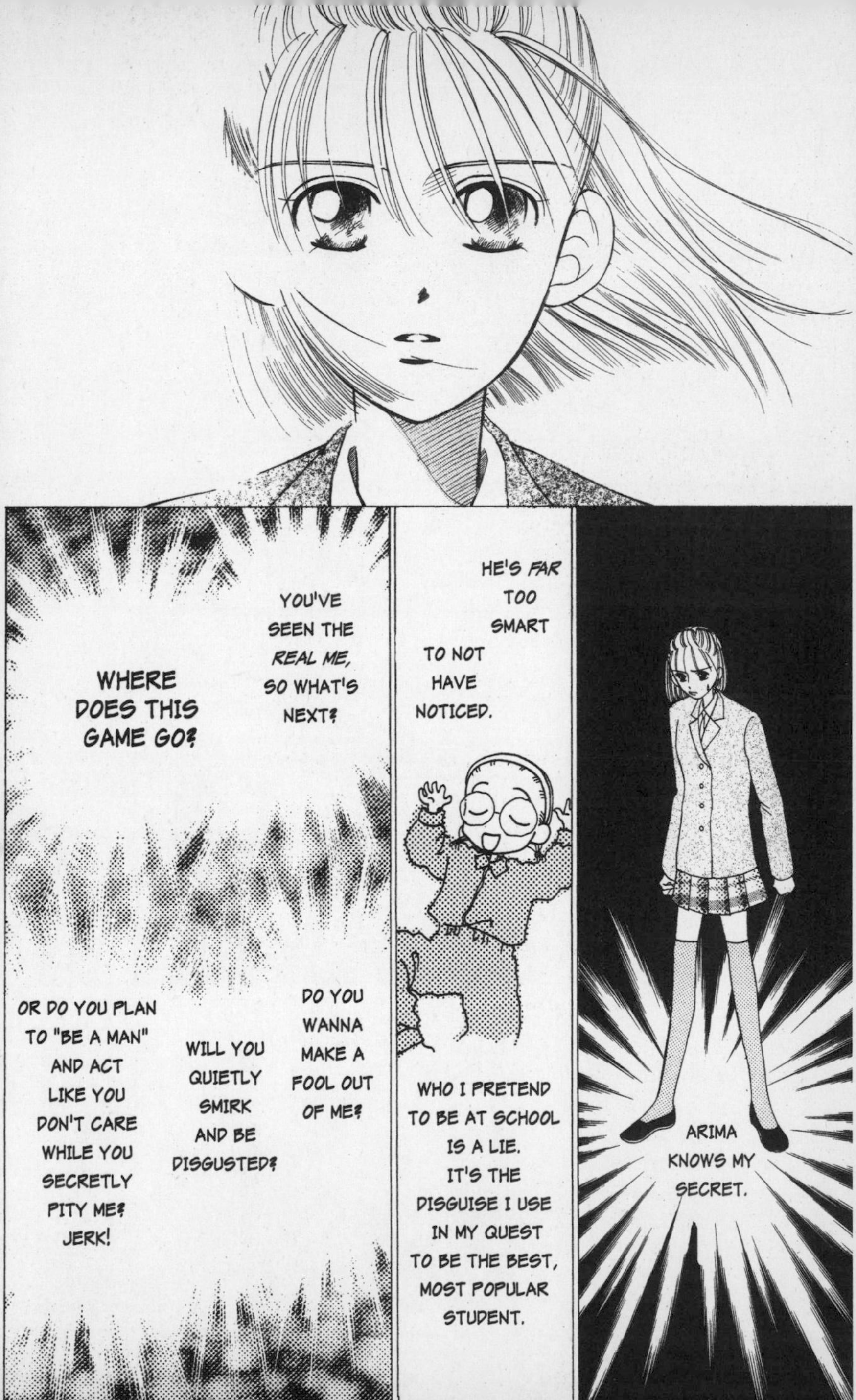
ARIMA KNOWS MY SECRET.
HE'S *FAR* TOO SMART TO NOT HAVE NOTICED.
WHO I PRETEND TO BE AT SCHOOL IS A LIE. IT'S THE DISGUISE I USE IN MY QUEST TO BE THE BEST, MOST POPULAR STUDENT.
YOU'VE SEEN THE *REAL ME,* SO WHAT'S NEXT?
WHERE DOES THIS GAME GO?
DO YOU WANNA MAKE A FOOL OUT OF ME?
WILL YOU QUIETLY SMIRK AND BE DISGUSTED?
OR DO YOU PLAN TO "BE A MAN" AND ACT LIKE YOU DON'T CARE WHILE YOU SECRETLY PITY ME? JERK!

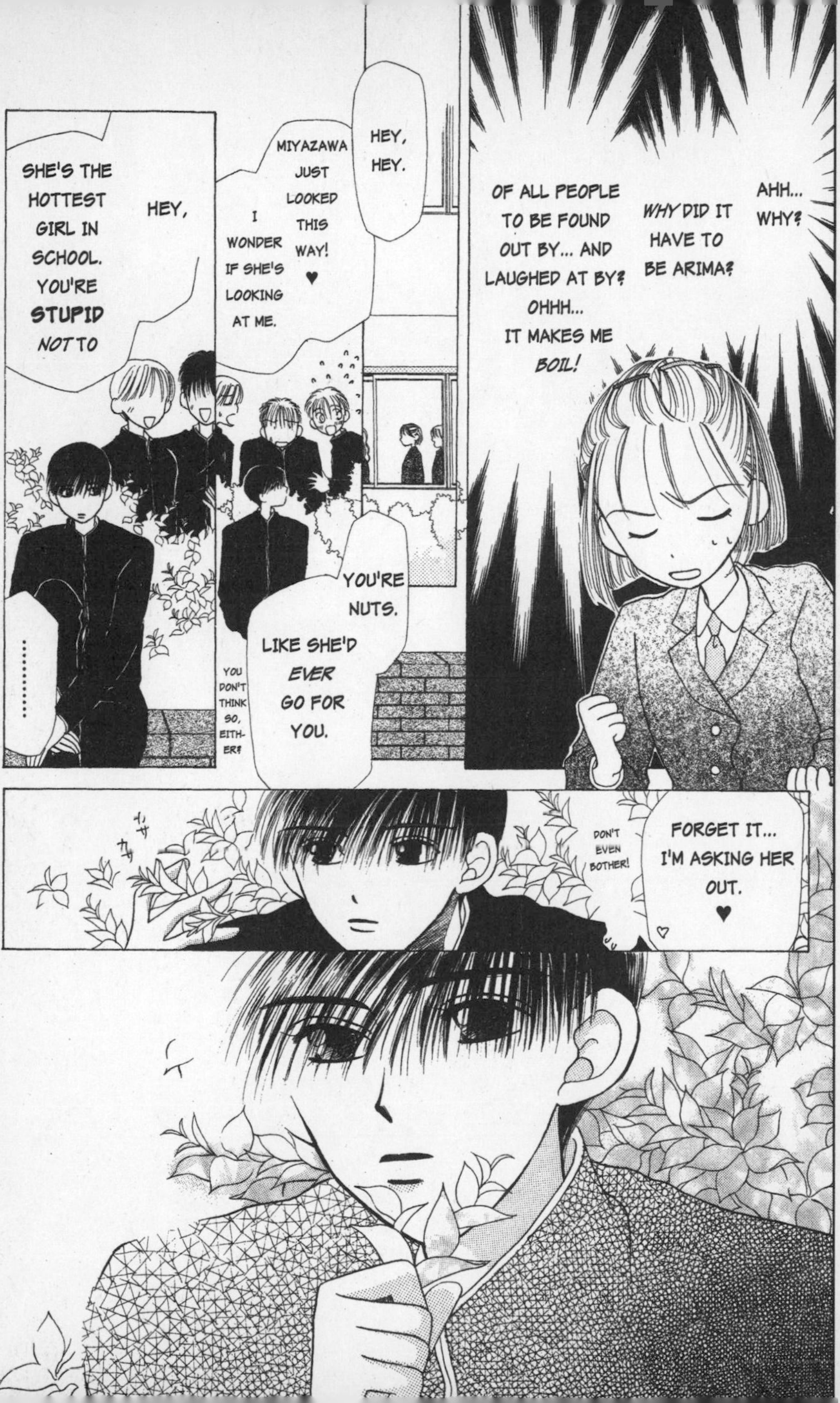
AHH... WHY?
WHY DID IT HAVE TO BE ARIMA?
OF ALL PEOPLE TO BE FOUND OUT BY... AND LAUGHED AT BY? OHHH... IT MAKES ME *BOIL!*
HEY, HEY.
MIYAZAWA JUST LOOKED THIS WAY! ♥
I WONDER IF SHE'S LOOKING AT ME.
YOU'RE NUTS.
LIKE SHE'D *EVER* GO FOR YOU.
YOU DON'T THINK SO, EITHER?
HEY,
SHE'S THE HOTTEST GIRL IN SCHOOL. YOU'RE **STUPID** *NOT* TO
....
FORGET IT... I'M ASKING HER OUT. ♥
DON'T EVEN BOTHER!

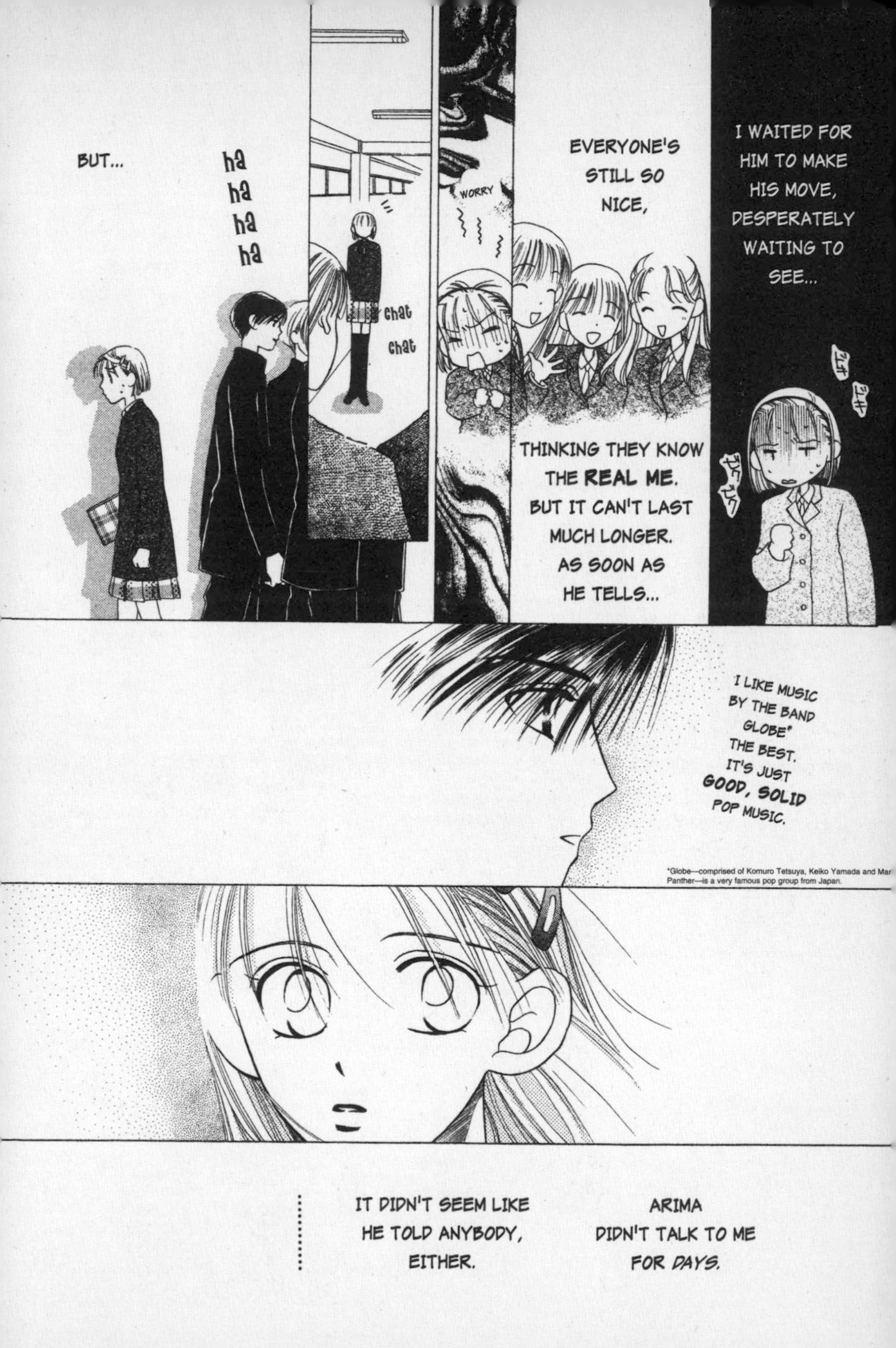
I WAITED FOR HIM TO MAKE HIS MOVE, DESPERATELY WAITING TO SEE...
EVERYONE'S STILL SO NICE,
THINKING THEY KNOW THE REAL ME. BUT IT CAN'T LAST MUCH LONGER. AS SOON AS HE TELLS...
WORRY
chat
chat
ha
ha
ha
ha
BUT...
I LIKE MUSIC BY THE BAND GLOBE* THE BEST. IT'S JUST GOOD, SOLID POP MUSIC.
ARIMA DIDN'T TALK TO ME FOR DAYS.
IT DIDN'T SEEM LIKE HE TOLD ANYBODY, EITHER.

*Globe—comprised of Komuro Tetsuya, Keiko Yamada and Mar Panther—is a very famous pop group from Japan.

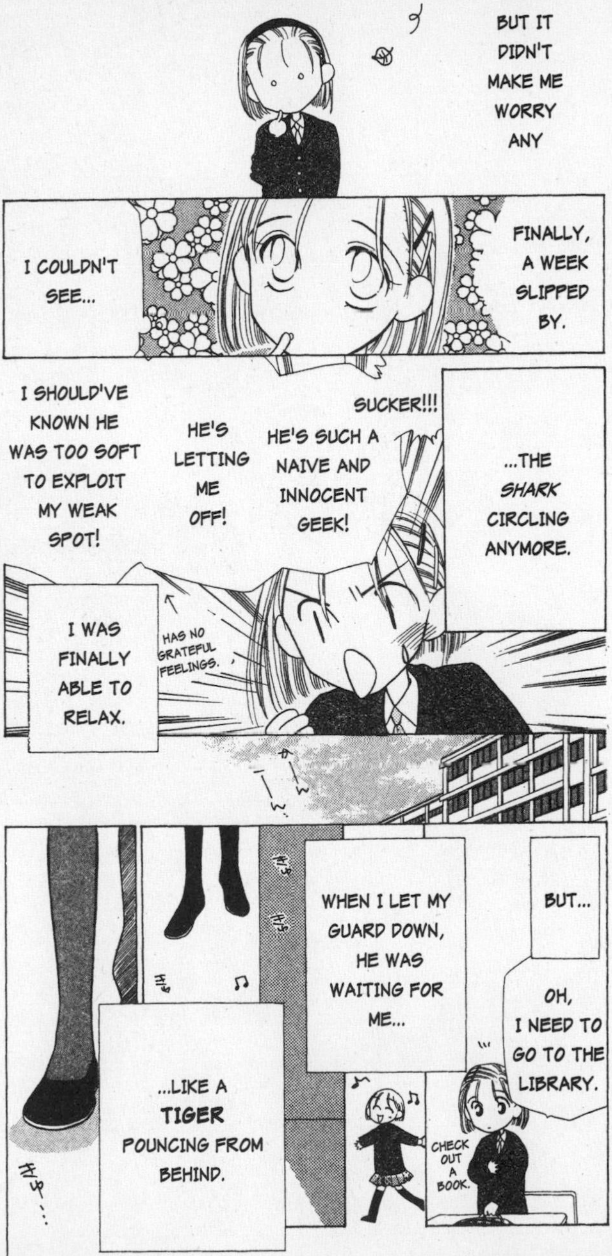
BUT IT DIDN'T MAKE ME WORRY ANY
FINALLY, A WEEK SLIPPED BY.
I COULDN'T SEE...
...THE SHARK CIRCLING ANYMORE.
SUCKER!!!
HE'S SUCH A NAIVE AND INNOCENT GEEK!
HE'S LETTING ME OFF!
I SHOULD'VE KNOWN HE WAS TOO SOFT TO EXPLOIT MY WEAK SPOT!
HAS NO GRATEFUL FEELINGS.
I WAS FINALLY ABLE TO RELAX.
BUT...
OH, I NEED TO GO TO THE LIBRARY.
CHECK OUT A BOOK.
WHEN I LET MY GUARD DOWN, HE WAS WAITING FOR ME...
...LIKE A TIGER POUNCING FROM BEHIND.

2

When I wrote my report, I got lots of paper cuts.

I cut myself with my own paper and magazines.

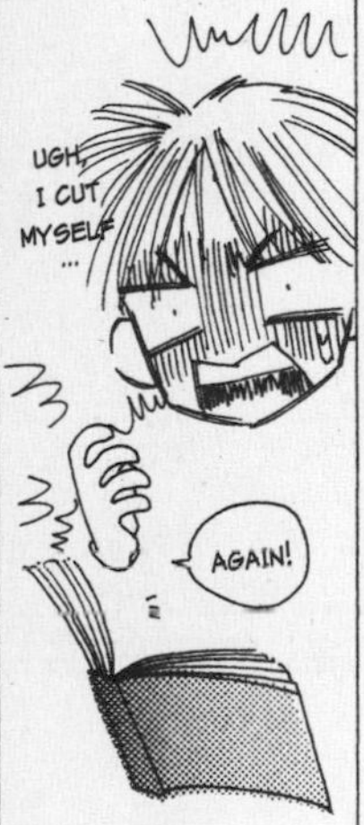
UGH, I CUT MYSELF...
AGAIN!

Well, they were only paper cuts, so I didn't actually bleed... but I was really sore.

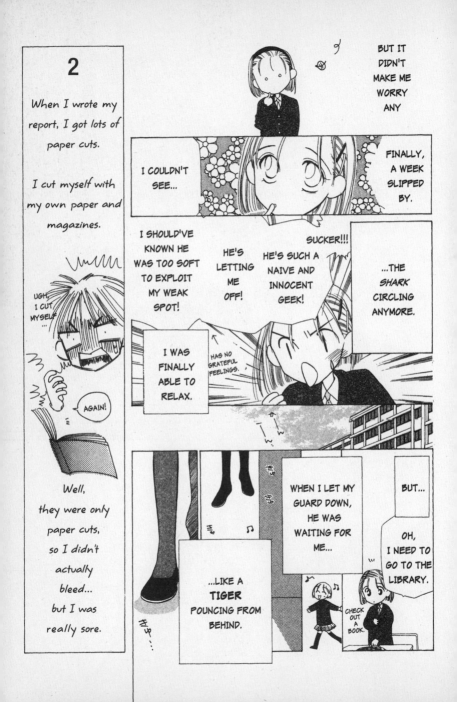

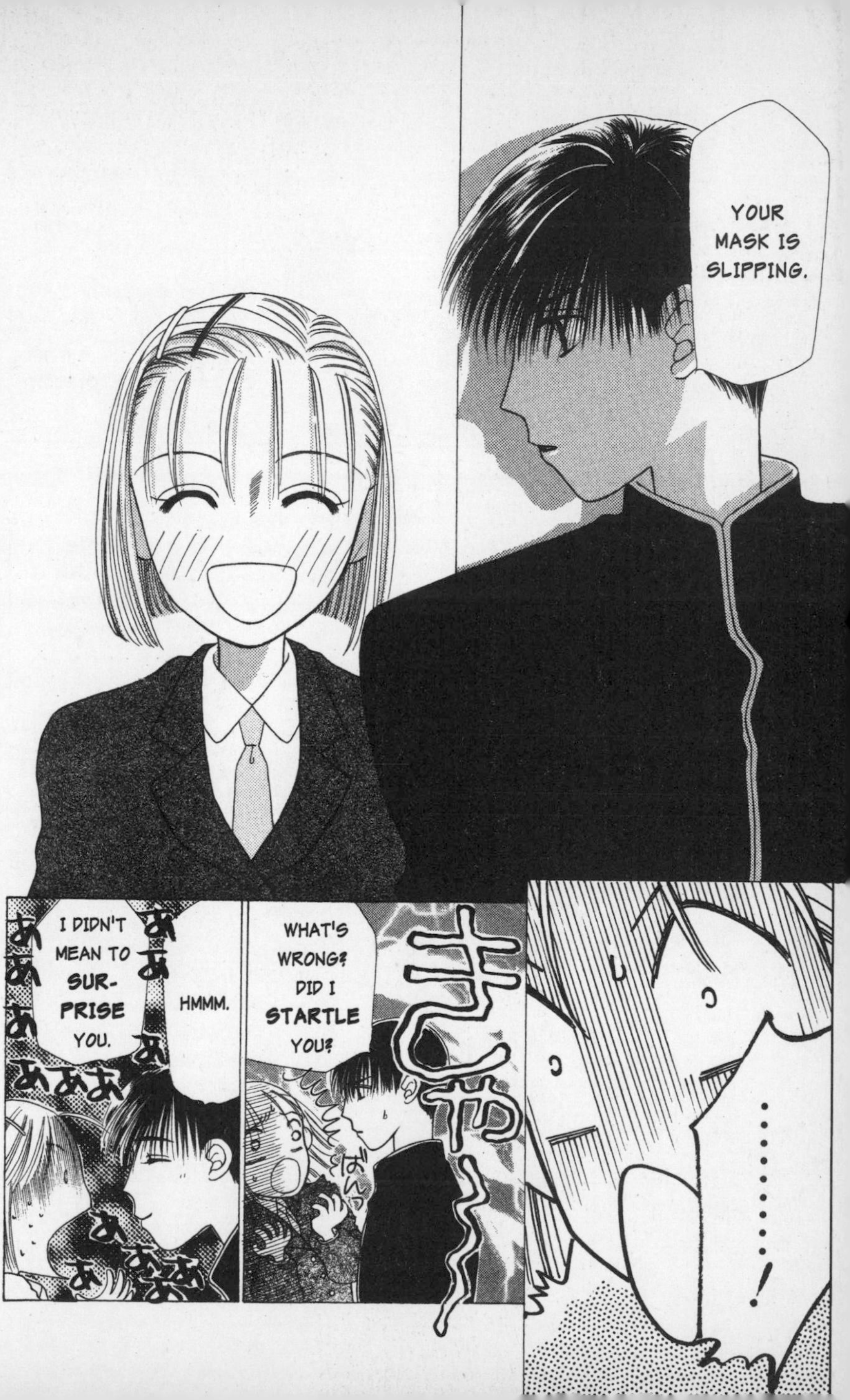

YOUR MASK IS SLIPPING.
......!
きゃ〜
WHAT'S WRONG? DID I STARTLE YOU?
HMMM.
I DIDN'T MEAN TO SURPRISE YOU.

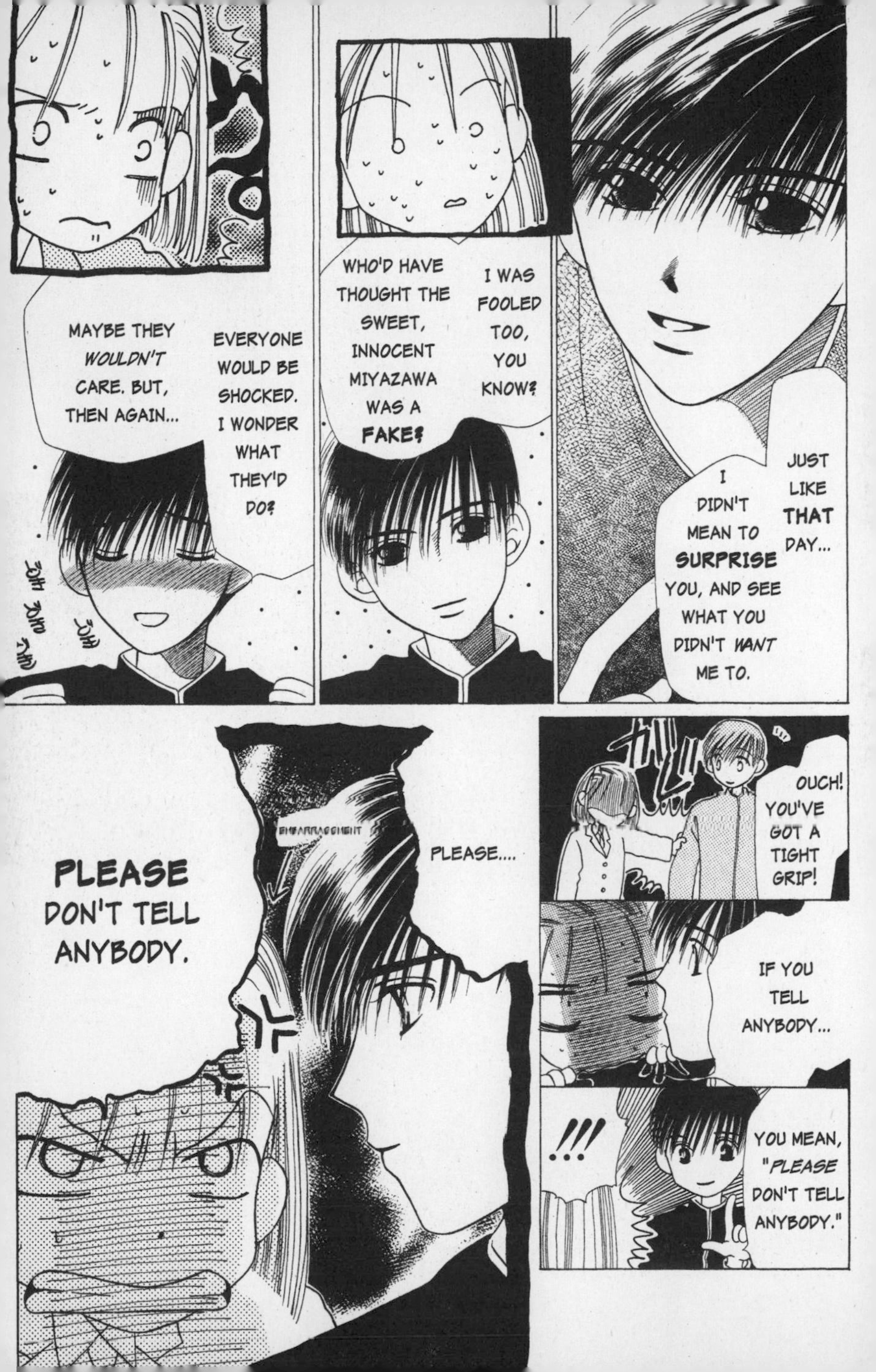
JUST LIKE THAT DAY...
I DIDN'T MEAN TO SURPRISE YOU, AND SEE WHAT YOU DIDN'T WANT ME TO.
I WAS FOOLED TOO, YOU KNOW?
WHO'D HAVE THOUGHT THE SWEET, INNOCENT MIYAZAWA WAS A FAKE?
EVERYONE WOULD BE SHOCKED. I WONDER WHAT THEY'D DO?
MAYBE THEY WOULDN'T CARE. BUT, THEN AGAIN...
OUCH! YOU'VE GOT A TIGHT GRIP!
IF YOU TELL ANYBODY...
YOU MEAN, "PLEASE DON'T TELL ANYBODY."
!!!
PLEASE....
EMBARRASSMENT
PLEASE DON'T TELL ANYBODY.

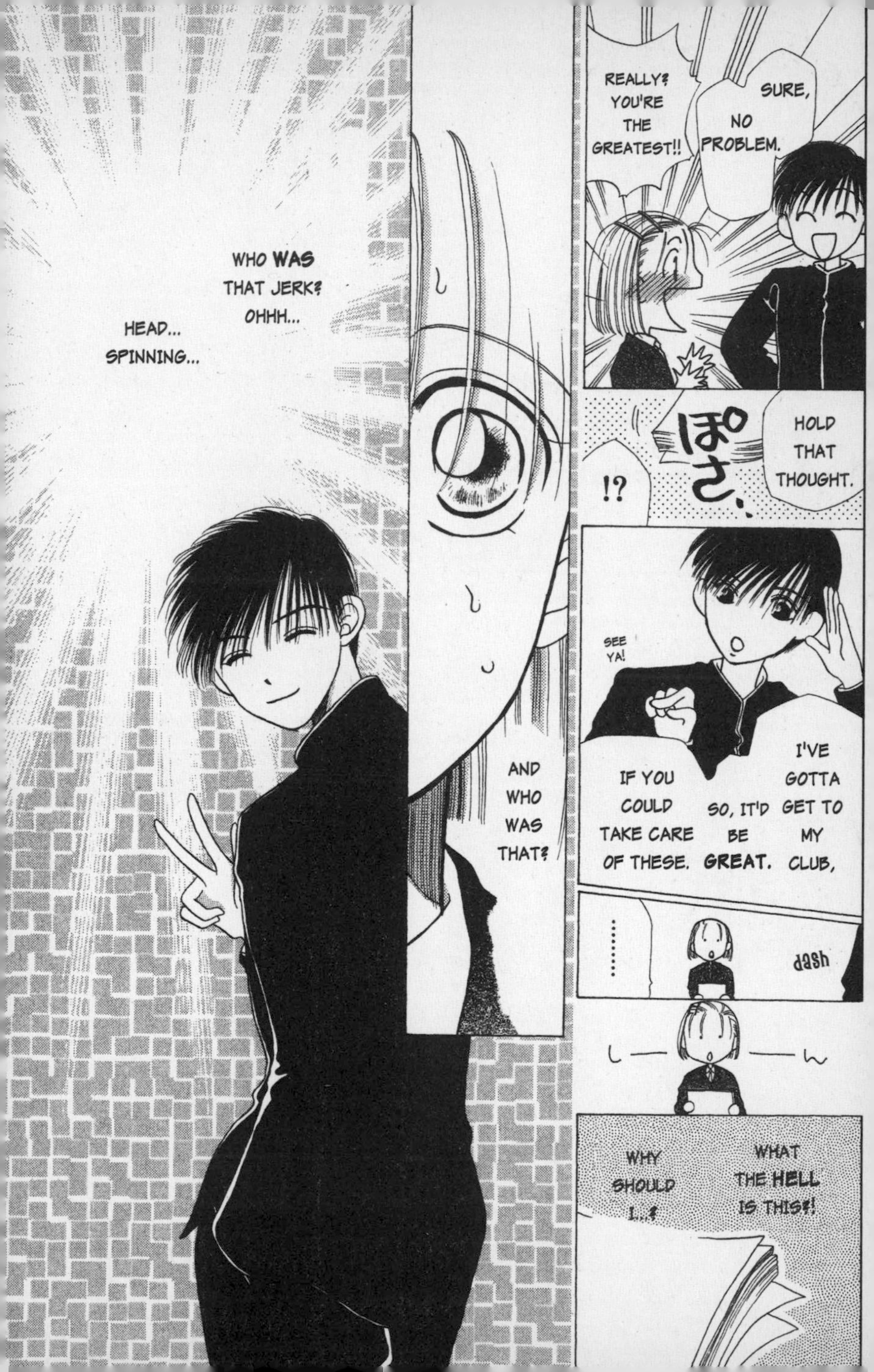
SURE, NO PROBLEM.
REALLY? YOU'RE THE GREATEST!!
HOLD THAT THOUGHT.
ぽさ
!?
I'VE GOTTA GET TO MY CLUB,
SO, IT'D BE GREAT.
IF YOU COULD TAKE CARE OF THESE.
SEE YA!
dash
......
し————ん
WHAT THE HELL IS THIS?!
WHY SHOULD I...?
AND WHO WAS THAT?
WHO WAS THAT JERK? OHHH...
HEAD... SPINNING...

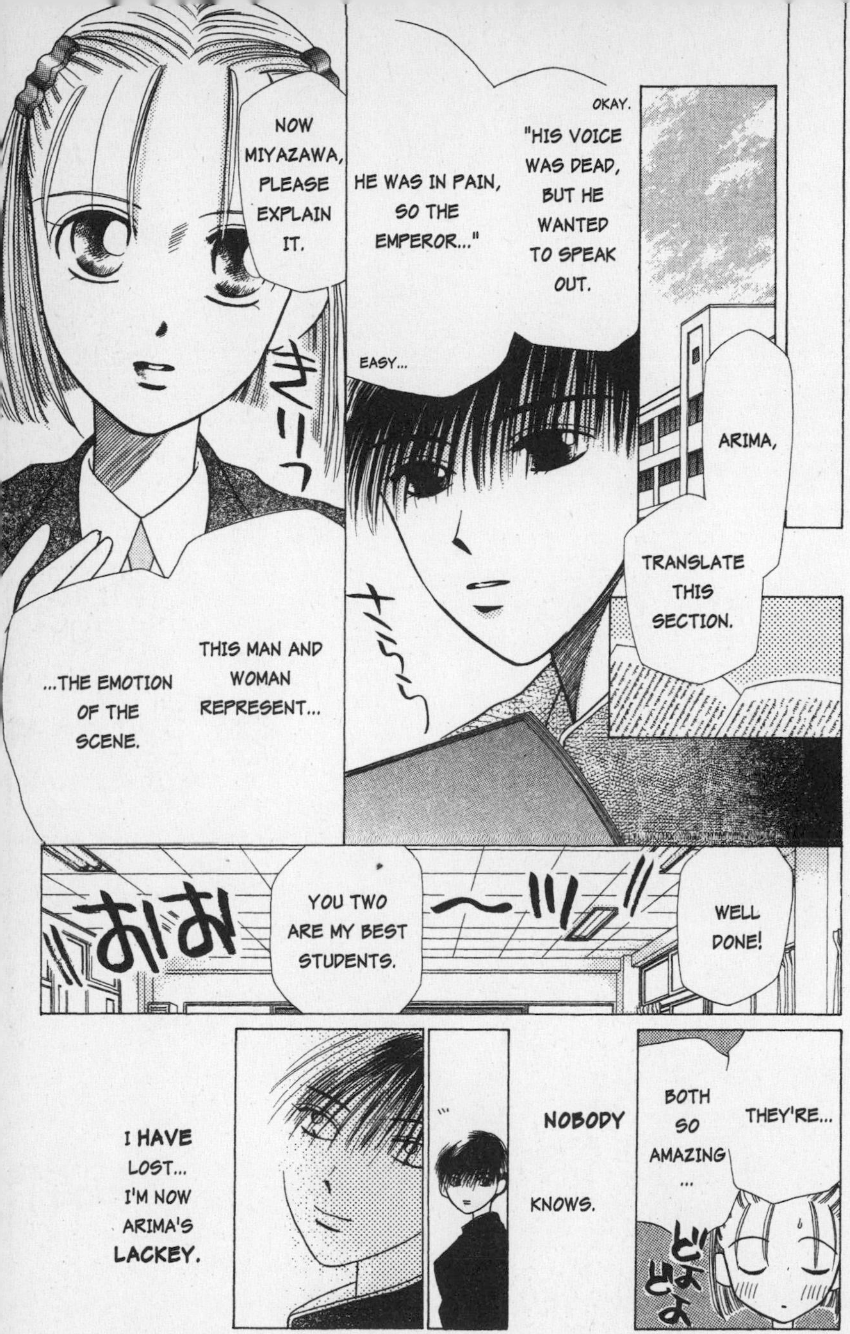
ARIMA,
TRANSLATE THIS SECTION.
OKAY.
"HIS VOICE WAS DEAD, BUT HE WANTED TO SPEAK OUT.
HE WAS IN PAIN, SO THE EMPEROR..."
EASY...
さらっ
NOW MIYAZAWA, PLEASE EXPLAIN IT.
きりっ
THIS MAN AND WOMAN REPRESENT...
...THE EMOTION OF THE SCENE.
WELL DONE!
YOU TWO ARE MY BEST STUDENTS.
おお〜〜ッ
THEY'RE...
BOTH SO AMAZING...
どよどよ
NOBODY KNOWS.
I HAVE LOST... I'M NOW ARIMA'S LACKEY.

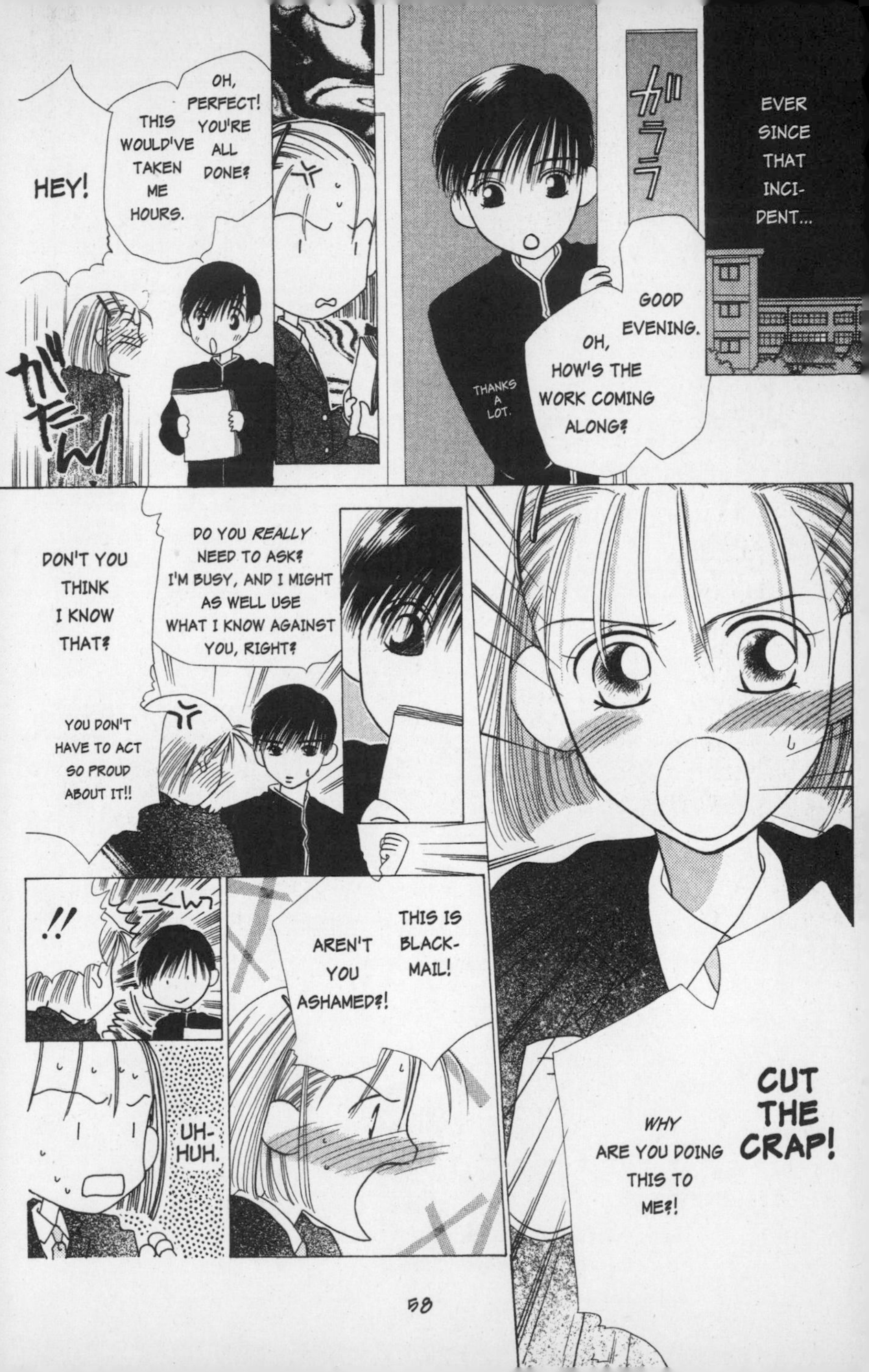
EVER SINCE THAT INCIDENT...
ガララ
GOOD EVENING.
OH, HOW'S THE WORK COMING ALONG?
THANKS A LOT.
OH, PERFECT! YOU'RE ALL DONE?
THIS WOULD'VE TAKEN ME HOURS.
HEY!
CUT THE CRAP!
WHY ARE YOU DOING THIS TO ME?!
DO YOU *REALLY* NEED TO ASK? I'M BUSY, AND I MIGHT AS WELL USE WHAT I KNOW AGAINST YOU, RIGHT?
DON'T YOU THINK I KNOW THAT?
YOU DON'T HAVE TO ACT SO PROUD ABOUT IT!!
THIS IS BLACK-MAIL!
AREN'T YOU ASHAMED?!
!!
UH-HUH.

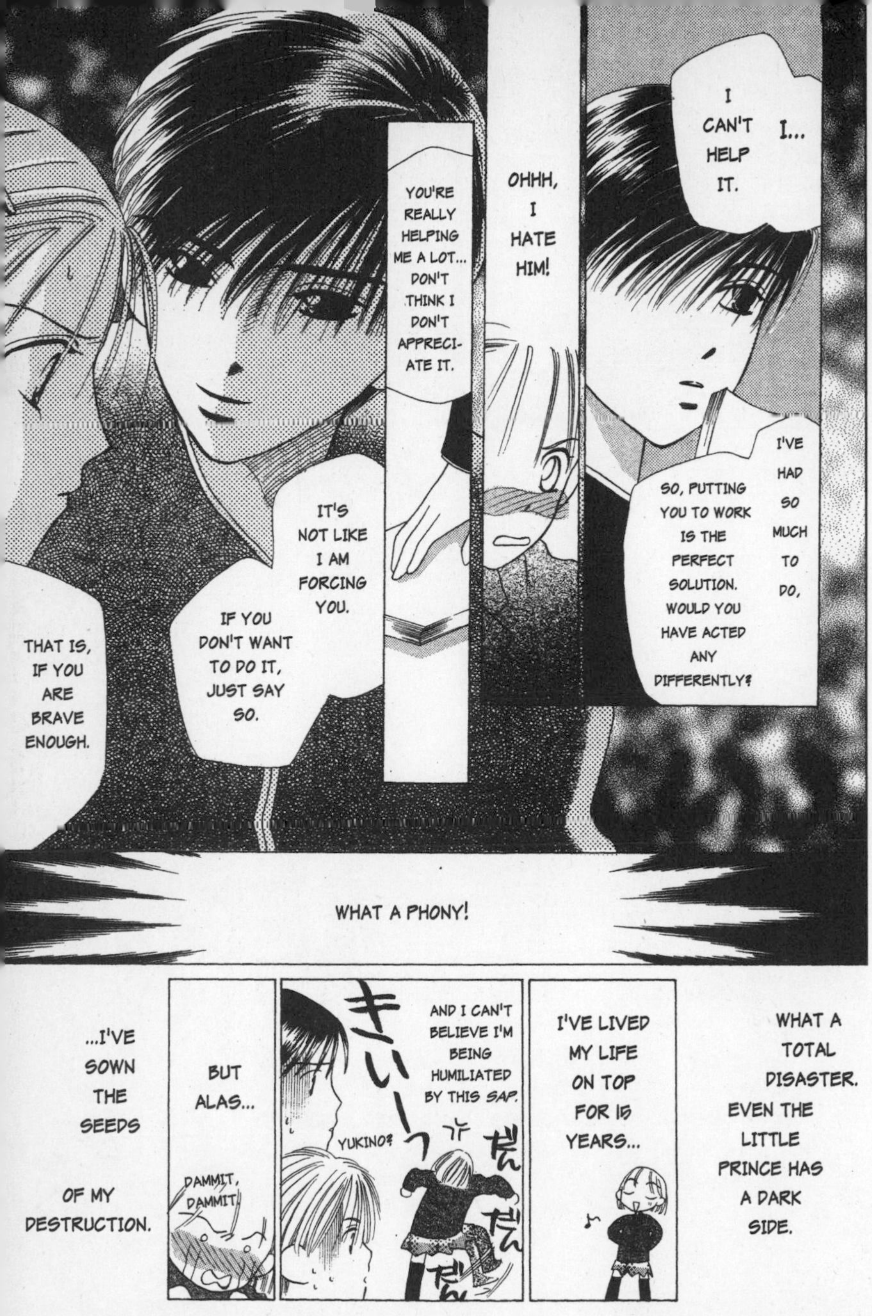
I...
I CAN'T HELP IT.
I'VE HAD SO MUCH TO DO,
SO, PUTTING YOU TO WORK IS THE PERFECT SOLUTION. WOULD YOU HAVE ACTED ANY DIFFERENTLY?
OHHH, I HATE HIM!
YOU'RE REALLY HELPING ME A LOT... DON'T THINK I DON'T APPRECIATE IT.
IT'S NOT LIKE I AM FORCING YOU.
IF YOU DON'T WANT TO DO IT, JUST SAY SO.
THAT IS, IF YOU ARE BRAVE ENOUGH.
WHAT A PHONY!
WHAT A TOTAL DISASTER. EVEN THE LITTLE PRINCE HAS A DARK SIDE.
I'VE LIVED MY LIFE ON TOP FOR 15 YEARS...
AND I CAN'T BELIEVE I'M BEING HUMILIATED BY THIS *SAP.*
きぃーっ
YUKINO?
だん
だん
だん
BUT ALAS...
DAMMIT, DAMMIT
...I'VE SOWN THE SEEDS
OF MY DESTRUCTION.

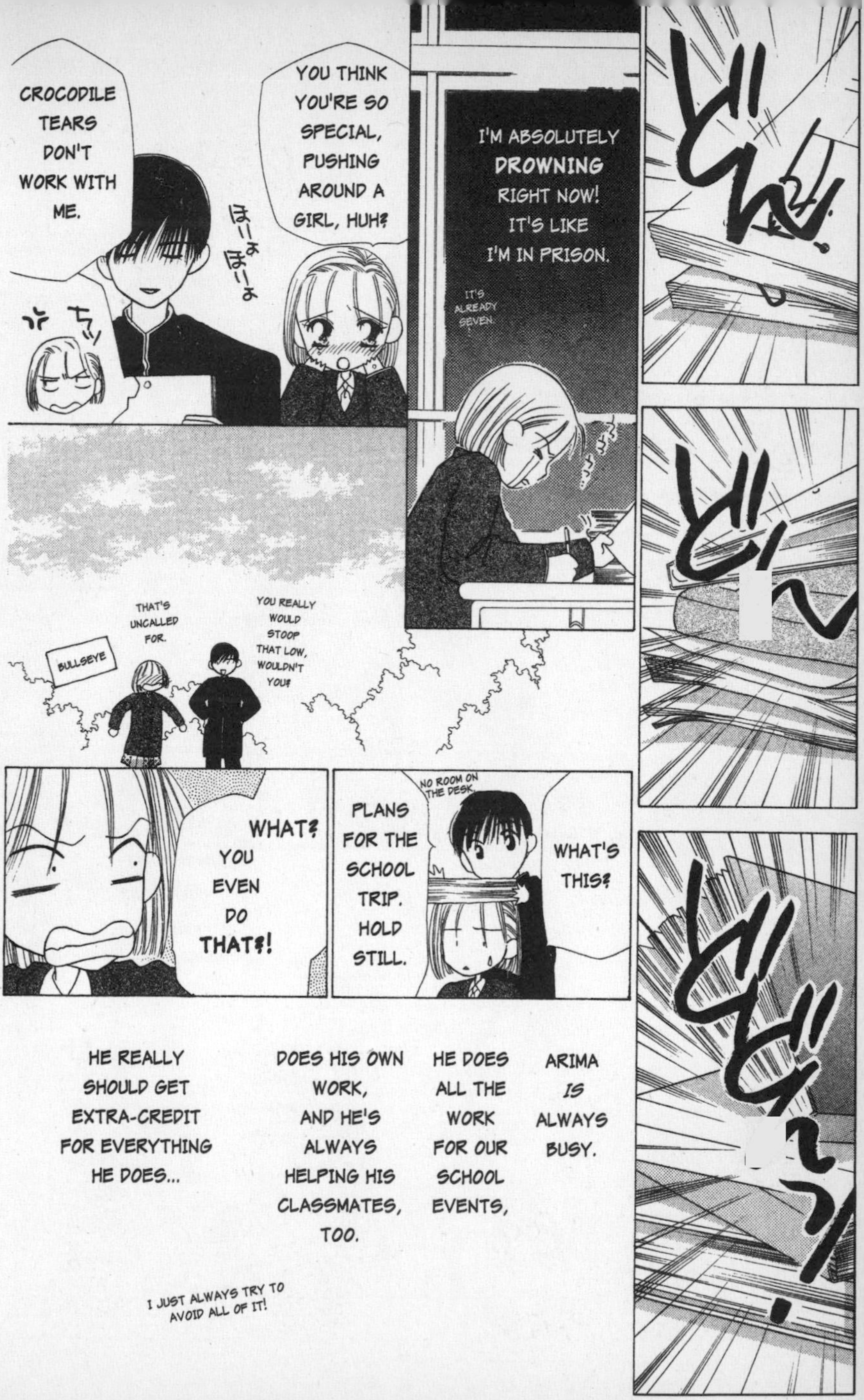
どん！
どん
どどっ！
I'M ABSOLUTELY DROWNING RIGHT NOW! IT'S LIKE I'M IN PRISON.
IT'S ALREADY SEVEN.
YOU THINK YOU'RE SO SPECIAL, PUSHING AROUND A GIRL, HUH?
CROCODILE TEARS DON'T WORK WITH ME.
YOU REALLY WOULD STOOP THAT LOW, WOULDN'T YOU?
THAT'S UNCALLED FOR.
BULLSEYE
WHAT'S THIS?
NO ROOM ON THE DESK.
PLANS FOR THE SCHOOL TRIP. HOLD STILL.
WHAT? YOU EVEN DO THAT?!
ARIMA IS ALWAYS BUSY.
HE DOES ALL THE WORK FOR OUR SCHOOL EVENTS,
DOES HIS OWN WORK, AND HE'S ALWAYS HELPING HIS CLASSMATES, TOO.
HE REALLY SHOULD GET EXTRA-CREDIT FOR EVERYTHING HE DOES...
I JUST ALWAYS TRY TO AVOID ALL OF IT!

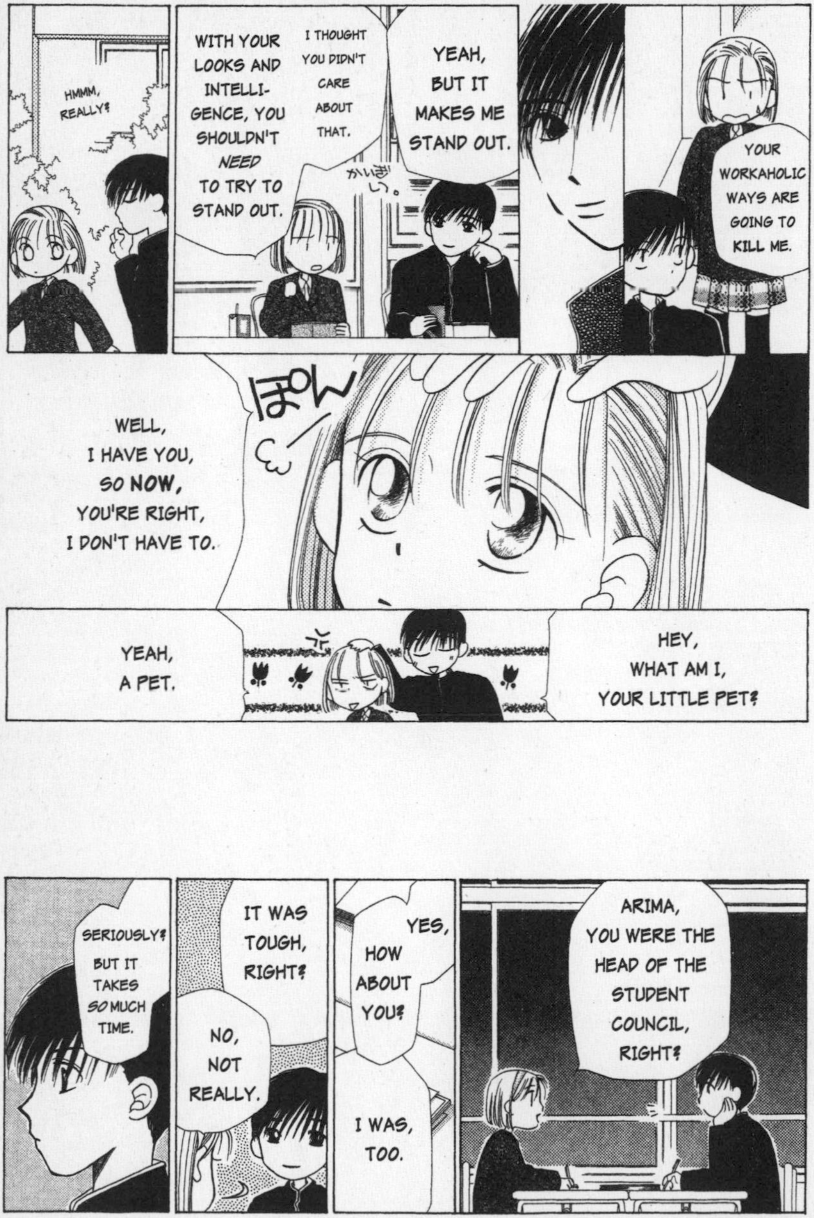
YOUR WORKAHOLIC WAYS ARE GOING TO KILL ME.
YEAH, BUT IT MAKES ME STAND OUT.
I THOUGHT YOU DIDN'T CARE ABOUT THAT.
かいぎしつ。
WITH YOUR LOOKS AND INTELLI- GENCE, YOU SHOULDN'T *NEED* TO TRY TO STAND OUT.
HMMM, REALLY?
ぽん
WELL, I HAVE YOU, SO **NOW**, YOU'RE RIGHT, I DON'T HAVE TO.
HEY, WHAT AM I, YOUR LITTLE PET?
YEAH, A PET.
ARIMA, YOU WERE THE HEAD OF THE STUDENT COUNCIL, RIGHT?
YES, HOW ABOUT YOU?
I WAS, TOO.
IT WAS TOUGH, RIGHT?
NO, NOT REALLY.
SERIOUSLY? BUT IT TAKES SO MUCH TIME.

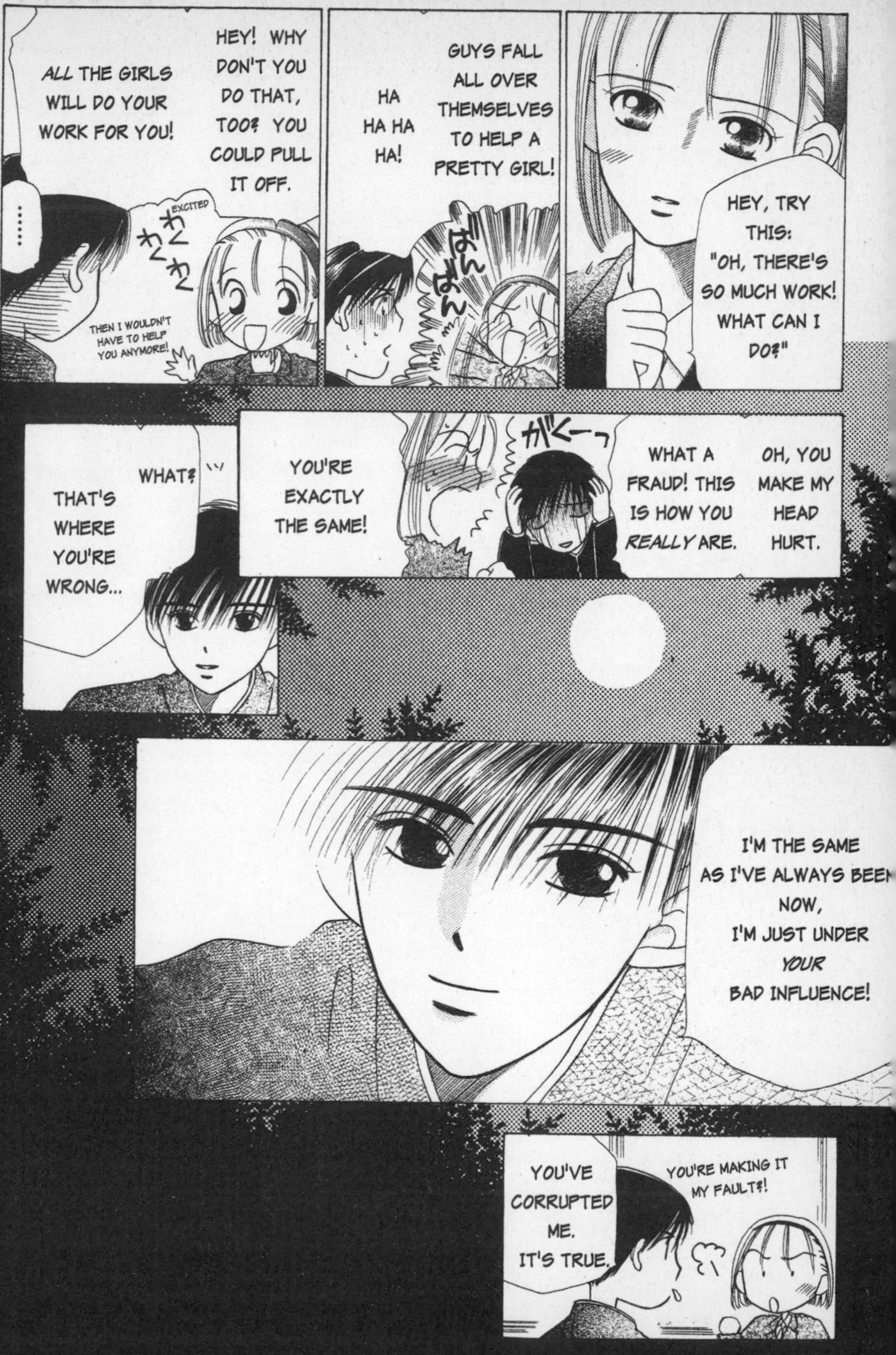
HEY, TRY THIS: "OH, THERE'S SO MUCH WORK! WHAT CAN I DO?"
GUYS FALL ALL OVER THEMSELVES TO HELP A PRETTY GIRL!
HA HA HA HA!
ばんばん
HEY! WHY DON'T YOU DO THAT, TOO? YOU COULD PULL IT OFF.
ALL THE GIRLS WILL DO YOUR WORK FOR YOU!
EXCITED
わくわく
......
THEN I WOULDN'T HAVE TO HELP YOU ANYMORE!
OH, YOU MAKE MY HEAD HURT.
WHAT A FRAUD! THIS IS HOW YOU REALLY ARE.
がくーっ
YOU'RE EXACTLY THE SAME!
WHAT?
THAT'S WHERE YOU'RE WRONG...
I'M THE SAME AS I'VE ALWAYS BEEN NOW, I'M JUST UNDER YOUR BAD INFLUENCE!
YOU'VE CORRUPTED ME. IT'S TRUE.
YOU'RE MAKING IT MY FAULT?!

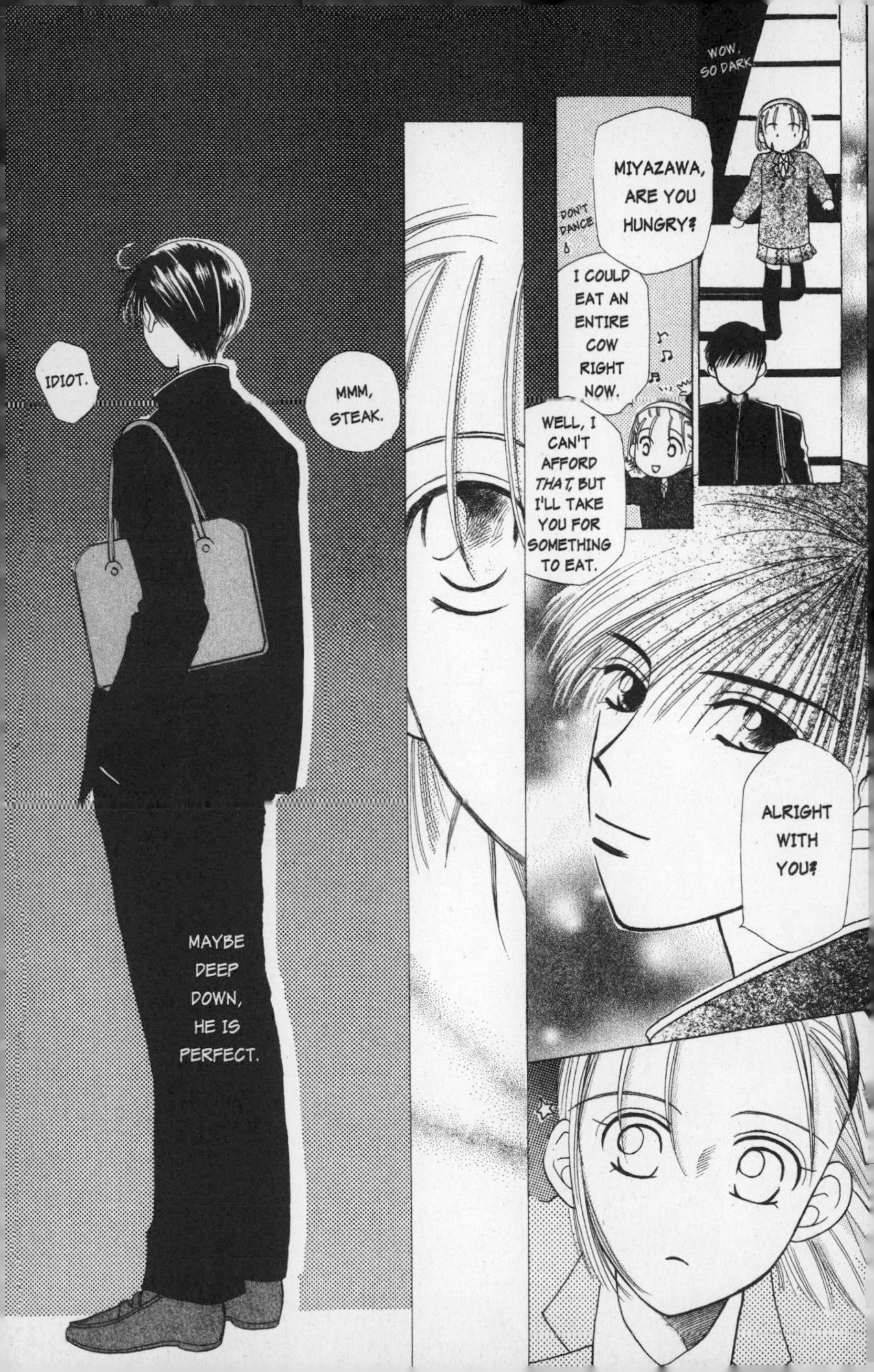
WOW, SO DARK.
MIYAZAWA, ARE YOU HUNGRY?
DON'T DANCE
I COULD EAT AN ENTIRE COW RIGHT NOW.
WELL, I CAN'T AFFORD *THAT*, BUT I'LL TAKE YOU FOR SOMETHING TO EAT.
ALRIGHT WITH YOU?
MMM, STEAK.
IDIOT.
MAYBE DEEP DOWN, HE IS PERFECT.

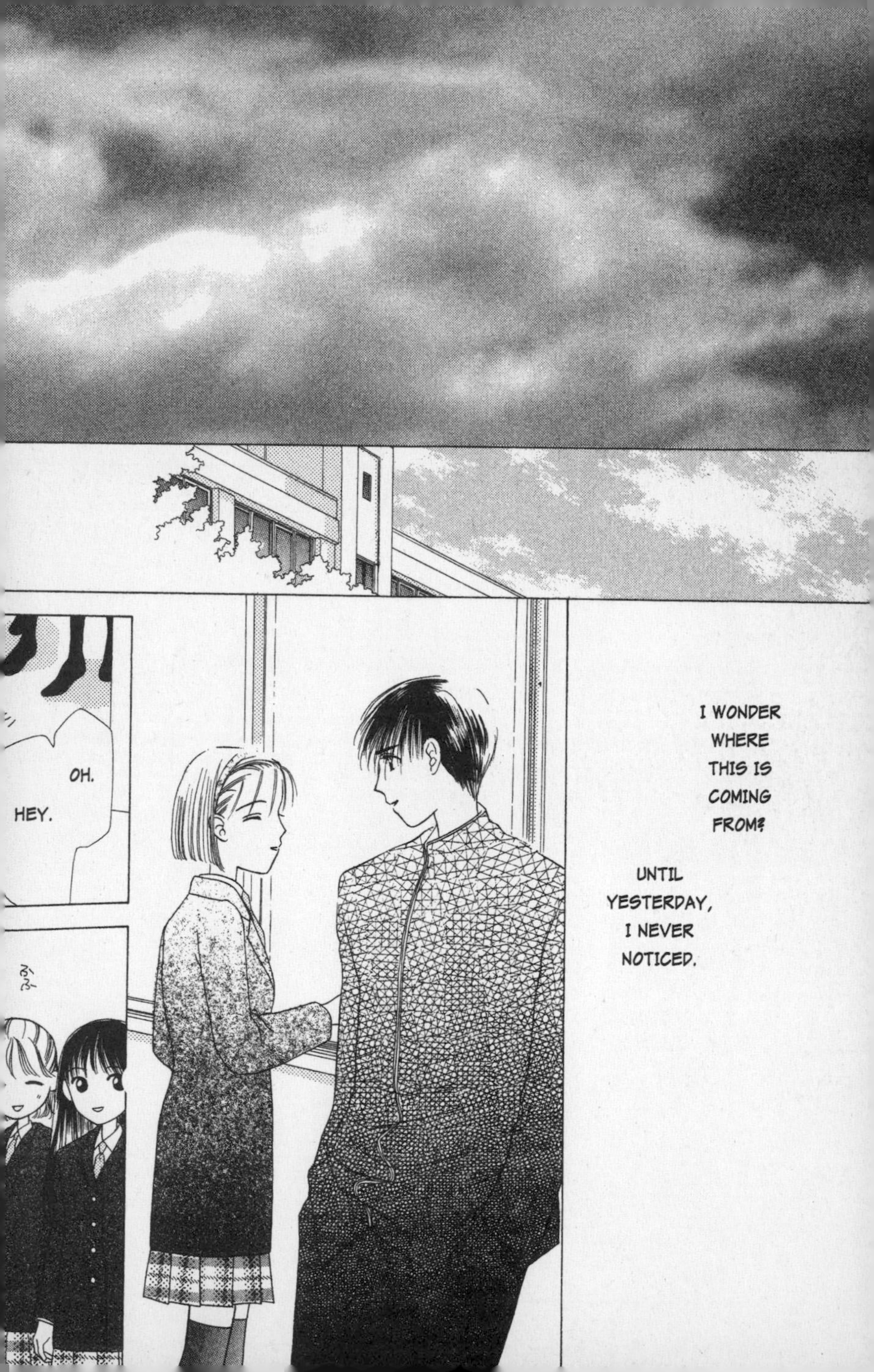
I WONDER WHERE THIS IS COMING FROM?
UNTIL YESTERDAY, I NEVER NOTICED.
OH.
HEY.
ふふ

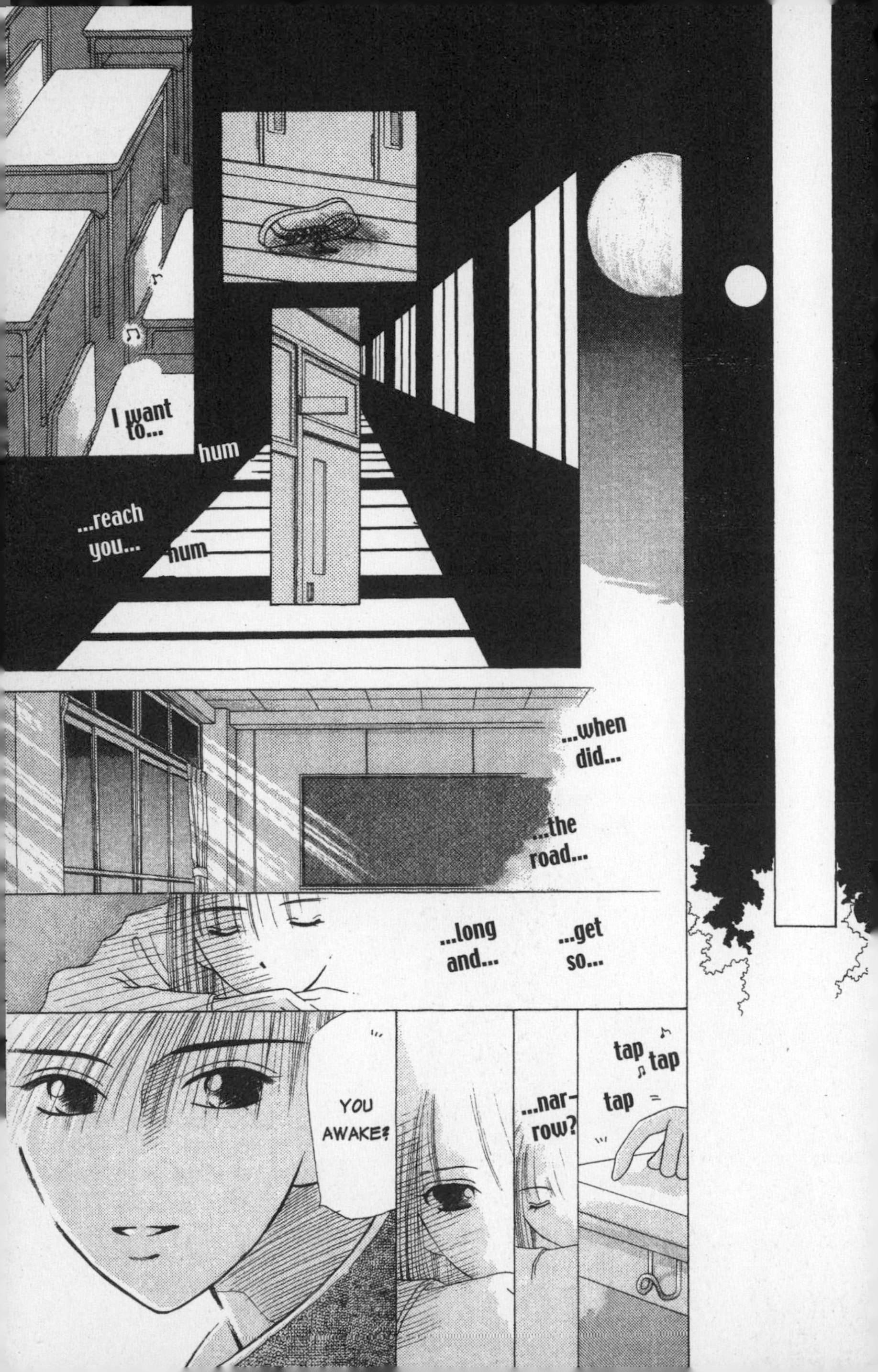

I want to...
hum
...reach you...
hum
...when did...
...the road...
...get so...
...long and...
tap tap
tap
...nar-row?
YOU AWAKE?

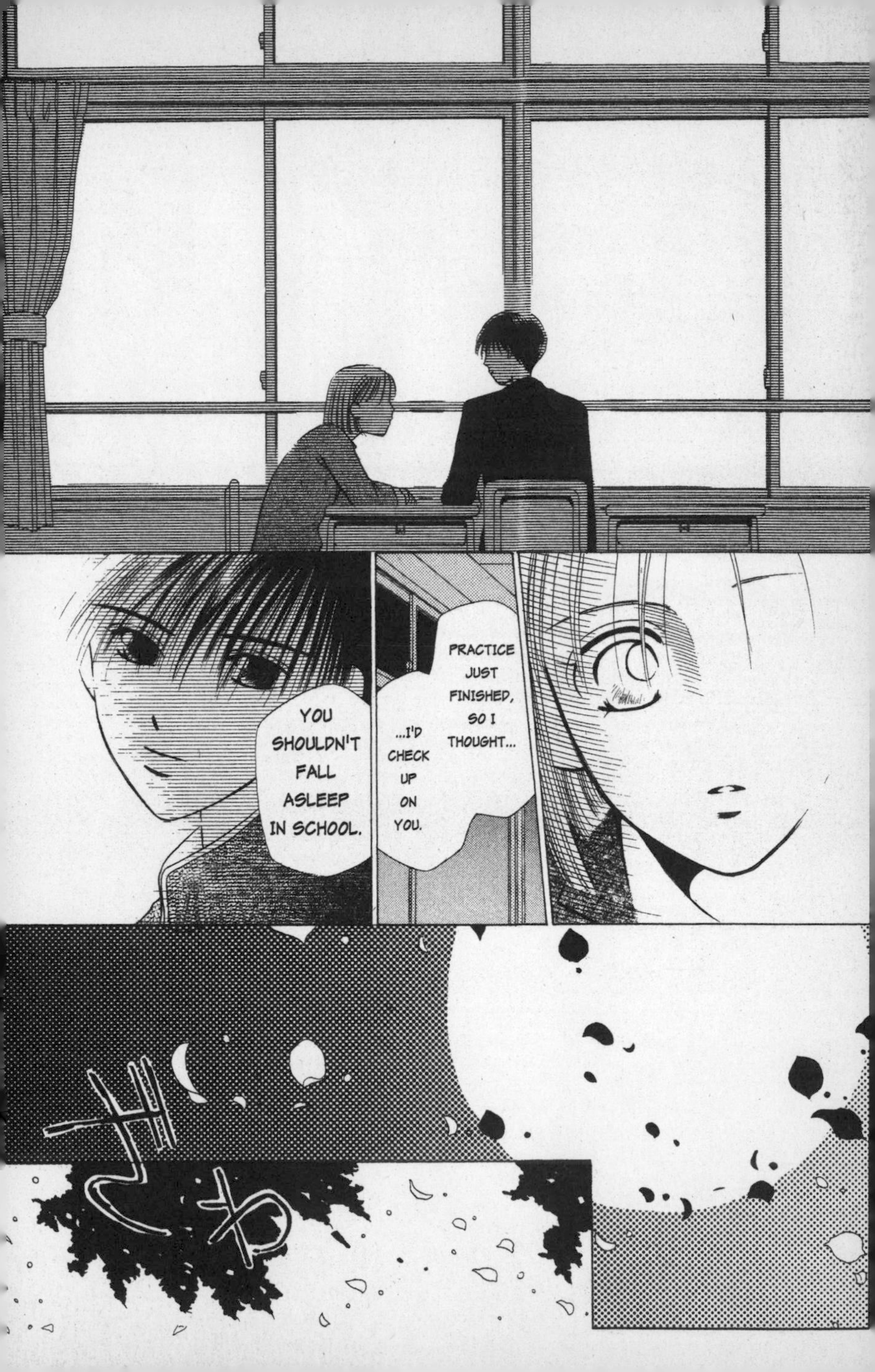
PRACTICE JUST FINISHED, SO I THOUGHT...
...I'D CHECK UP ON YOU.
YOU SHOULDN'T FALL ASLEEP IN SCHOOL.

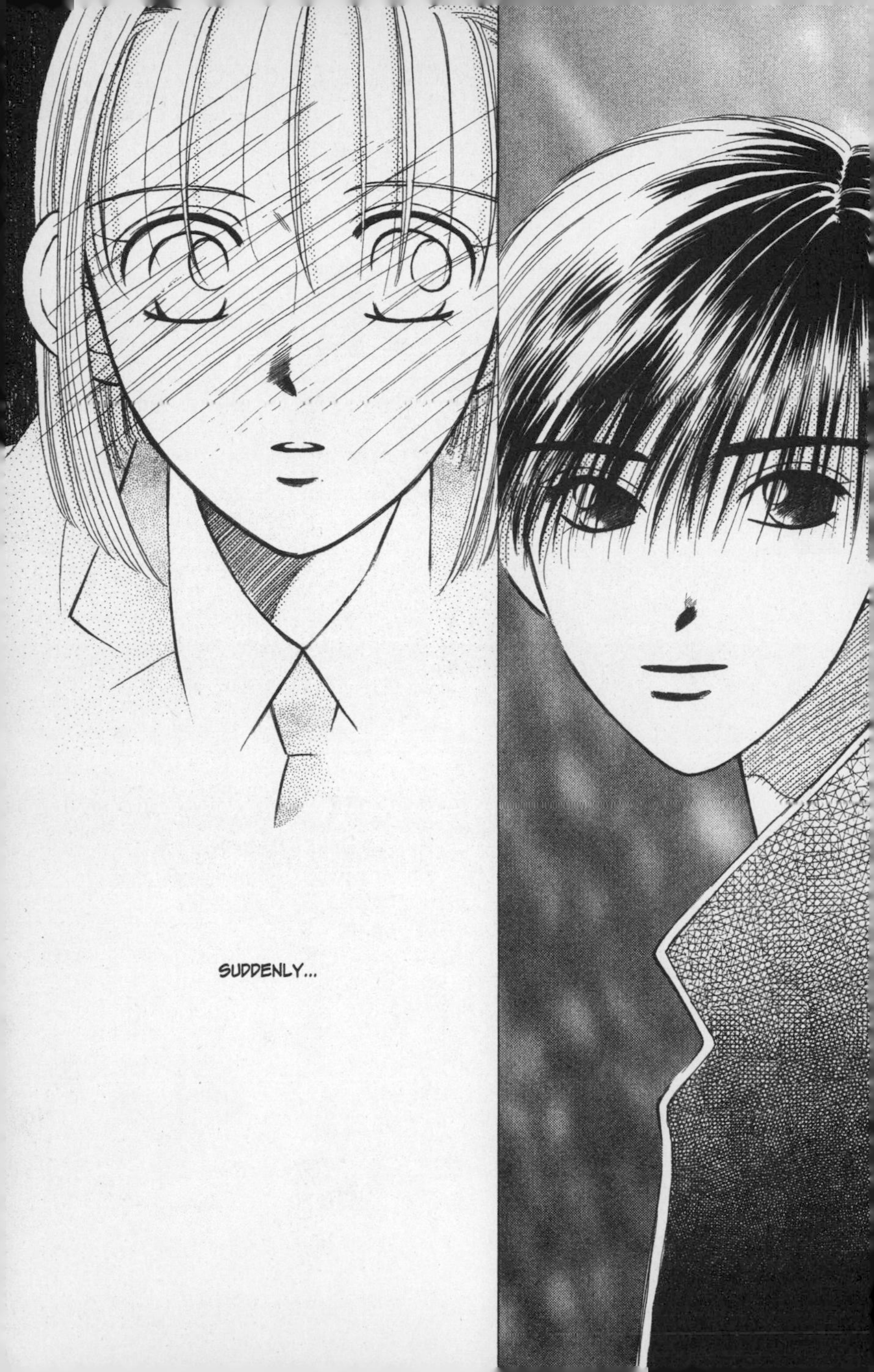
SUDDENLY...

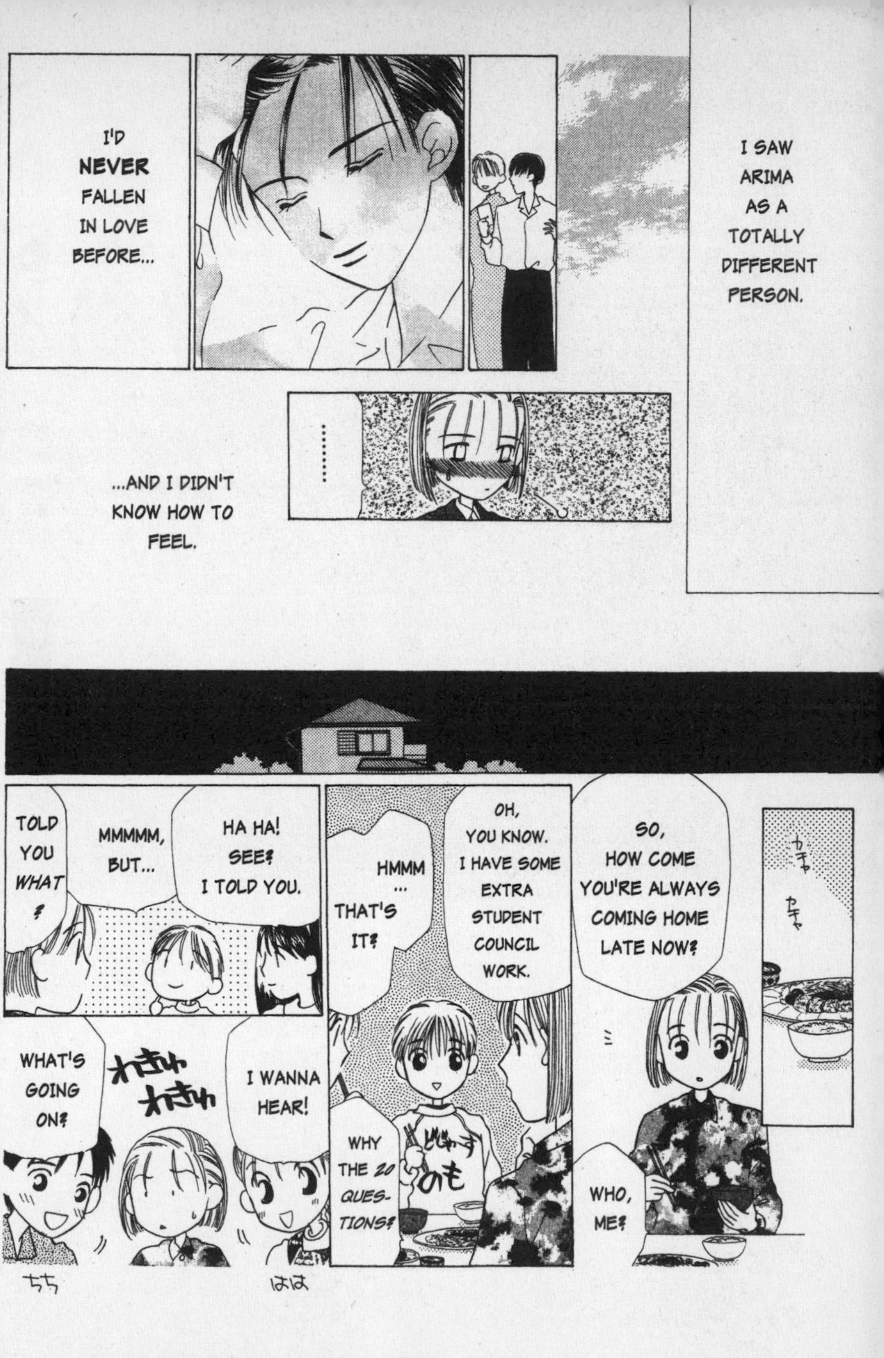
I SAW ARIMA AS A TOTALLY DIFFERENT PERSON.
I'D NEVER FALLEN IN LOVE BEFORE...
....
...AND I DIDN'T KNOW HOW TO FEEL.
カチャ
カチャ
SO, HOW COME YOU'RE ALWAYS COMING HOME LATE NOW?
WHO, ME?
OH, YOU KNOW. I HAVE SOME EXTRA STUDENT COUNCIL WORK.
HMMM ... THAT'S IT?
WHY THE 20 QUESTIONS?
HA HA! SEE? I TOLD YOU.
MMMMM, BUT...
TOLD YOU WHAT?
I WANNA HEAR!
わきゃ わきゃ
WHAT'S GOING ON?
はは
ちち

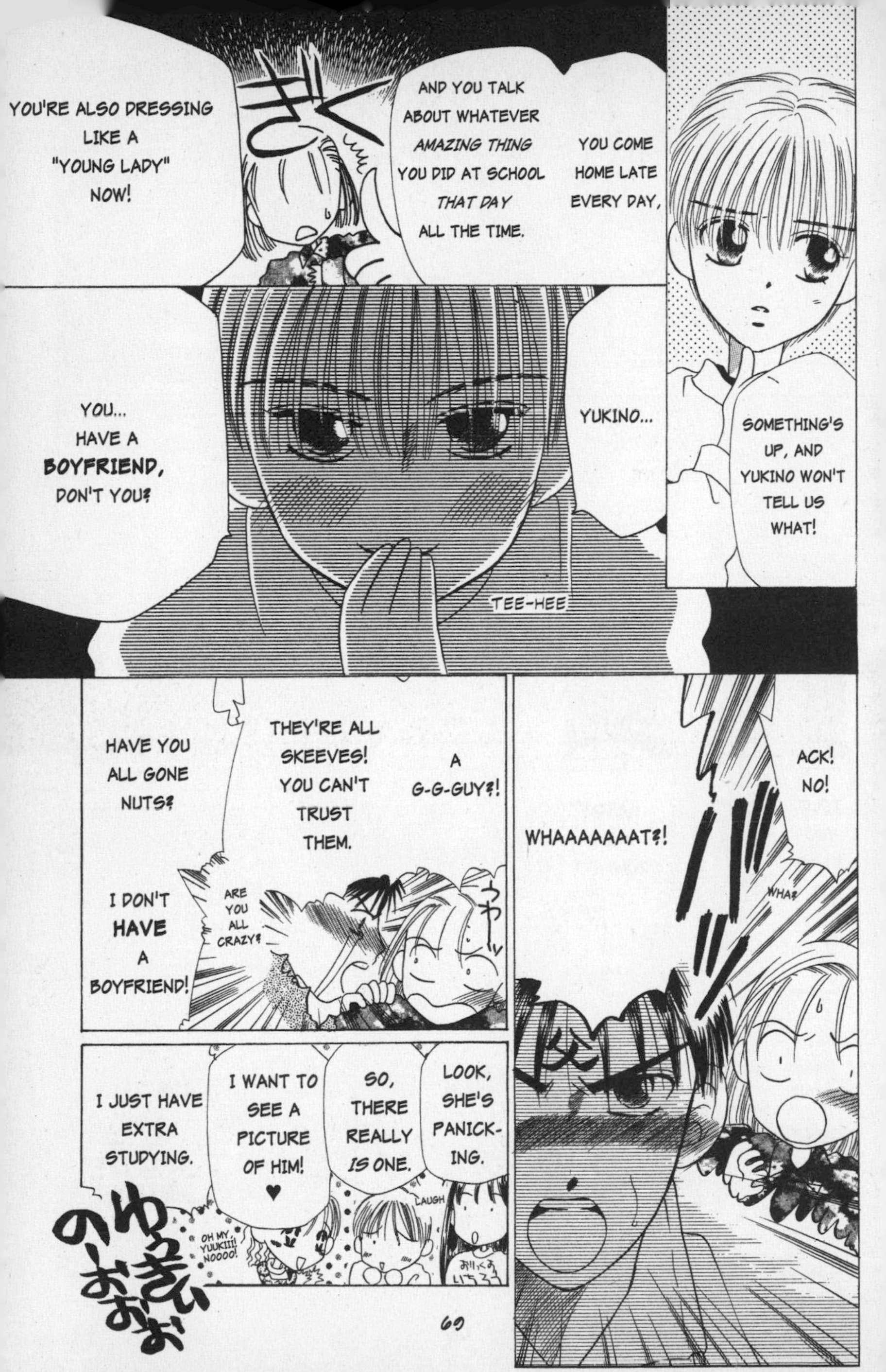
SOMETHING'S UP, AND YUKINO WON'T TELL US WHAT!
YOU COME HOME LATE EVERY DAY,
AND YOU TALK ABOUT WHATEVER *AMAZING THING* YOU DID AT SCHOOL *THAT DAY* ALL THE TIME.
YOU'RE ALSO DRESSING LIKE A "YOUNG LADY" NOW!
YUKINO...
YOU... HAVE A **BOYFRIEND,** DON'T YOU?
TEE-HEE
ACK! NO!
WHA?
WHAAAAAAAT?!
A G-G-GUY?!
THEY'RE ALL SKEEVES! YOU CAN'T TRUST THEM.
HAVE YOU ALL GONE NUTS?
ARE YOU ALL CRAZY?
I DON'T **HAVE** A BOYFRIEND!
LOOK, SHE'S PANICK-ING.
SO, THERE REALLY *IS* ONE.
I WANT TO SEE A PICTURE OF HIM! ♥
I JUST HAVE EXTRA STUDYING.
LAUGH
OH MY, YUUKIII! NOOOO!
ゆきいのおおお

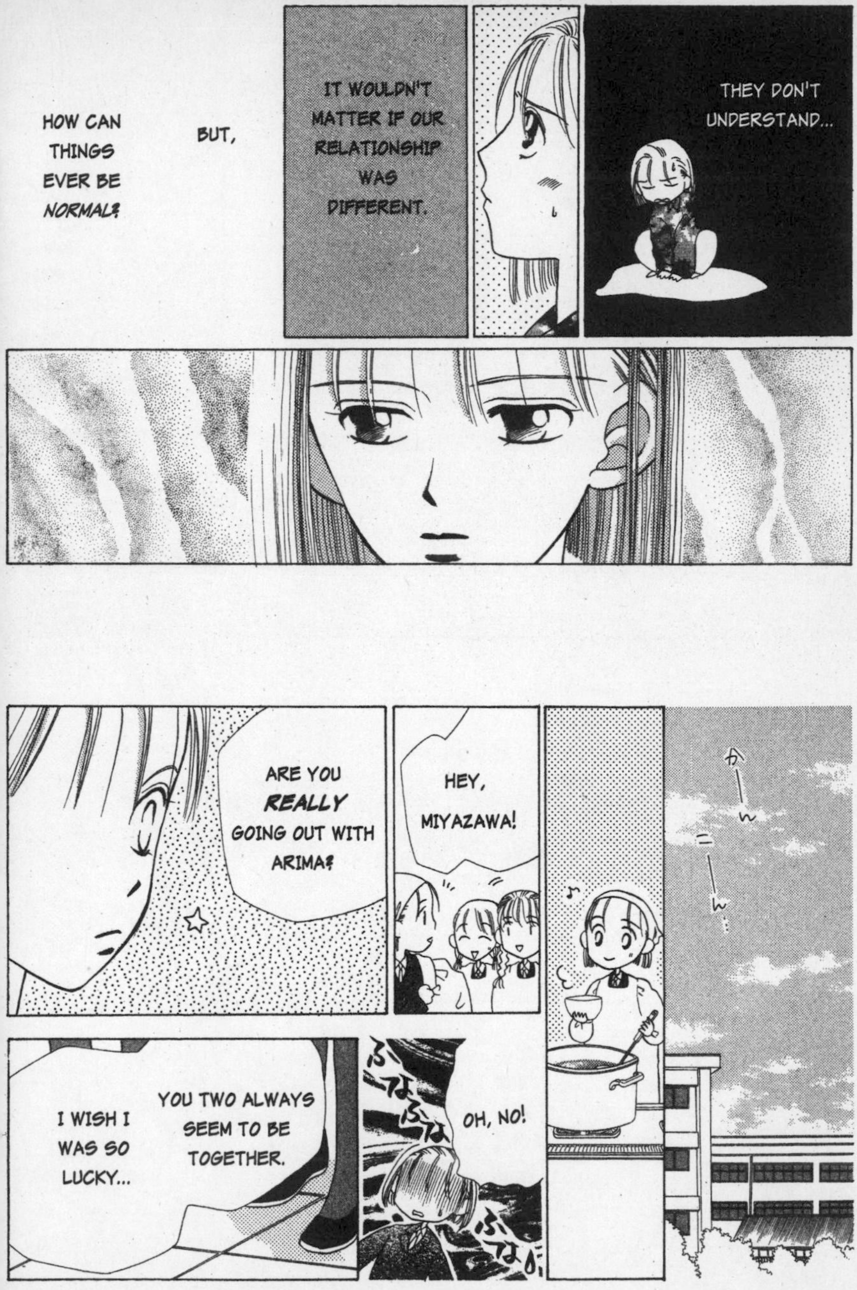
THEY DON'T UNDERSTAND...
IT WOULDN'T MATTER IF OUR RELATIONSHIP WAS DIFFERENT.
BUT,
HOW CAN THINGS EVER BE *NORMAL*?
かーん
こーん…
HEY, MIYAZAWA!
ARE YOU *REALLY* GOING OUT WITH ARIMA?
OH, NO!
ふなふな
ふな
YOU TWO ALWAYS SEEM TO BE TOGETHER.
I WISH I WAS SO LUCKY...

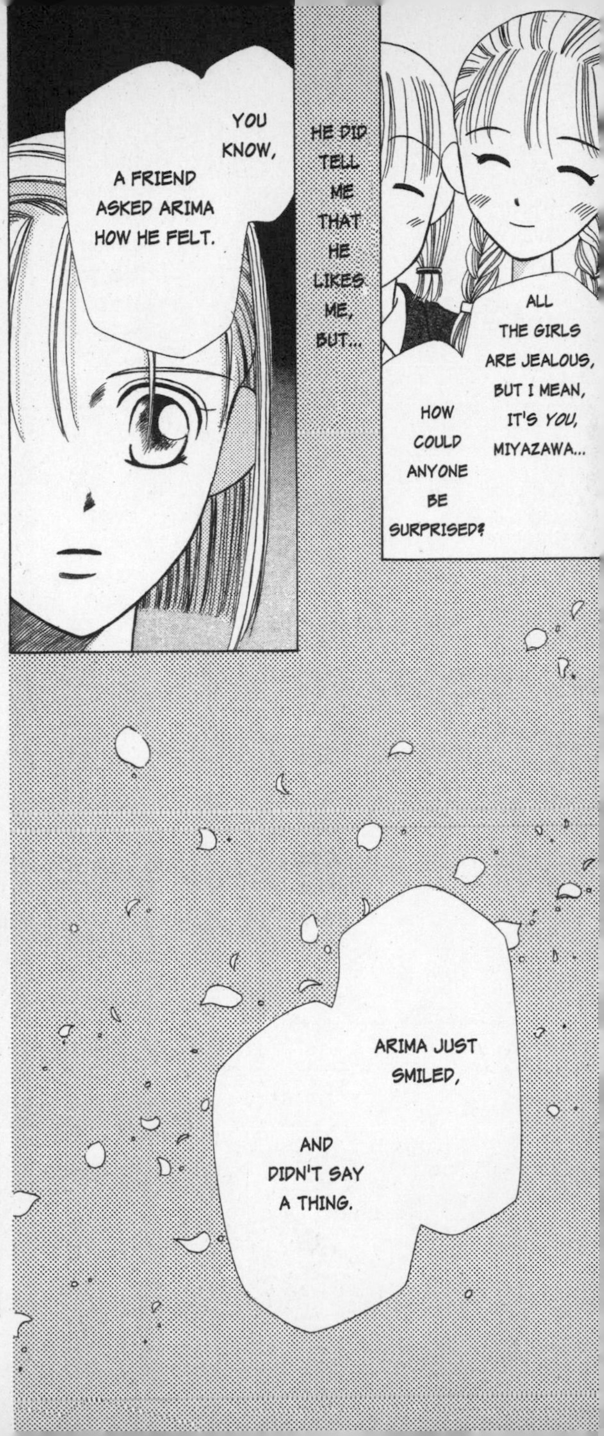
ALL THE GIRLS ARE JEALOUS, BUT I MEAN, IT'S *YOU*, MIYAZAWA...
HOW COULD ANYONE BE SURPRISED?
HE DID TELL ME THAT HE LIKES ME, BUT...
YOU KNOW, A FRIEND ASKED ARIMA HOW HE FELT.
ARIMA JUST SMILED,
AND DIDN'T SAY A THING.

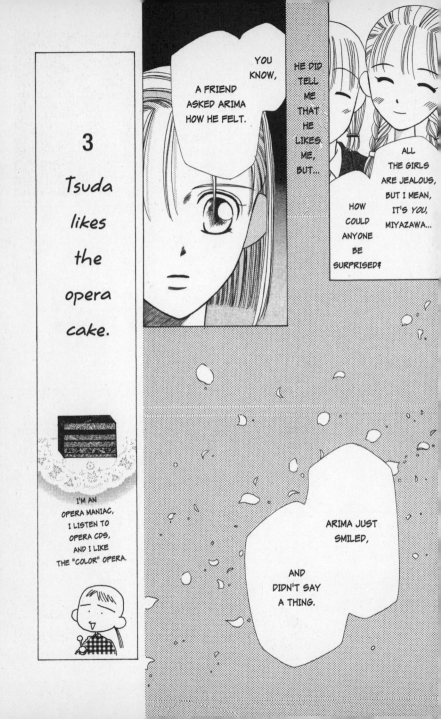

3

Tsuda likes the opera cake.

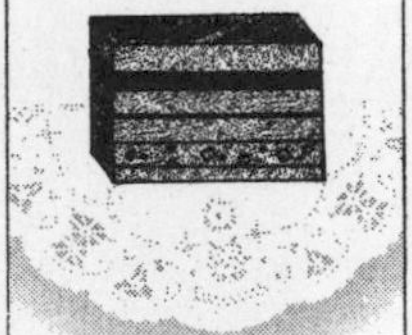

I'M AN OPERA MANIAC, I LISTEN TO OPERA CDS, AND I LIKE THE "COLOR" OPERA.

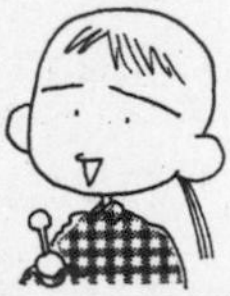

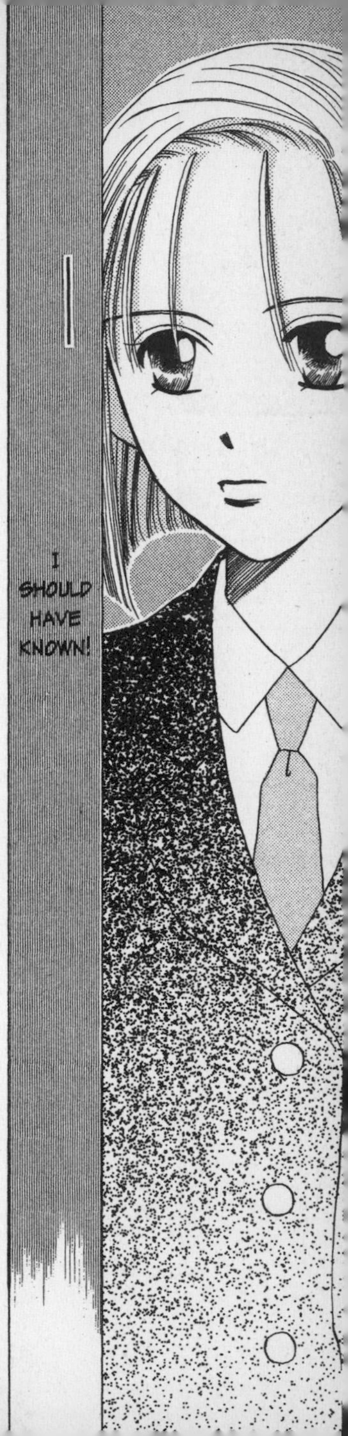
I SHOULD HAVE KNOWN!

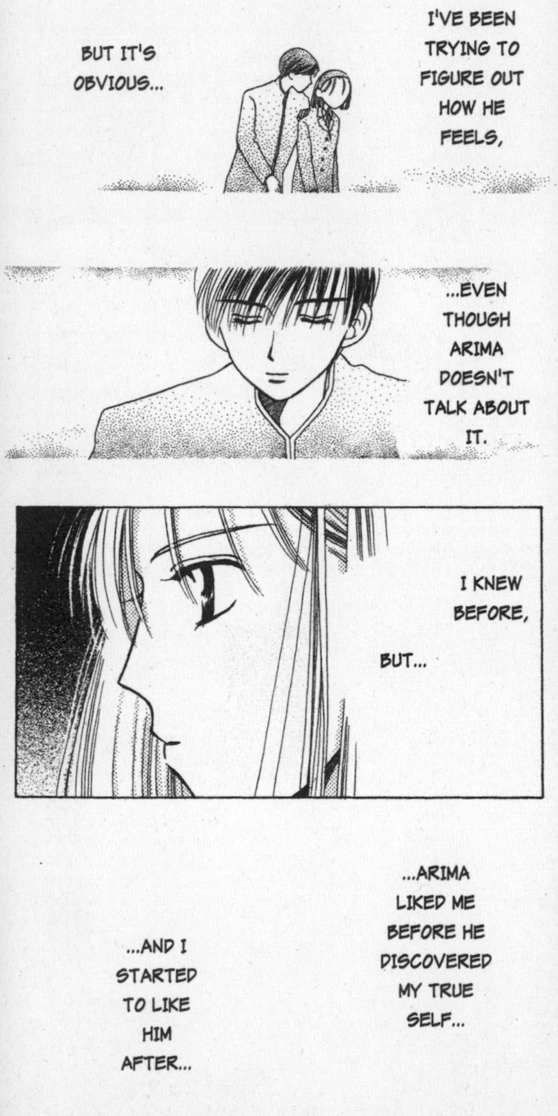
I'VE BEEN TRYING TO FIGURE OUT HOW HE FEELS,
BUT IT'S OBVIOUS...
...EVEN THOUGH ARIMA DOESN'T TALK ABOUT IT.
I KNEW BEFORE,
BUT...
...ARIMA LIKED ME BEFORE HE DISCOVERED MY TRUE SELF...
...AND I STARTED TO LIKE HIM AFTER...

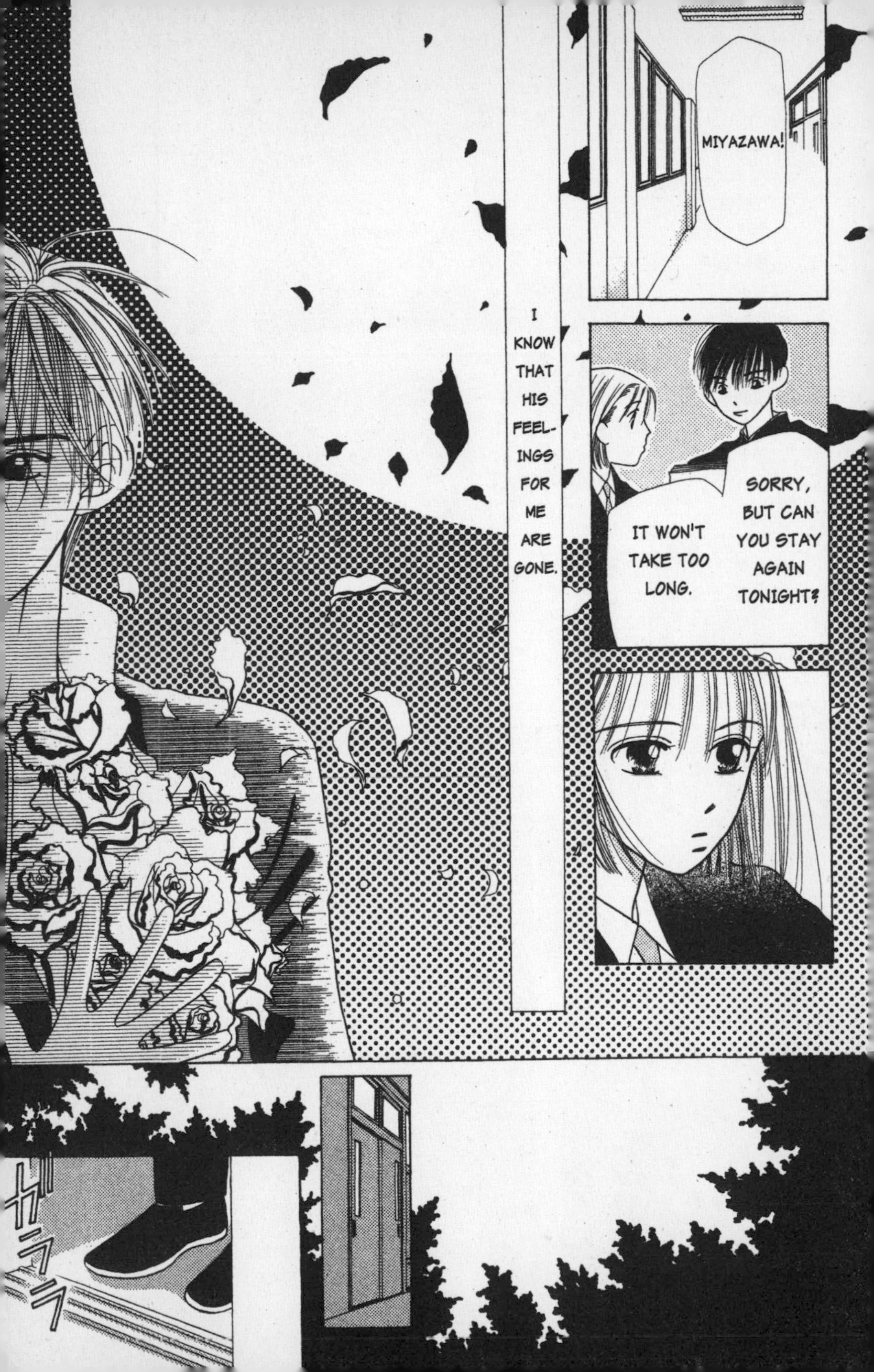
MIYAZAWA!
SORRY, BUT CAN YOU STAY AGAIN TONIGHT?
IT WON'T TAKE TOO LONG.
I KNOW THAT HIS FEEL-INGS FOR ME ARE GONE.

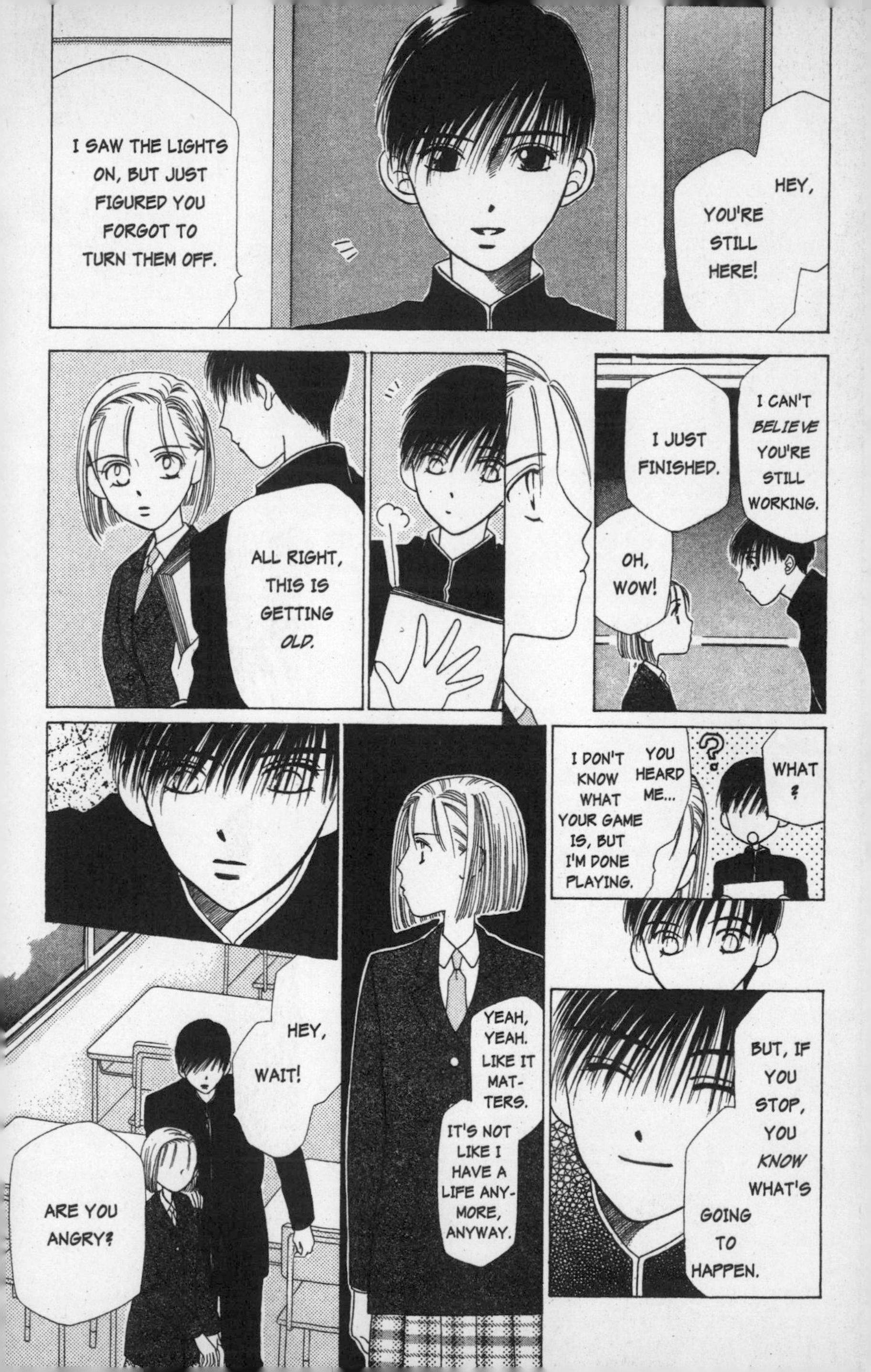
HEY, YOU'RE STILL HERE!
I SAW THE LIGHTS ON, BUT JUST FIGURED YOU FORGOT TO TURN THEM OFF.
I CAN'T *BELIEVE* YOU'RE STILL WORKING.
I JUST FINISHED.
OH, WOW!
ALL RIGHT, THIS IS GETTING *OLD.*
WHAT?
YOU HEARD ME...
I DON'T KNOW WHAT YOUR GAME IS, BUT I'M DONE PLAYING.
BUT, IF YOU STOP, YOU *KNOW* WHAT'S GOING TO HAPPEN.
YEAH, YEAH. LIKE IT MAT-TERS.
IT'S NOT LIKE I HAVE A LIFE ANY-MORE, ANYWAY.
HEY, WAIT!
ARE YOU ANGRY?

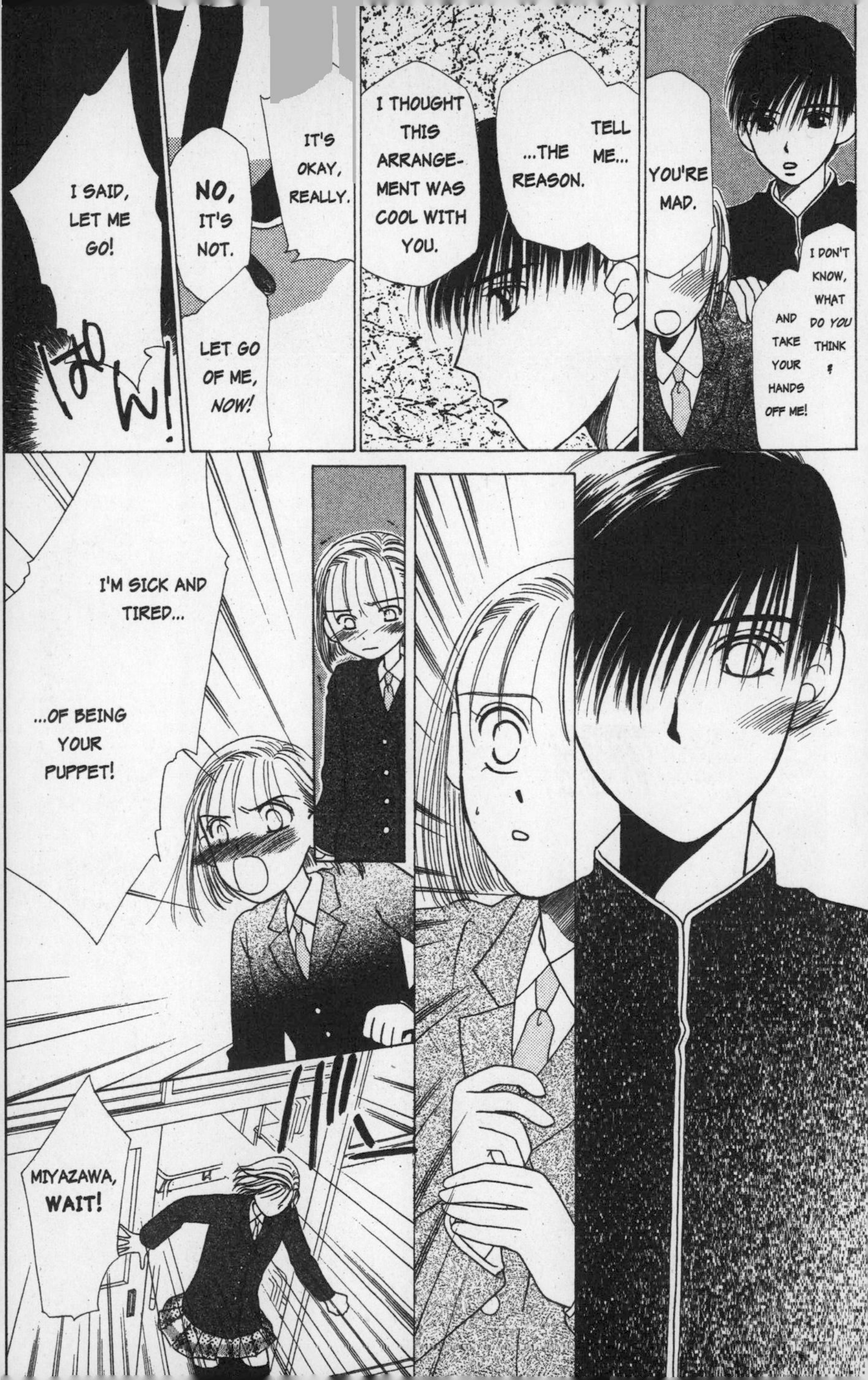
YOU'RE MAD.
I DON'T KNOW, WHAT DO YOU THINK?
AND TAKE YOUR HANDS OFF ME!
TELL ME...
...THE REASON.
I THOUGHT THIS ARRANGEMENT WAS COOL WITH YOU.
IT'S OKAY, REALLY.
NO, IT'S NOT.
LET GO OF ME, NOW!
I SAID, LET ME GO!
I'M SICK AND TIRED...
...OF BEING YOUR PUPPET!
MIYAZAWA, WAIT!

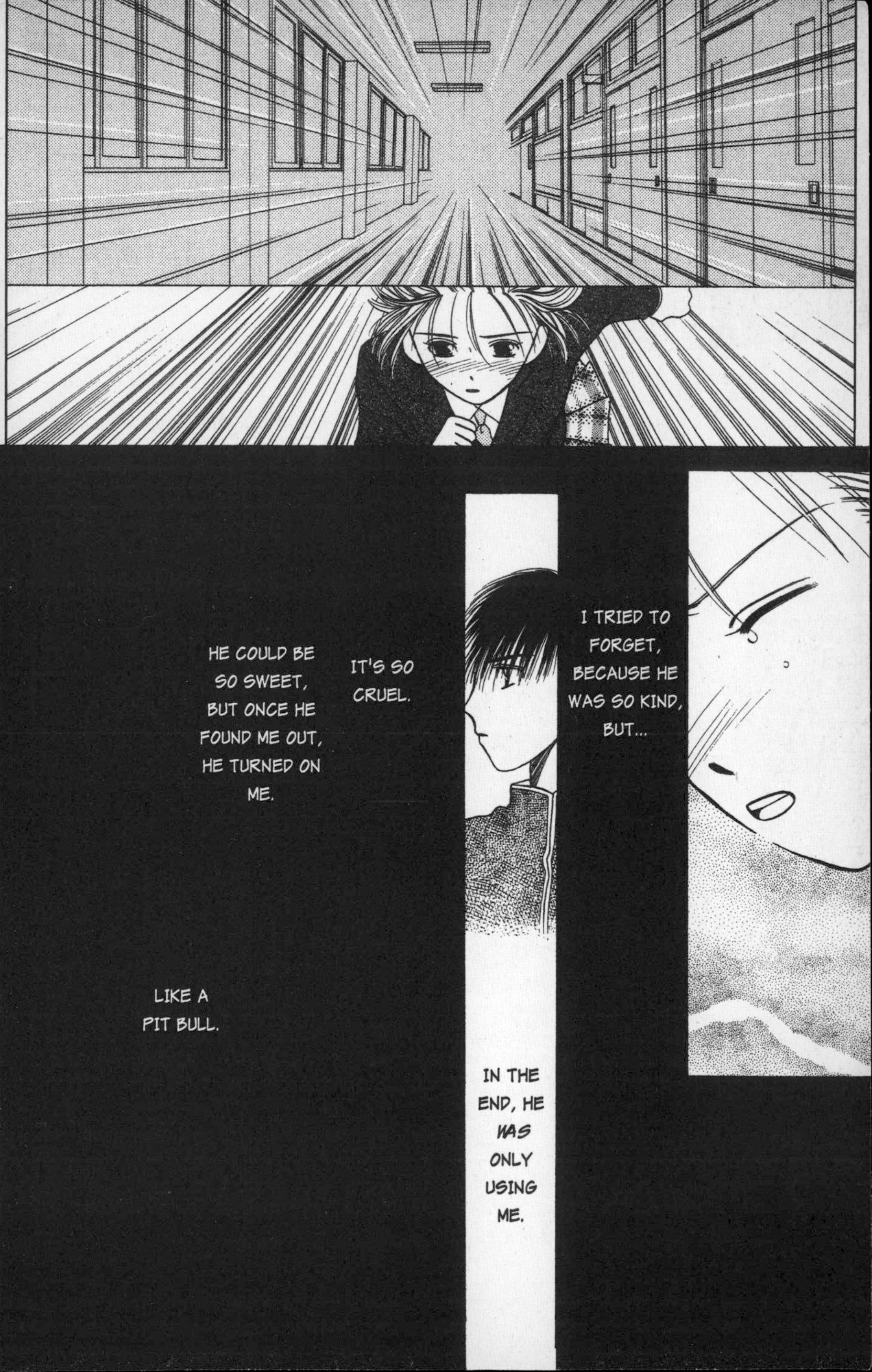
I TRIED TO FORGET, BECAUSE HE WAS SO KIND, BUT...
IN THE END, HE WAS ONLY USING ME.
IT'S SO CRUEL.
HE COULD BE SO SWEET, BUT ONCE HE FOUND ME OUT, HE TURNED ON ME.
LIKE A PIT BULL.

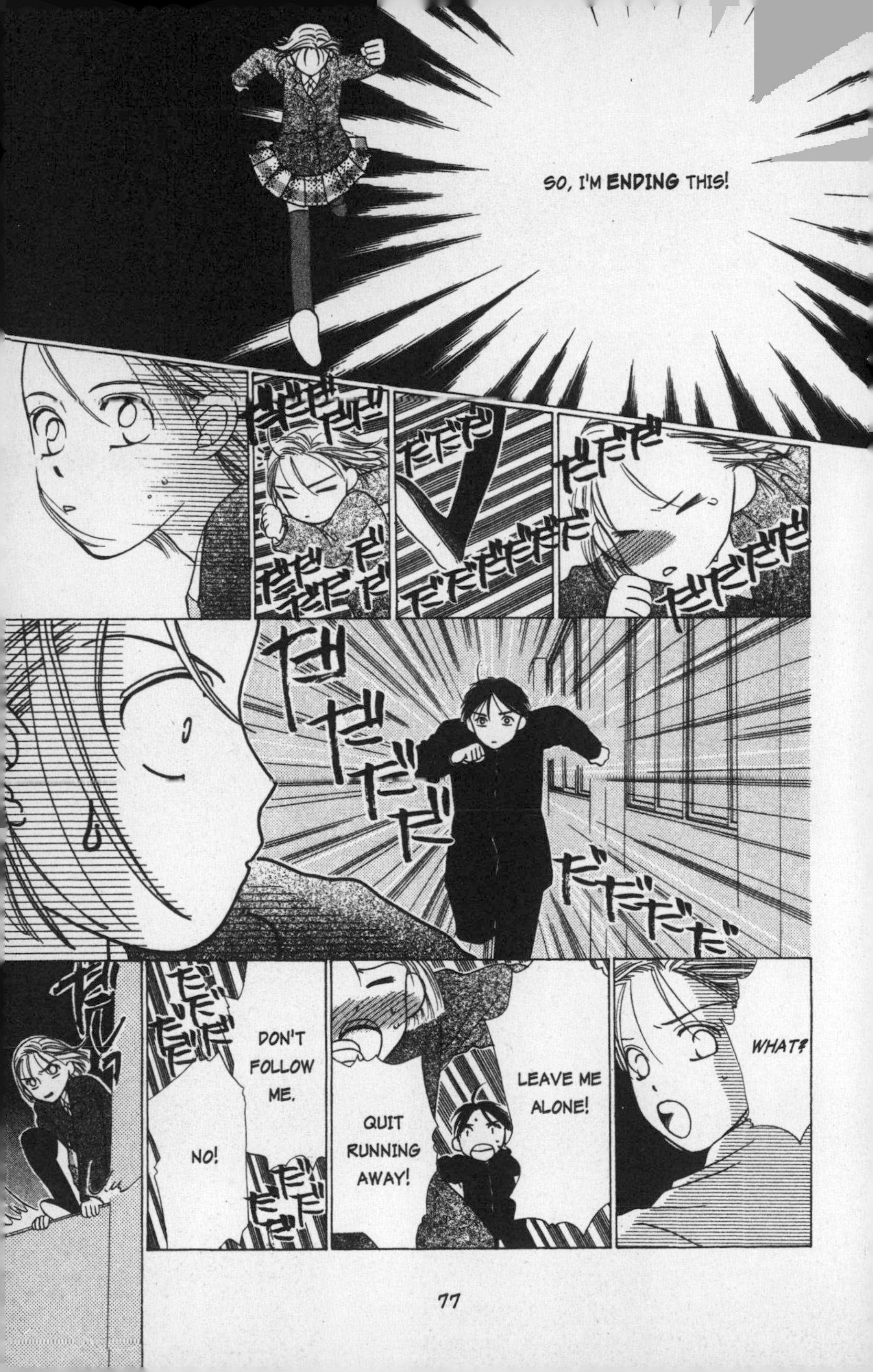
SO, I'M **ENDING** THIS!
WHAT?
LEAVE ME ALONE!
QUIT RUNNING AWAY!
DON'T FOLLOW ME.
NO!

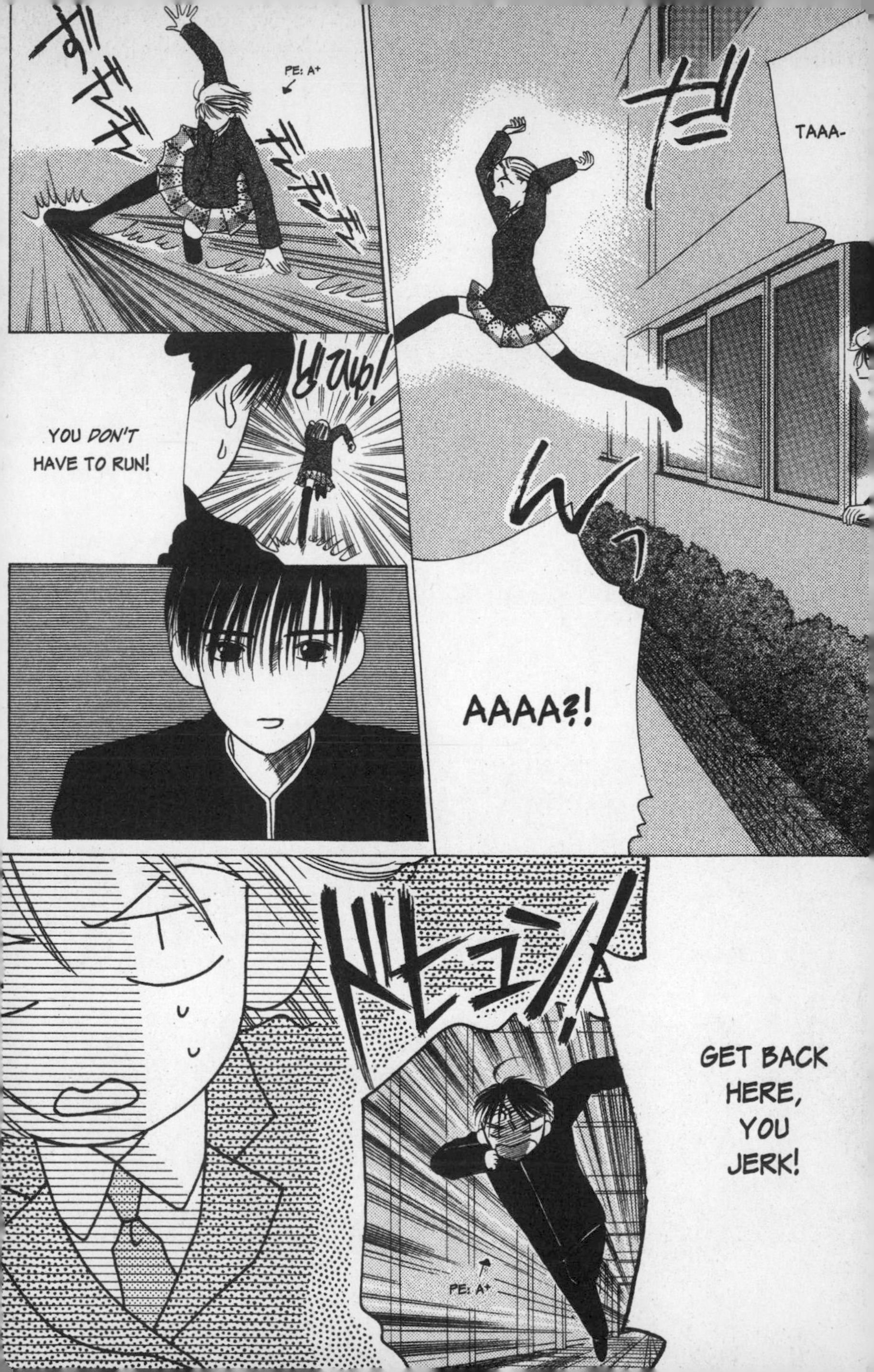
TAAA-
AAAA?!
PE: A+
YOU DON'T HAVE TO RUN!
GET BACK HERE, YOU JERK!
PE: A+

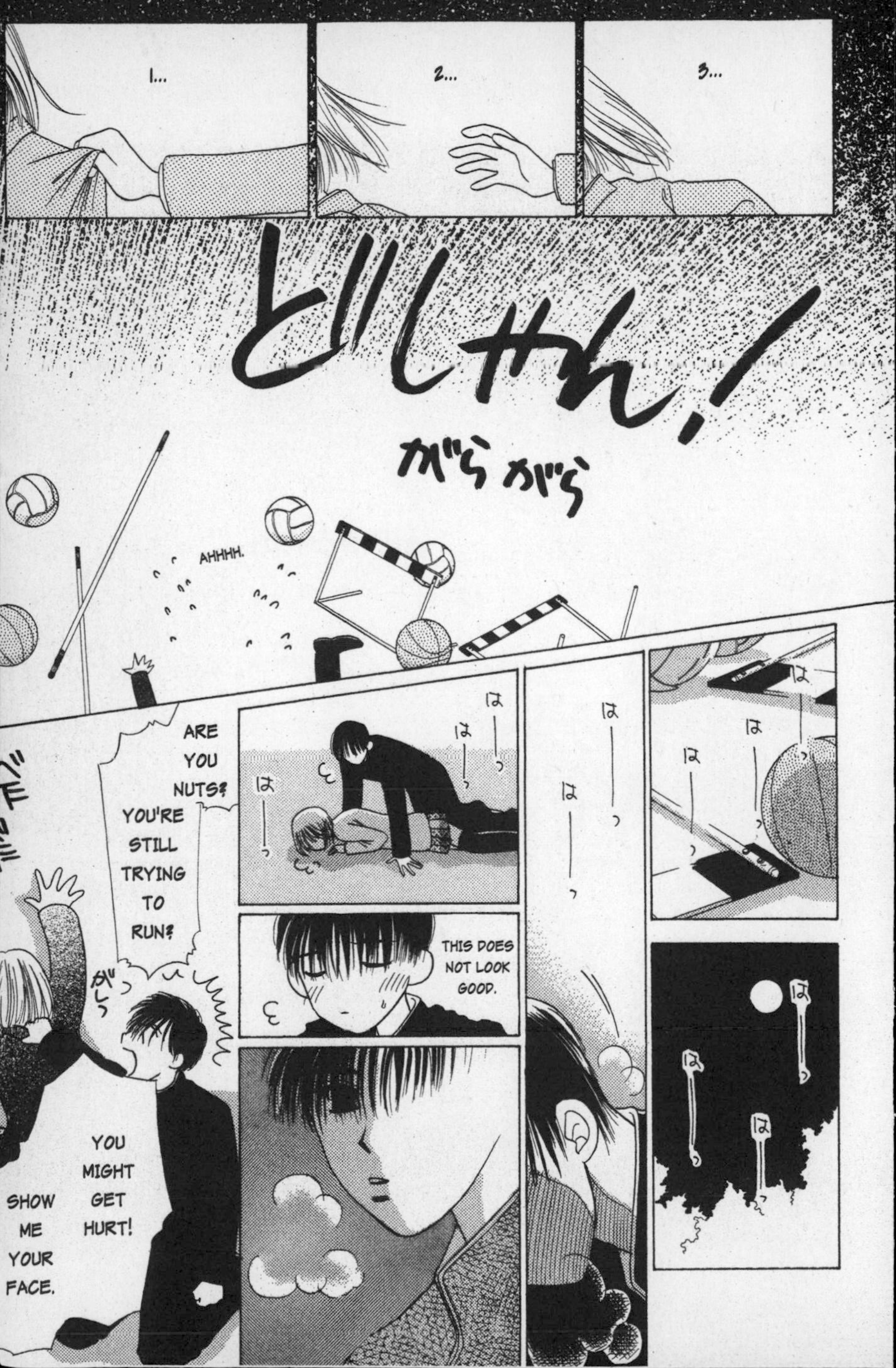

1...
2...
3...
どしゃん!
がらがら
AHHHH.
ARE YOU NUTS?
YOU'RE STILL TRYING TO RUN?
がしっ
YOU MIGHT GET HURT!
SHOW ME YOUR FACE.
はーっ はーっ はーっ
THIS DOES NOT LOOK GOOD.
はーっ はーっ
はっ はーっ はーっ
はっ はーっ はーっ

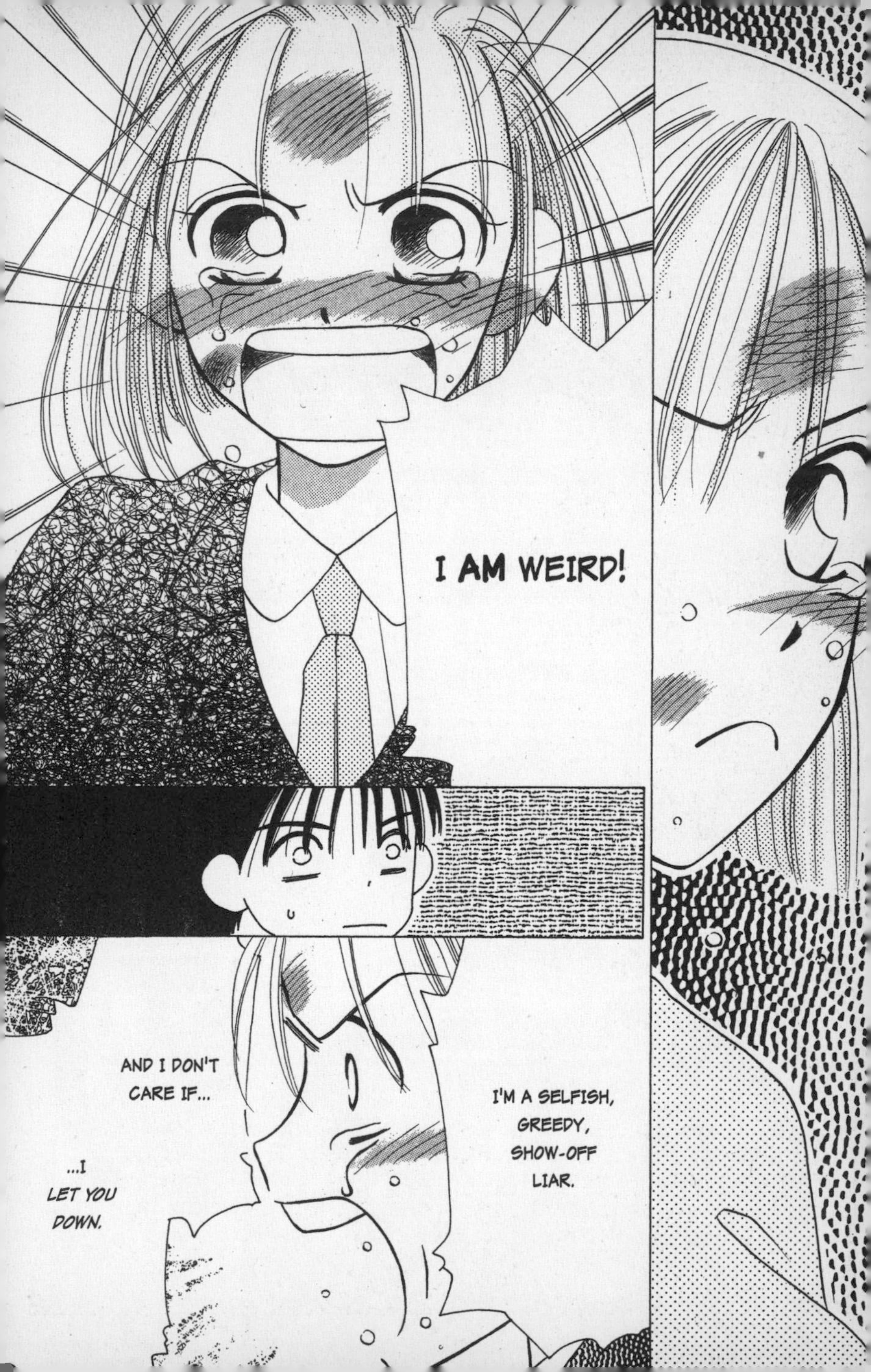
I AM WEIRD!
I'M A SELFISH, GREEDY, SHOW-OFF LIAR.
AND I DON'T CARE IF...
...I LET YOU DOWN.

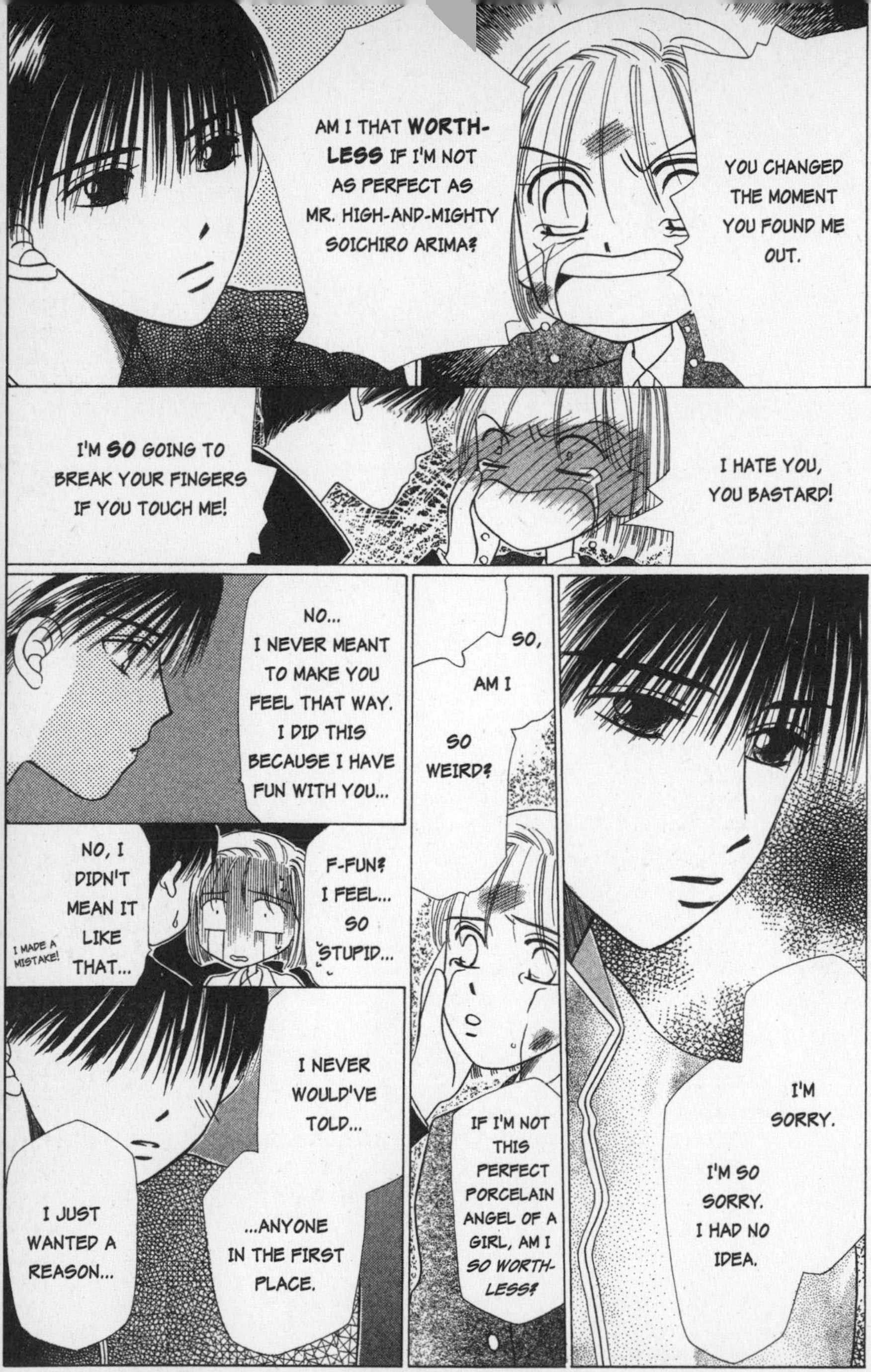
YOU CHANGED THE MOMENT YOU FOUND ME OUT.
AM I THAT WORTHLESS IF I'M NOT AS PERFECT AS MR. HIGH-AND-MIGHTY SOICHIRO ARIMA?
I HATE YOU, YOU BASTARD!
I'M SO GOING TO BREAK YOUR FINGERS IF YOU TOUCH ME!
I'M SORRY.
I'M SO SORRY. I HAD NO IDEA.
SO, AM I SO WEIRD?
IF I'M NOT THIS PERFECT PORCELAIN ANGEL OF A GIRL, AM I SO WORTHLESS?
NO... I NEVER MEANT TO MAKE YOU FEEL THAT WAY. I DID THIS BECAUSE I HAVE FUN WITH YOU...
F-FUN? I FEEL... SO STUPID...
NO, I DIDN'T MEAN IT LIKE THAT...
I MADE A MISTAKE!
I NEVER WOULD'VE TOLD...
...ANYONE IN THE FIRST PLACE.
I JUST WANTED A REASON...

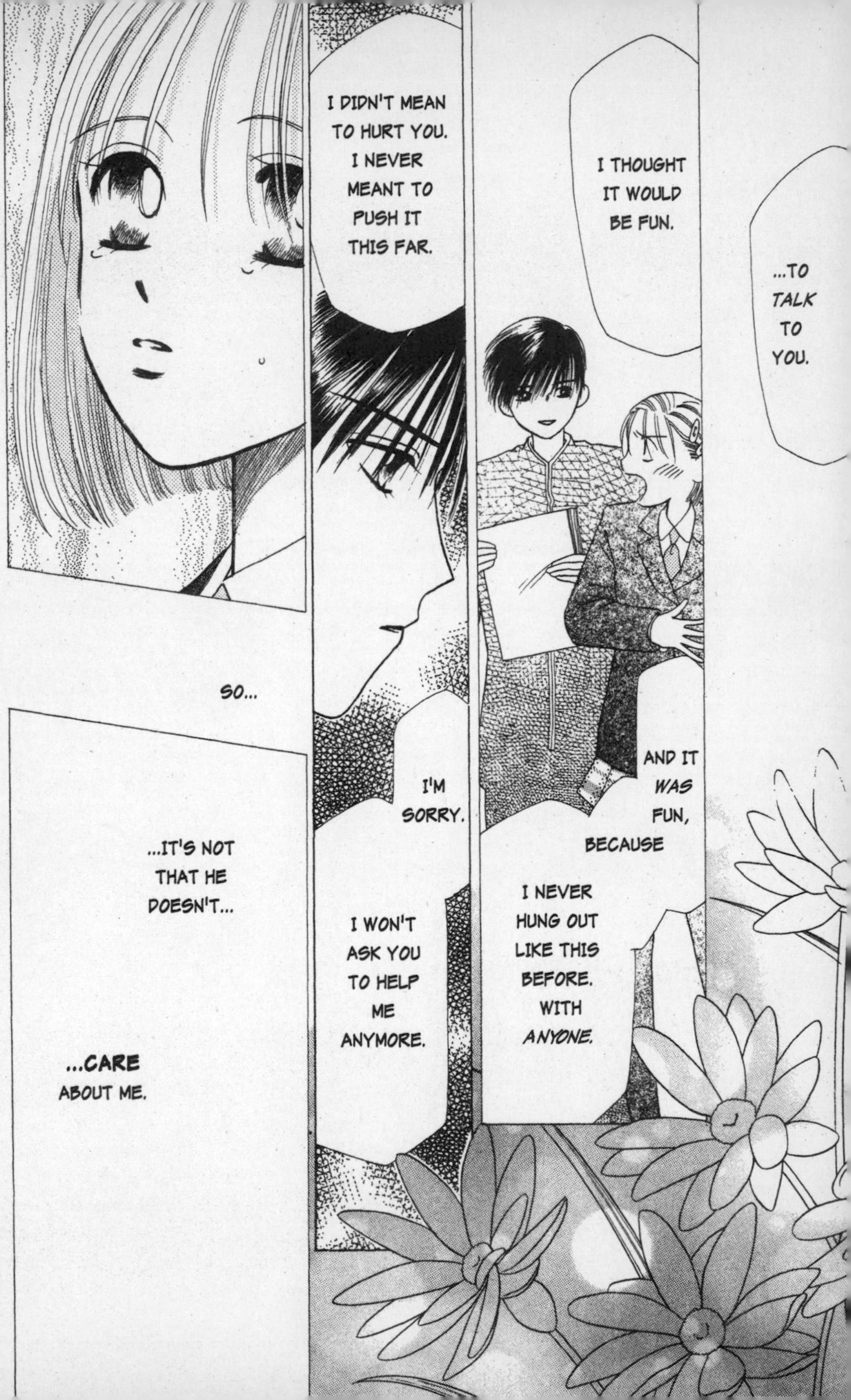
...TO TALK TO YOU.
I THOUGHT IT WOULD BE FUN.
AND IT WAS FUN, BECAUSE
I NEVER HUNG OUT LIKE THIS BEFORE. WITH ANYONE.
I DIDN'T MEAN TO HURT YOU. I NEVER MEANT TO PUSH IT THIS FAR.
I'M SORRY.
I WON'T ASK YOU TO HELP ME ANYMORE.
SO...
...IT'S NOT THAT HE DOESN'T...
...CARE ABOUT ME.

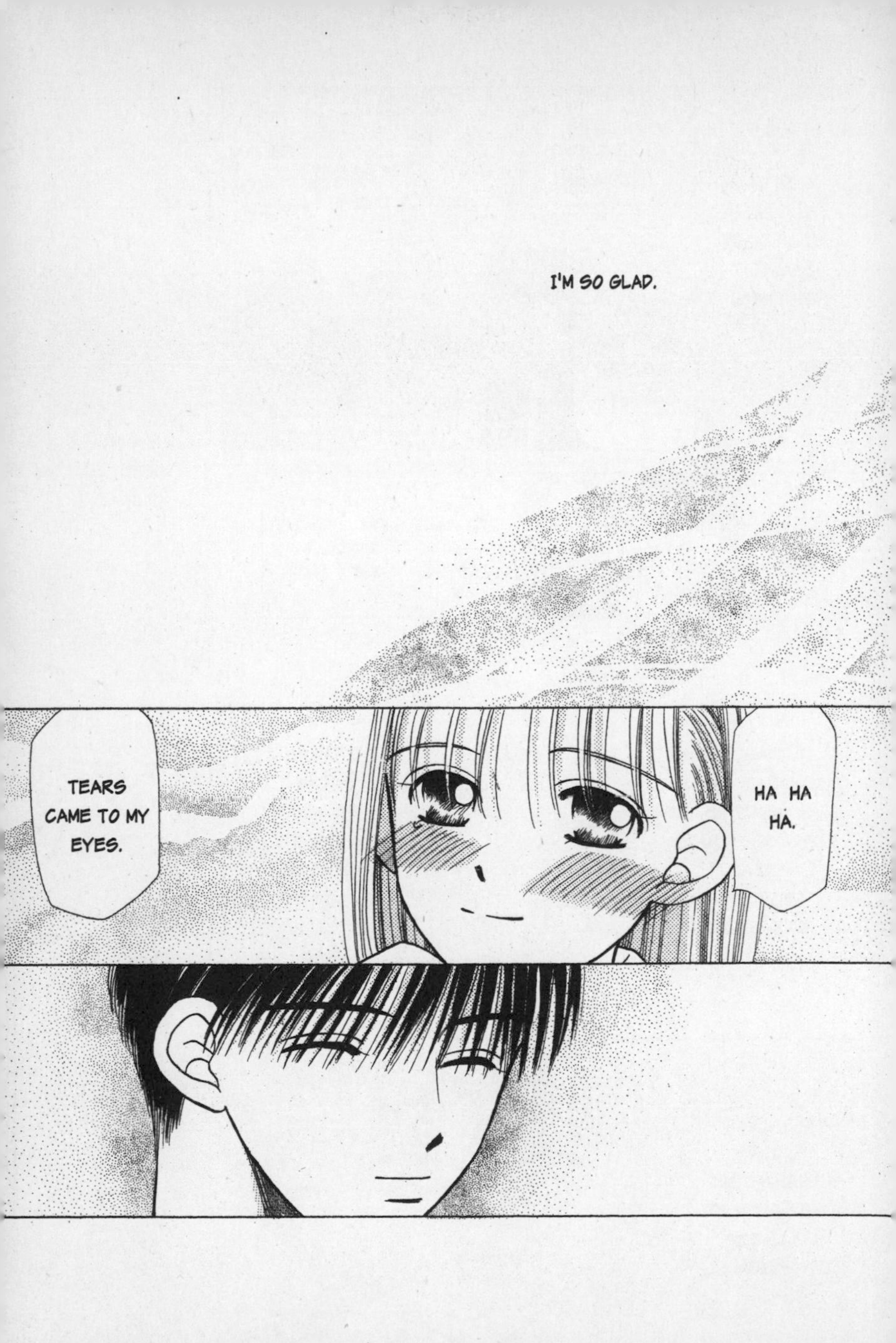
I'M SO GLAD.
HA HA HA.
TEARS CAME TO MY EYES.

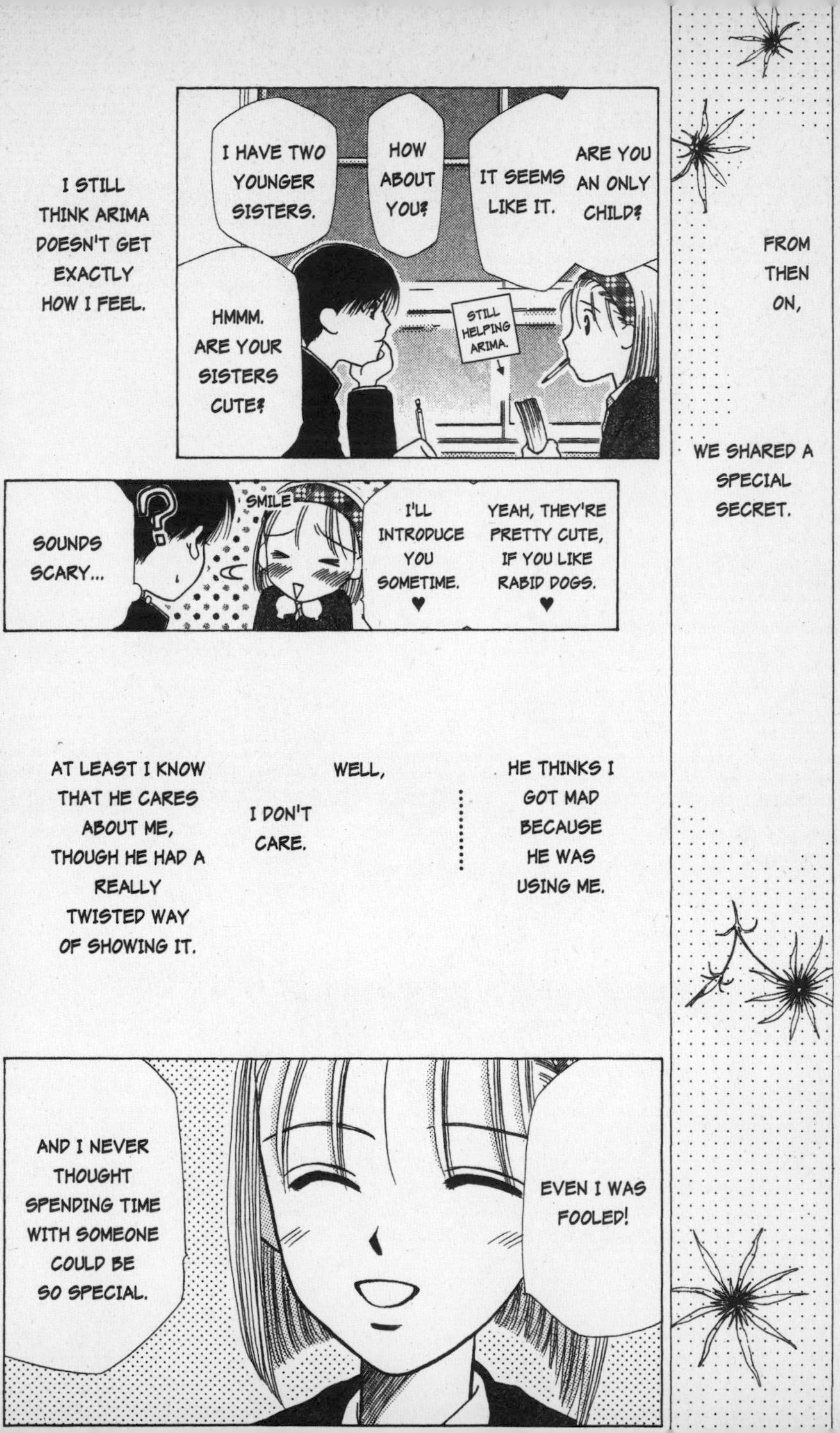
FROM THEN ON,
WE SHARED A SPECIAL SECRET.
ARE YOU AN ONLY CHILD?
IT SEEMS LIKE IT.
HOW ABOUT YOU?
I HAVE TWO YOUNGER SISTERS.
STILL HELPING ARIMA.
HMMM. ARE YOUR SISTERS CUTE?
I STILL THINK ARIMA DOESN'T GET EXACTLY HOW I FEEL.
YEAH, THEY'RE PRETTY CUTE, IF YOU LIKE RABID DOGS. ♥
I'LL INTRODUCE YOU SOMETIME. ♥
SMILE
SOUNDS SCARY...
HE THINKS I GOT MAD BECAUSE HE WAS USING ME.
......
WELL,
I DON'T CARE.
AT LEAST I KNOW THAT HE CARES ABOUT ME, THOUGH HE HAD A REALLY TWISTED WAY OF SHOWING IT.
EVEN I WAS FOOLED!
AND I NEVER THOUGHT SPENDING TIME WITH SOMEONE COULD BE SO SPECIAL.

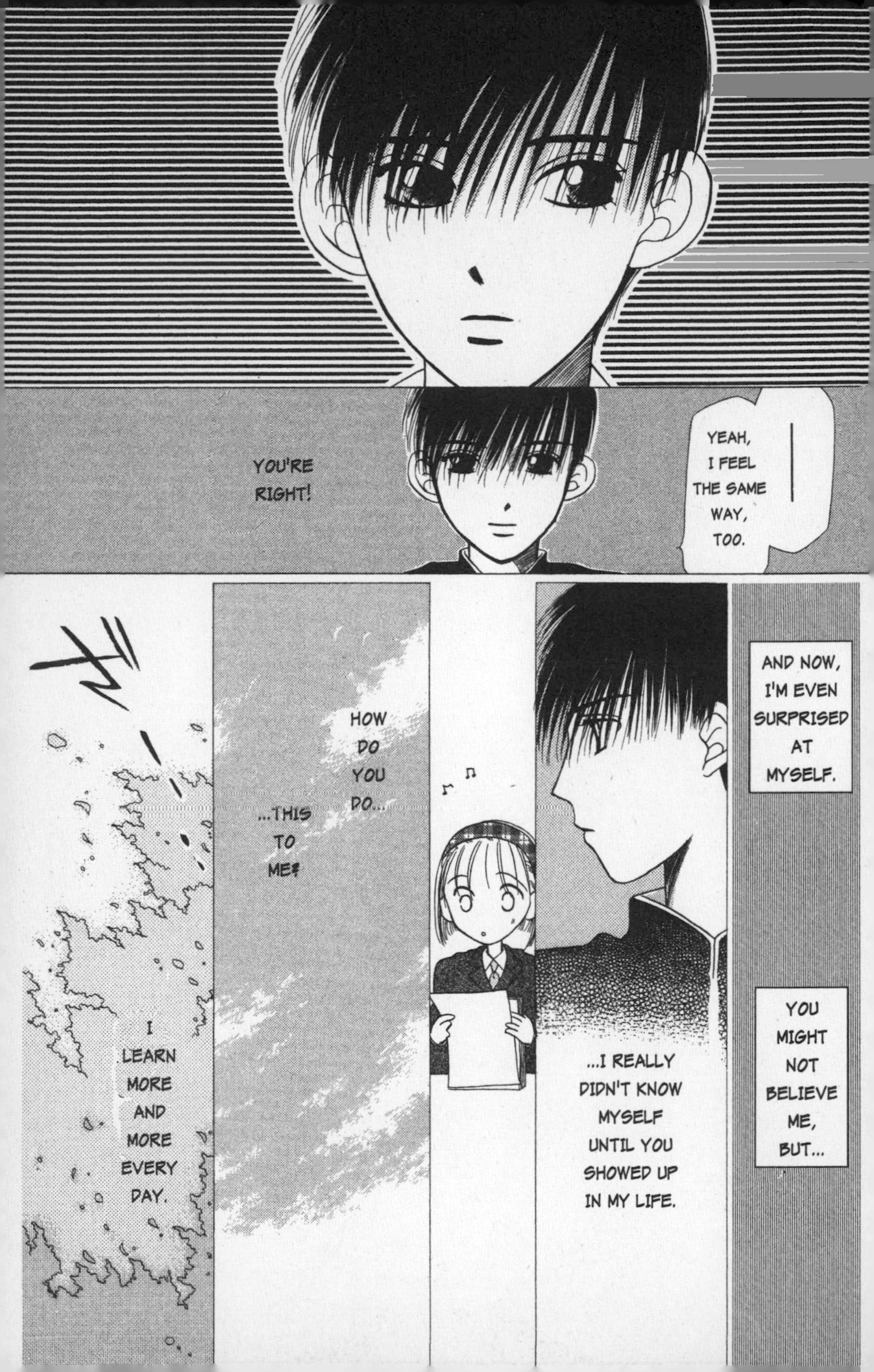
YEAH, I FEEL THE SAME WAY, TOO.
YOU'RE RIGHT!
AND NOW, I'M EVEN SURPRISED AT MYSELF.
YOU MIGHT NOT BELIEVE ME, BUT...
...I REALLY DIDN'T KNOW MYSELF UNTIL YOU SHOWED UP IN MY LIFE.
HOW DO YOU DO...
...THIS TO ME?
I LEARN MORE AND MORE EVERY DAY.

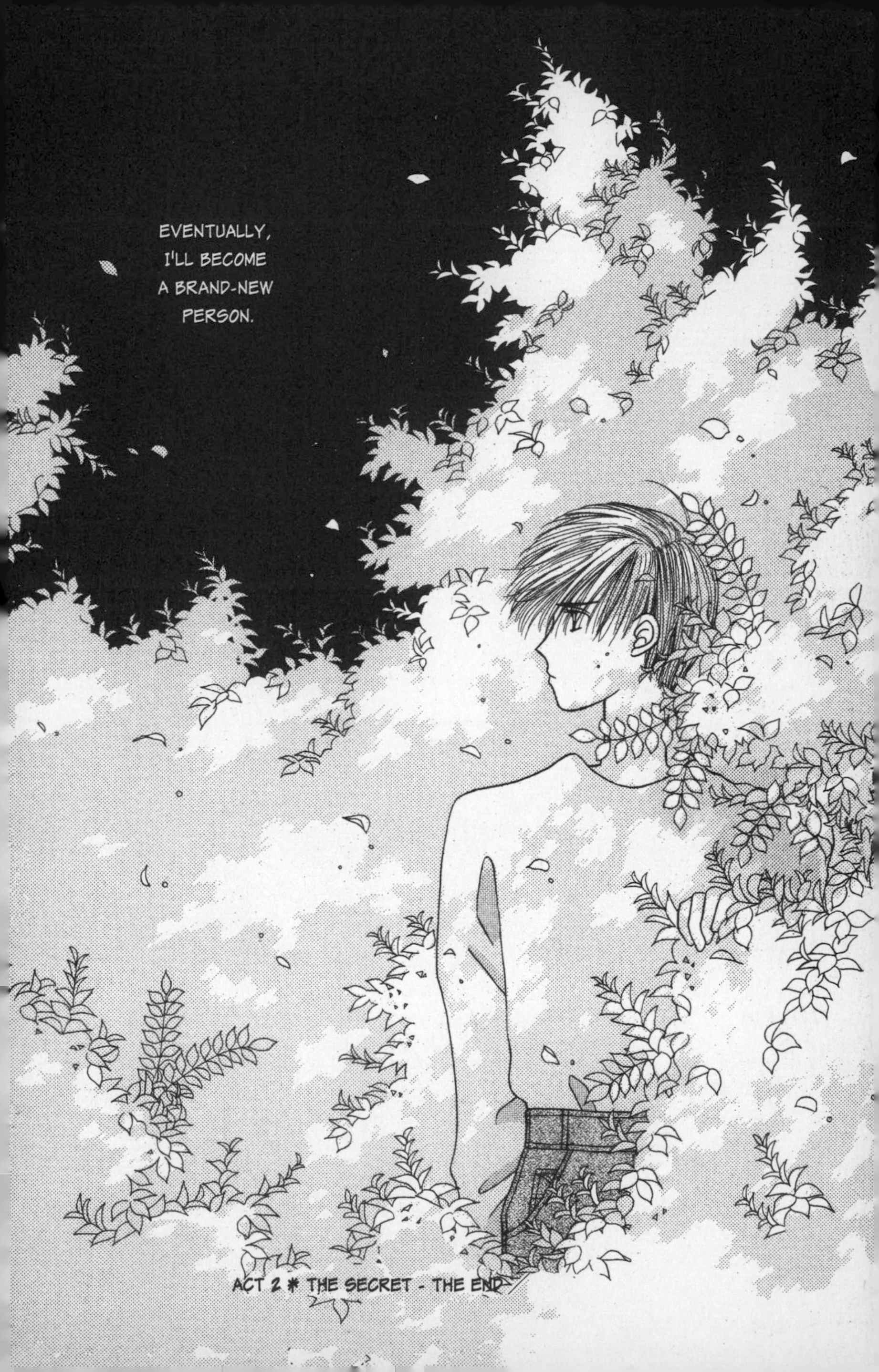
EVENTUALLY,
I'LL BECOME
A BRAND-NEW
PERSON.
ACT 2 * THE SECRET - THE END

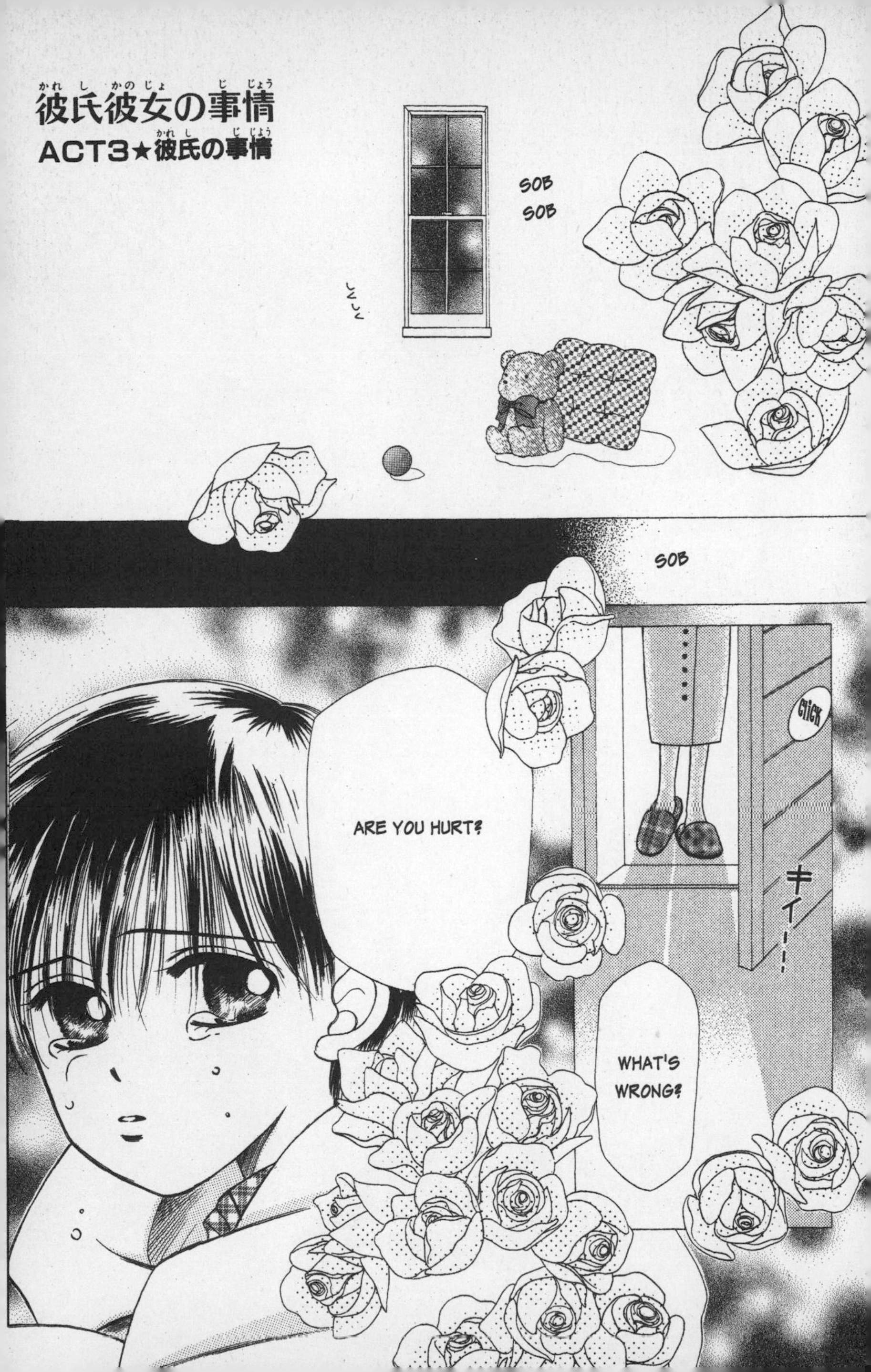
彼氏彼女の事情
ACT3★彼氏の事情
SOB
SOB
しくしく
SOB
CLICK
キイ…
WHAT'S WRONG?
ARE YOU HURT?

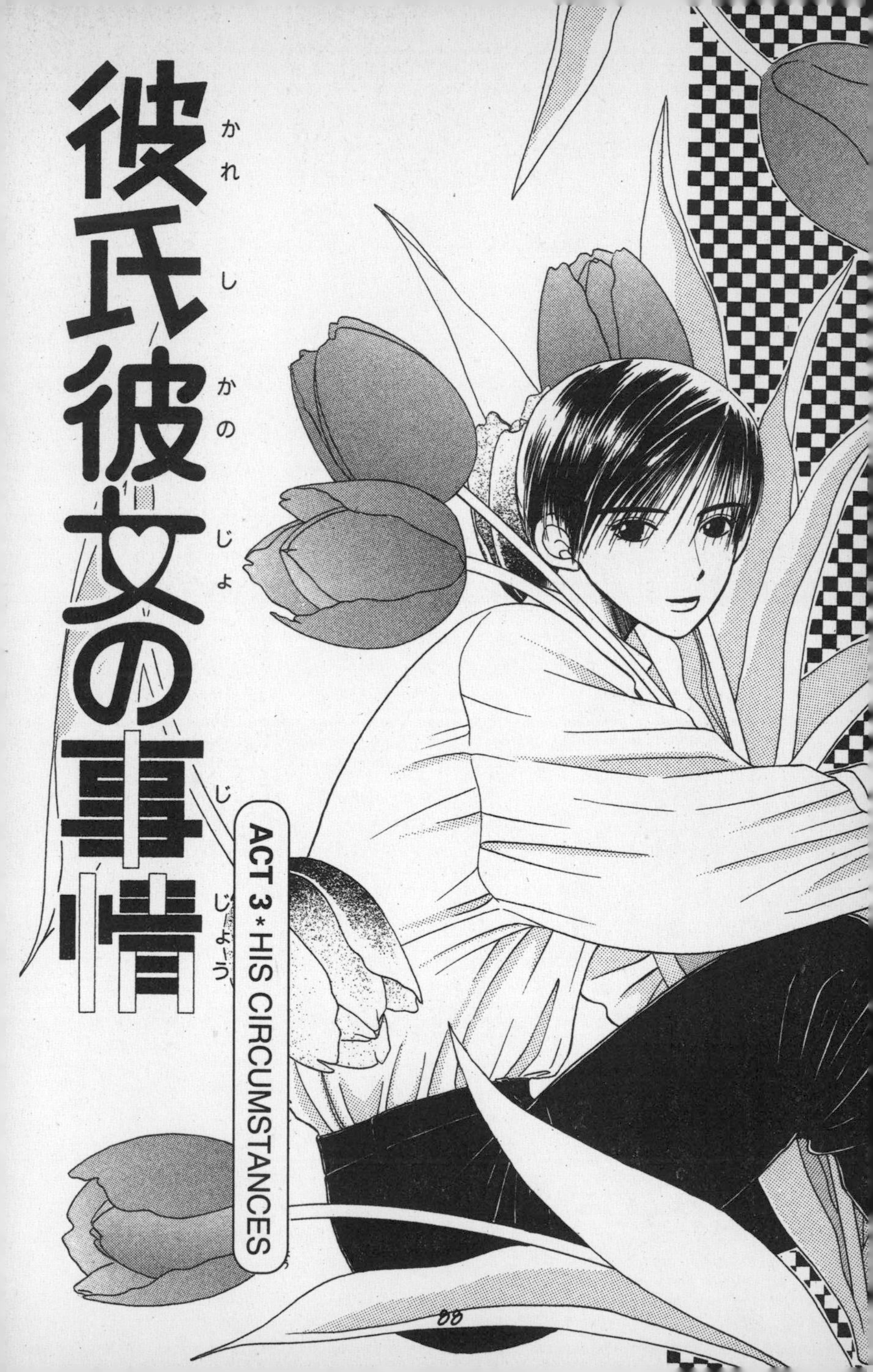
彼氏彼女の事情
ACT 3 * HIS CIRCUMSTANCES

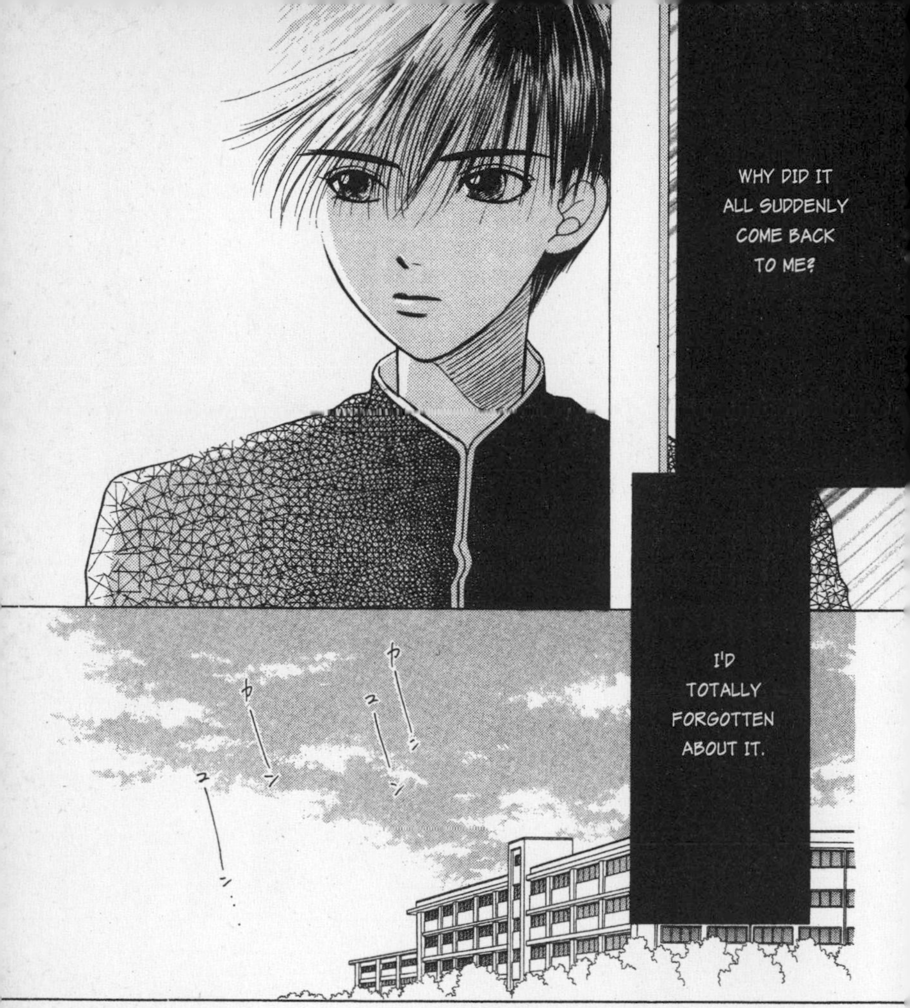
WHY DID IT ALL SUDDENLY COME BACK TO ME?
I'D TOTALLY FORGOTTEN ABOUT IT.

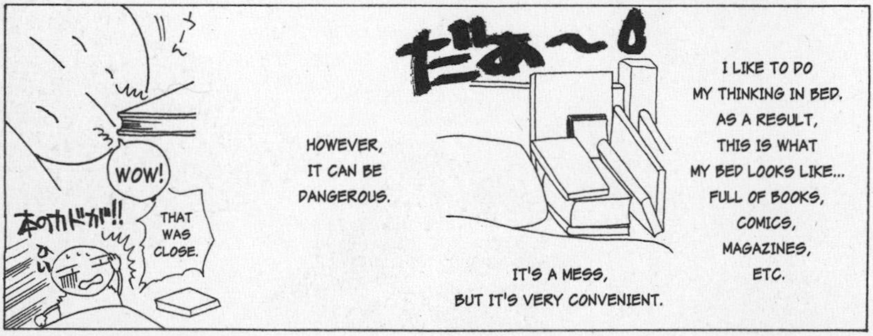
I LIKE TO DO MY THINKING IN BED. AS A RESULT, THIS IS WHAT MY BED LOOKS LIKE... FULL OF BOOKS, COMICS, MAGAZINES, ETC.
だあ～
IT'S A MESS, BUT IT'S VERY CONVENIENT.
HOWEVER, IT CAN BE DANGEROUS.
WOW!
本のカドが!!
THAT WAS CLOSE.
ひい

THE EDGE OF THE BOOKS...

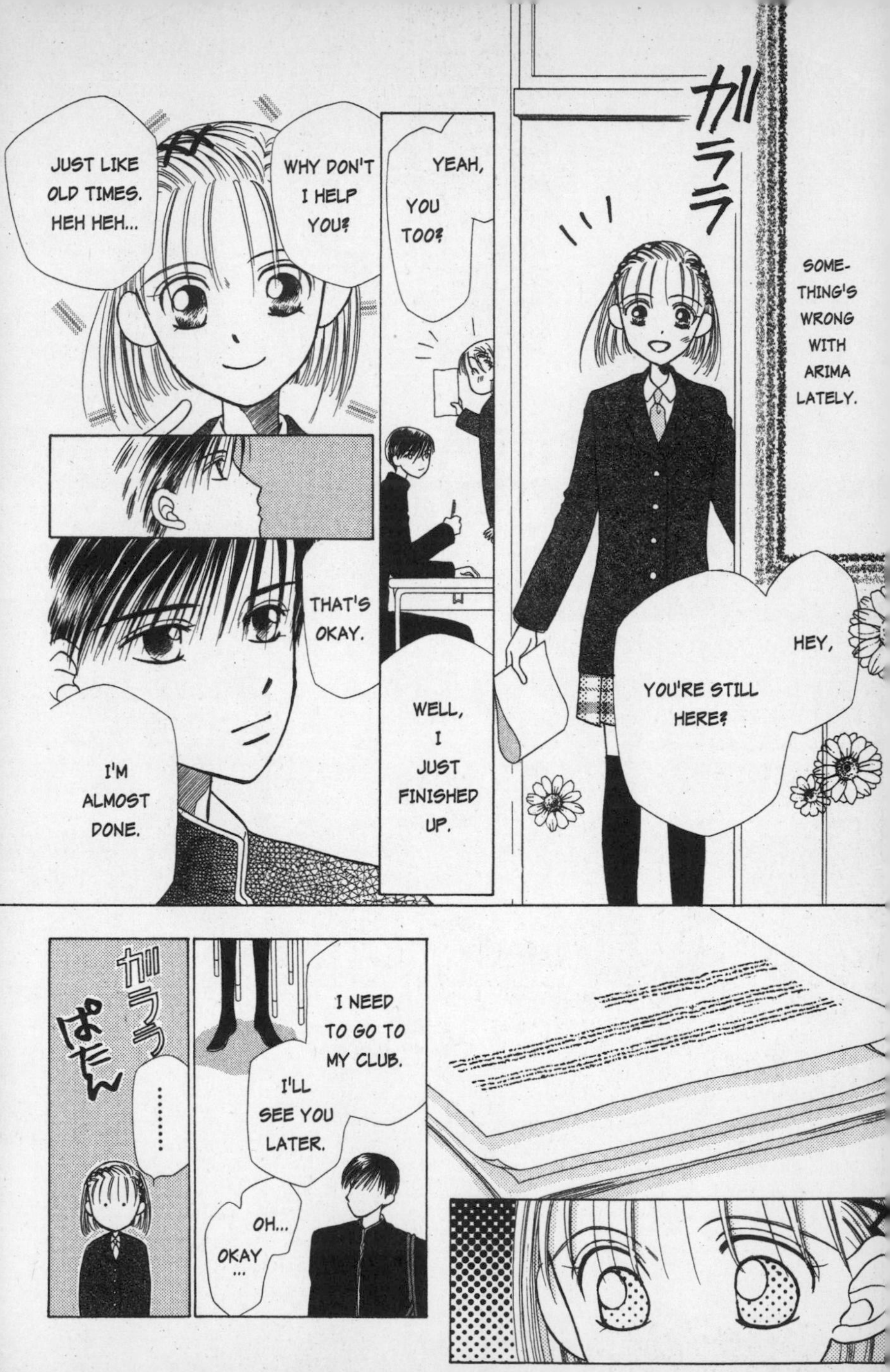
ガララ
SOME-THING'S WRONG WITH ARIMA LATELY.
HEY,
YOU'RE STILL HERE?
YEAH,
YOU TOO?
WELL, I JUST FINISHED UP.
WHY DON'T I HELP YOU?
JUST LIKE OLD TIMES. HEH HEH...
THAT'S OKAY.
I'M ALMOST DONE.
I NEED TO GO TO MY CLUB.
I'LL SEE YOU LATER.
OH... OKAY ...
ガララ
ぱたん
......

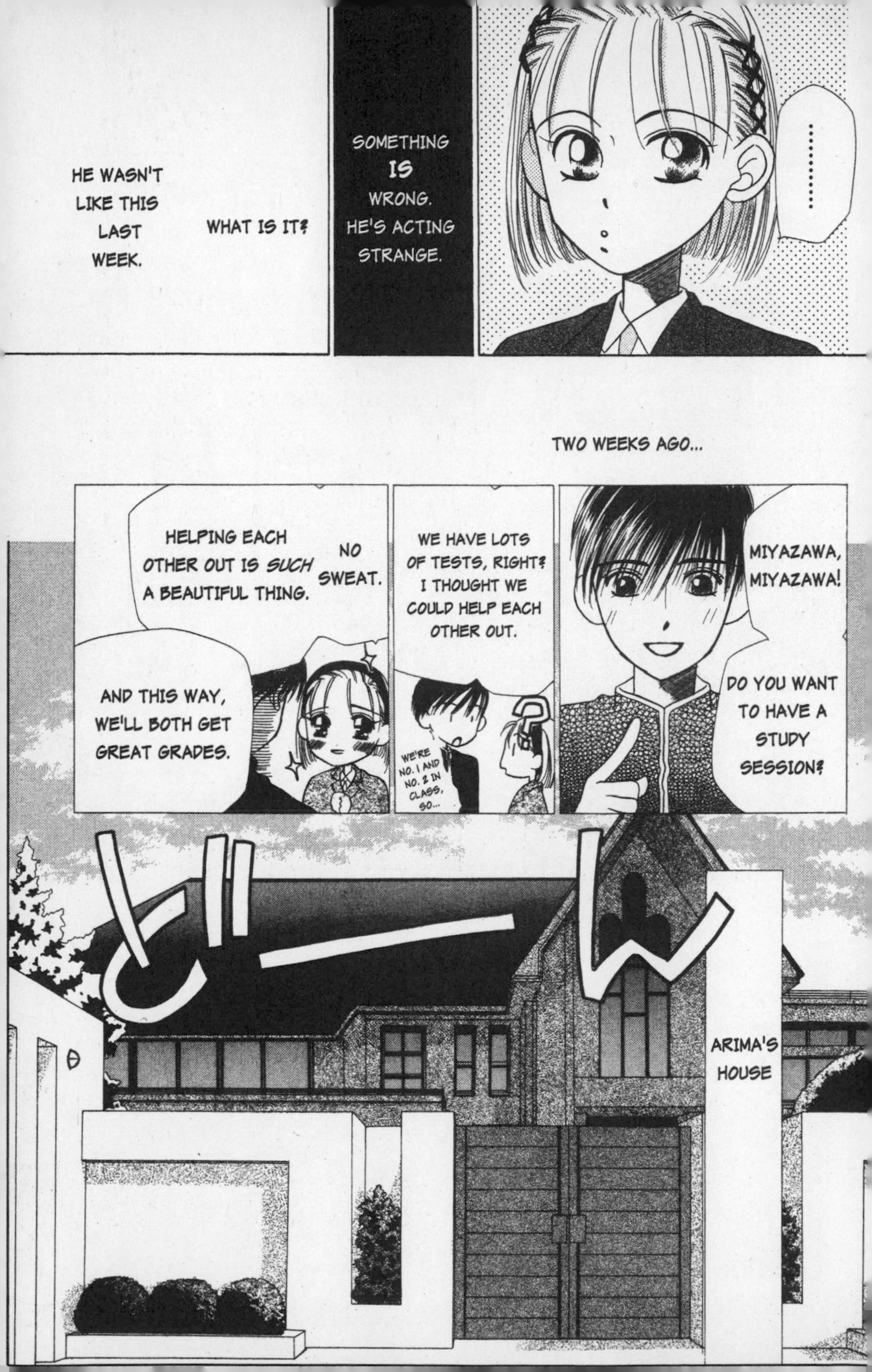
......
SOMETHING IS WRONG. HE'S ACTING STRANGE.
WHAT IS IT?
HE WASN'T LIKE THIS LAST WEEK.
TWO WEEKS AGO...
MIYAZAWA, MIYAZAWA!
DO YOU WANT TO HAVE A STUDY SESSION?
WE HAVE LOTS OF TESTS, RIGHT? I THOUGHT WE COULD HELP EACH OTHER OUT.
WE'RE NO. 1 AND NO. 2 IN CLASS, SO...
NO SWEAT.
HELPING EACH OTHER OUT IS *SUCH* A BEAUTIFUL THING.
AND THIS WAY, WE'LL BOTH GET GREAT GRADES.
ARIMA'S HOUSE
じーん

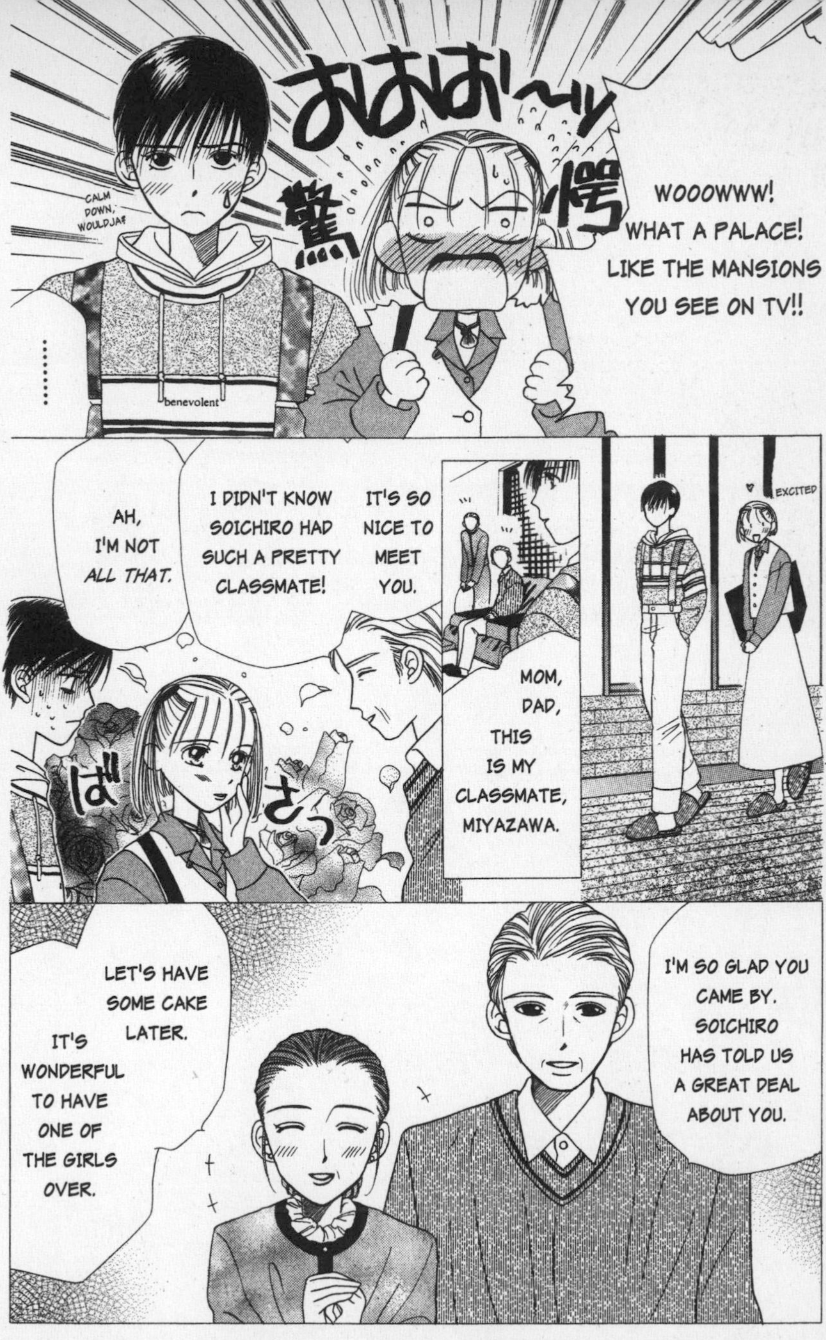
おおお〜ッ
驚愕
WOOOWWW! WHAT A PALACE! LIKE THE MANSIONS YOU SEE ON TV!!
CALM DOWN, WOULDJA?
......
benevolent
EXCITED
MOM, DAD, THIS IS MY CLASSMATE, MIYAZAWA.
IT'S SO NICE TO MEET YOU.
I DIDN'T KNOW SOICHIRO HAD SUCH A PRETTY CLASSMATE!
AH, I'M NOT *ALL THAT.*
ばさっ
I'M SO GLAD YOU CAME BY. SOICHIRO HAS TOLD US A GREAT DEAL ABOUT YOU.
LET'S HAVE SOME CAKE LATER.
IT'S WONDERFUL TO HAVE ONE OF THE GIRLS OVER.

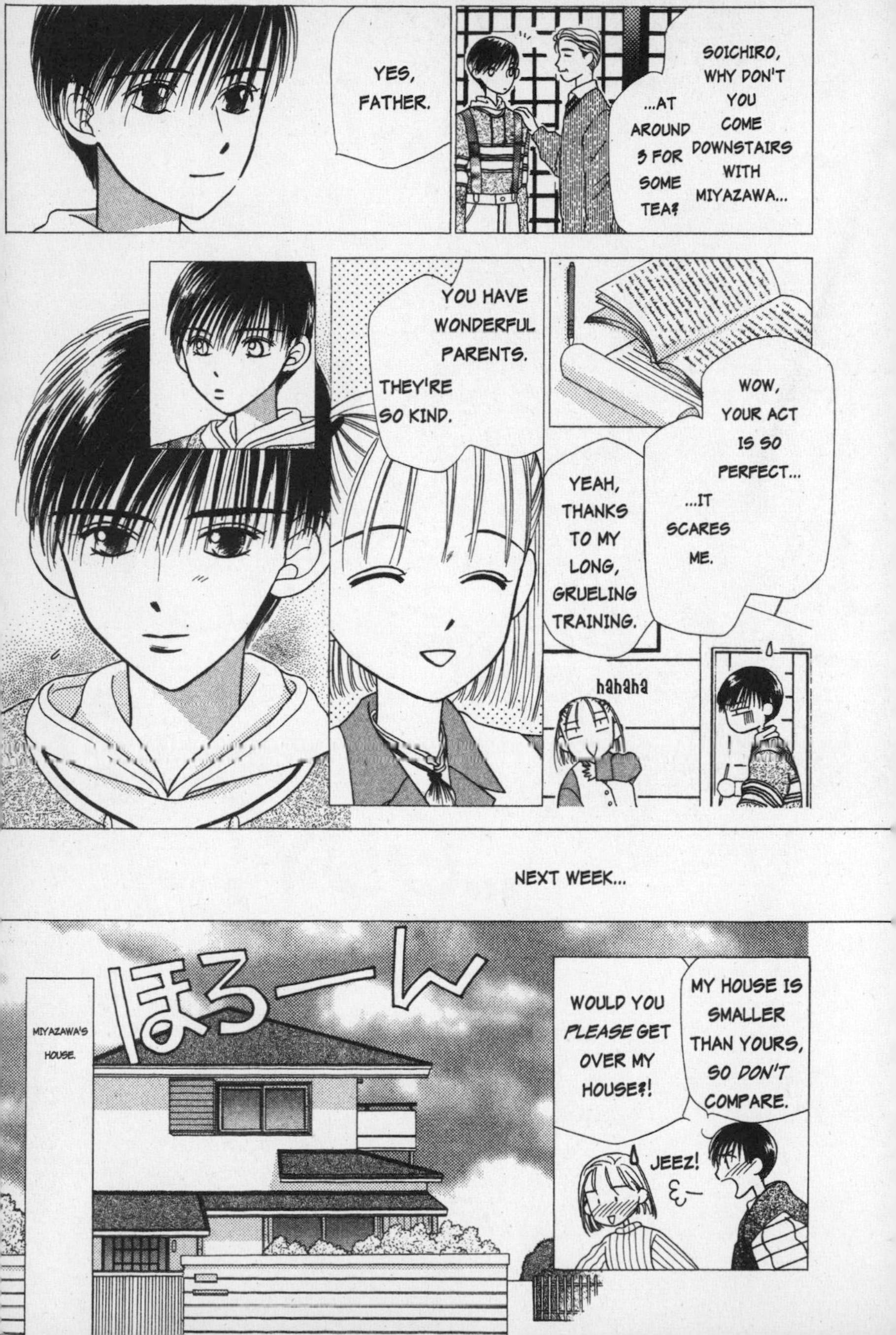
SOICHIRO, WHY DON'T YOU COME DOWNSTAIRS WITH MIYAZAWA...
...AT AROUND 3 FOR SOME TEA?
YES, FATHER.
WOW, YOUR ACT IS SO PERFECT...
...IT SCARES ME.
YEAH, THANKS TO MY LONG, GRUELING TRAINING.
hahaha
YOU HAVE WONDERFUL PARENTS.
THEY'RE SO KIND.
NEXT WEEK...
MY HOUSE IS SMALLER THAN YOURS, SO *DON'T* COMPARE.
WOULD YOU *PLEASE* GET OVER MY HOUSE?!
JEEZ!
ほろーん
MIYAZAWA'S HOUSE.

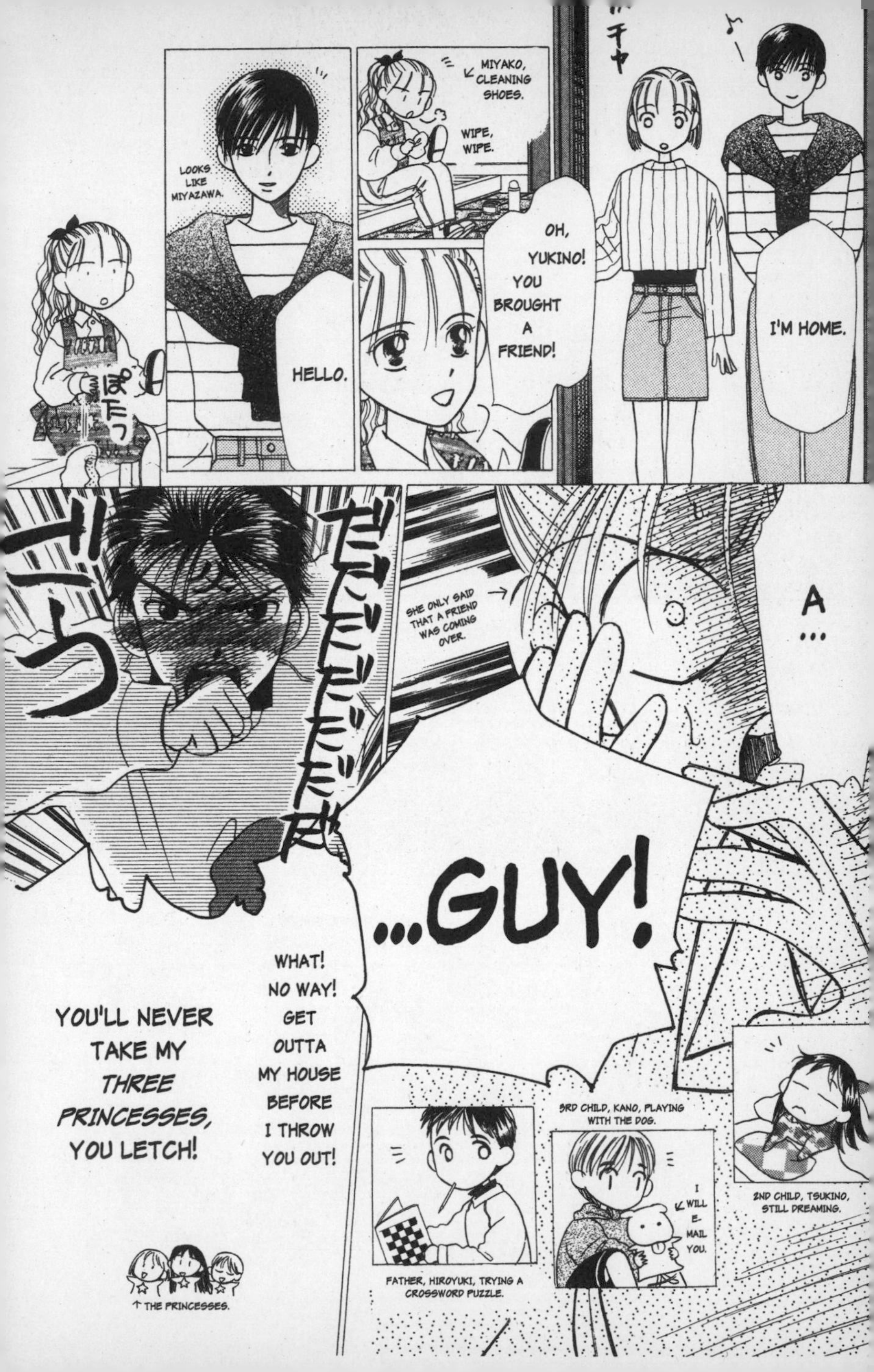
ガチャ
I'M HOME.
MIYAKO, CLEANING SHOES.
WIPE, WIPE.
OH, YUKINO! YOU BROUGHT A FRIEND!
LOOKS LIKE MIYAZAWA.
HELLO.
ぽてっ
A...
SHE ONLY SAID THAT A FRIEND WAS COMING OVER.
...GUY!
WHAT! NO WAY! GET OUTTA MY HOUSE BEFORE I THROW YOU OUT!
YOU'LL NEVER TAKE MY *THREE PRINCESSES,* YOU LETCH!
2ND CHILD, TSUKINO, STILL DREAMING.
3RD CHILD, KANO, PLAYING WITH THE DOG.
I WILL E-MAIL YOU.
FATHER, HIROYUKI, TRYING A CROSSWORD PUZZLE.
THE PRINCESSES.

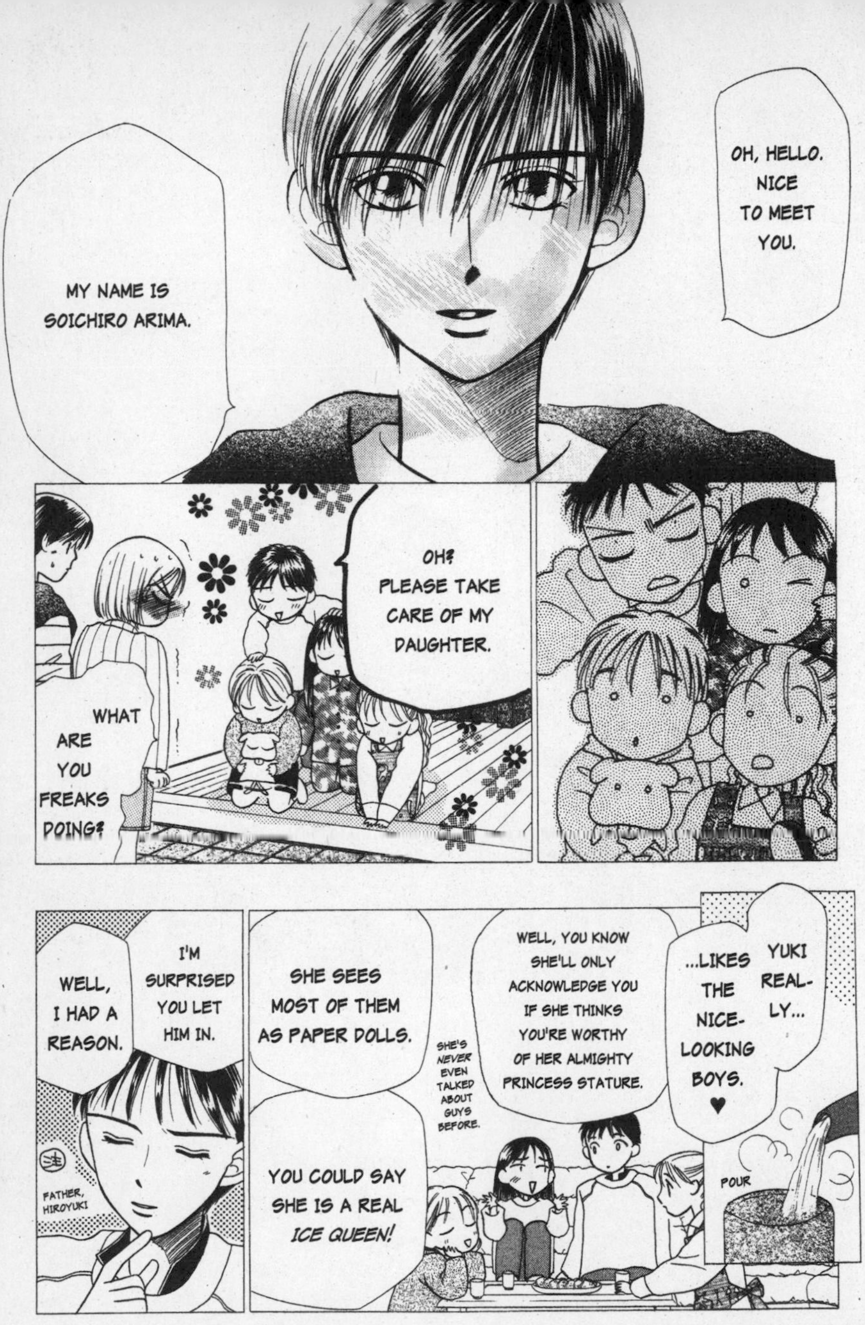
OH, HELLO. NICE TO MEET YOU.
MY NAME IS SOICHIRO ARIMA.
OH? PLEASE TAKE CARE OF MY DAUGHTER.
WHAT ARE YOU FREAKS DOING?
YUKI REALLY...
...LIKES THE NICE-LOOKING BOYS. ♥
POUR
WELL, YOU KNOW SHE'LL ONLY ACKNOWLEDGE YOU IF SHE THINKS YOU'RE WORTHY OF HER ALMIGHTY PRINCESS STATURE.
SHE'S *NEVER* EVEN TALKED ABOUT GUYS BEFORE.
SHE SEES MOST OF THEM AS PAPER DOLLS.
YOU COULD SAY SHE IS A REAL *ICE QUEEN!*
I'M SURPRISED YOU LET HIM IN.
WELL, I HAD A REASON.
FATHER, HIROYUKI

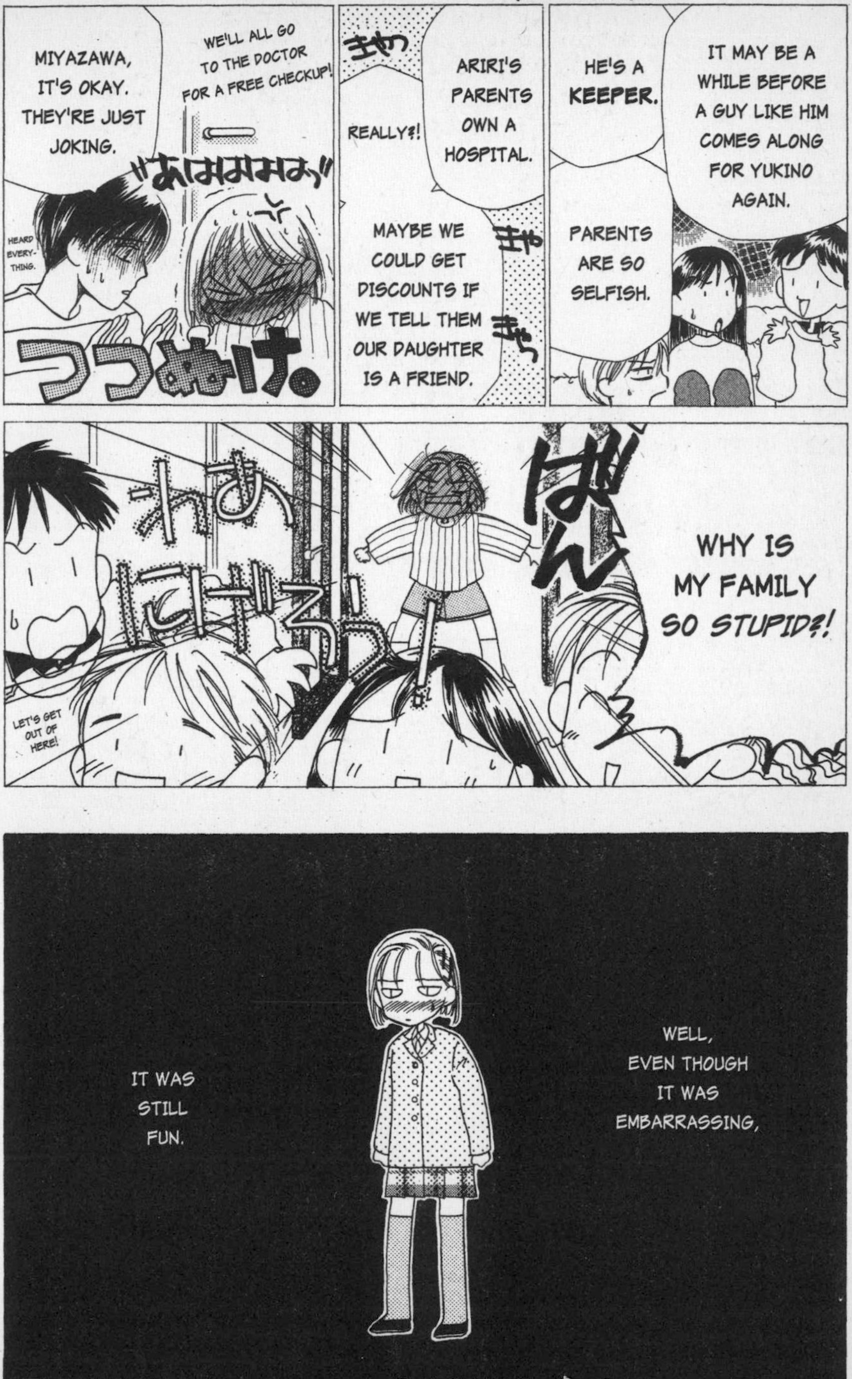
↓ALREADY GIVING HIM NICKNAMES.
IT MAY BE A WHILE BEFORE A GUY LIKE HIM COMES ALONG FOR YUKINO AGAIN.
HE'S A KEEPER.
PARENTS ARE SO SELFISH.
きゃっ
ARIRI'S PARENTS OWN A HOSPITAL.
REALLY?!
きゃ
MAYBE WE COULD GET DISCOUNTS IF WE TELL THEM OUR DAUGHTER IS A FRIEND.
きゃっ
WE'LL ALL GO TO THE DOCTOR FOR A FREE CHECKUP!
MIYAZAWA, IT'S OKAY. THEY'RE JUST JOKING.
あははははっ
HEARD EVERY-THING.
つつぬけ。
ばん
WHY IS MY FAMILY SO STUPID?!
わあ
にげろぉ
LET'S GET OUT OF HERE!
WELL, EVEN THOUGH IT WAS EMBARRASSING,
IT WAS STILL FUN.

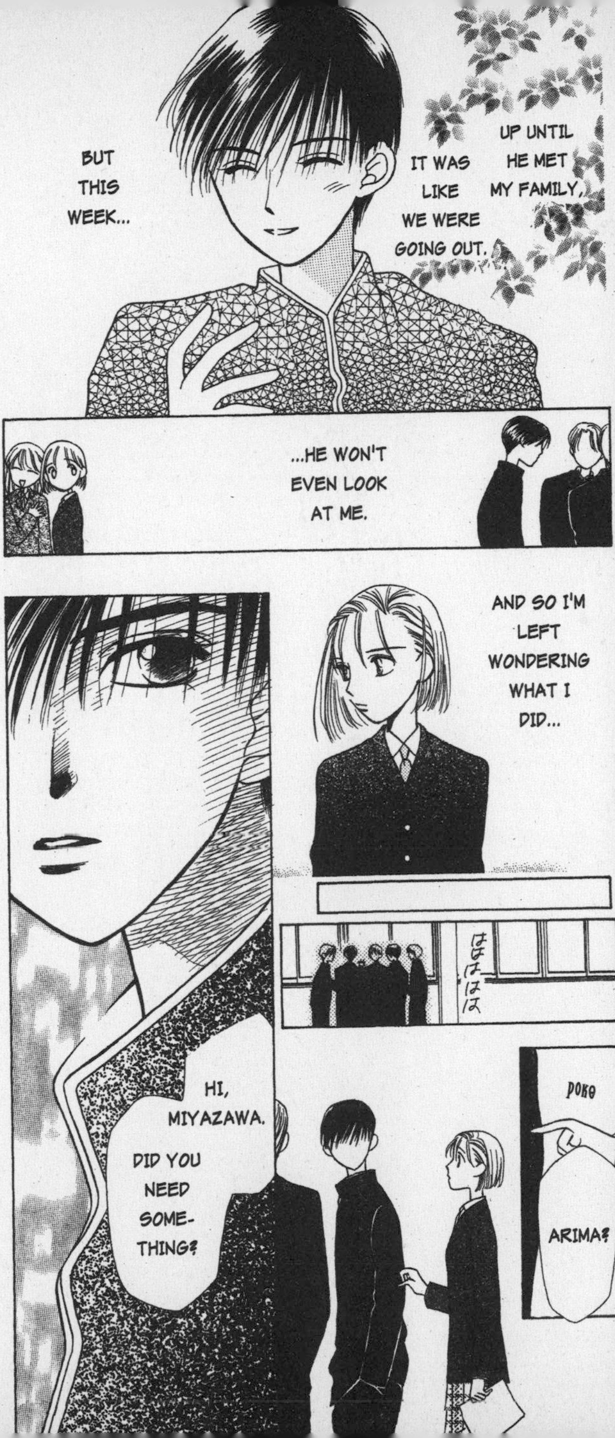
UP UNTIL HE MET MY FAMILY,
IT WAS LIKE WE WERE GOING OUT.
BUT THIS WEEK...
...HE WON'T EVEN LOOK AT ME.
AND SO I'M LEFT WONDERING WHAT I DID...
はははは
POKO
ARIMA?
HI, MIYAZAWA.
DID YOU NEED SOME-THING?

4

While I was writing this comic, I went to go see the Ken Hill version of The Phantom of the Opera.

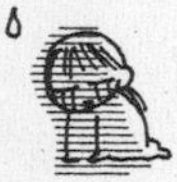

The song "While Floating High Above" is the greatest song ever! It makes me feel lucky to be alive.

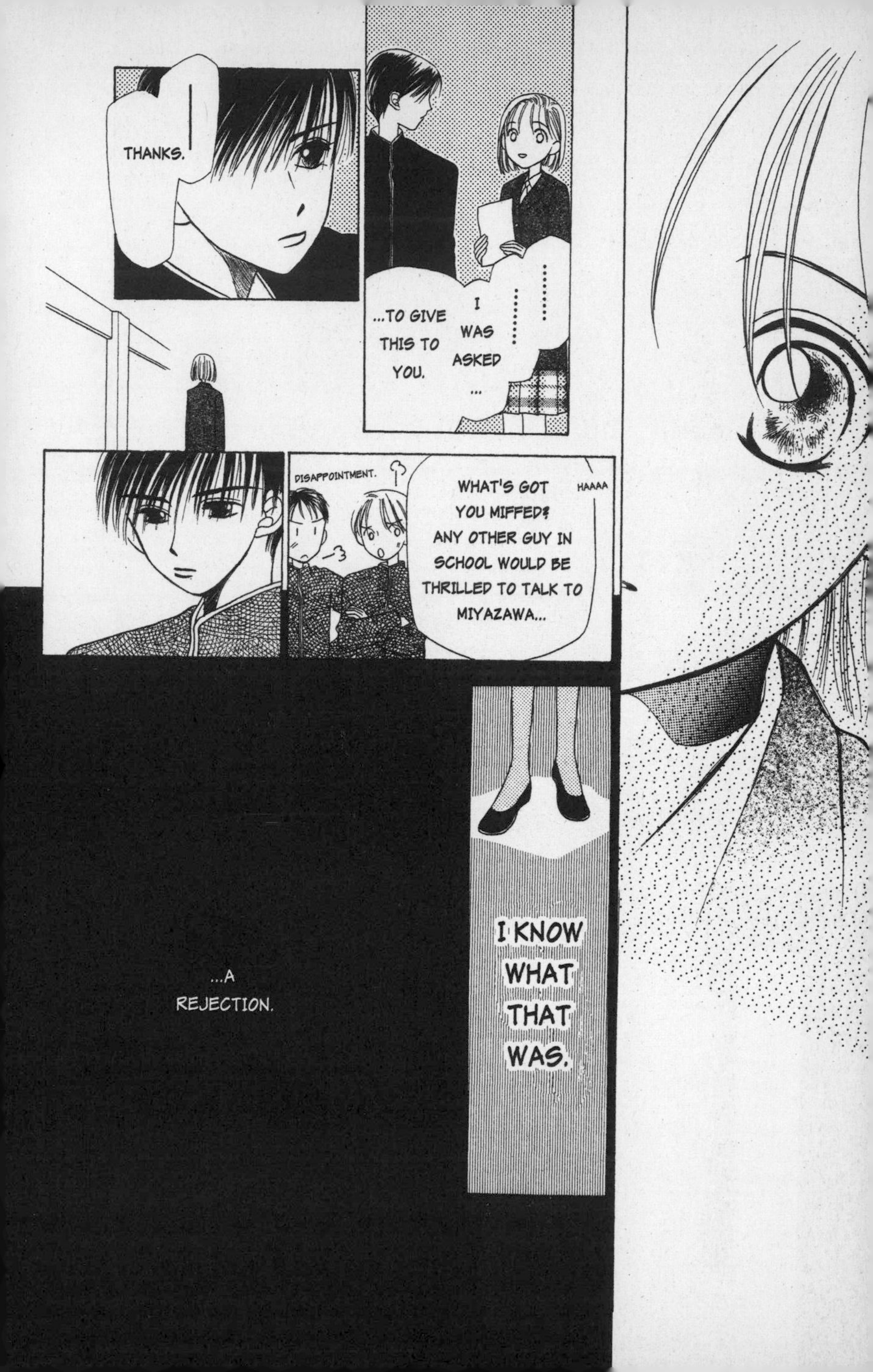
I WAS ASKED...
...TO GIVE THIS TO YOU.
....
THANKS.
HAAAA
WHAT'S GOT YOU MIFFED? ANY OTHER GUY IN SCHOOL WOULD BE THRILLED TO TALK TO MIYAZAWA...
DISAPPOINTMENT.
I KNOW WHAT THAT WAS.
...A REJECTION.

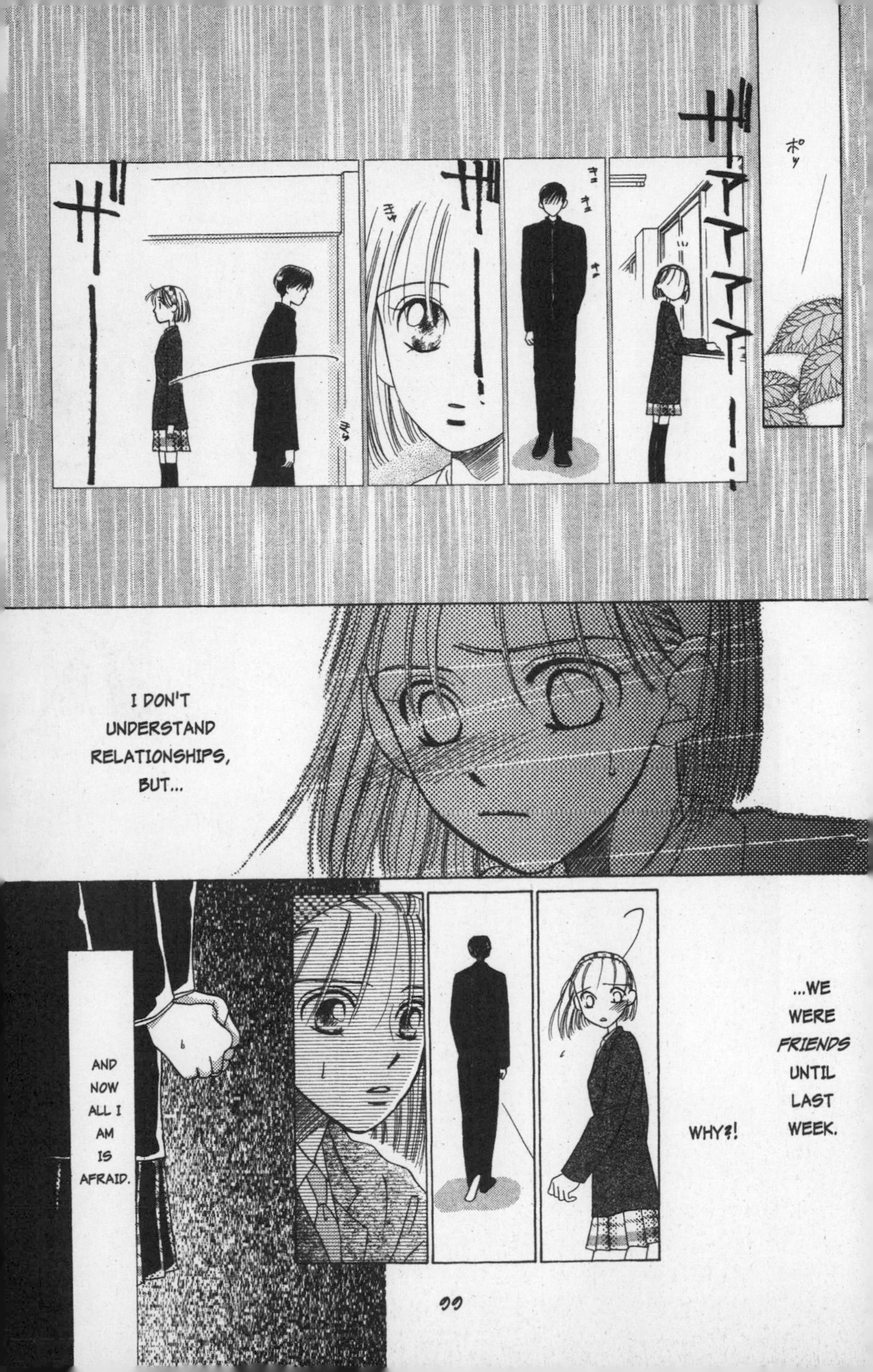
ポッ
ザァァァー
ザー
I DON'T UNDERSTAND RELATIONSHIPS, BUT...
...WE WERE FRIENDS UNTIL LAST WEEK.
WHY?!
AND NOW ALL I AM IS AFRAID.

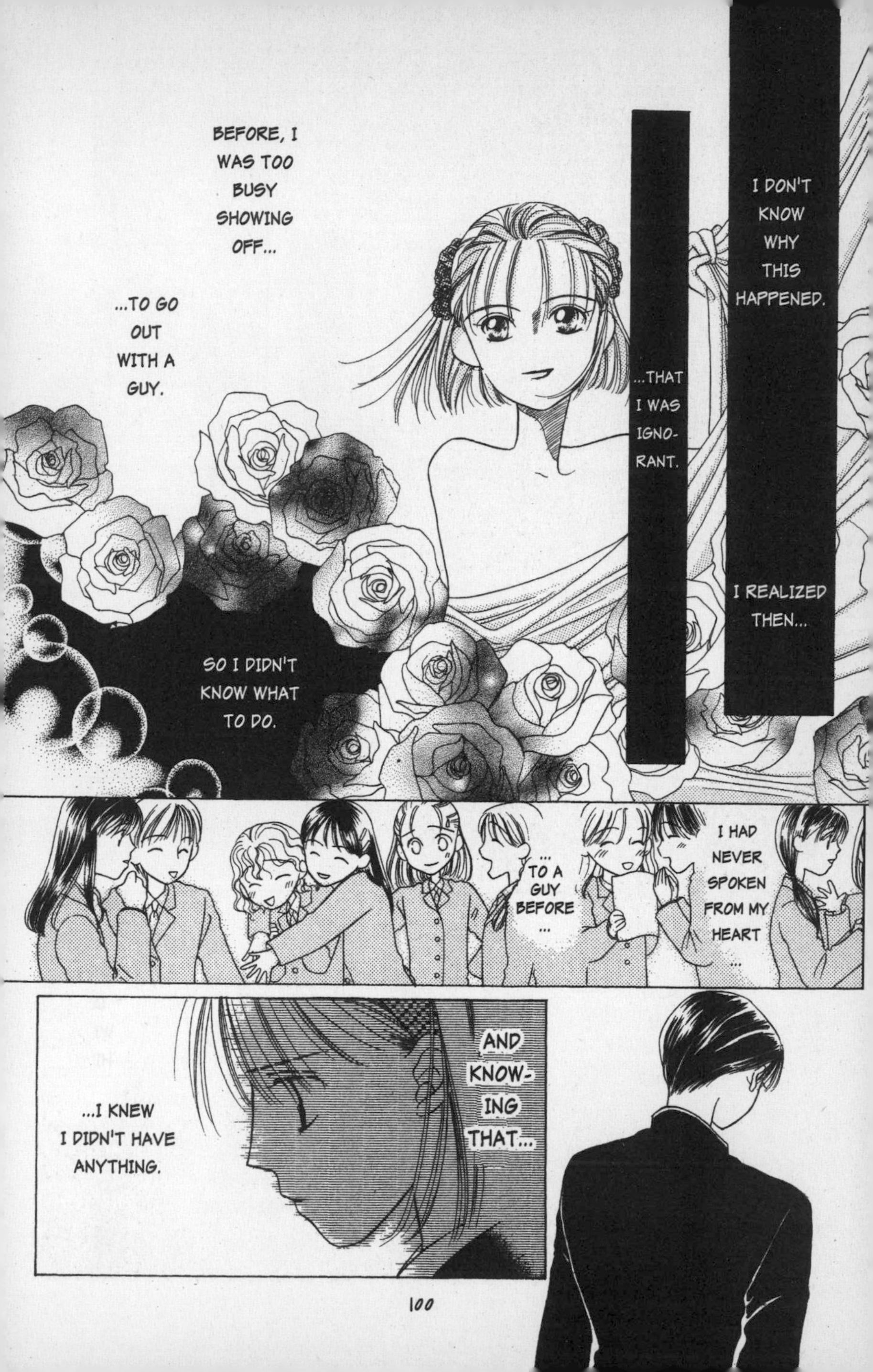
I DON'T KNOW WHY THIS HAPPENED.
I REALIZED THEN...
...THAT I WAS IGNO-RANT.
BEFORE, I WAS TOO BUSY SHOWING OFF...
...TO GO OUT WITH A GUY.
SO I DIDN'T KNOW WHAT TO DO.
I HAD NEVER SPOKEN FROM MY HEART...
...TO A GUY BEFORE...
AND KNOW-ING THAT...
...I KNEW I DIDN'T HAVE ANYTHING.

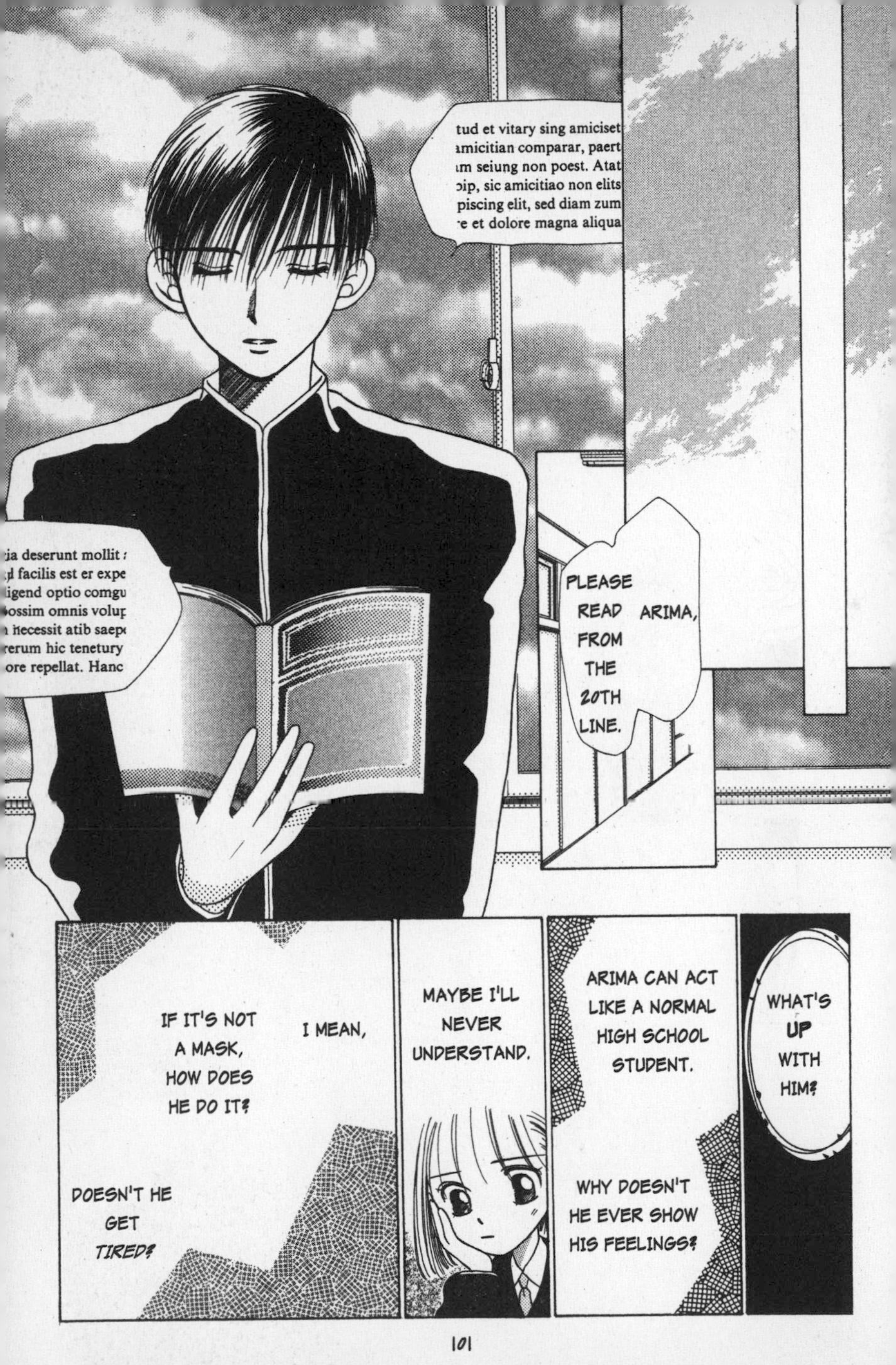
PLEASE READ ARIMA, FROM THE 20TH LINE.
tud et vitary sing amiciset amicitian comparar, paert ım seiung non poest. Atat ɔip, sic amicitiao non elits piscing elit, sed diam zum e et dolore magna aliqua
ia deserunt mollit d facilis est er expe ligend optio compu ossim omnis volup necessit atib saep erum hic tenetury ore repellat. Hanc
WHAT'S UP WITH HIM?
ARIMA CAN ACT LIKE A NORMAL HIGH SCHOOL STUDENT.
WHY DOESN'T HE EVER SHOW HIS FEELINGS?
MAYBE I'LL NEVER UNDERSTAND.
I MEAN,
IF IT'S NOT A MASK, HOW DOES HE DO IT?
DOESN'T HE GET TIRED?

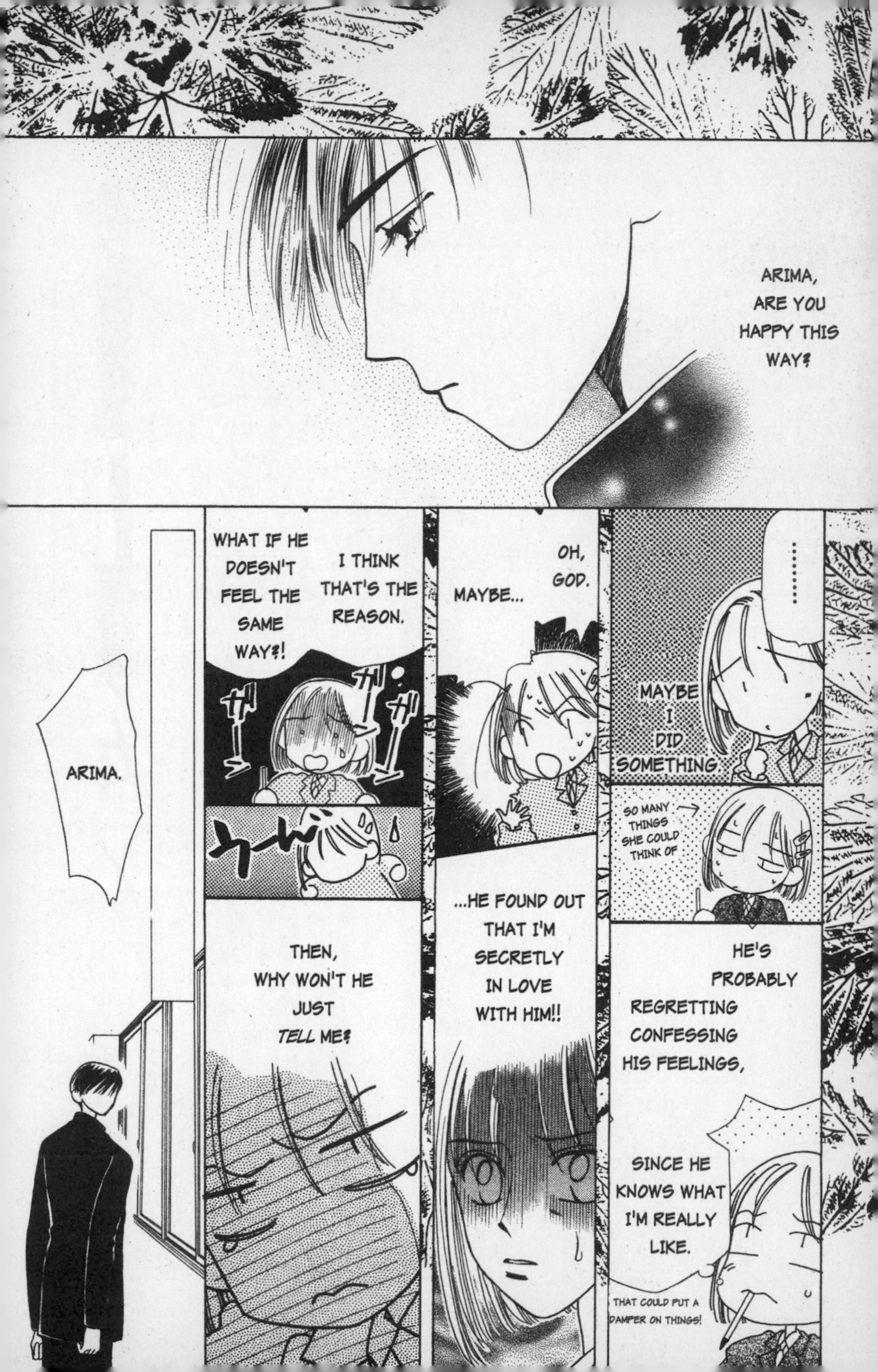
ARIMA, ARE YOU HAPPY THIS WAY?
......
MAYBE I DID SOMETHING.
SO MANY THINGS SHE COULD THINK OF
HE'S PROBABLY REGRETTING CONFESSING HIS FEELINGS,
SINCE HE KNOWS WHAT I'M REALLY LIKE.
THAT COULD PUT A DAMPER ON THINGS!
OH, GOD.
MAYBE...
...HE FOUND OUT THAT I'M SECRETLY IN LOVE WITH HIM!!
I THINK THAT'S THE REASON.
WHAT IF HE DOESN'T FEEL THE SAME WAY?!
THEN, WHY WON'T HE JUST *TELL* ME?
ARIMA.

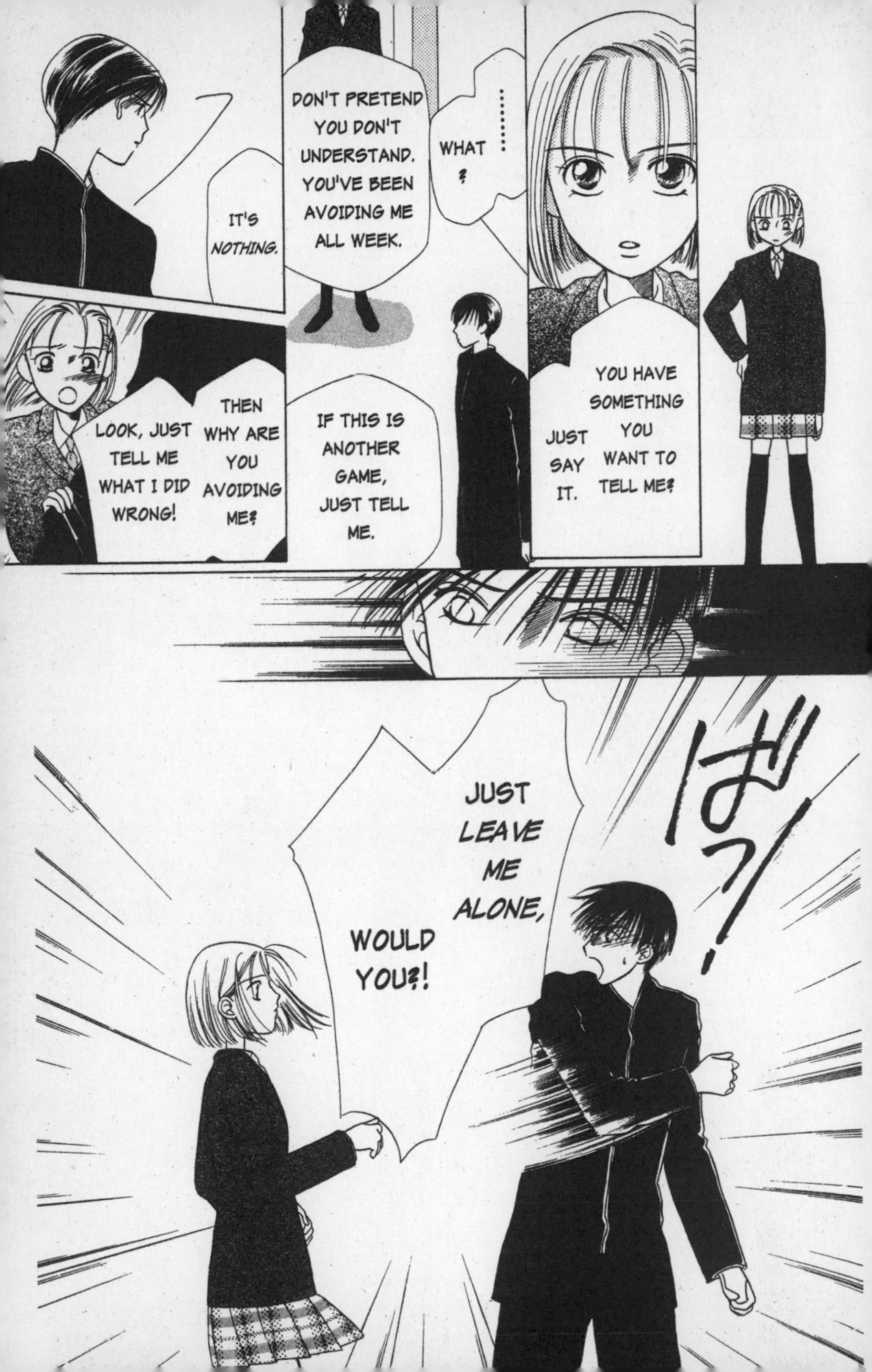
YOU HAVE SOMETHING YOU WANT TO TELL ME?
JUST SAY IT.
WHAT......?
DON'T PRETEND YOU DON'T UNDERSTAND. YOU'VE BEEN AVOIDING ME ALL WEEK.
IT'S NOTHING.
IF THIS IS ANOTHER GAME, JUST TELL ME.
THEN WHY ARE YOU AVOIDING ME?
LOOK, JUST TELL ME WHAT I DID WRONG!
ばっ!
JUST LEAVE ME ALONE, WOULD YOU?!

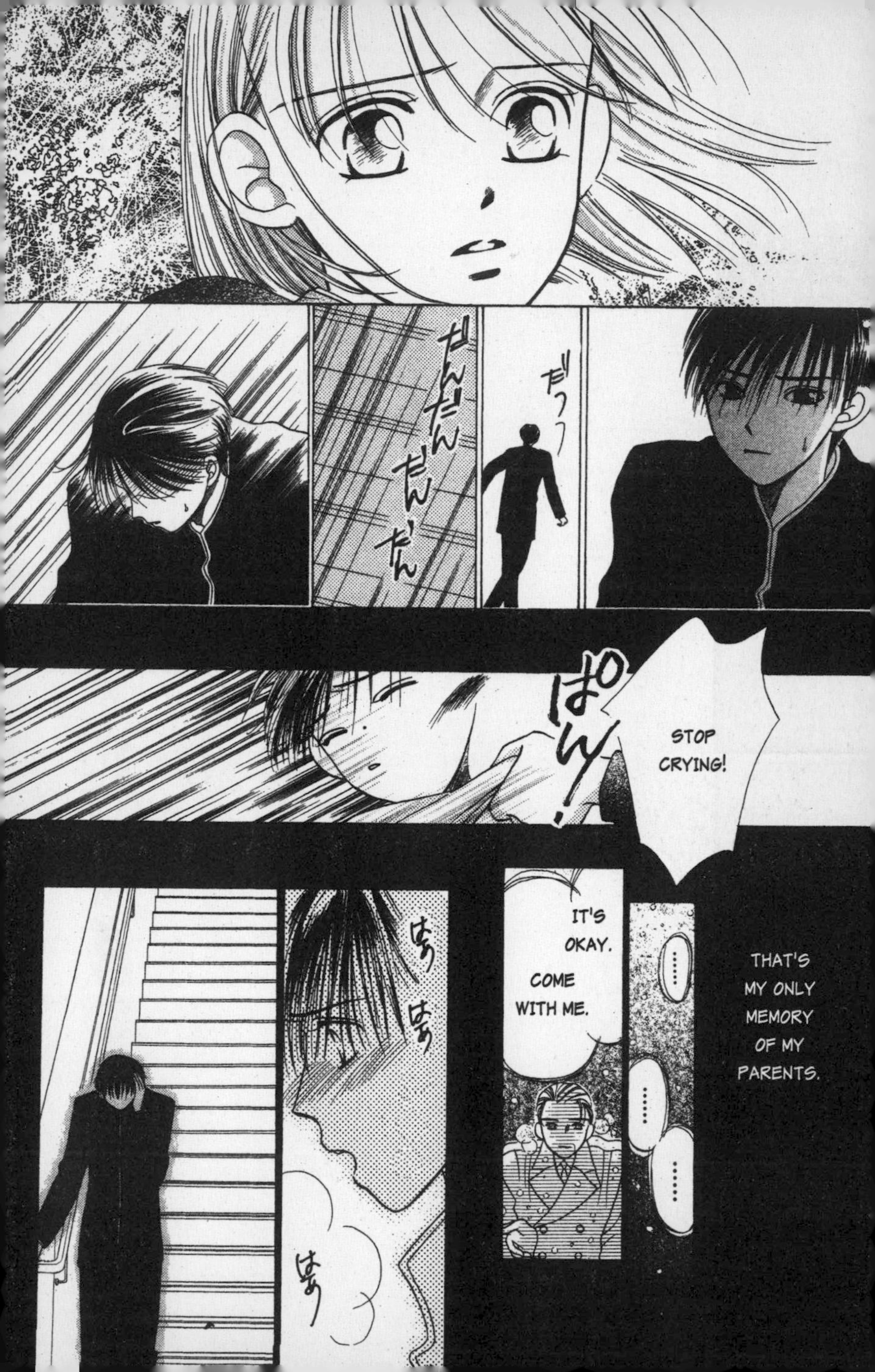
だっ
だんだん だんだん
ぱん!
STOP CRYING!
THAT'S MY ONLY MEMORY OF MY PARENTS.
......
......
......
IT'S OKAY.
COME WITH ME.
はぁ はぁ
はぁ

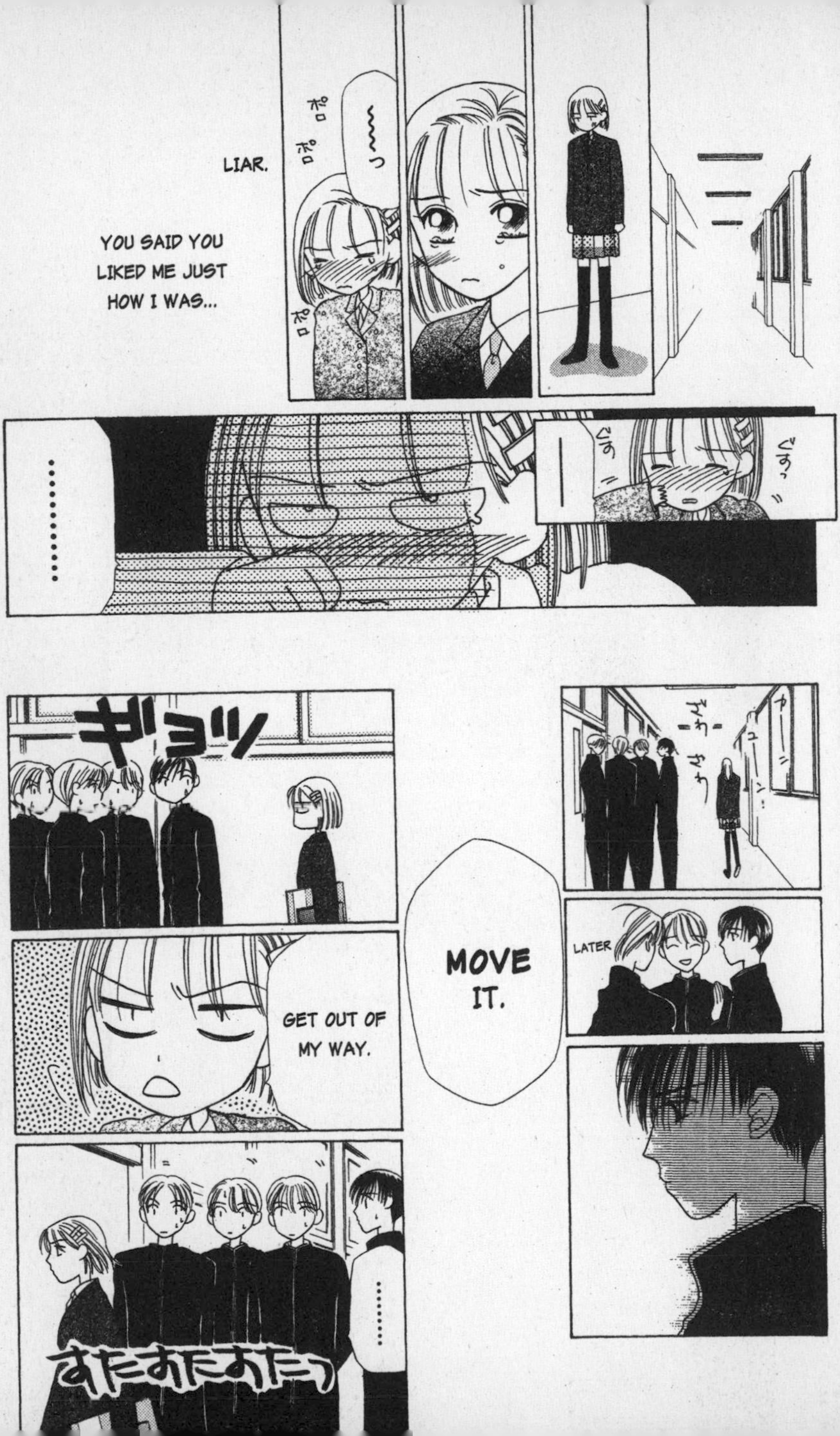
ポロ
ポロ
ポロ
LIAR.
YOU SAID YOU LIKED ME JUST HOW I WAS...
ぐすっ
ぐす
……
ざわ
ざわ
LATER
MOVE IT.
ギョッ
GET OUT OF MY WAY.
……
すたすたすたっ

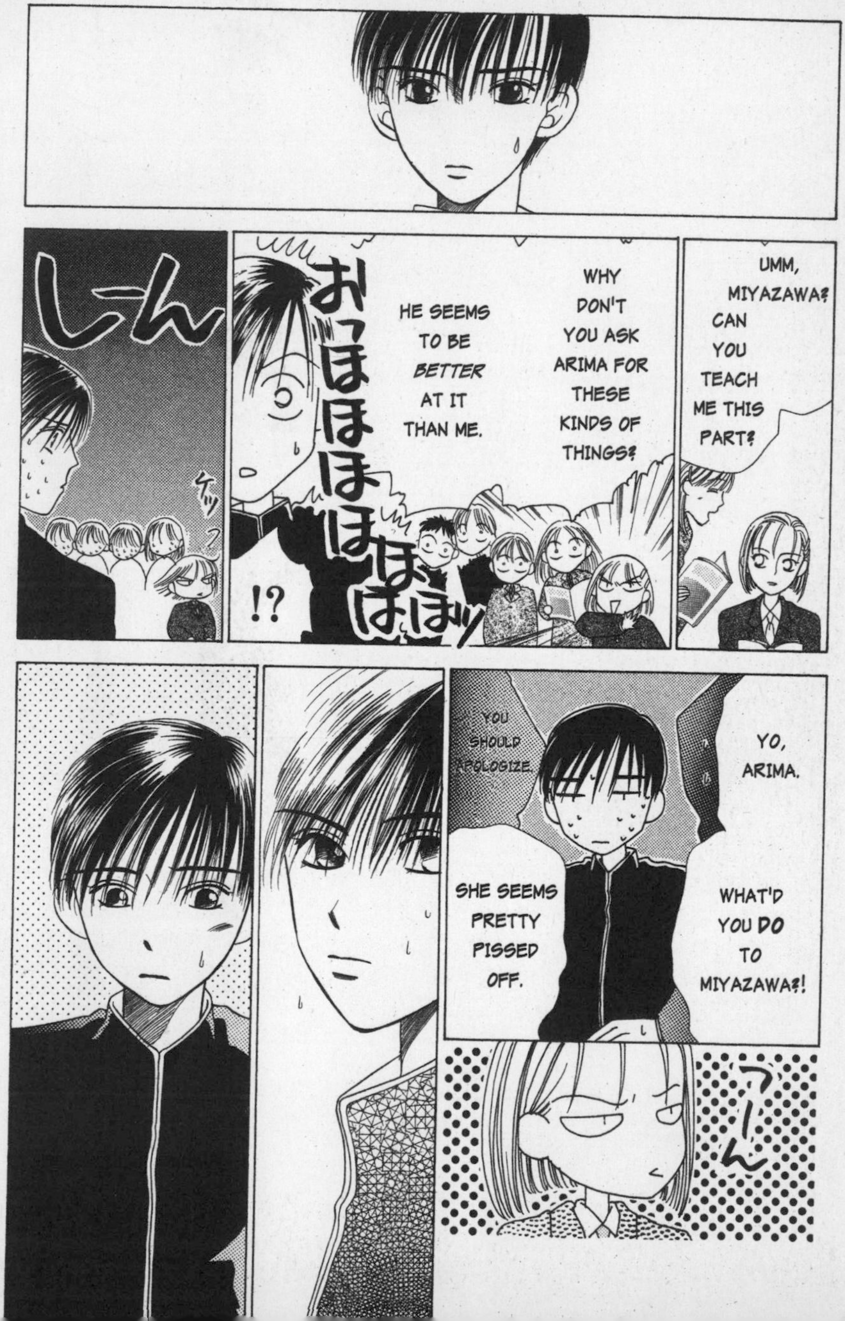
UMM, MIYAZAWA? CAN YOU TEACH ME THIS PART?
WHY DON'T YOU ASK ARIMA FOR THESE KINDS OF THINGS?
HE SEEMS TO BE *BETTER* AT IT THAN ME.
おっほほほほほほほッ
!?
しーん
ケッ
YO, ARIMA.
YOU SHOULD APOLOGIZE.
WHAT'D YOU DO TO MIYAZAWA?!
SHE SEEMS PRETTY PISSED OFF.
つーん

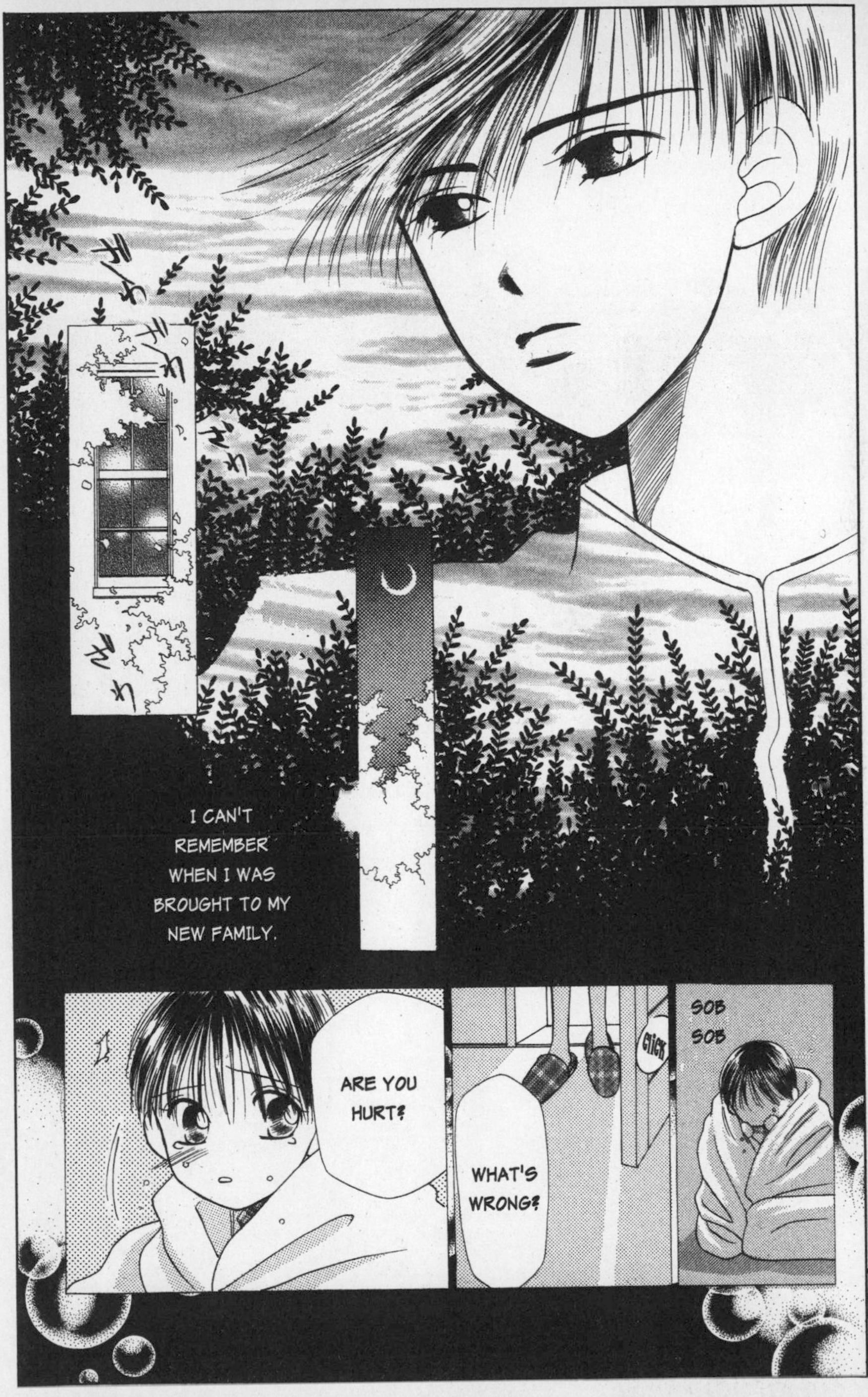
I CAN'T REMEMBER WHEN I WAS BROUGHT TO MY NEW FAMILY.
SOB SOB
CLICK
WHAT'S WRONG?
ARE YOU HURT?

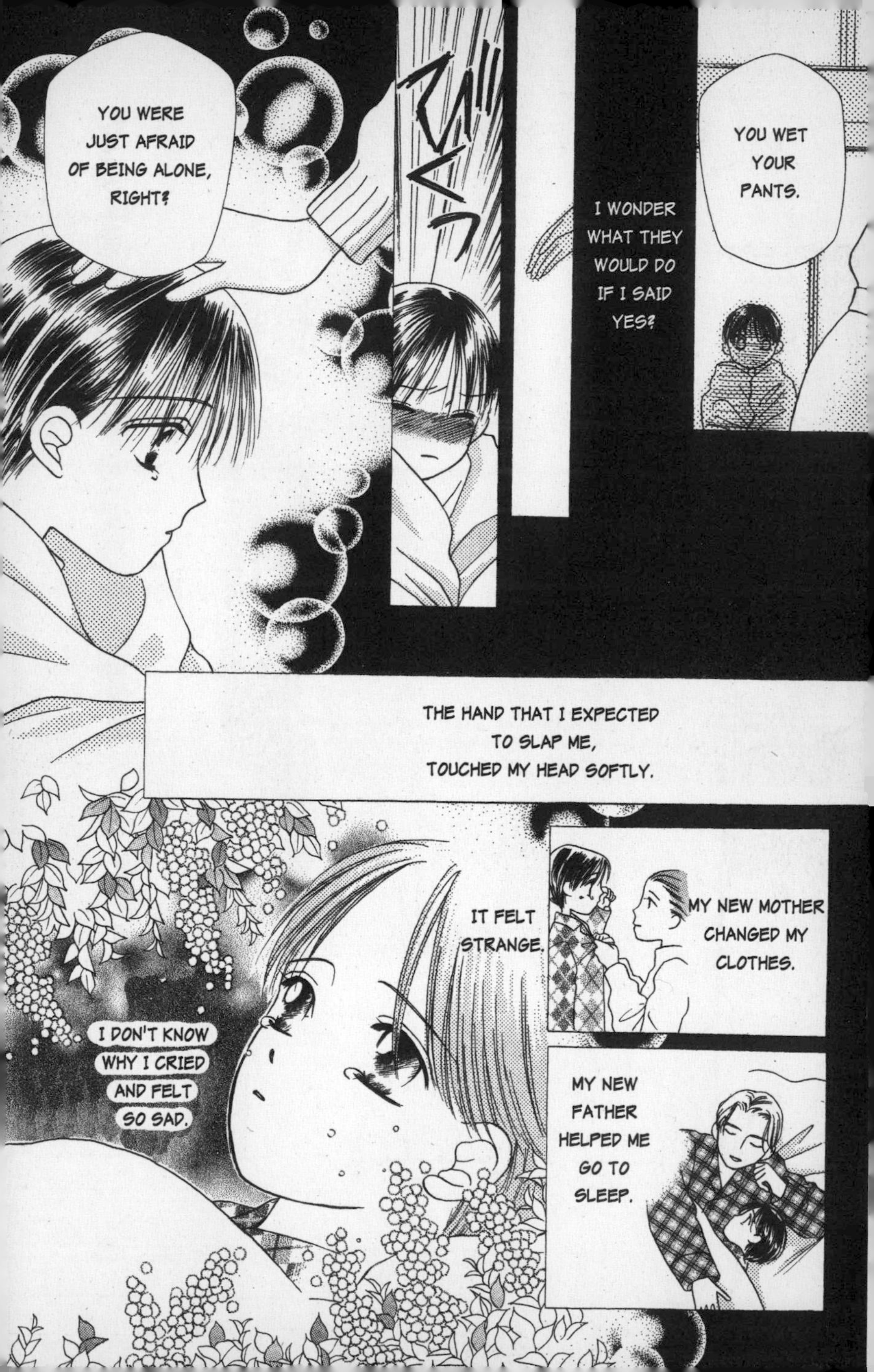
YOU WET YOUR PANTS.
I WONDER WHAT THEY WOULD DO IF I SAID YES?
YOU WERE JUST AFRAID OF BEING ALONE, RIGHT?
THE HAND THAT I EXPECTED TO SLAP ME, TOUCHED MY HEAD SOFTLY.
MY NEW MOTHER CHANGED MY CLOTHES.
MY NEW FATHER HELPED ME GO TO SLEEP.
IT FELT STRANGE.
I DON'T KNOW WHY I CRIED AND FELT SO SAD.

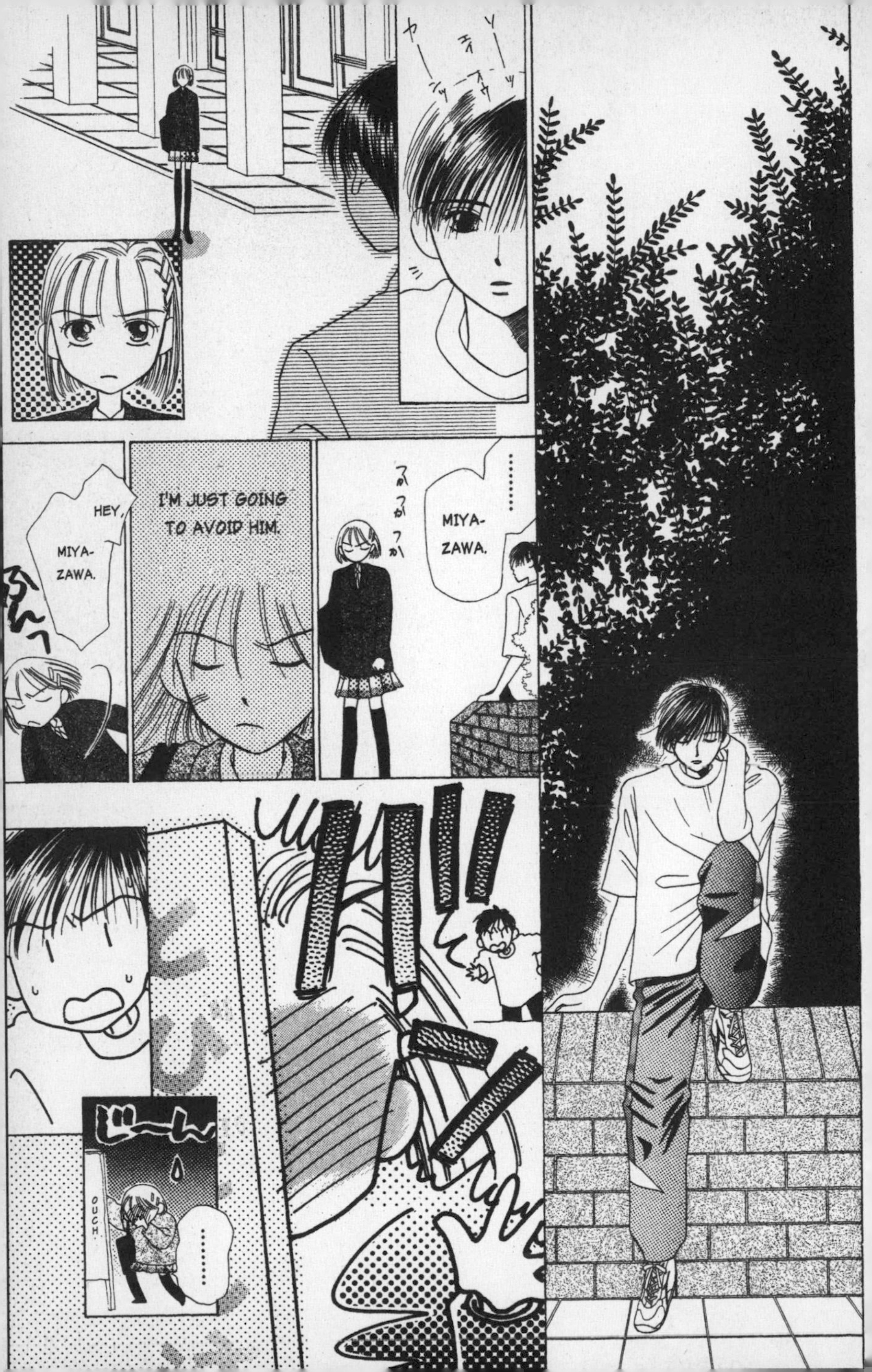

......
MIYA-ZAWA.
I'M JUST GOING TO AVOID HIM.
HEY, MIYA-ZAWA.
OUCH.
......

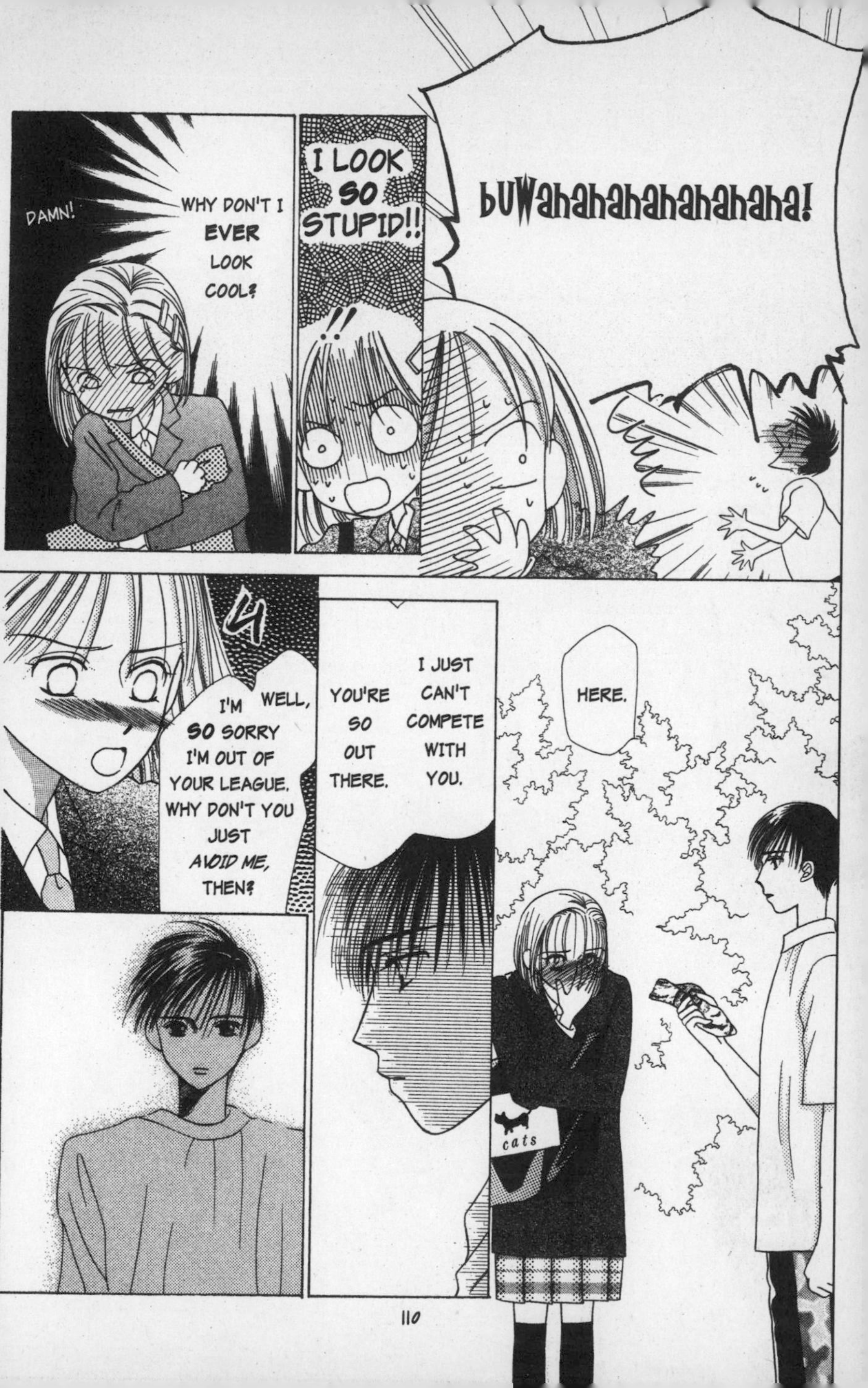
bUWahahahahahahaha!
!!
I LOOK SO STUPID!!
DAMN!
WHY DON'T I EVER LOOK COOL?
HERE.
I JUST CAN'T COMPETE WITH YOU.
YOU'RE SO OUT THERE.
WELL, I'M SO SORRY I'M OUT OF YOUR LEAGUE. WHY DON'T YOU JUST AVOID ME, THEN?

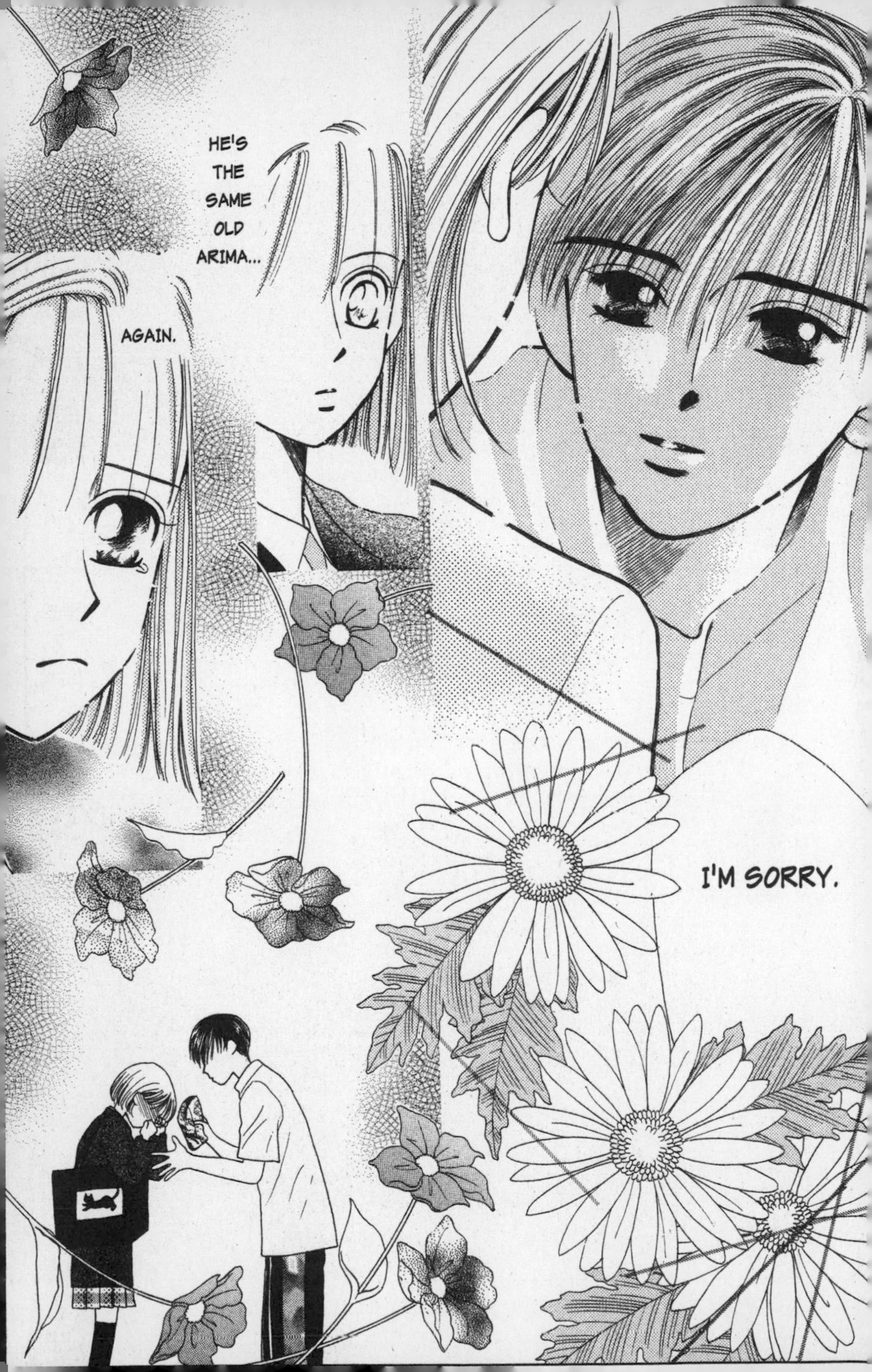
I'M SORRY.
HE'S THE SAME OLD ARIMA...
AGAIN.

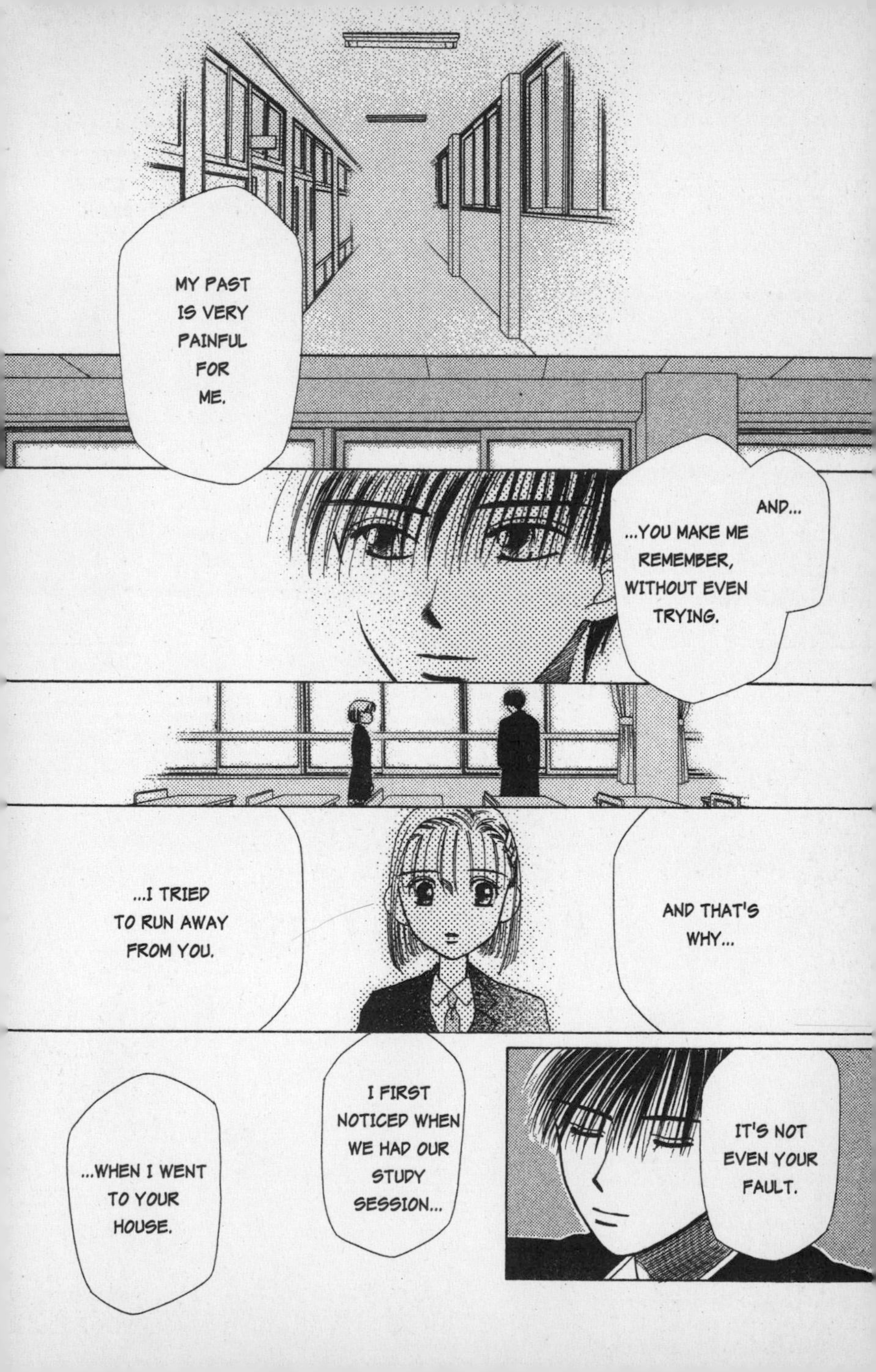
MY PAST IS VERY PAINFUL FOR ME.
AND... ...YOU MAKE ME REMEMBER, WITHOUT EVEN TRYING.
AND THAT'S WHY...
...I TRIED TO RUN AWAY FROM YOU.
IT'S NOT EVEN YOUR FAULT.
I FIRST NOTICED WHEN WE HAD OUR STUDY SESSION...
...WHEN I WENT TO YOUR HOUSE.

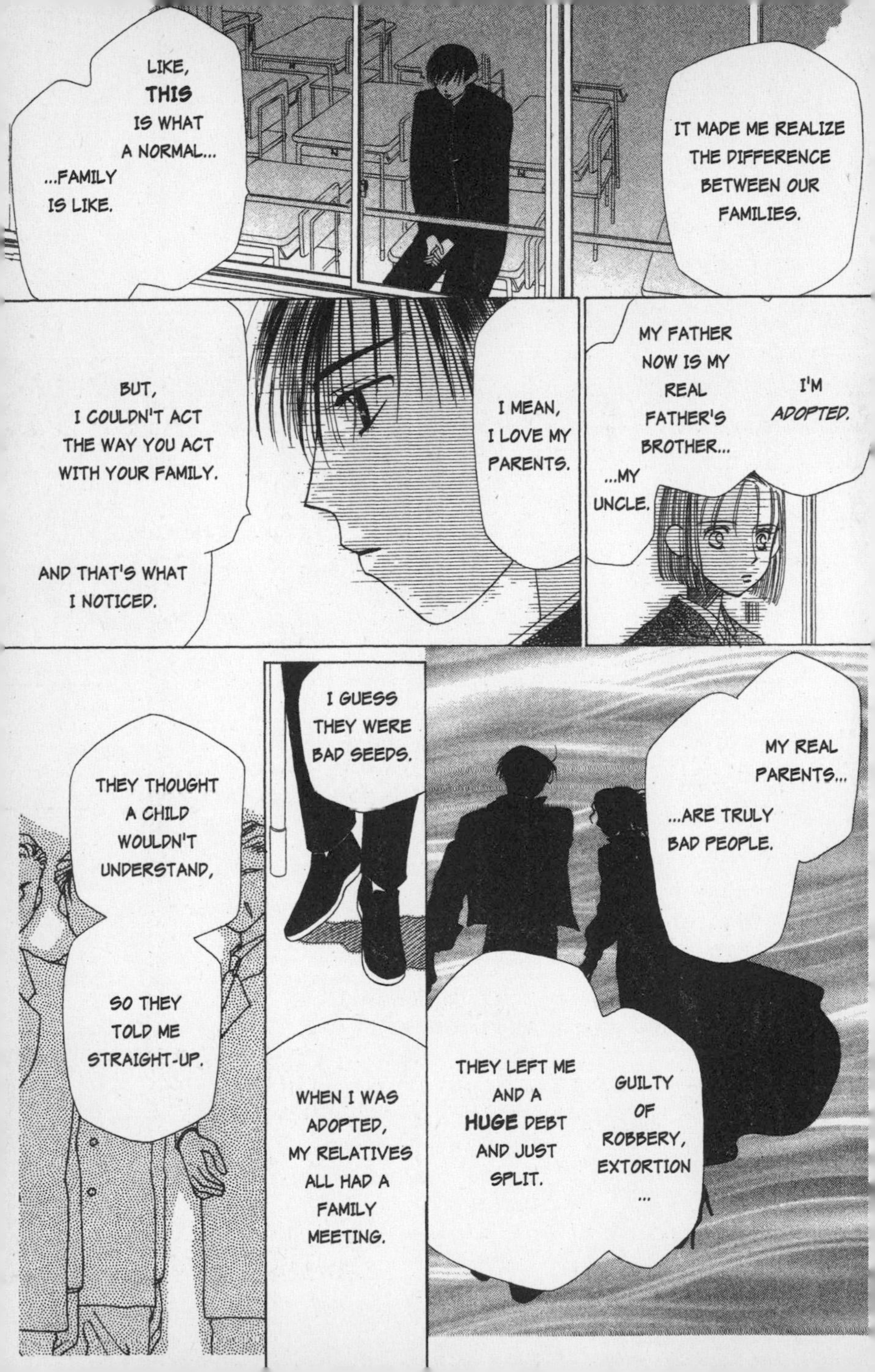
IT MADE ME REALIZE THE DIFFERENCE BETWEEN OUR FAMILIES.
LIKE, **THIS** IS WHAT A NORMAL... ...FAMILY IS LIKE.
I'M *ADOPTED.*
MY FATHER NOW IS MY REAL FATHER'S BROTHER...
...MY UNCLE.
I MEAN, I LOVE MY PARENTS.
BUT, I COULDN'T ACT THE WAY YOU ACT WITH YOUR FAMILY.
AND THAT'S WHAT I NOTICED.
MY REAL PARENTS...
...ARE TRULY BAD PEOPLE.
GUILTY OF ROBBERY, EXTORTION ...
THEY LEFT ME AND A **HUGE** DEBT AND JUST SPLIT.
I GUESS THEY WERE BAD SEEDS.
WHEN I WAS ADOPTED, MY RELATIVES ALL HAD A FAMILY MEETING.
THEY THOUGHT A CHILD WOULDN'T UNDERSTAND,
SO THEY TOLD ME STRAIGHT-UP.

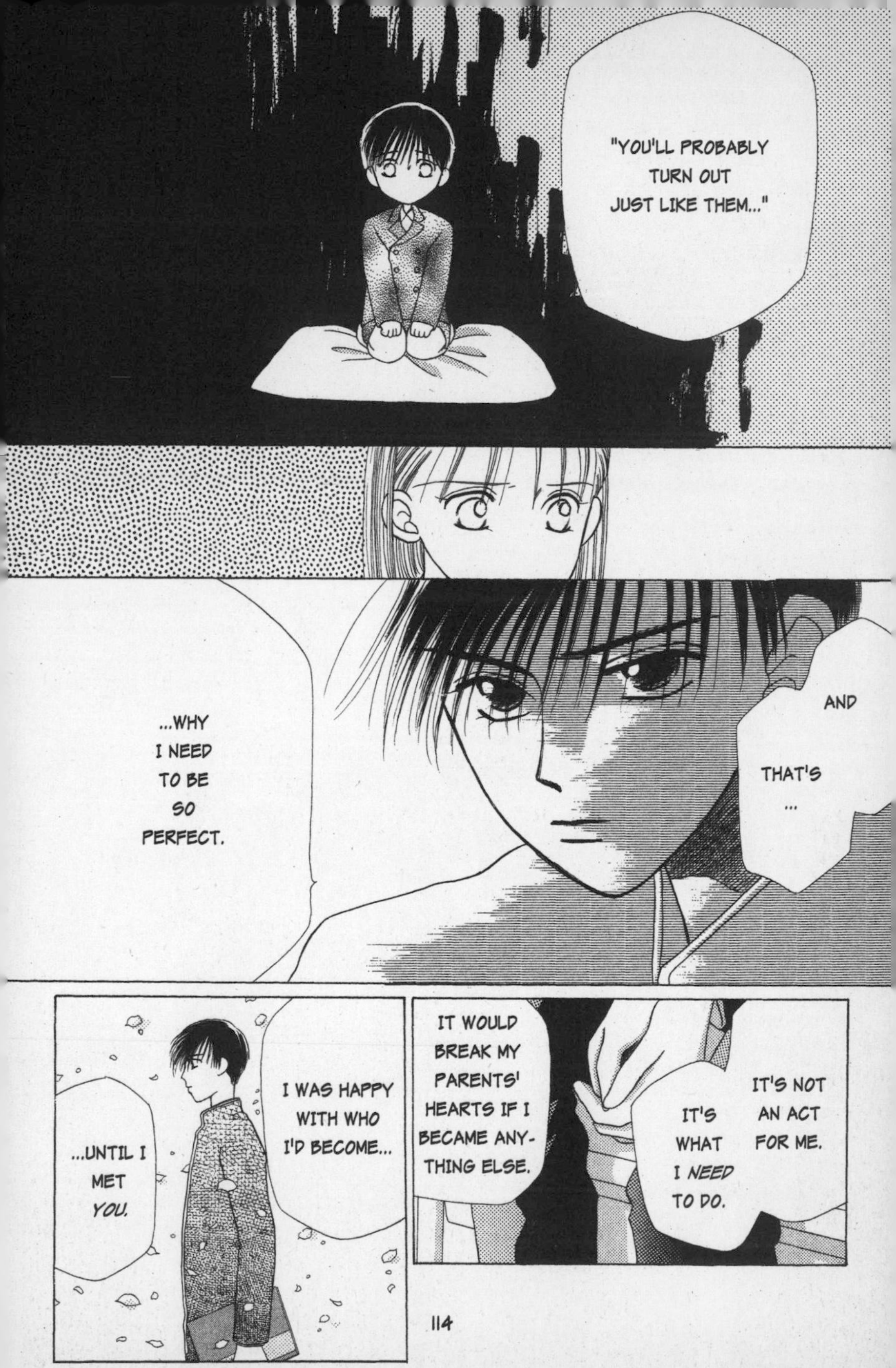
"YOU'LL PROBABLY TURN OUT JUST LIKE THEM..."
AND THAT'S ...
...WHY I NEED TO BE SO PERFECT.
IT'S NOT AN ACT FOR ME.
IT'S WHAT I *NEED* TO DO.
IT WOULD BREAK MY PARENTS' HEARTS IF I BECAME ANY-THING ELSE.
I WAS HAPPY WITH WHO I'D BECOME...
...UNTIL I MET *YOU*.

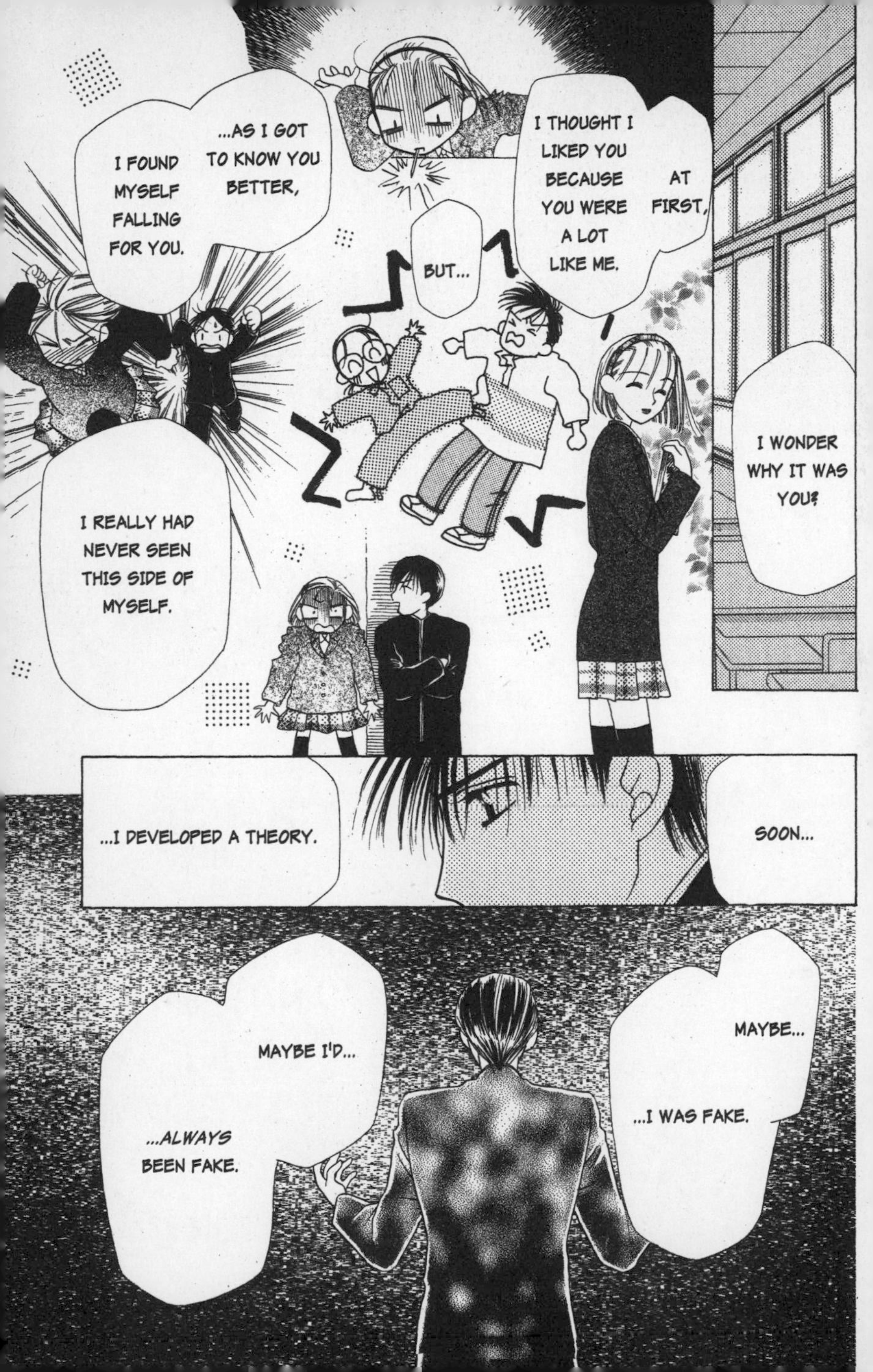
AT FIRST, I THOUGHT I LIKED YOU BECAUSE YOU WERE A LOT LIKE ME.
BUT...
...AS I GOT TO KNOW YOU BETTER, I FOUND MYSELF FALLING FOR YOU.
I WONDER WHY IT WAS YOU?
I REALLY HAD NEVER SEEN THIS SIDE OF MYSELF.
SOON...
...I DEVELOPED A THEORY.
MAYBE...
...I WAS FAKE.
MAYBE I'D...
...ALWAYS BEEN FAKE.

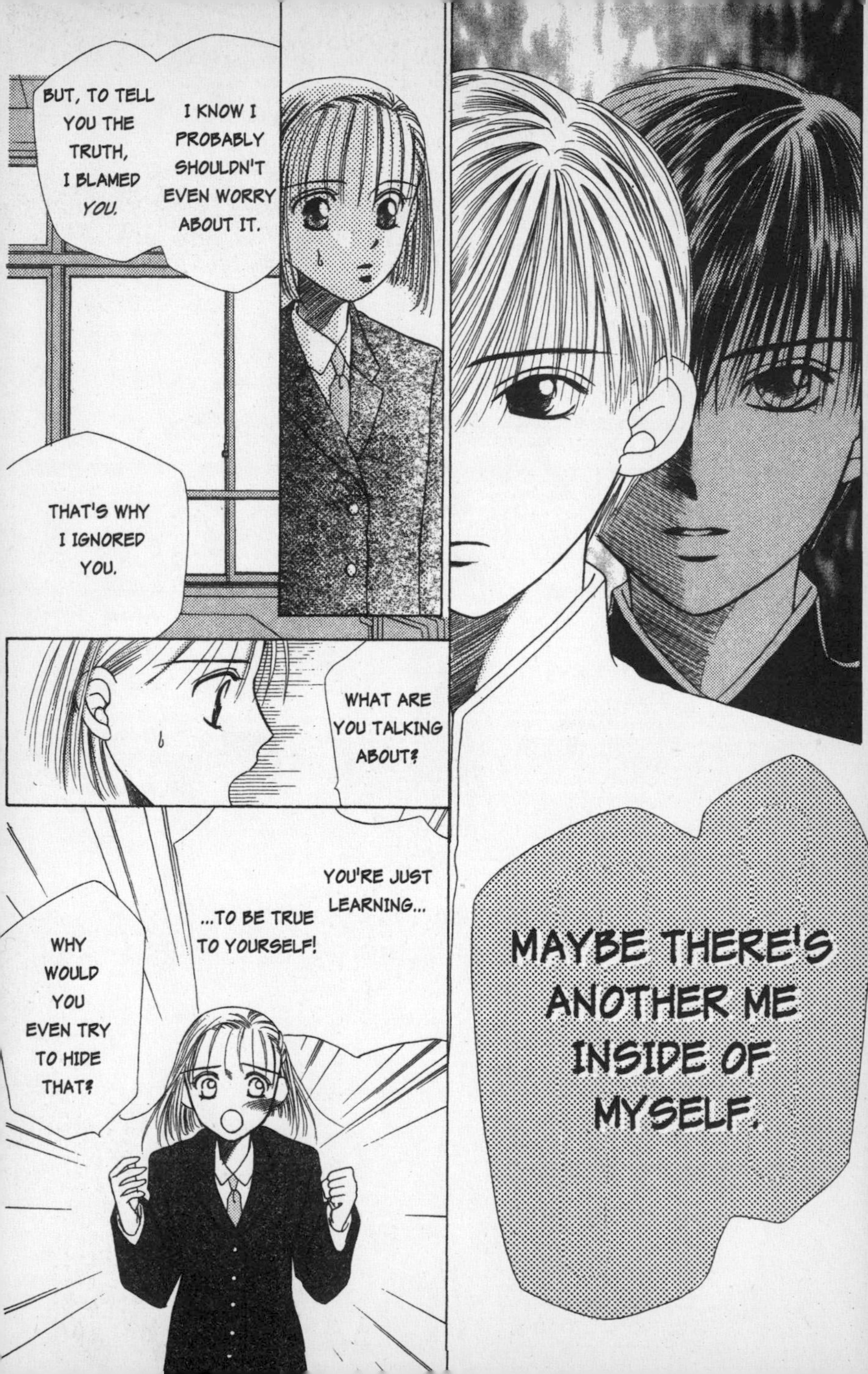
MAYBE THERE'S ANOTHER ME INSIDE OF MYSELF.
I KNOW I PROBABLY SHOULDN'T EVEN WORRY ABOUT IT.
BUT, TO TELL YOU THE TRUTH, I BLAMED *YOU.*
THAT'S WHY I IGNORED YOU.
WHAT ARE YOU TALKING ABOUT?
YOU'RE JUST LEARNING...
...TO BE TRUE TO YOURSELF!
WHY WOULD YOU EVEN TRY TO HIDE THAT?

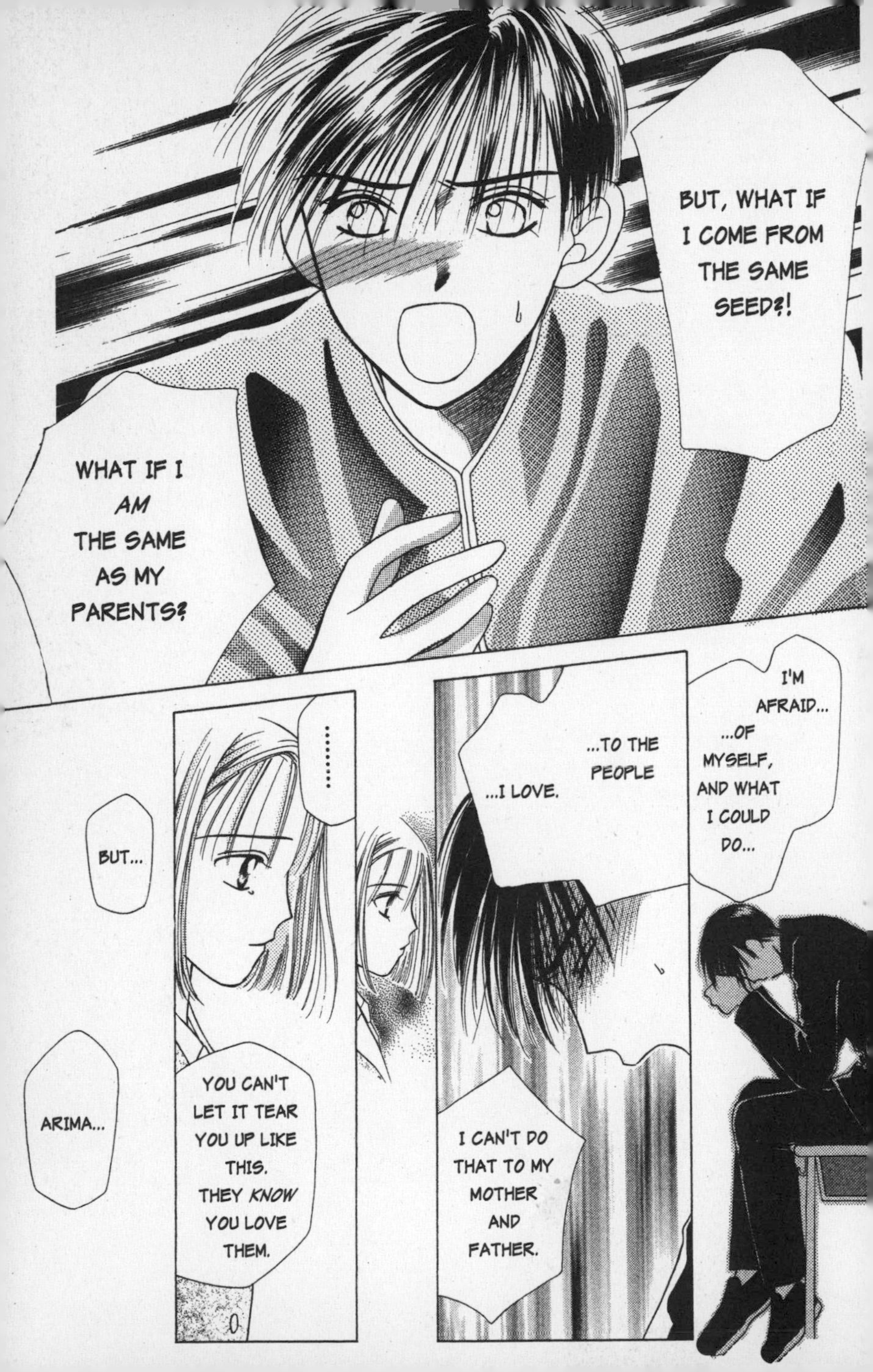
BUT, WHAT IF I COME FROM THE SAME SEED?!
WHAT IF I *AM* THE SAME AS MY PARENTS?
I'M AFRAID...
...OF MYSELF, AND WHAT I COULD DO...
...TO THE PEOPLE
...I LOVE.
I CAN'T DO THAT TO MY MOTHER AND FATHER.
....
BUT...
YOU CAN'T LET IT TEAR YOU UP LIKE THIS. THEY *KNOW* YOU LOVE THEM.
ARIMA...

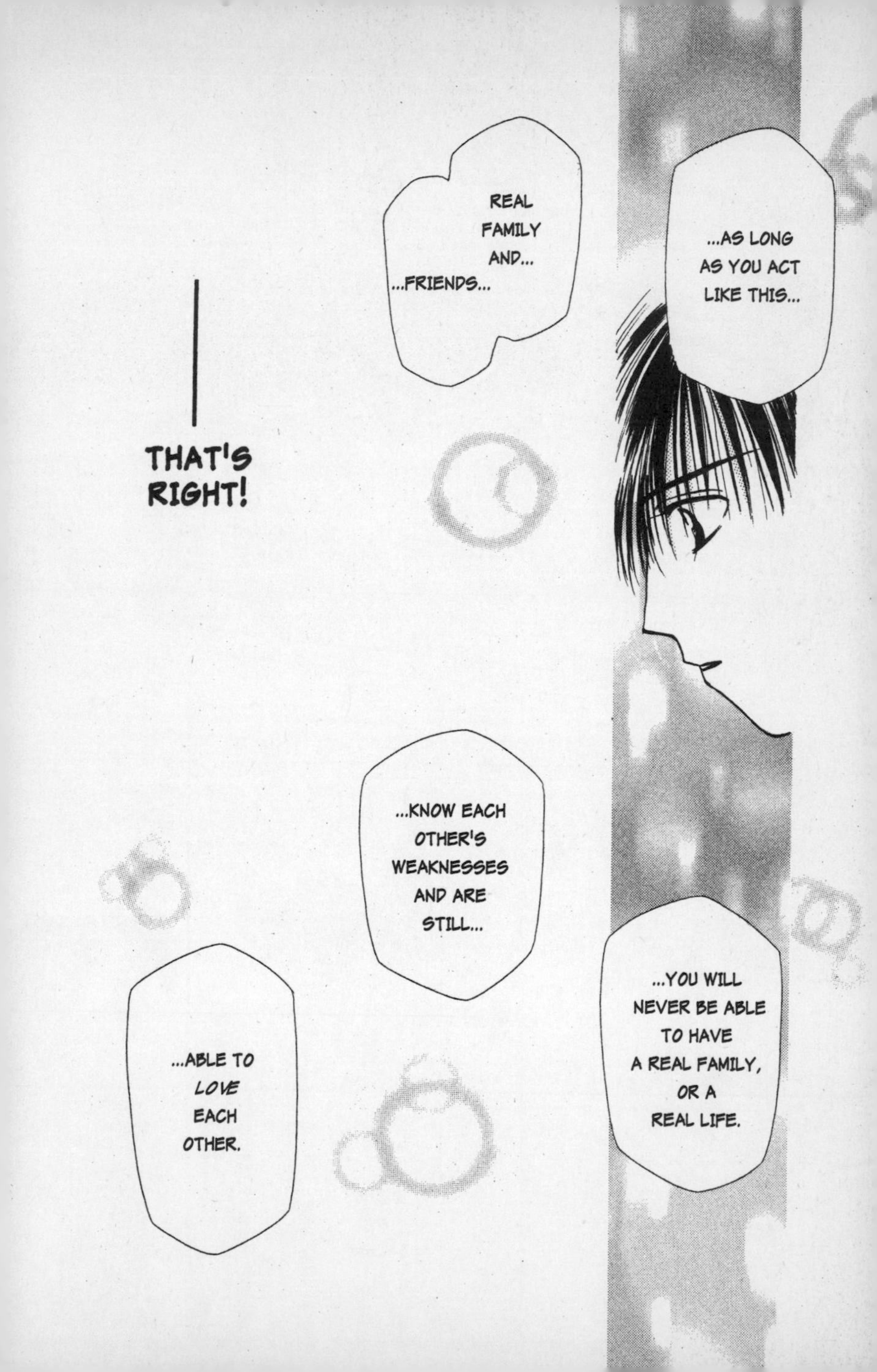
...AS LONG AS YOU ACT LIKE THIS...
...YOU WILL NEVER BE ABLE TO HAVE A REAL FAMILY, OR A REAL LIFE.
THAT'S RIGHT!
REAL FAMILY AND... ...FRIENDS...
...KNOW EACH OTHER'S WEAKNESSES AND ARE STILL...
...ABLE TO *LOVE* EACH OTHER.

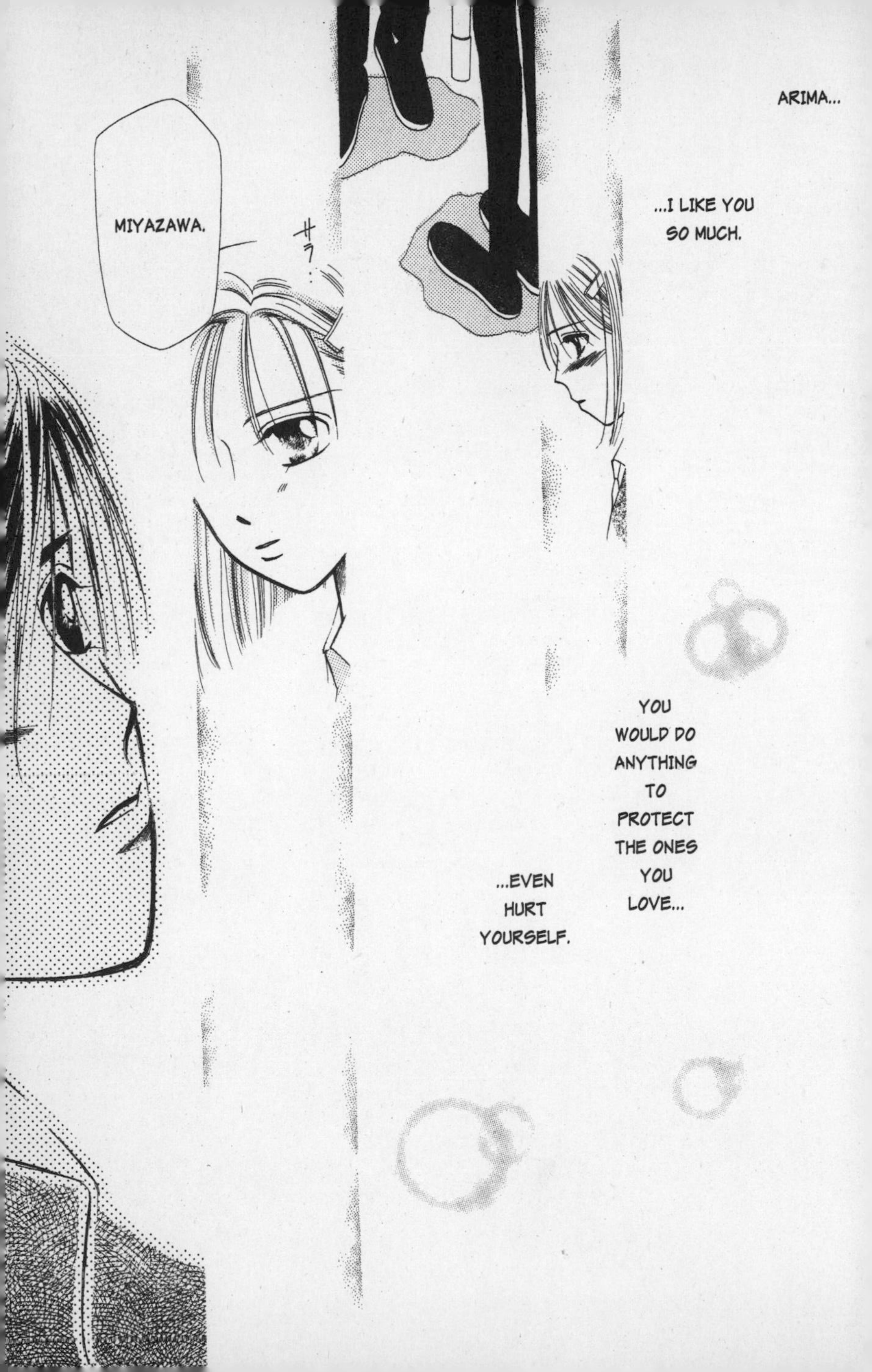
ARIMA...
...I LIKE YOU SO MUCH.
YOU WOULD DO ANYTHING TO PROTECT THE ONES YOU LOVE...
...EVEN HURT YOURSELF.
MIYAZAWA.

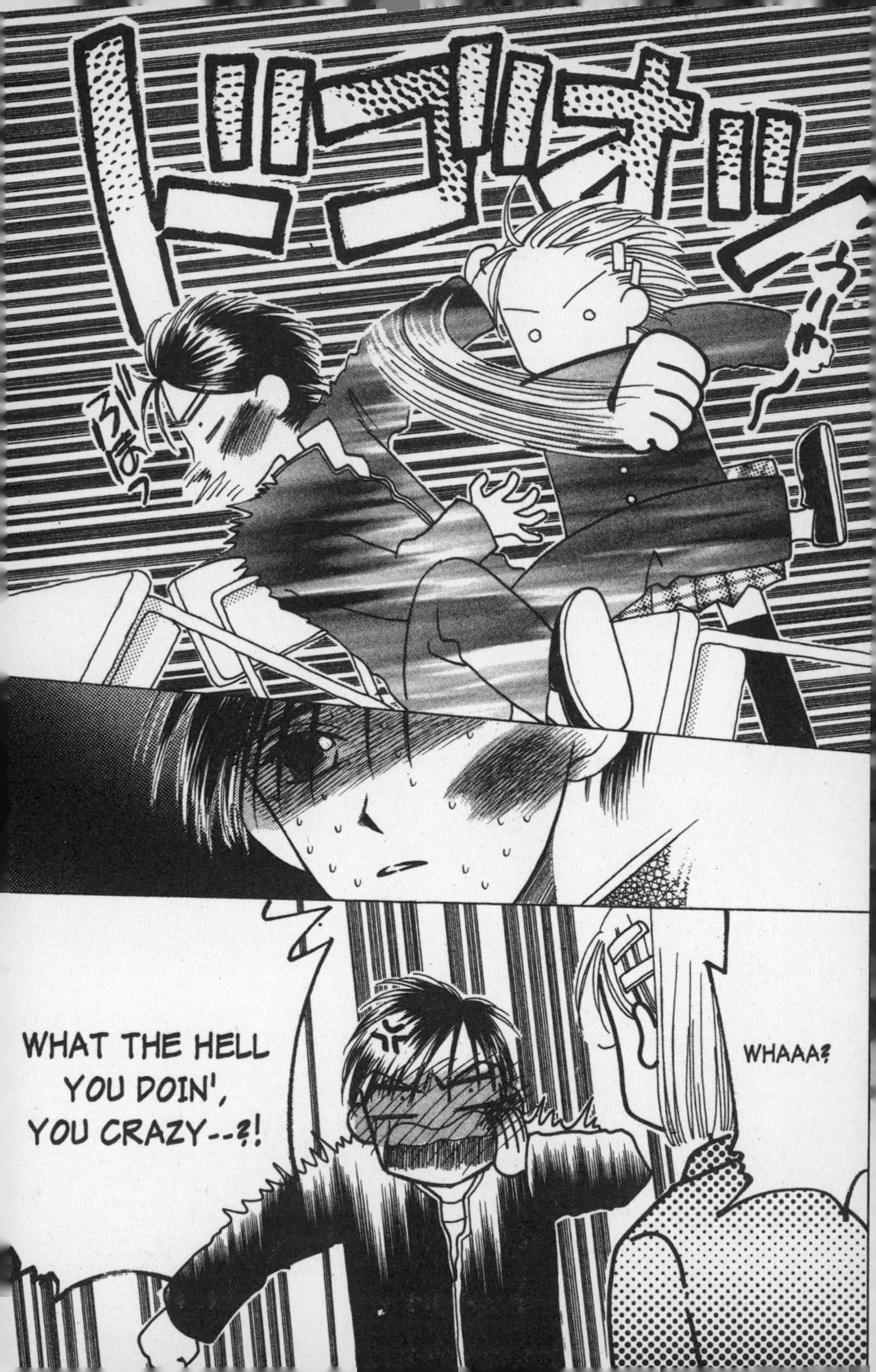
WHAAA?
WHAT THE HELL YOU DOIN', YOU CRAZY--?!

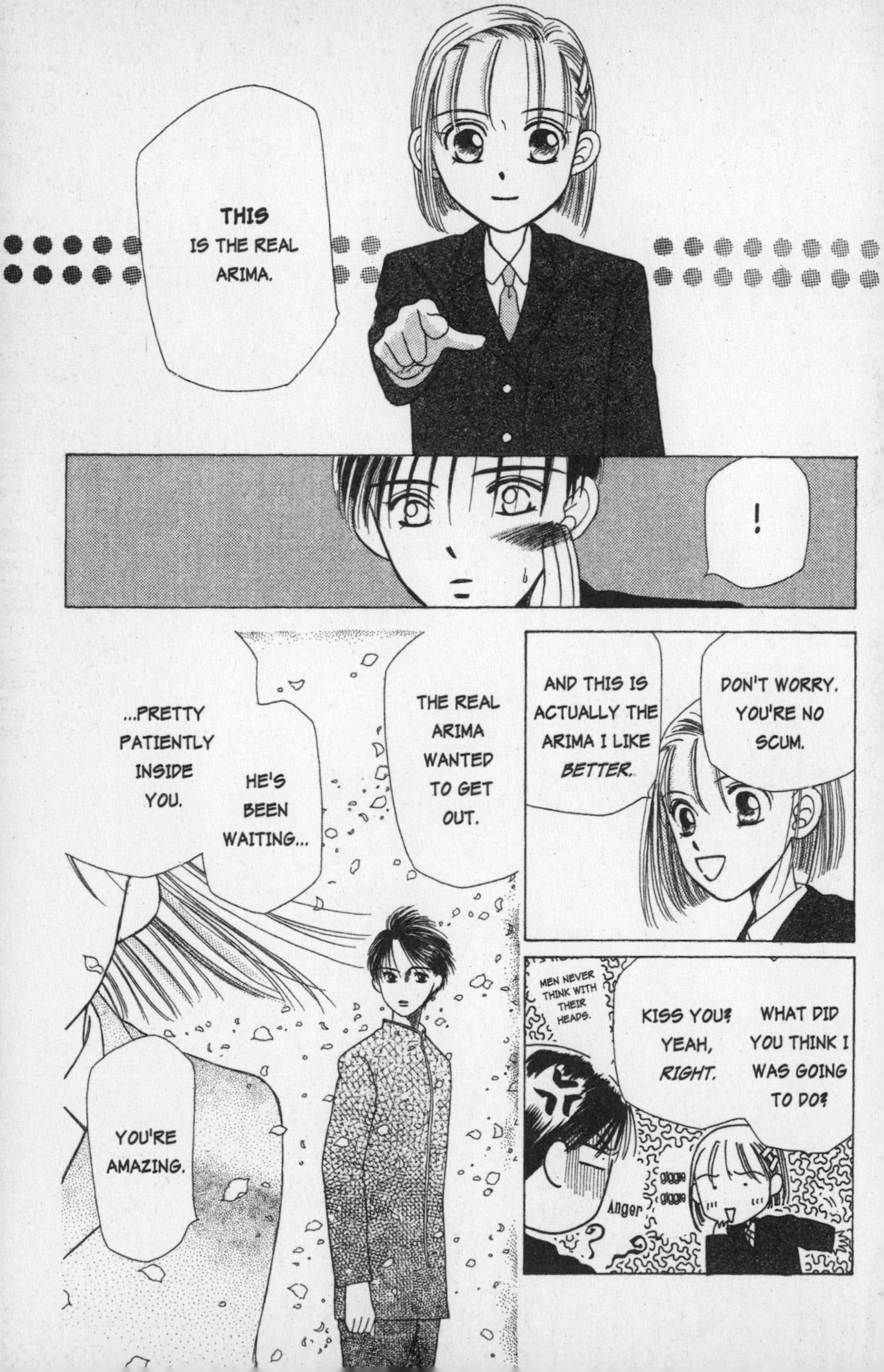
THIS IS THE REAL ARIMA.
!
DON'T WORRY. YOU'RE NO SCUM.
AND THIS IS ACTUALLY THE ARIMA I LIKE *BETTER.*
WHAT DID YOU THINK I WAS GOING TO DO?
KISS YOU? YEAH, *RIGHT.*
MEN NEVER THINK WITH THEIR HEADS.
giggle giggle
Anger
THE REAL ARIMA WANTED TO GET OUT.
HE'S BEEN WAITING...
...PRETTY PATIENTLY INSIDE YOU.
YOU'RE AMAZING.

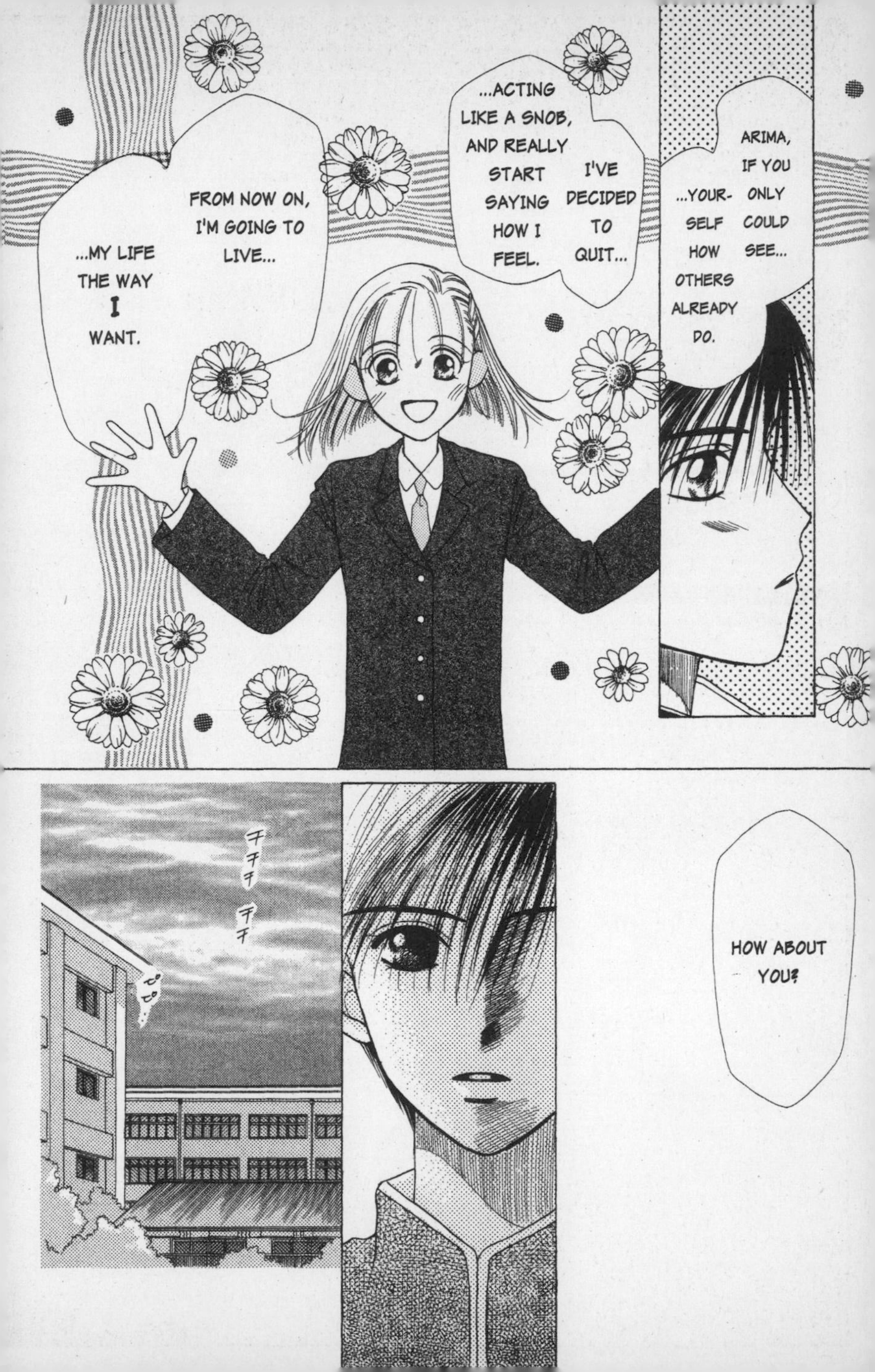
ARIMA, IF YOU ONLY COULD SEE...
...YOURSELF HOW OTHERS ALREADY DO.
I'VE DECIDED TO QUIT...
...ACTING LIKE A SNOB, AND REALLY START SAYING HOW I FEEL.
FROM NOW ON, I'M GOING TO LIVE...
...MY LIFE THE WAY I WANT.
HOW ABOUT YOU?
チチチ
チチ

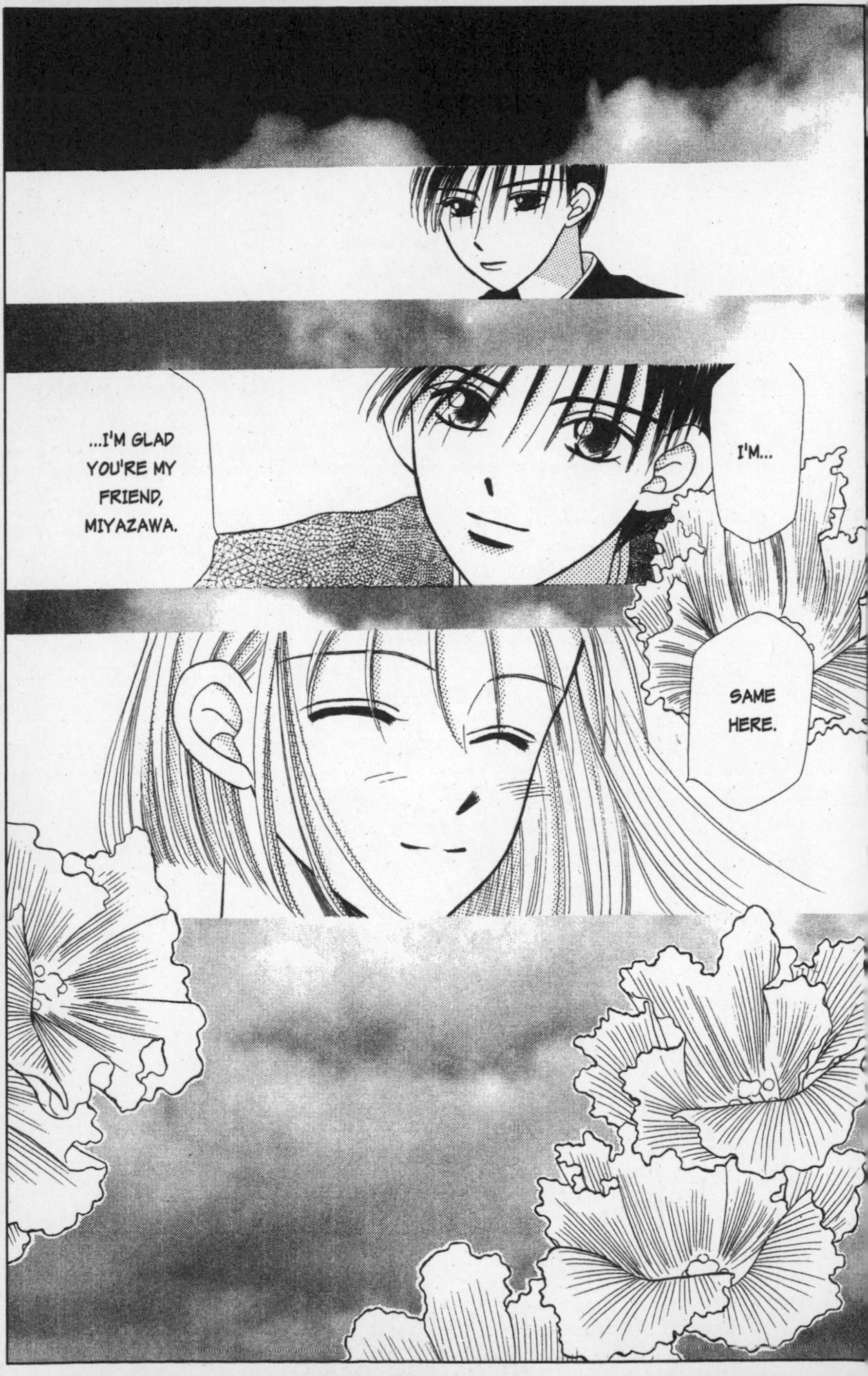
I'M...
...I'M GLAD YOU'RE MY FRIEND, MIYAZAWA.
SAME HERE.

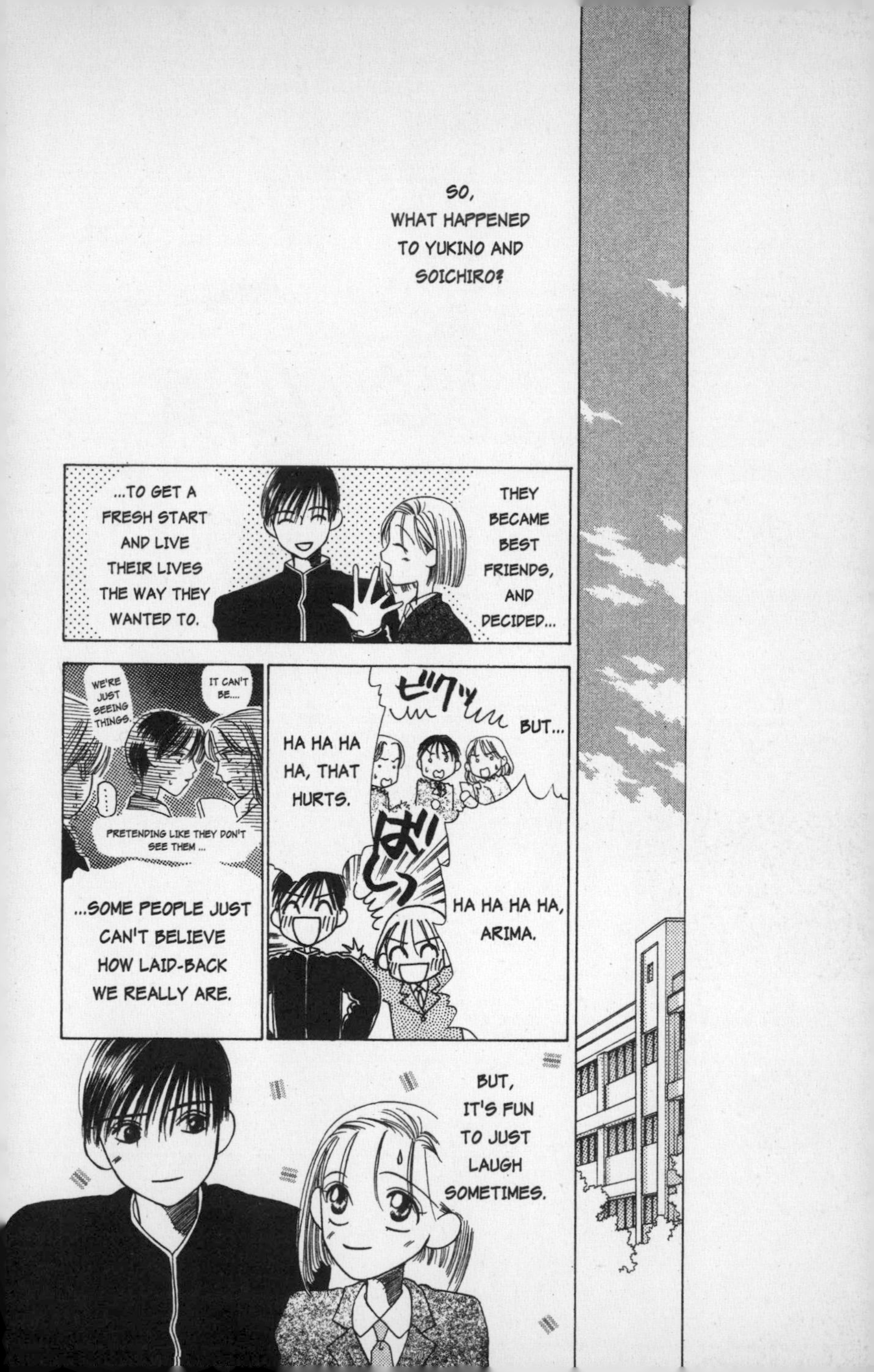
SO, WHAT HAPPENED TO YUKINO AND SOICHIRO?
THEY BECAME BEST FRIENDS, AND DECIDED...
...TO GET A FRESH START AND LIVE THEIR LIVES THE WAY THEY WANTED TO.
BUT...
HA HA HA HA, THAT HURTS.
HA HA HA HA, ARIMA.
IT CAN'T BE....
WE'RE JUST SEEING THINGS.
...
PRETENDING LIKE THEY DON'T SEE THEM ...
...SOME PEOPLE JUST CAN'T BELIEVE HOW LAID-BACK WE REALLY ARE.
BUT, IT'S FUN TO JUST LAUGH SOMETIMES.

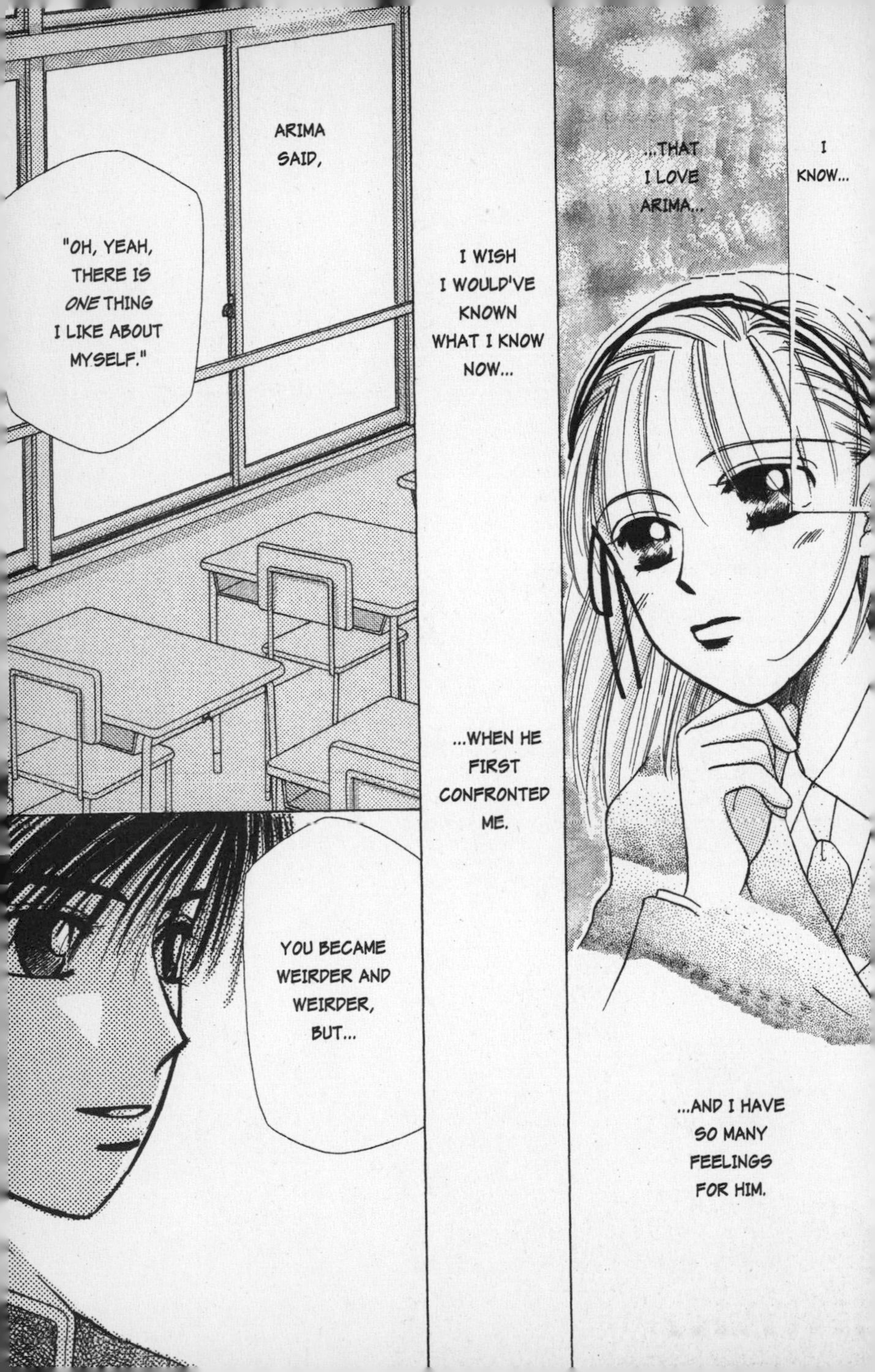
I KNOW...
...THAT I LOVE ARIMA...
...AND I HAVE SO MANY FEELINGS FOR HIM.
I WISH I WOULD'VE KNOWN WHAT I KNOW NOW...
...WHEN HE FIRST CONFRONTED ME.
ARIMA SAID,
"OH, YEAH, THERE IS *ONE* THING I LIKE ABOUT MYSELF."
YOU BECAME WEIRDER AND WEIRDER, BUT...

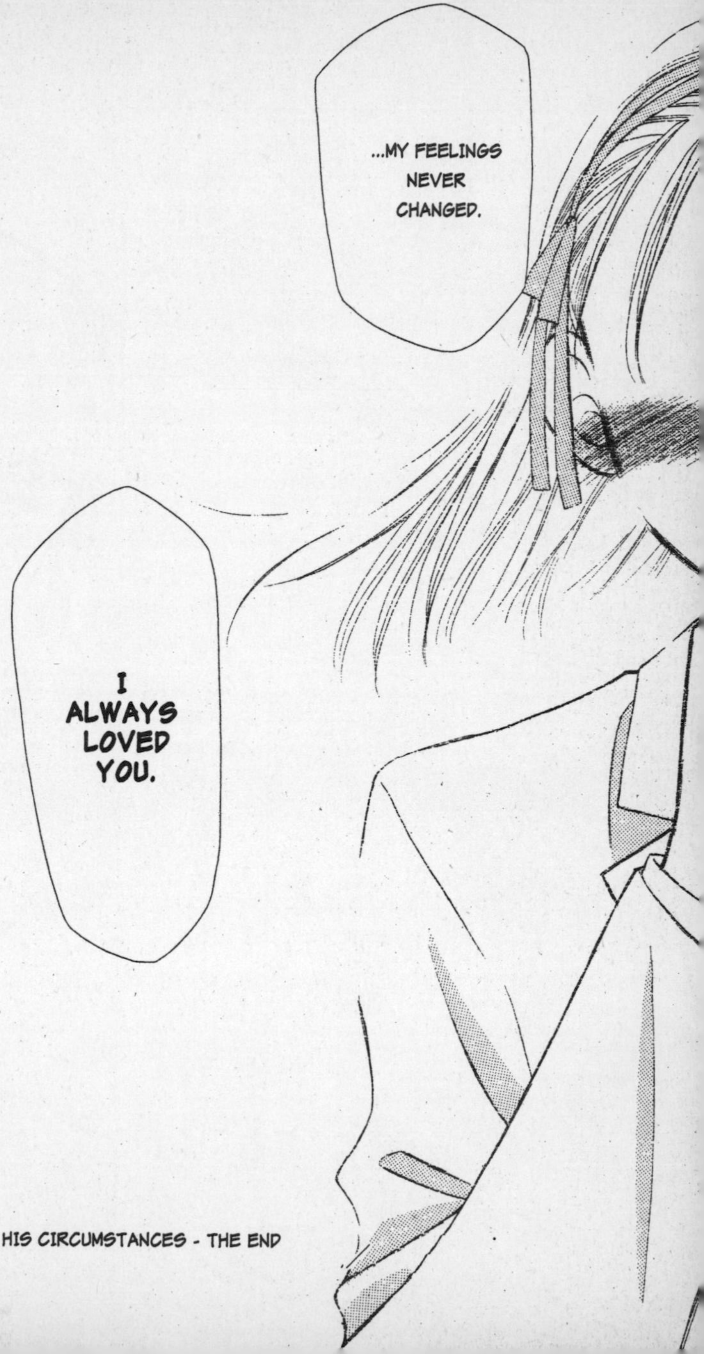
...MY FEELINGS NEVER CHANGED.
I ALWAYS LOVED YOU.

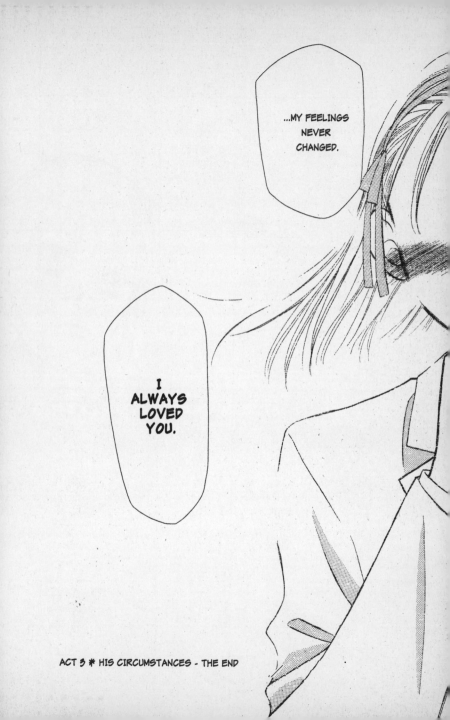

ACT 3 * HIS CIRCUMSTANCES - THE END

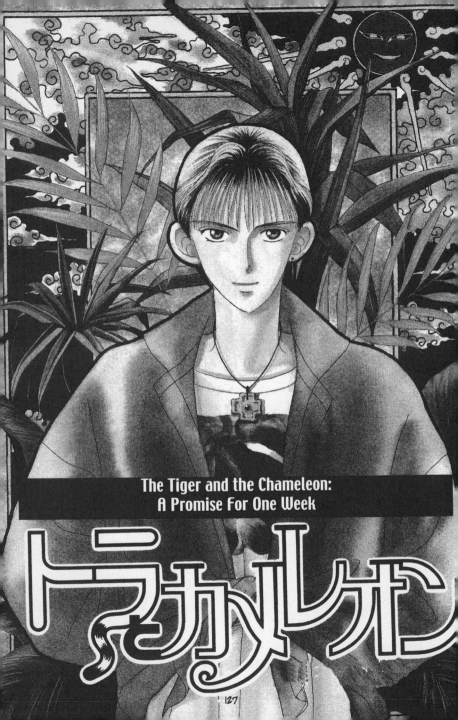

The Tiger and the Chameleon:
A Promise For One Week

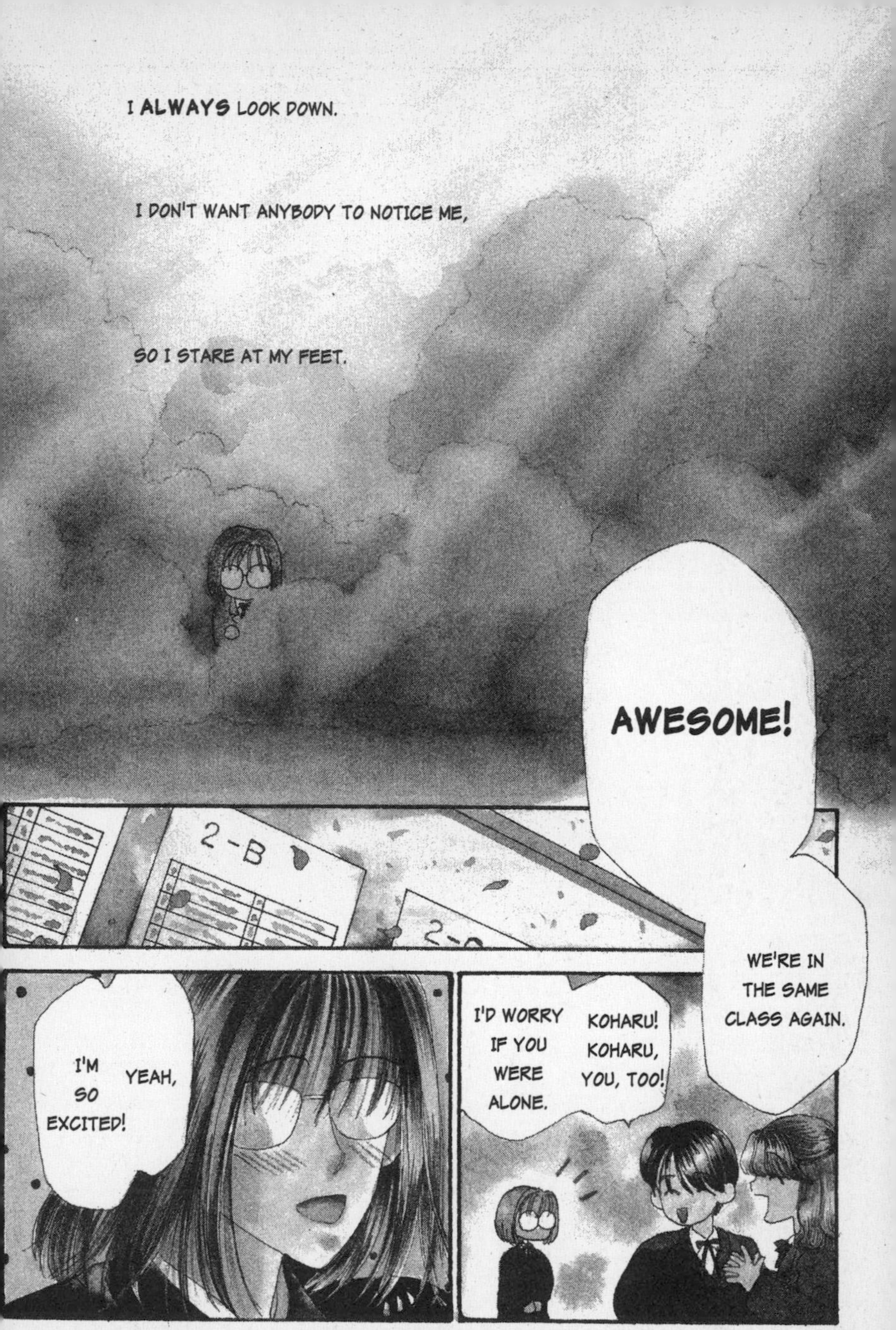
I ALWAYS LOOK DOWN.
I DON'T WANT ANYBODY TO NOTICE ME,
SO I STARE AT MY FEET.
AWESOME!
2-B
WE'RE IN THE SAME CLASS AGAIN.
KOHARU! KOHARU, YOU, TOO!
I'D WORRY IF YOU WERE ALONE.
YEAH, I'M SO EXCITED!

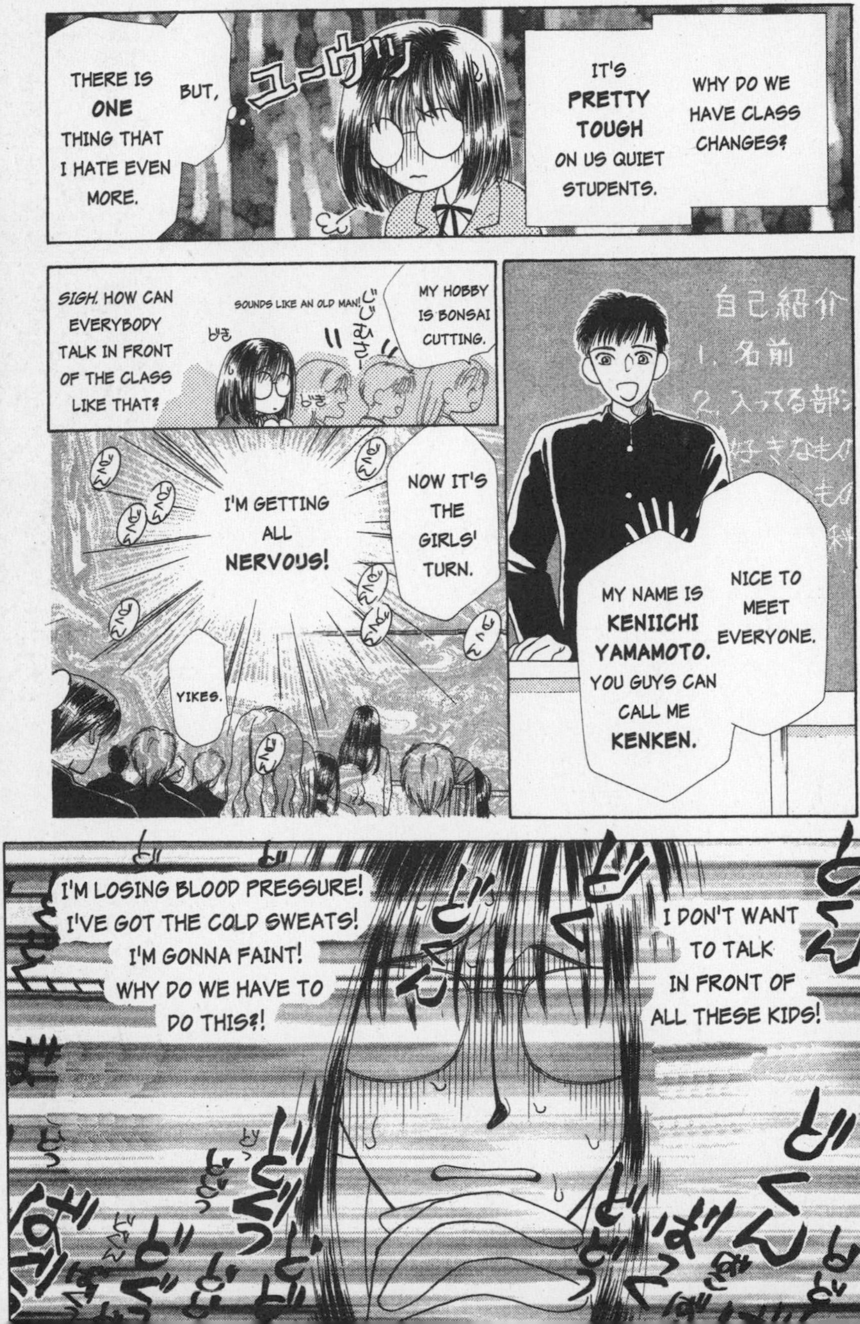
WHY DO WE HAVE CLASS CHANGES?
IT'S PRETTY TOUGH ON US QUIET STUDENTS.
ユーウツ
BUT,
THERE IS ONE THING THAT I HATE EVEN MORE.
自己紹介
1. 名前
2. 入ってる部
NICE TO MEET EVERYONE.
MY NAME IS KENIICHI YAMAMOTO. YOU GUYS CAN CALL ME KENKEN.
MY HOBBY IS BONSAI CUTTING.
SOUNDS LIKE AN OLD MAN!
SIGH. HOW CAN EVERYBODY TALK IN FRONT OF THE CLASS LIKE THAT?
NOW IT'S THE GIRLS' TURN.
I'M GETTING ALL NERVOUS!
YIKES.
I DON'T WANT TO TALK IN FRONT OF ALL THESE KIDS!
I'M LOSING BLOOD PRESSURE! I'VE GOT THE COLD SWEATS! I'M GONNA FAINT! WHY DO WE HAVE TO DO THIS?!

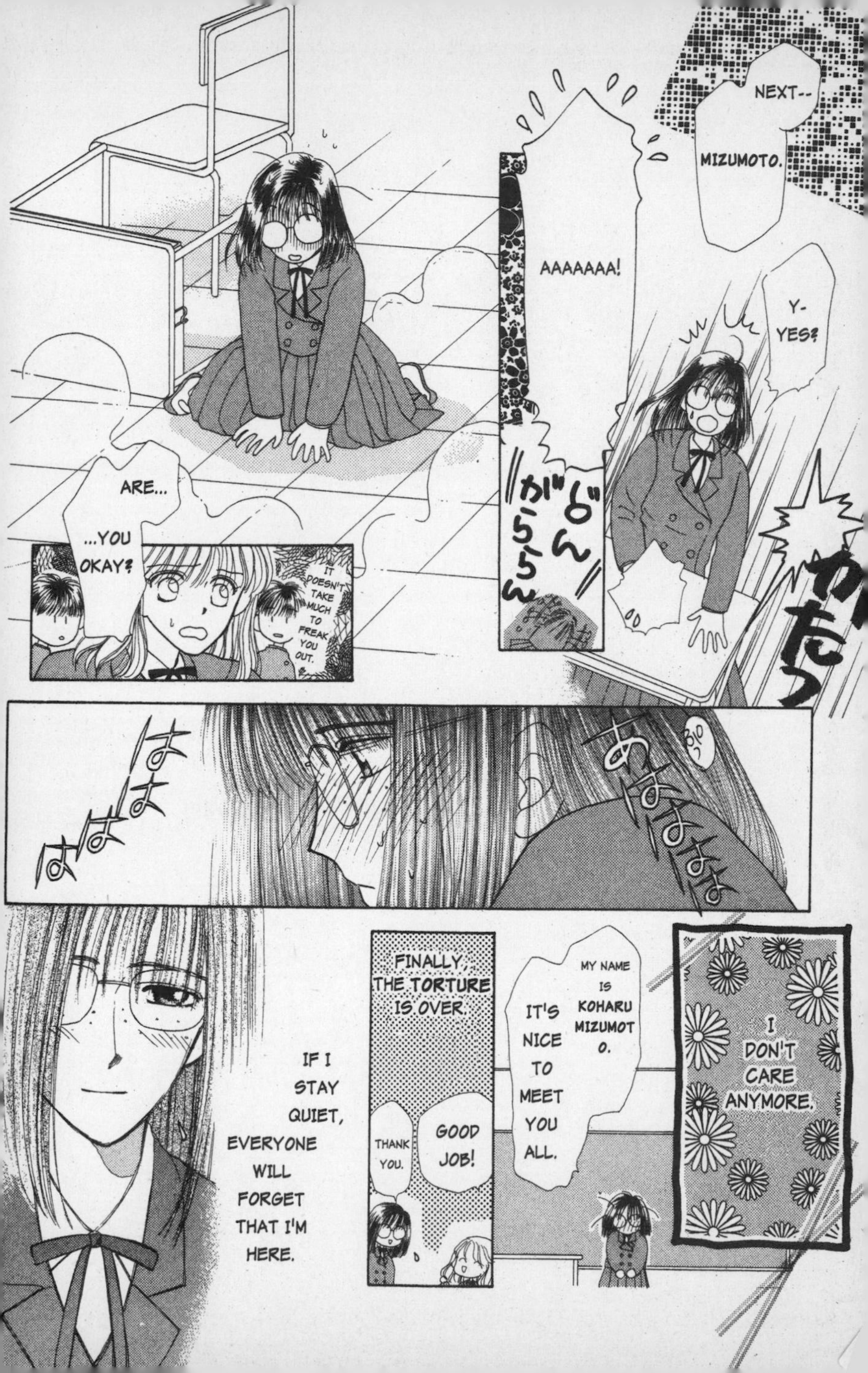
NEXT--
MIZUMOTO.
Y-YES?
かたっ
AAAAAAA!
どん
がららん
ARE...
...YOU OKAY?
IT DOESN'T TAKE MUCH TO FREAK YOU OUT.
I DON'T CARE ANYMORE.
MY NAME IS KOHARU MIZUMOTO.
IT'S NICE TO MEET YOU ALL.
FINALLY, THE TORTURE IS OVER.
GOOD JOB!
THANK YOU.
IF I STAY QUIET, EVERYONE WILL FORGET THAT I'M HERE.

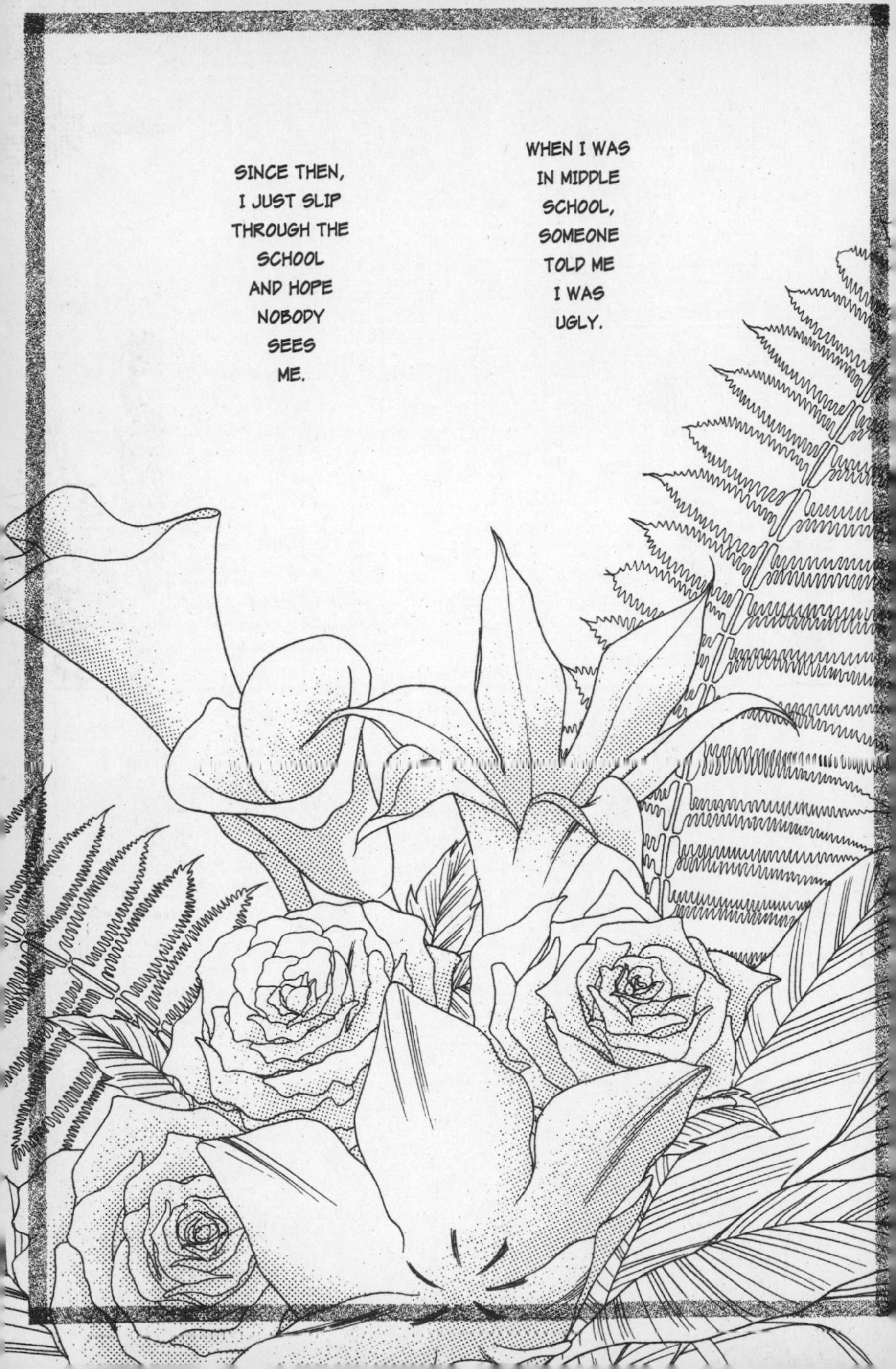
WHEN I WAS IN MIDDLE SCHOOL, SOMEONE TOLD ME I WAS UGLY.
SINCE THEN, I JUST SLIP THROUGH THE SCHOOL AND HOPE NOBODY SEES ME.

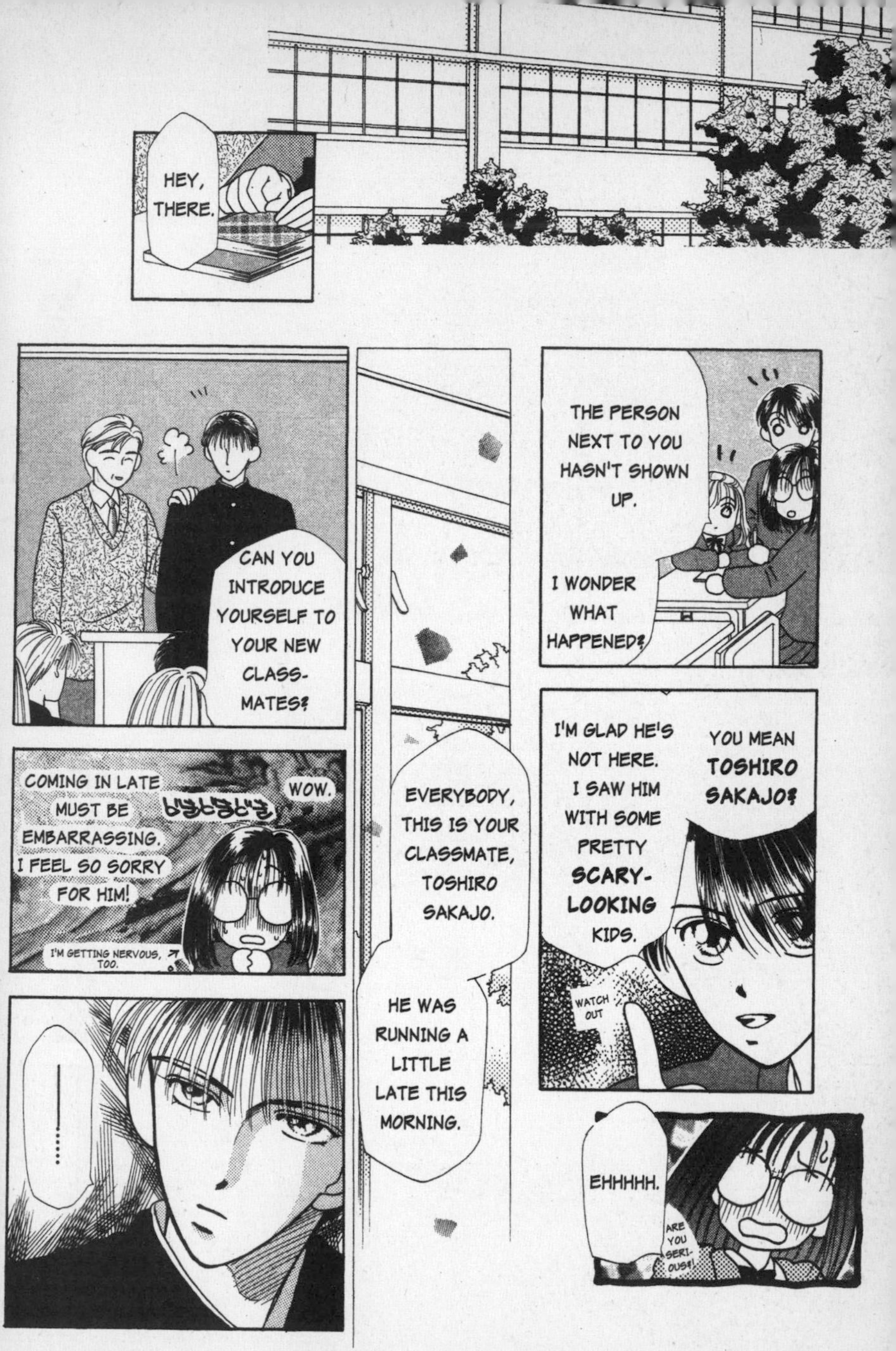
HEY, THERE.
THE PERSON NEXT TO YOU HASN'T SHOWN UP.
I WONDER WHAT HAPPENED?
YOU MEAN TOSHIRO SAKAJO?
I'M GLAD HE'S NOT HERE. I SAW HIM WITH SOME PRETTY SCARY-LOOKING KIDS.
WATCH OUT
EHHHHH.
ARE YOU SERI-OUS?!
EVERYBODY, THIS IS YOUR CLASSMATE, TOSHIRO SAKAJO.
HE WAS RUNNING A LITTLE LATE THIS MORNING.
CAN YOU INTRODUCE YOURSELF TO YOUR NEW CLASS-MATES?
WOW.
COMING IN LATE MUST BE EMBARRASSING. I FEEL SO SORRY FOR HIM!
I'M GETTING NERVOUS, TOO.
……

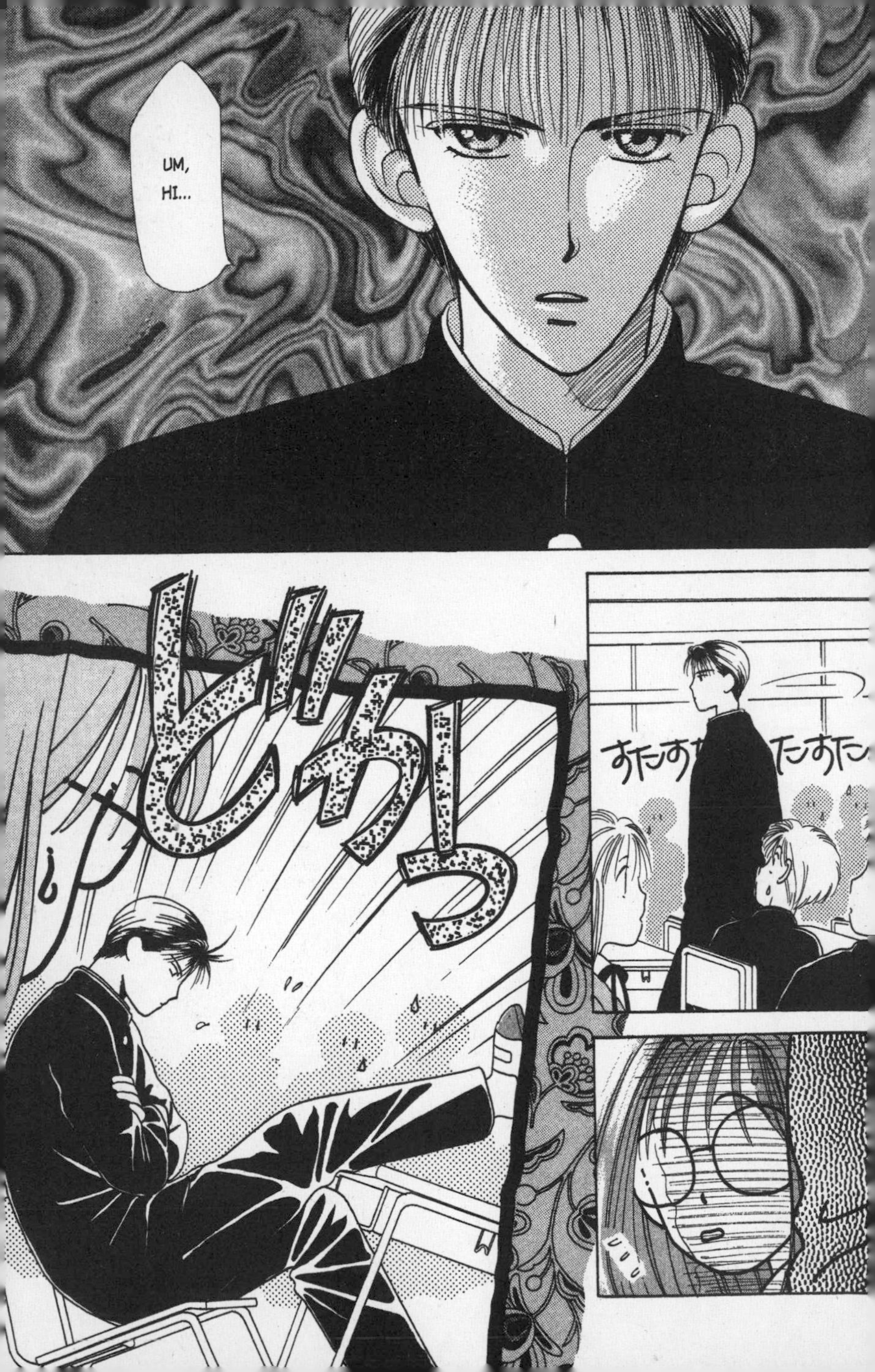
UM, HI...
すたすた
たすた
どわっ!

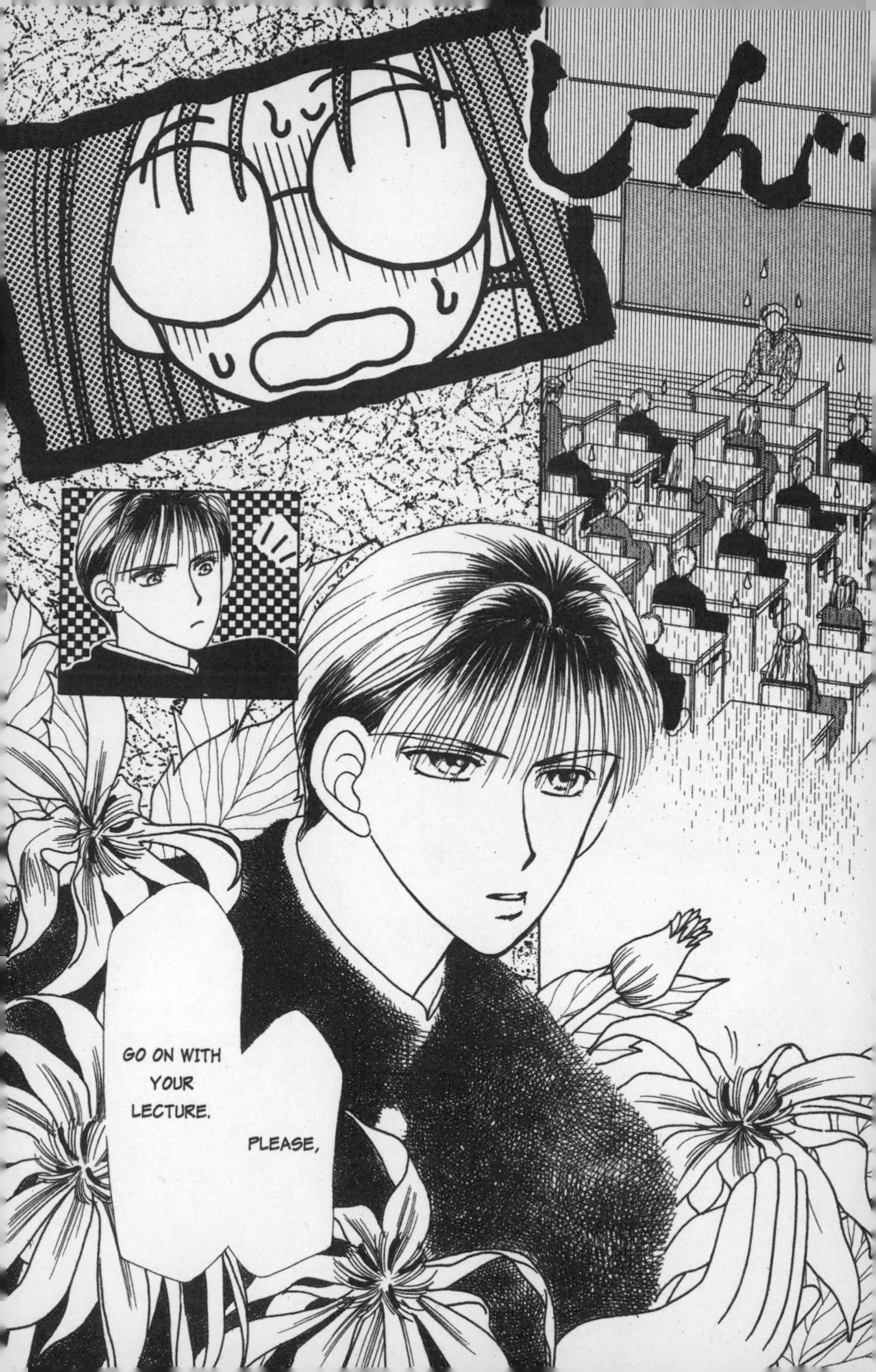
しーん
PLEASE,
GO ON WITH YOUR LECTURE.

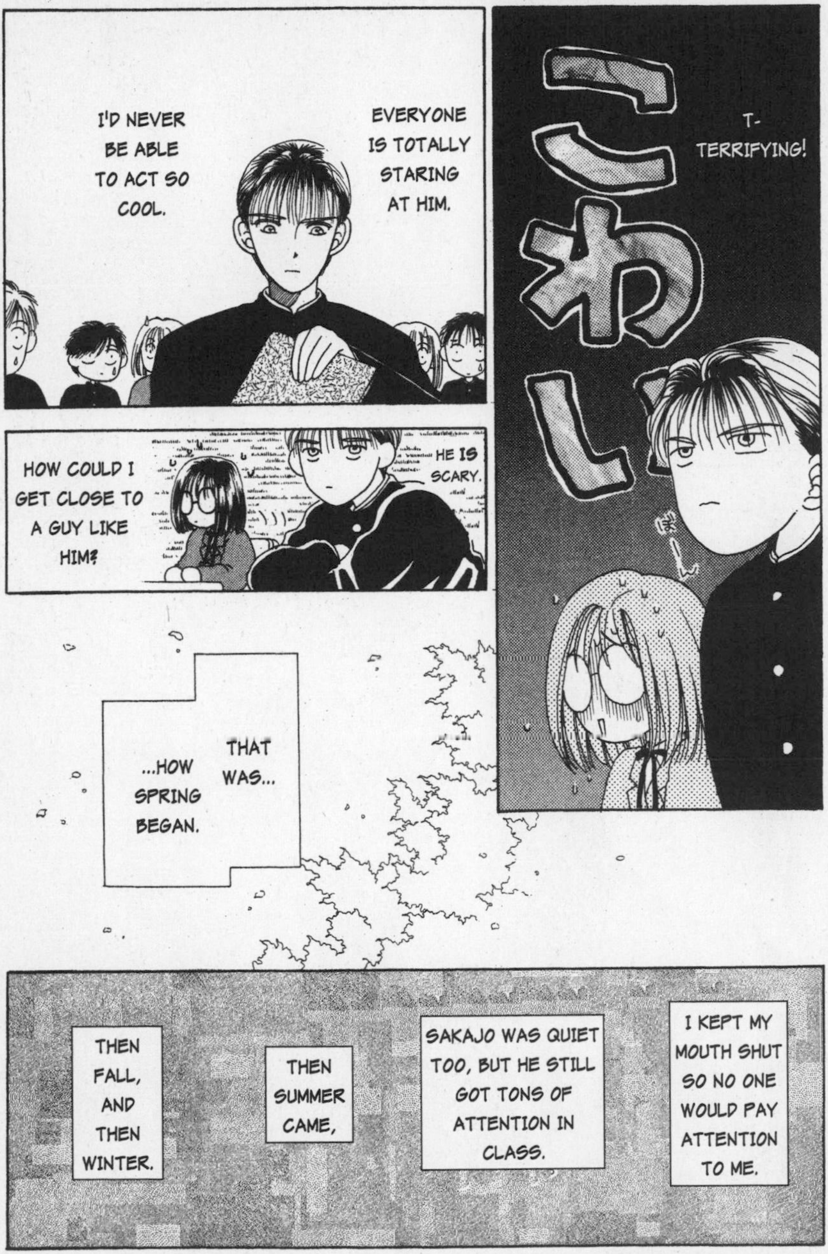
こわい
T-TERRIFYING!
EVERYONE IS TOTALLY STARING AT HIM.
I'D NEVER BE ABLE TO ACT SO COOL.
HE IS SCARY.
HOW COULD I GET CLOSE TO A GUY LIKE HIM?
THAT WAS...
...HOW SPRING BEGAN.
I KEPT MY MOUTH SHUT SO NO ONE WOULD PAY ATTENTION TO ME.
SAKAJO WAS QUIET TOO, BUT HE STILL GOT TONS OF ATTENTION IN CLASS.
THEN SUMMER CAME,
THEN FALL, AND THEN WINTER.

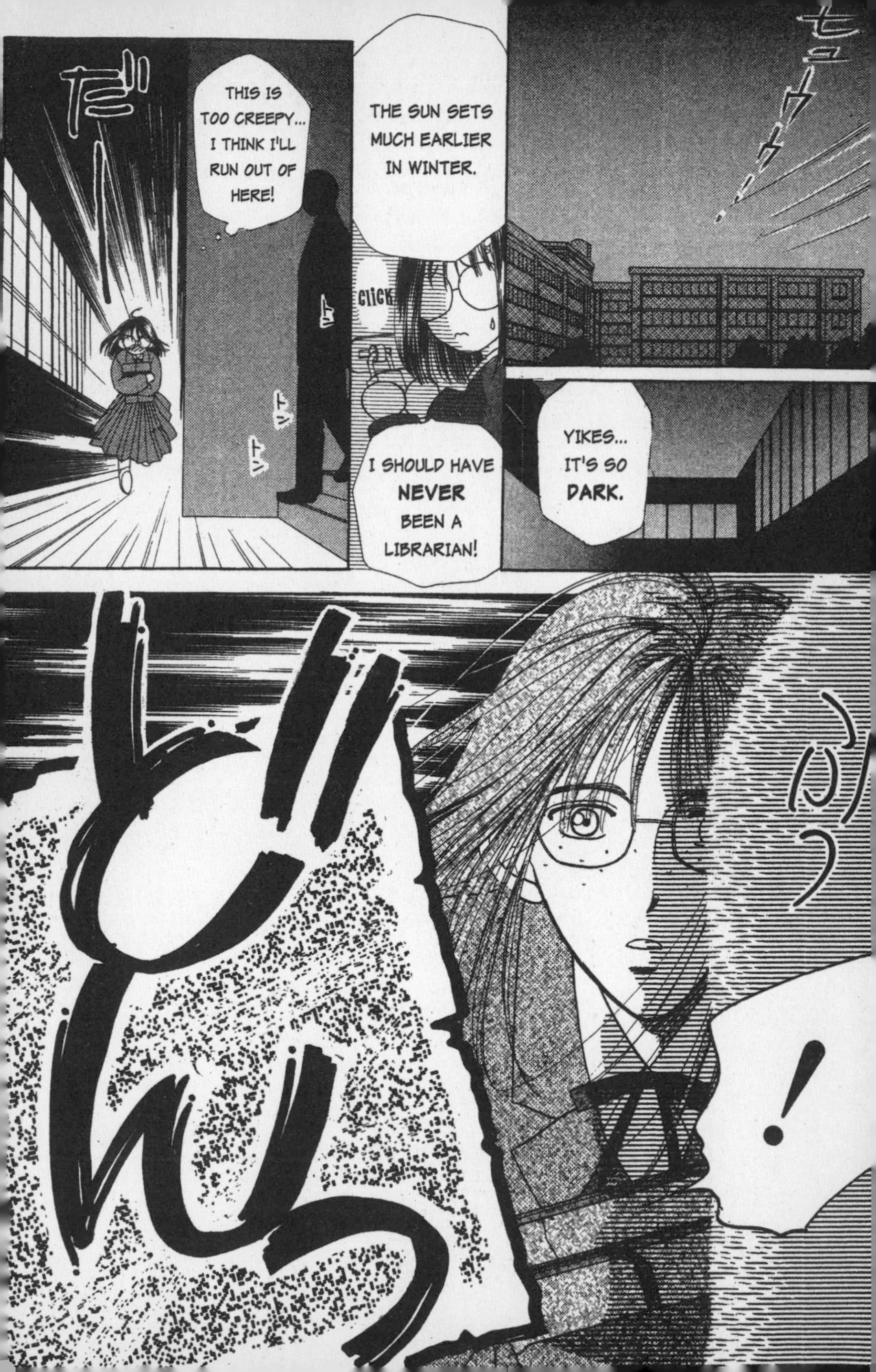
YIKES... IT'S SO DARK.
THE SUN SETS MUCH EARLIER IN WINTER.
CLICK
I SHOULD HAVE NEVER BEEN A LIBRARIAN!
THIS IS TOO CREEPY... I THINK I'LL RUN OUT OF HERE!
!

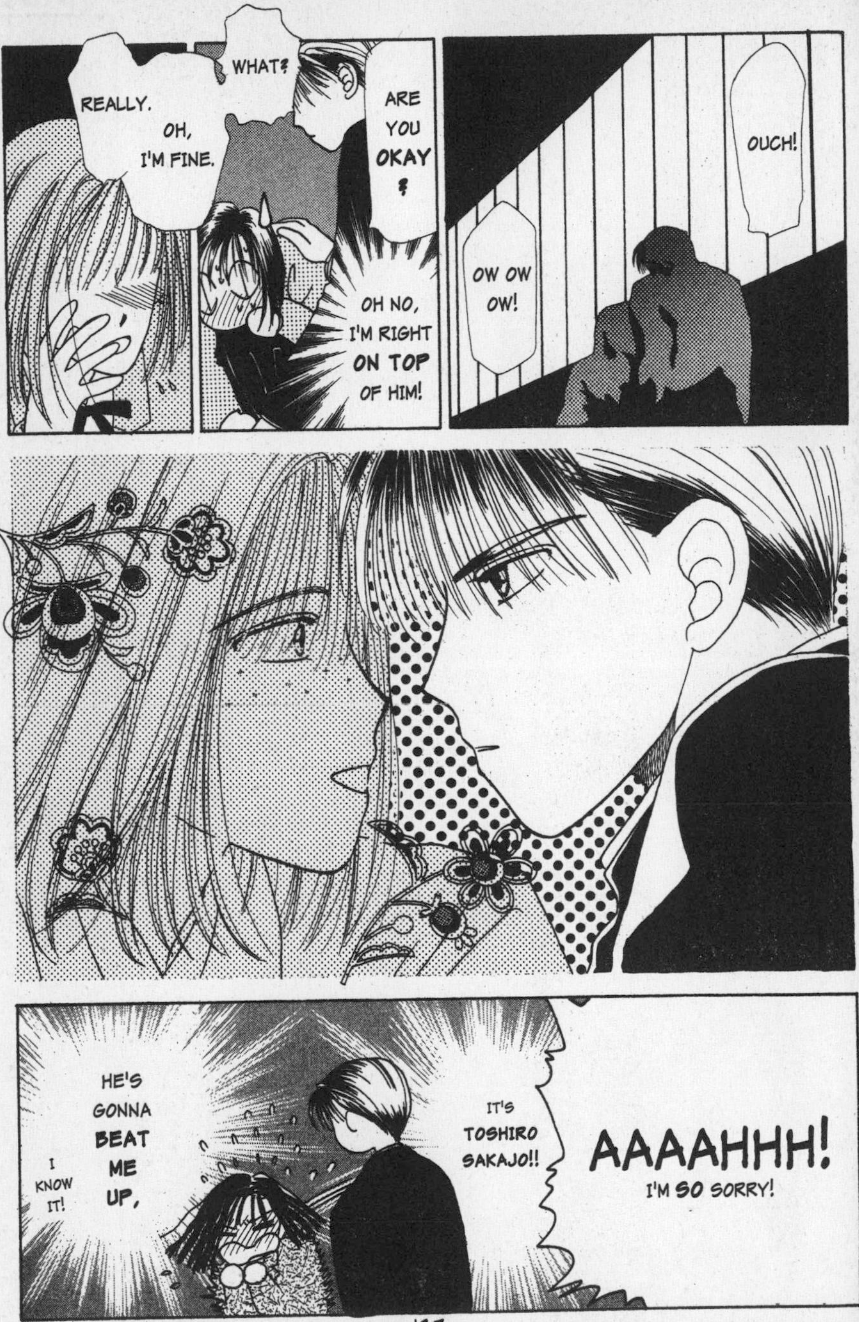
OUCH!
OW OW OW!
ARE YOU OKAY?
WHAT?
OH NO, I'M RIGHT ON TOP OF HIM!
REALLY. OH, I'M FINE.
AAAAHHH! I'M SO SORRY!
IT'S TOSHIRO SAKAJO!!
HE'S GONNA BEAT ME UP,
I KNOW IT!

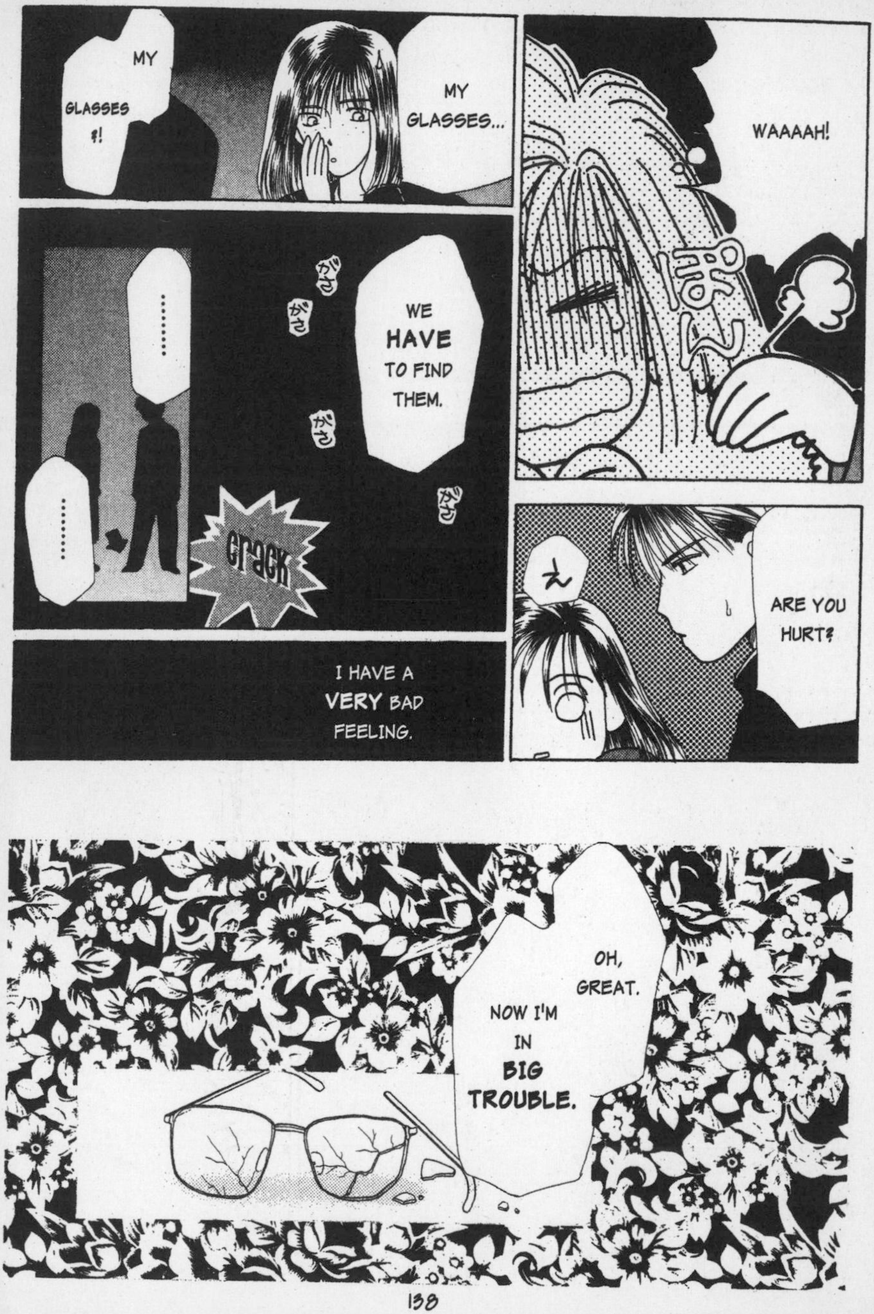
WAAAAH!
ぽん
MY GLASSES...
MY GLASSES ?!
がさ
がさ
WE HAVE TO FIND THEM.
がさ
がさ
crack
......
......
ARE YOU HURT?
え
I HAVE A VERY BAD FEELING.
OH, GREAT.
NOW I'M IN BIG TROUBLE.

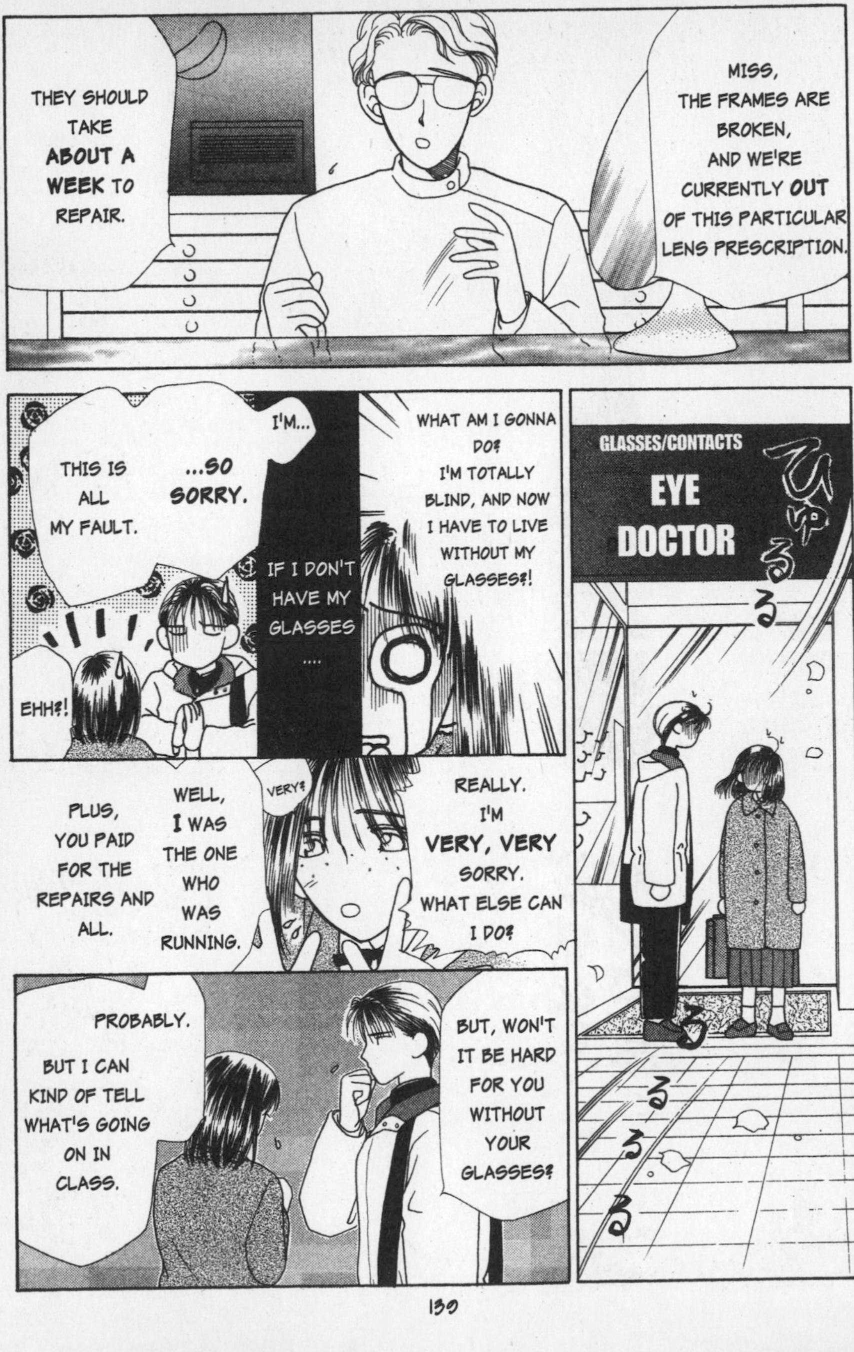
MISS, THE FRAMES ARE BROKEN, AND WE'RE CURRENTLY OUT OF THIS PARTICULAR LENS PRESCRIPTION.
THEY SHOULD TAKE ABOUT A WEEK TO REPAIR.
GLASSES/CONTACTS
EYE DOCTOR
ひゅるる
るるるる
WHAT AM I GONNA DO? I'M TOTALLY BLIND, AND NOW I HAVE TO LIVE WITHOUT MY GLASSES?!
IF I DON'T HAVE MY GLASSES ....
I'M...
...SO SORRY.
THIS IS ALL MY FAULT.
EHH?!
REALLY. I'M VERY, VERY SORRY. WHAT ELSE CAN I DO?
VERY?
WELL, I WAS THE ONE WHO WAS RUNNING.
PLUS, YOU PAID FOR THE REPAIRS AND ALL.
BUT, WON'T IT BE HARD FOR YOU WITHOUT YOUR GLASSES?
PROBABLY.
BUT I CAN KIND OF TELL WHAT'S GOING ON IN CLASS.

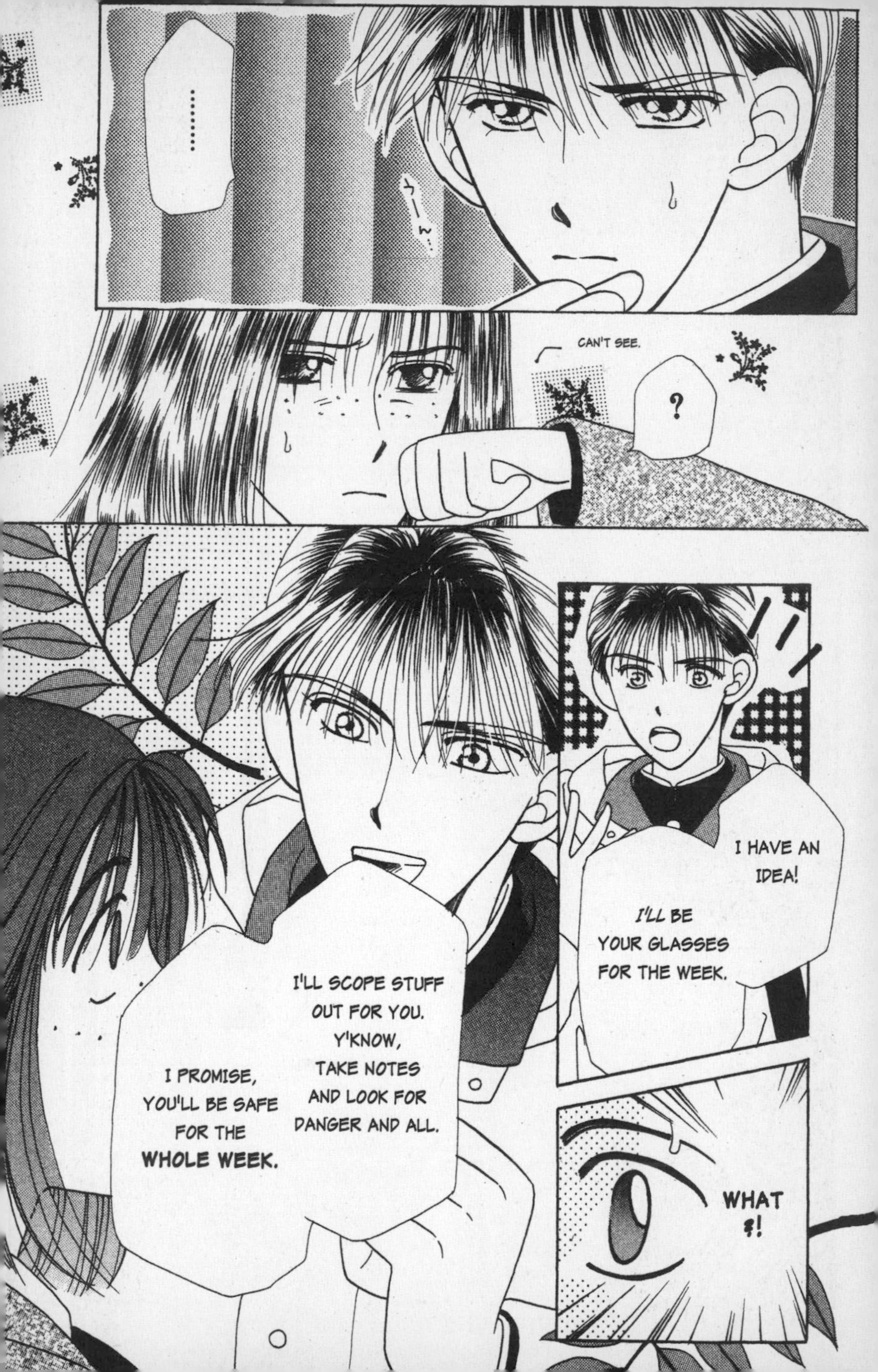
......
CAN'T SEE.
?
I HAVE AN IDEA!
I'LL BE YOUR GLASSES FOR THE WEEK.
WHAT?!
I'LL SCOPE STUFF OUT FOR YOU. Y'KNOW, TAKE NOTES AND LOOK FOR DANGER AND ALL.
I PROMISE, YOU'LL BE SAFE FOR THE WHOLE WEEK.

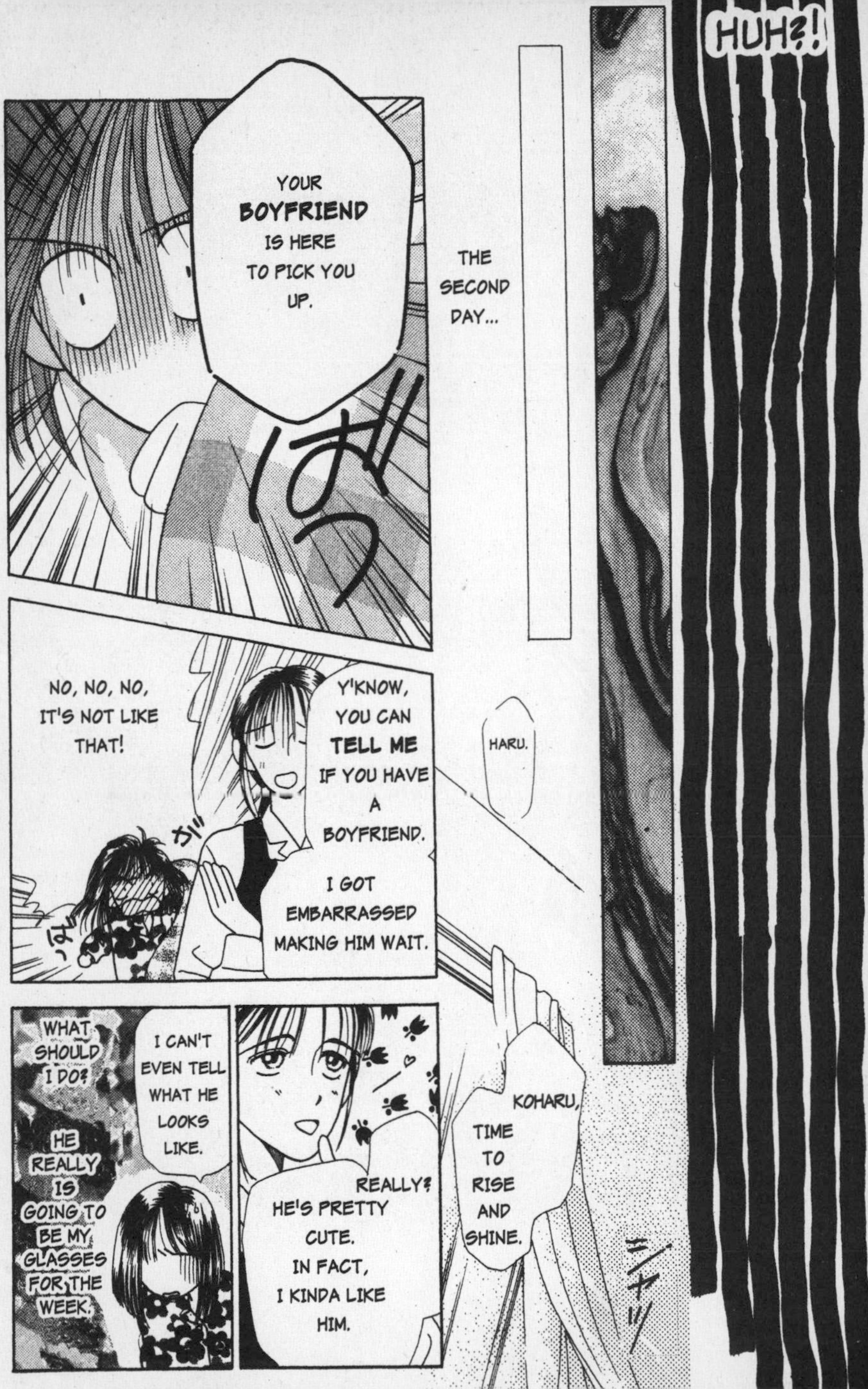
HUH?!
THE SECOND DAY...
HARU.
KOHARU, TIME TO RISE AND SHINE.
YOUR BOYFRIEND IS HERE TO PICK YOU UP.
Y'KNOW, YOU CAN TELL ME IF YOU HAVE A BOYFRIEND.
NO, NO, NO, IT'S NOT LIKE THAT!
I GOT EMBARRASSED MAKING HIM WAIT.
REALLY? HE'S PRETTY CUTE. IN FACT, I KINDA LIKE HIM.
I CAN'T EVEN TELL WHAT HE LOOKS LIKE.
WHAT SHOULD I DO?
HE REALLY IS GOING TO BE MY GLASSES FOR THE WEEK.

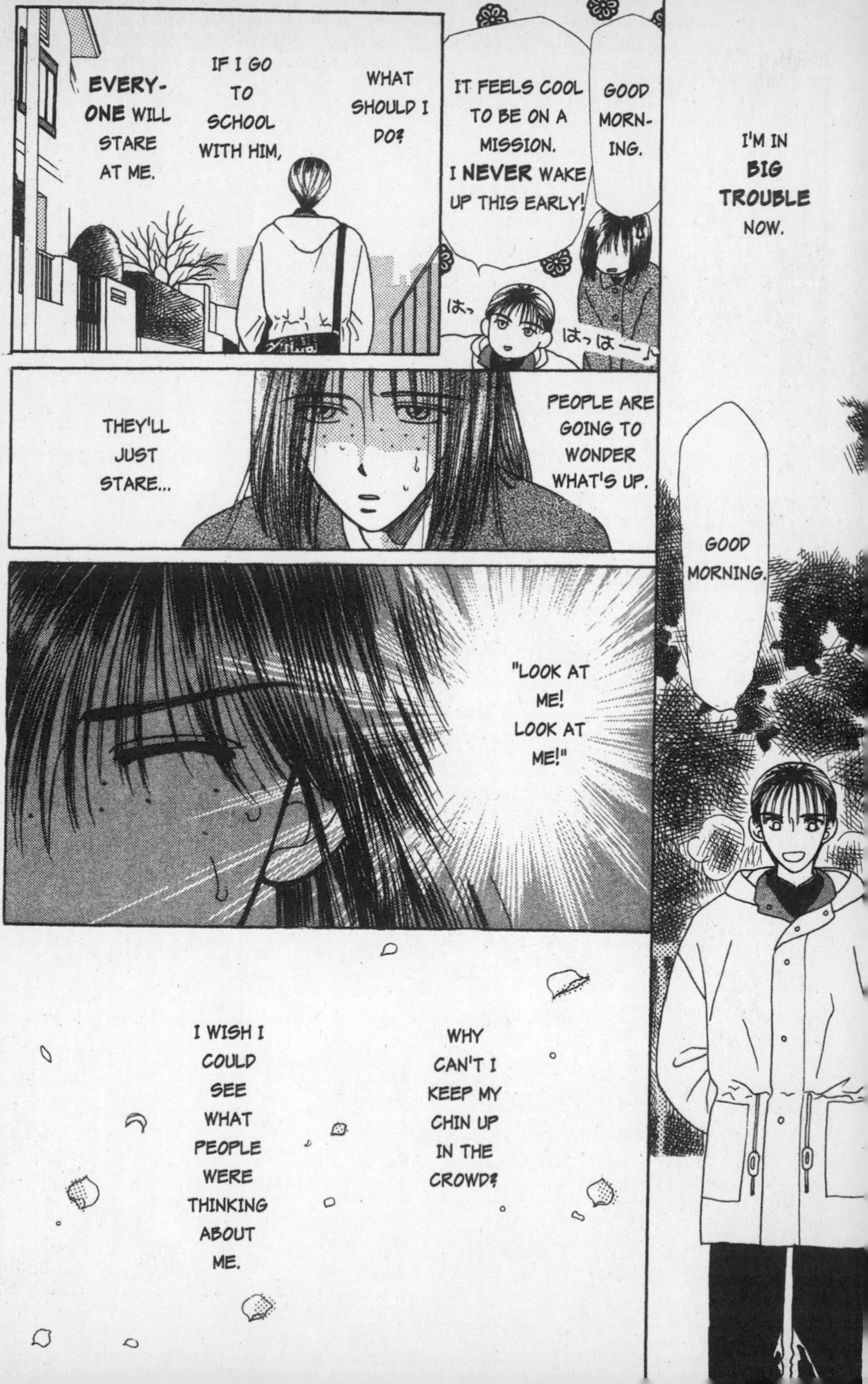
I'M IN BIG TROUBLE NOW.
GOOD MORNING.
GOOD MORNING.
IT FEELS COOL TO BE ON A MISSION. I NEVER WAKE UP THIS EARLY!
はっ
はっはー♪
WHAT SHOULD I DO?
IF I GO TO SCHOOL WITH HIM,
EVERYONE WILL STARE AT ME.
PEOPLE ARE GOING TO WONDER WHAT'S UP.
THEY'LL JUST STARE...
"LOOK AT ME! LOOK AT ME!"
WHY CAN'T I KEEP MY CHIN UP IN THE CROWD?
I WISH I COULD SEE WHAT PEOPLE WERE THINKING ABOUT ME.

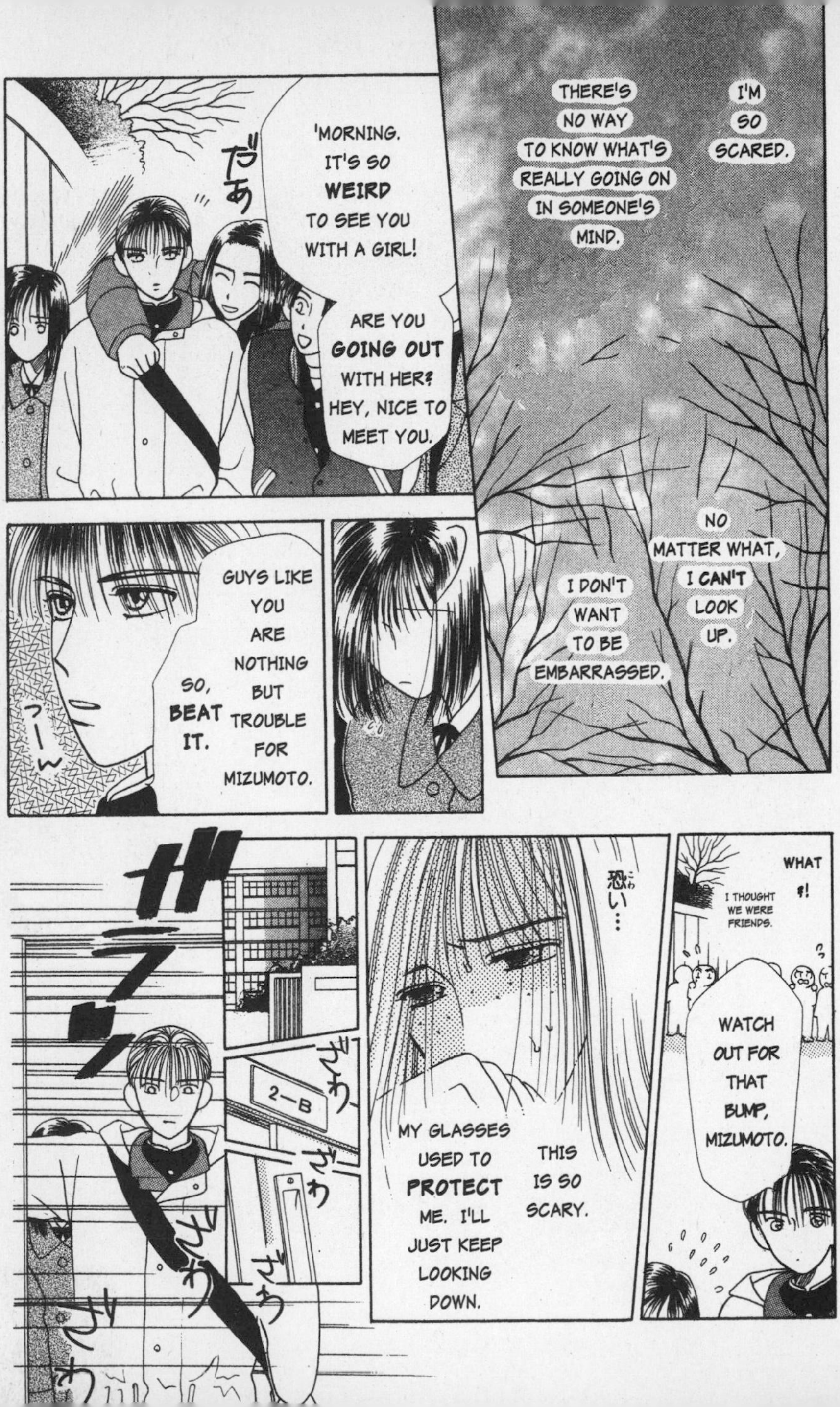
I'M SO SCARED.
THERE'S NO WAY TO KNOW WHAT'S REALLY GOING ON IN SOMEONE'S MIND.
NO MATTER WHAT, I CAN'T LOOK UP.
I DON'T WANT TO BE EMBARRASSED.
だあ
'MORNING. IT'S SO WEIRD TO SEE YOU WITH A GIRL!
ARE YOU GOING OUT WITH HER? HEY, NICE TO MEET YOU.
GUYS LIKE YOU ARE NOTHING BUT TROUBLE FOR MIZUMOTO.
SO, BEAT IT.
つーん
WHAT ?!
I THOUGHT WE WERE FRIENDS.
WATCH OUT FOR THAT BUMP, MIZUMOTO.
恐い…
THIS IS SO SCARY.
MY GLASSES USED TO PROTECT ME. I'LL JUST KEEP LOOKING DOWN.
ガラッ
2—B
ざわ
ざわ
ざわ
ざわ
ざわ

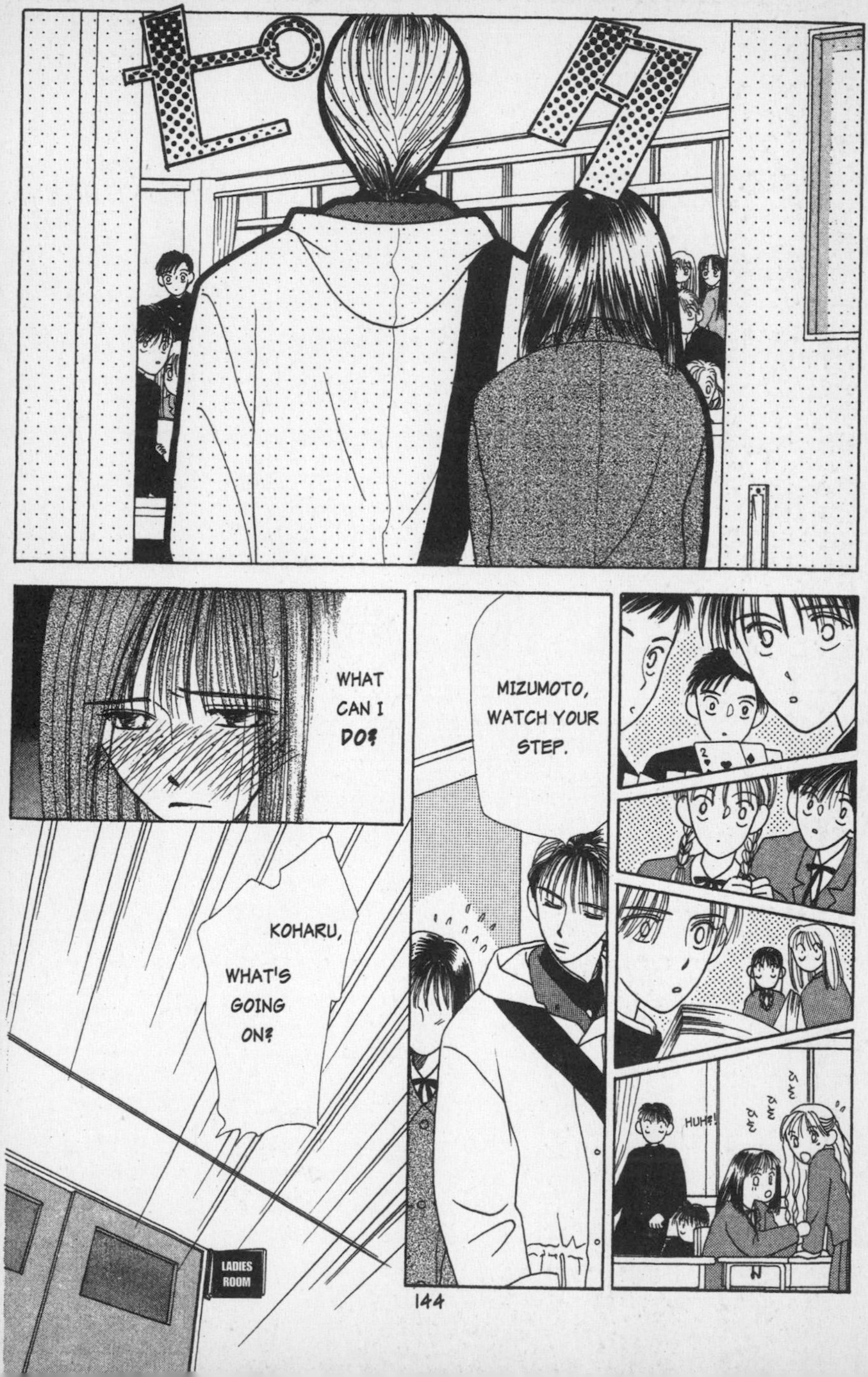
HUH?!
MIZUMOTO, WATCH YOUR STEP.
WHAT CAN I DO?
KOHARU,
WHAT'S GOING ON?
LADIES ROOM

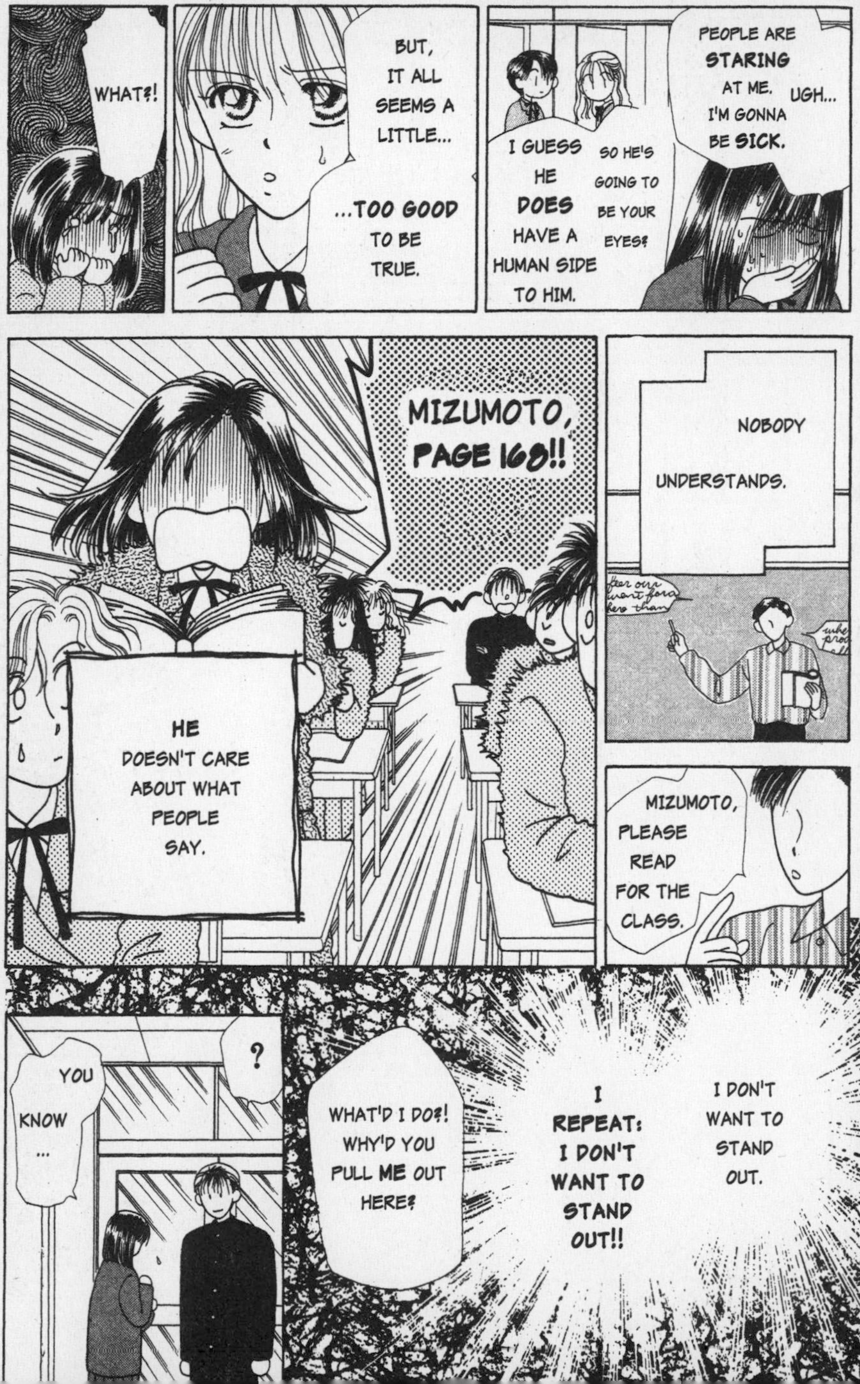

PEOPLE ARE STARING AT ME.
UGH...
I'M GONNA BE SICK.
SO HE'S GOING TO BE YOUR EYES?
I GUESS HE DOES HAVE A HUMAN SIDE TO HIM.
BUT, IT ALL SEEMS A LITTLE...
...TOO GOOD TO BE TRUE.
WHAT?!
NOBODY UNDERSTANDS.
MIZUMOTO, PLEASE READ FOR THE CLASS.
MIZUMOTO, PAGE 168!!
HE DOESN'T CARE ABOUT WHAT PEOPLE SAY.
I DON'T WANT TO STAND OUT.
I REPEAT: I DON'T WANT TO STAND OUT!!
WHAT'D I DO?! WHY'D YOU PULL ME OUT HERE?
?
YOU KNOW ...

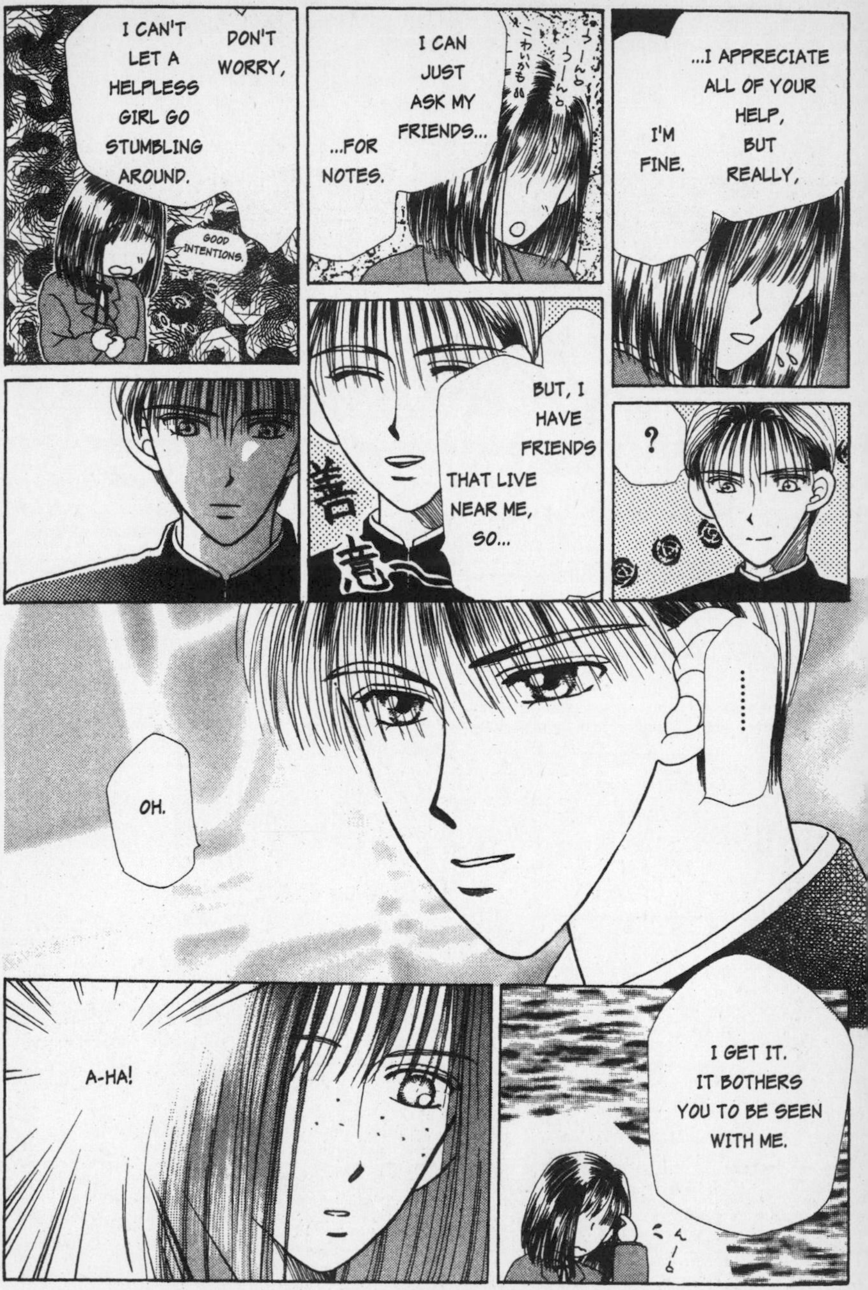

...I APPRECIATE ALL OF YOUR HELP, BUT REALLY,
I'M FINE.
I CAN JUST ASK MY FRIENDS...
...FOR NOTES.
DON'T WORRY,
I CAN'T LET A HELPLESS GIRL GO STUMBLING AROUND.
GOOD INTENTIONS.
?
BUT, I HAVE FRIENDS THAT LIVE NEAR ME, SO...
......
OH.
I GET IT. IT BOTHERS YOU TO BE SEEN WITH ME.
A-HA!

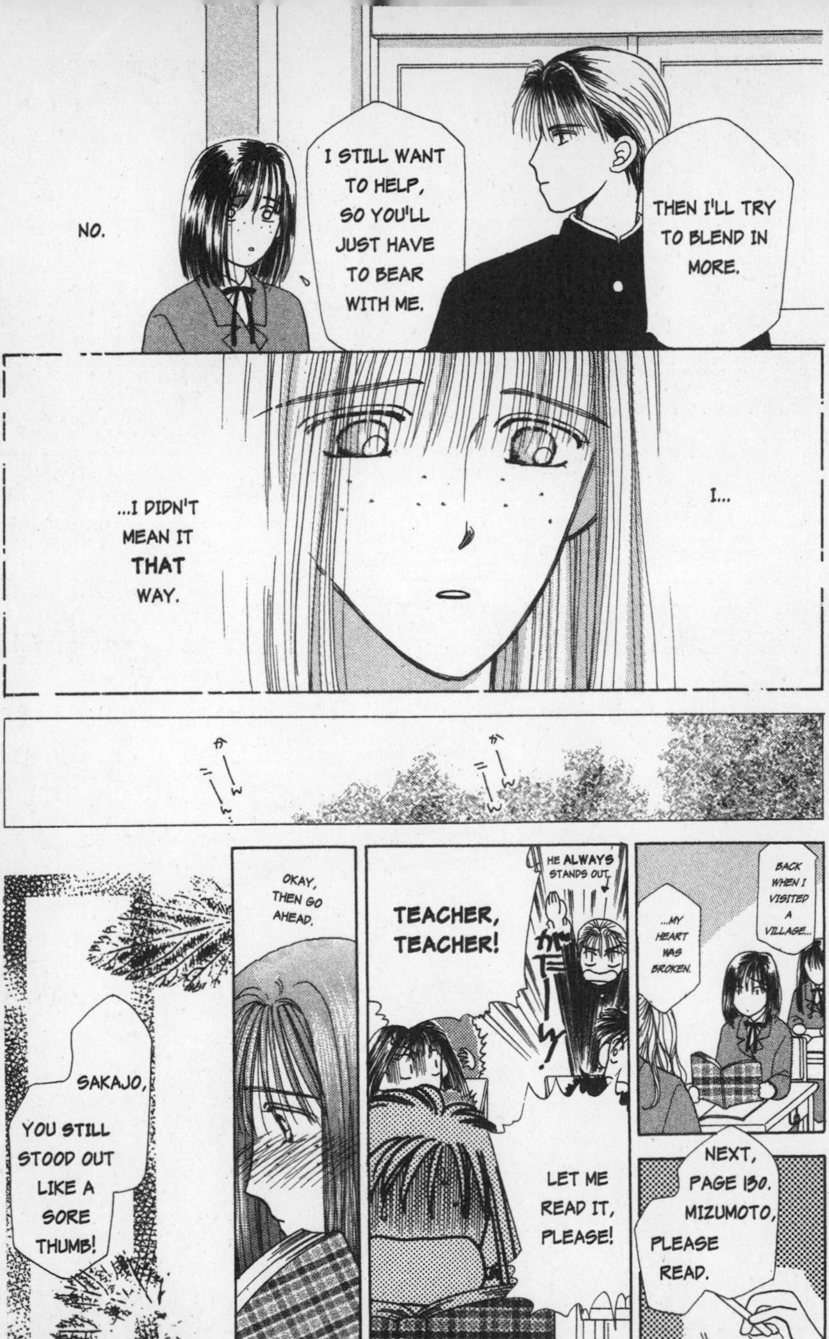
THEN I'LL TRY TO BLEND IN MORE.
I STILL WANT TO HELP, SO YOU'LL JUST HAVE TO BEAR WITH ME.
NO.
I...
...I DIDN'T MEAN IT THAT WAY.
BACK WHEN I VISITED A VILLAGE...
...MY HEART WAS BROKEN.
NEXT, PAGE 130. MIZUMOTO, PLEASE READ.
HE ALWAYS STANDS OUT.
TEACHER, TEACHER!
LET ME READ IT, PLEASE!
OKAY, THEN GO AHEAD.
SAKAJO, YOU STILL STOOD OUT LIKE A SORE THUMB!

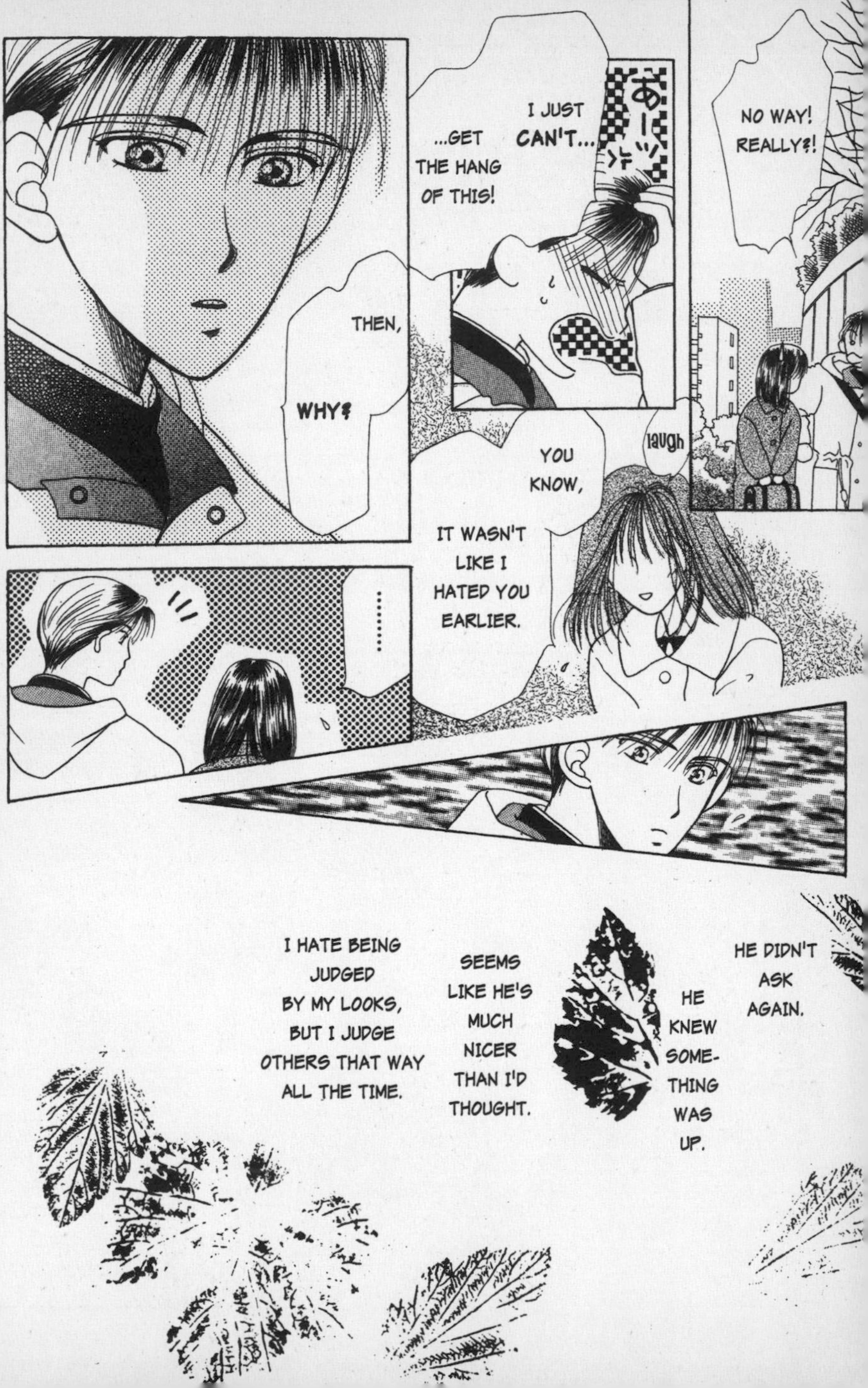
NO WAY! REALLY?!
I JUST CAN'T...
...GET THE HANG OF THIS!
laugh
YOU KNOW,
IT WASN'T LIKE I HATED YOU EARLIER.
THEN,
WHY?
......
HE DIDN'T ASK AGAIN.
HE KNEW SOME-THING WAS UP.
SEEMS LIKE HE'S MUCH NICER THAN I'D THOUGHT.
I HATE BEING JUDGED BY MY LOOKS, BUT I JUDGE OTHERS THAT WAY ALL THE TIME.

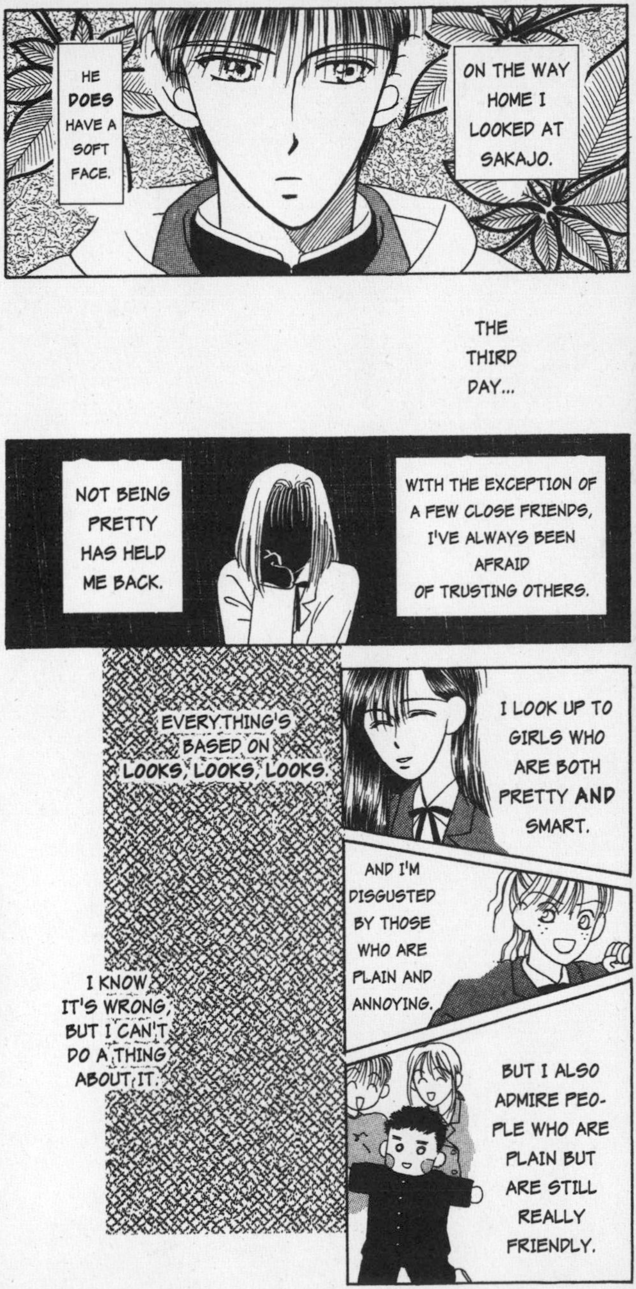
ON THE WAY HOME I LOOKED AT SAKAJO.
HE DOES HAVE A SOFT FACE.
THE THIRD DAY...
WITH THE EXCEPTION OF A FEW CLOSE FRIENDS, I'VE ALWAYS BEEN AFRAID OF TRUSTING OTHERS.
NOT BEING PRETTY HAS HELD ME BACK.
I LOOK UP TO GIRLS WHO ARE BOTH PRETTY AND SMART.
AND I'M DISGUSTED BY THOSE WHO ARE PLAIN AND ANNOYING.
BUT I ALSO ADMIRE PEOPLE WHO ARE PLAIN BUT ARE STILL REALLY FRIENDLY.
EVERYTHING'S BASED ON LOOKS, LOOKS, LOOKS.
I KNOW IT'S WRONG, BUT I CAN'T DO A THING ABOUT IT.

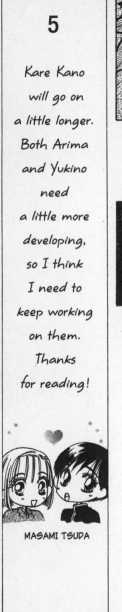

5

Kare Kano will go on a little longer. Both Arima and Yukino need a little more developing, so I think I need to keep working on them. Thanks for reading!

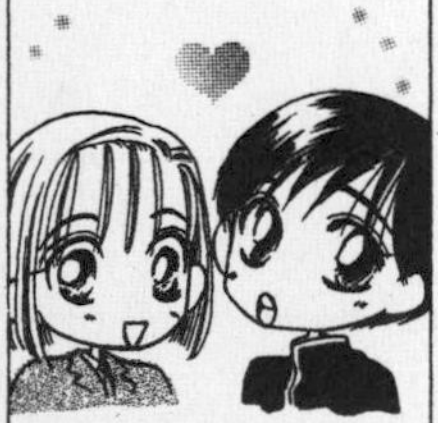

MASAMI TSUDA

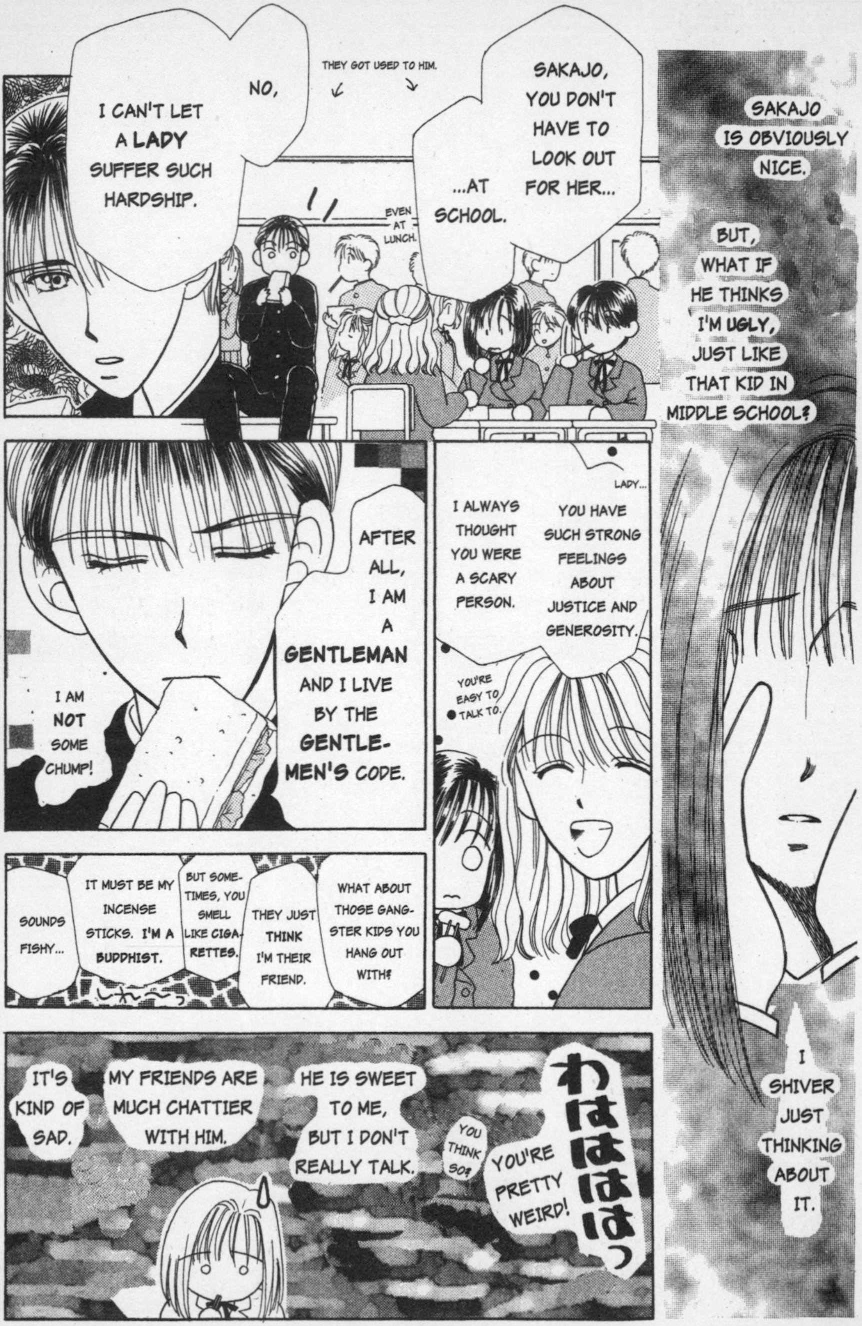
SAKAJO IS OBVIOUSLY NICE.
BUT, WHAT IF HE THINKS I'M UGLY, JUST LIKE THAT KID IN MIDDLE SCHOOL?
I SHIVER JUST THINKING ABOUT IT.
SAKAJO, YOU DON'T HAVE TO LOOK OUT FOR HER...
...AT SCHOOL.
EVEN AT LUNCH.
THEY GOT USED TO HIM.
NO,
I CAN'T LET A LADY SUFFER SUCH HARDSHIP.
LADY...
YOU HAVE SUCH STRONG FEELINGS ABOUT JUSTICE AND GENEROSITY.
I ALWAYS THOUGHT YOU WERE A SCARY PERSON.
YOU'RE EASY TO TALK TO.
AFTER ALL, I AM A GENTLEMAN AND I LIVE BY THE GENTLE-MEN'S CODE.
I AM NOT SOME CHUMP!
WHAT ABOUT THOSE GANG-STER KIDS YOU HANG OUT WITH?
THEY JUST THINK I'M THEIR FRIEND.
BUT SOME-TIMES, YOU SMELL LIKE CIGA-RETTES.
IT MUST BE MY INCENSE STICKS. I'M A BUDDHIST.
SOUNDS FISHY...
しれ〜っ
わははははっ
YOU'RE PRETTY WEIRD!
YOU THINK SO?
HE IS SWEET TO ME, BUT I DON'T REALLY TALK.
MY FRIENDS ARE MUCH CHATTIER WITH HIM.
IT'S KIND OF SAD.

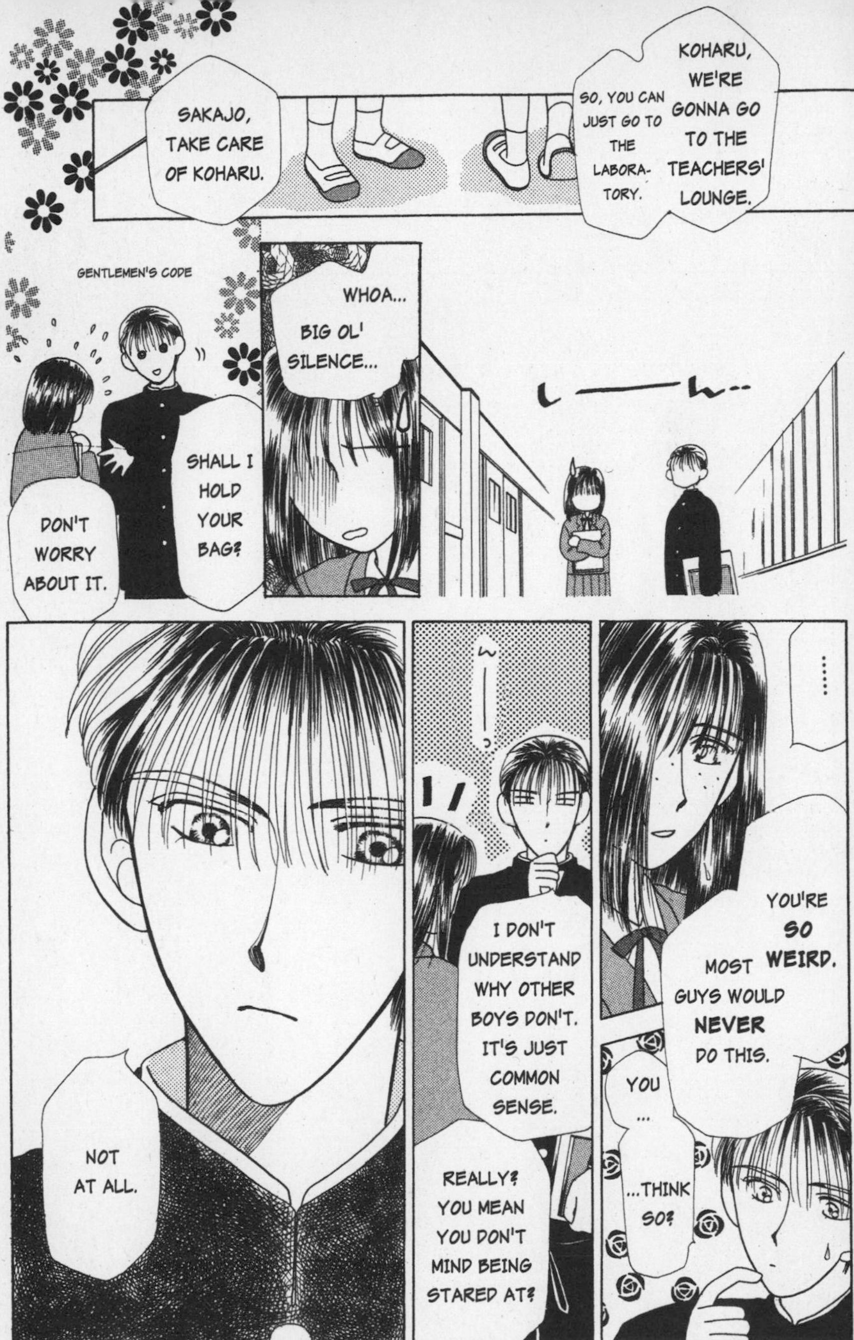
KOHARU, WE'RE GONNA GO TO THE TEACHERS' LOUNGE.
SO, YOU CAN JUST GO TO THE LABORA-TORY.
SAKAJO, TAKE CARE OF KOHARU.
し——ん‥
WHOA...
BIG OL' SILENCE...
GENTLEMEN'S CODE
SHALL I HOLD YOUR BAG?
DON'T WORRY ABOUT IT.
......
YOU'RE SO WEIRD.
MOST GUYS WOULD NEVER DO THIS.
YOU ...
...THINK SO?
I DON'T UNDERSTAND WHY OTHER BOYS DON'T. IT'S JUST COMMON SENSE.
REALLY? YOU MEAN YOU DON'T MIND BEING STARED AT?
NOT AT ALL.

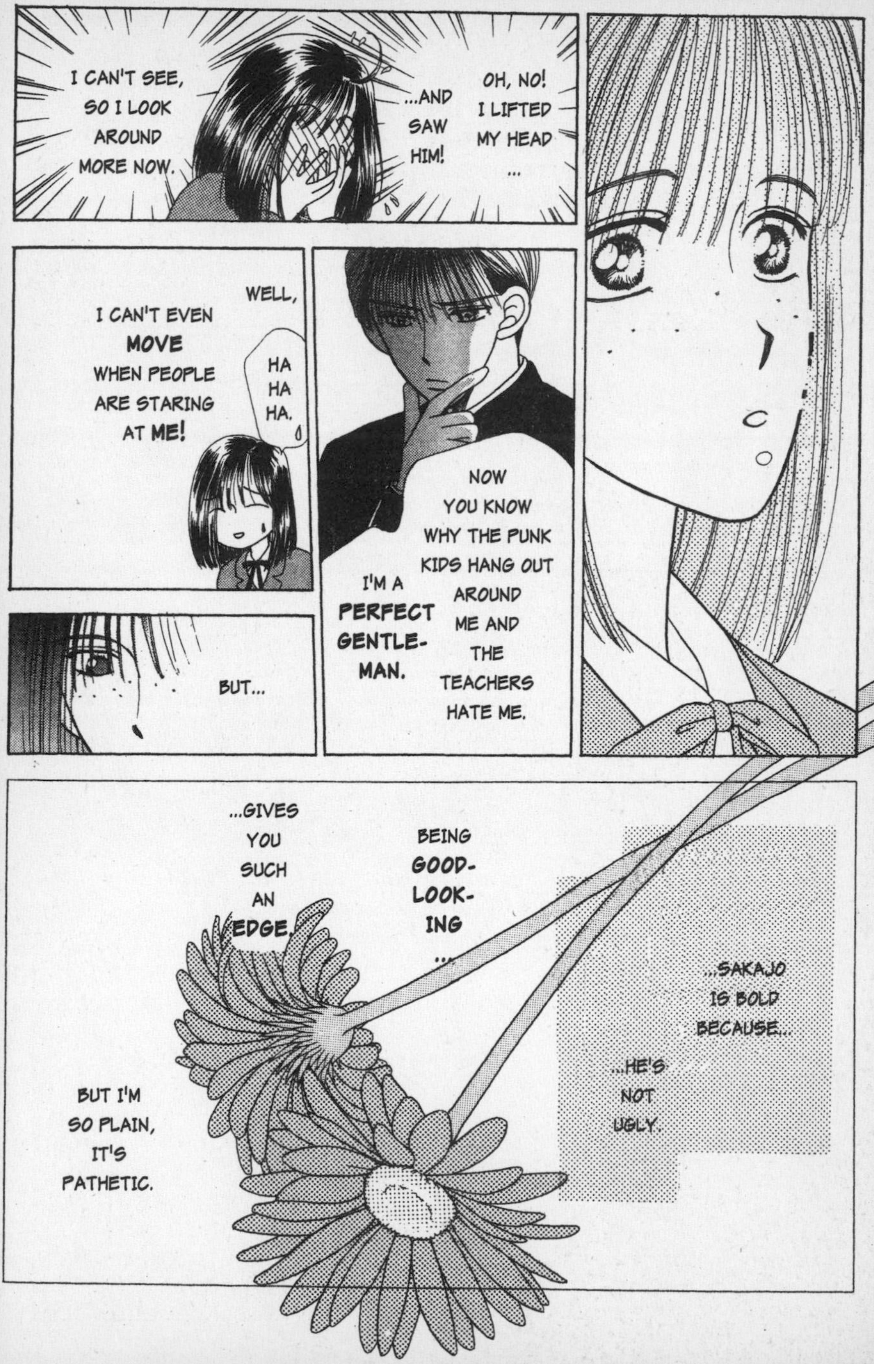
OH, NO! I LIFTED MY HEAD...
...AND SAW HIM!
I CAN'T SEE, SO I LOOK AROUND MORE NOW.
NOW YOU KNOW WHY THE PUNK KIDS HANG OUT AROUND ME AND THE TEACHERS HATE ME.
I'M A PERFECT GENTLEMAN.
WELL,
I CAN'T EVEN MOVE WHEN PEOPLE ARE STARING AT ME!
HA HA HA.
BUT...
...SAKAJO IS BOLD BECAUSE...
...HE'S NOT UGLY.
BEING GOOD-LOOKING...
...GIVES YOU SUCH AN EDGE.
BUT I'M SO PLAIN, IT'S PATHETIC.

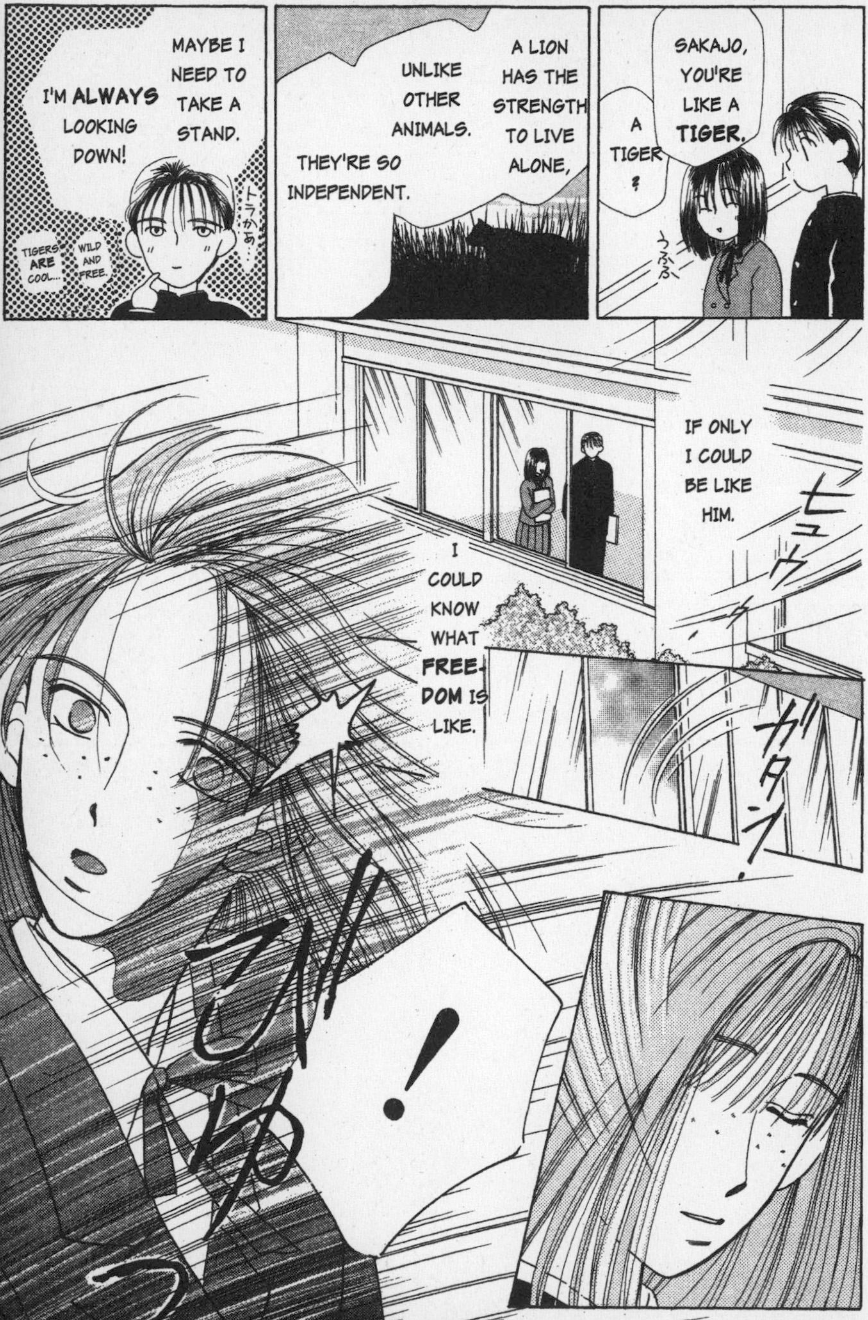
SAKAJO, YOU'RE LIKE A TIGER.
A TIGER?
うふふ
A LION HAS THE STRENGTH TO LIVE ALONE,
UNLIKE OTHER ANIMALS.
THEY'RE SO INDEPENDENT.
MAYBE I NEED TO TAKE A STAND.
I'M ALWAYS LOOKING DOWN!
トラかぁ…
WILD AND FREE.
TIGERS ARE COOL...
IF ONLY I COULD BE LIKE HIM.
I COULD KNOW WHAT FREEDOM IS LIKE.
ヒュウゥ
ガタン!
!

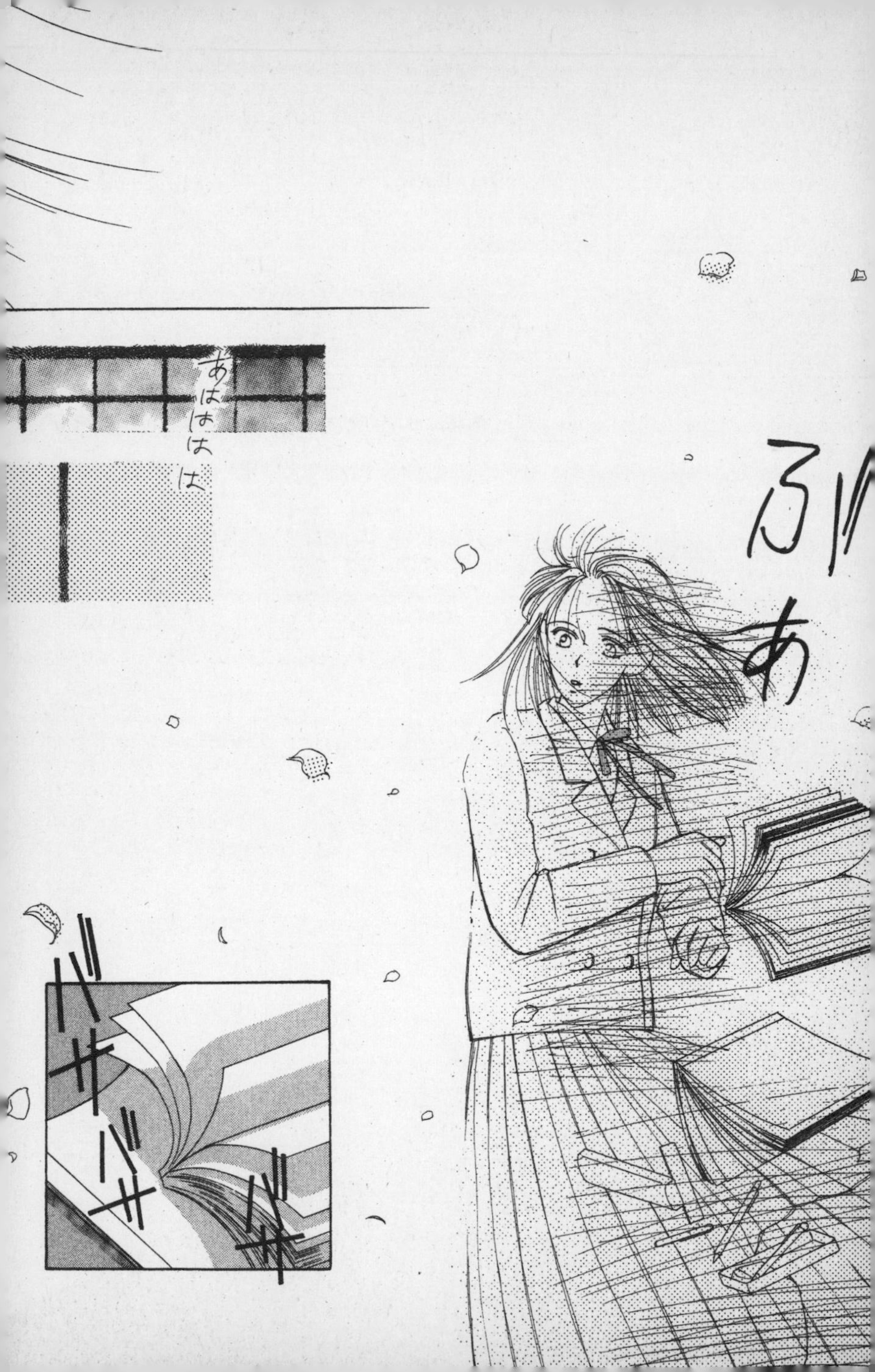
ふぁ
あははは
バサバサ
バサ

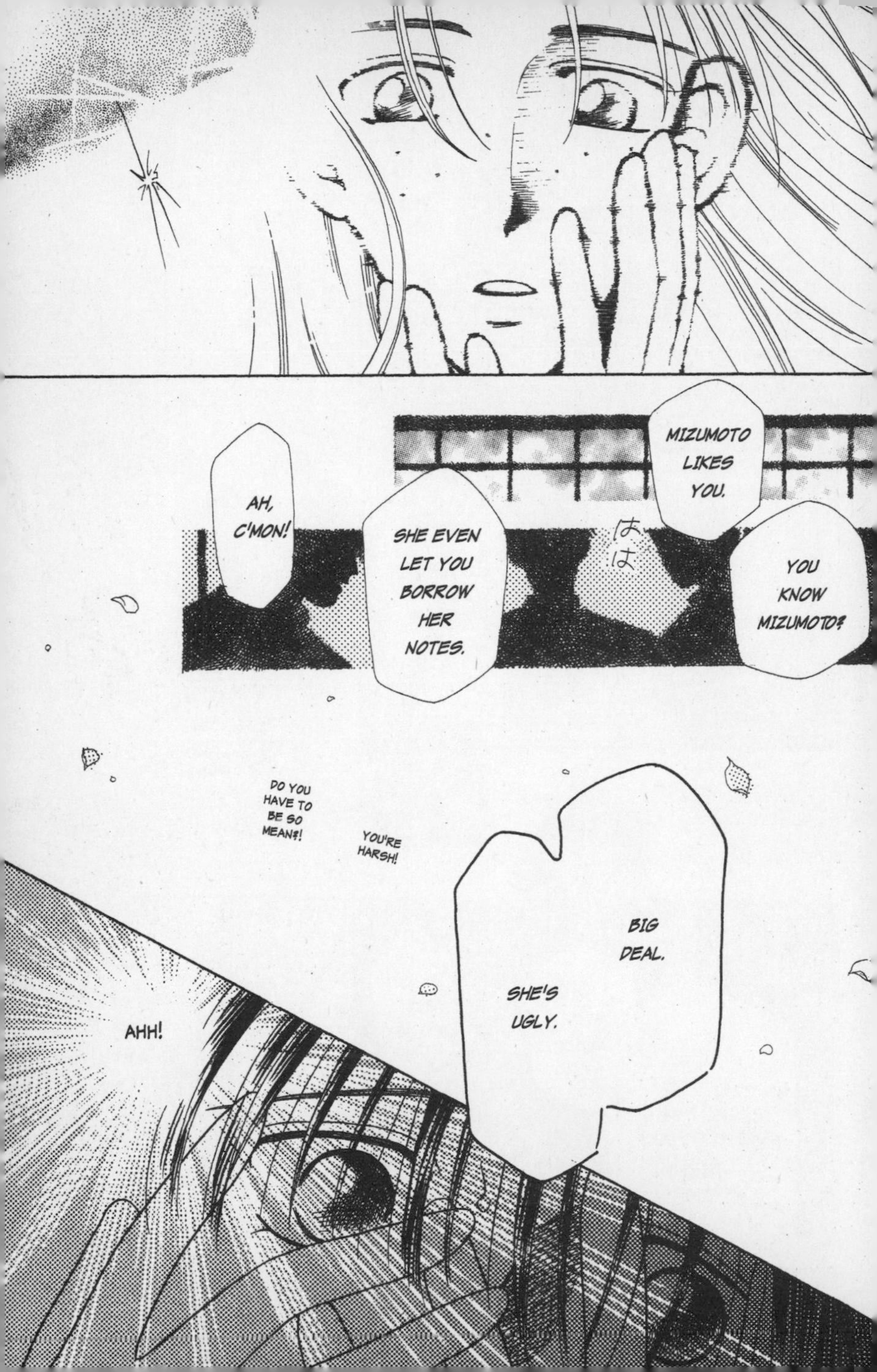
MIZUMOTO LIKES YOU.
YOU KNOW MIZUMOTO?
はは
SHE EVEN LET YOU BORROW HER NOTES.
AH, C'MON!
BIG DEAL. SHE'S UGLY.
YOU'RE HARSH!
DO YOU HAVE TO BE SO MEAN?!
AHH!

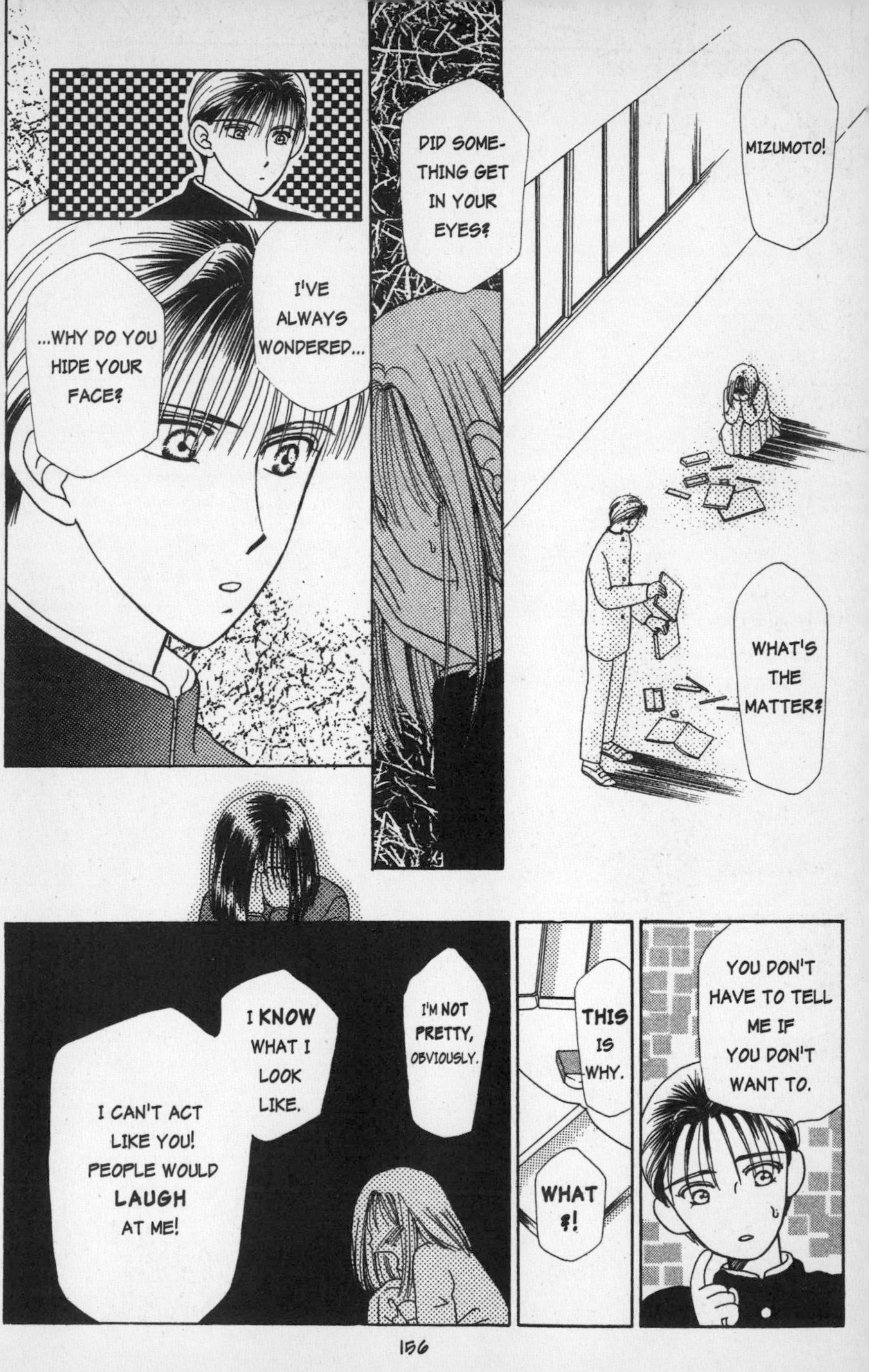
MIZUMOTO!
WHAT'S THE MATTER?
DID SOME-THING GET IN YOUR EYES?
I'VE ALWAYS WONDERED...
...WHY DO YOU HIDE YOUR FACE?
YOU DON'T HAVE TO TELL ME IF YOU DON'T WANT TO.
THIS IS WHY.
WHAT?!
I'M NOT PRETTY, OBVIOUSLY.
I KNOW WHAT I LOOK LIKE.
I CAN'T ACT LIKE YOU! PEOPLE WOULD LAUGH AT ME!

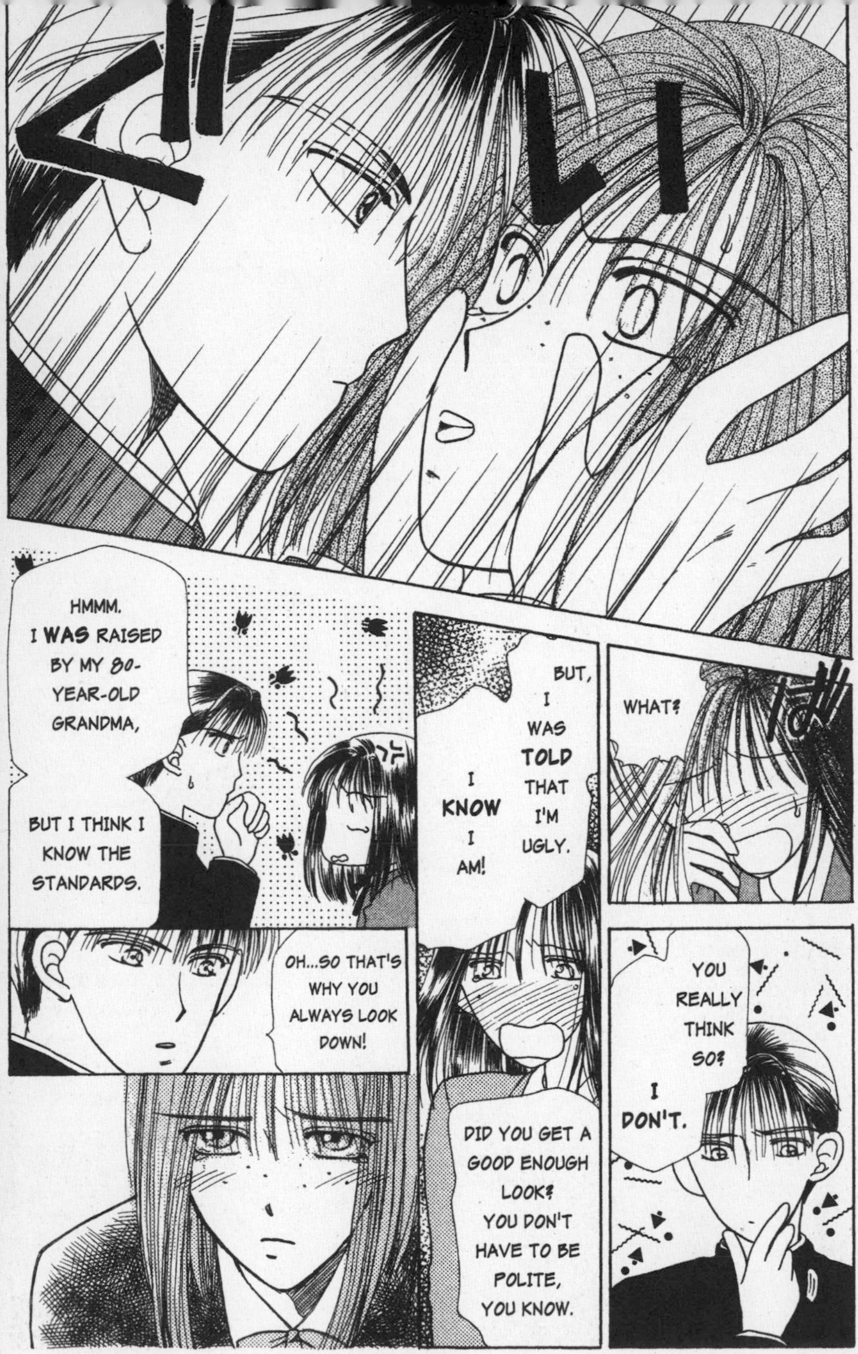
WHAT?
BUT, I WAS TOLD THAT I'M UGLY.
I KNOW I AM!
HMMM. I WAS RAISED BY MY 80-YEAR-OLD GRANDMA,
BUT I THINK I KNOW THE STANDARDS.
YOU REALLY THINK SO?
I DON'T.
OH...SO THAT'S WHY YOU ALWAYS LOOK DOWN!
DID YOU GET A GOOD ENOUGH LOOK? YOU DON'T HAVE TO BE POLITE, YOU KNOW.

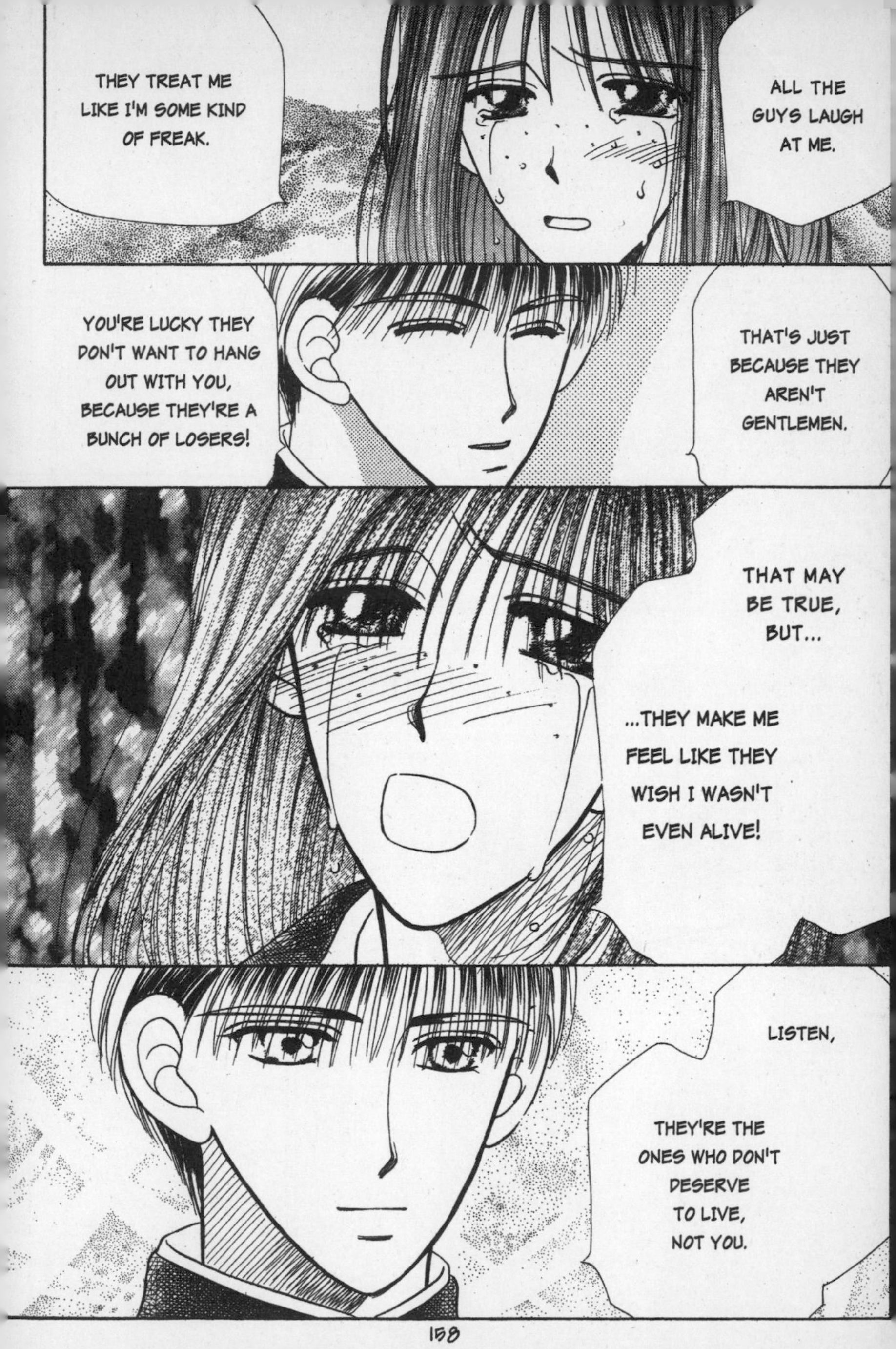
ALL THE GUYS LAUGH AT ME.
THEY TREAT ME LIKE I'M SOME KIND OF FREAK.
THAT'S JUST BECAUSE THEY AREN'T GENTLEMEN.
YOU'RE LUCKY THEY DON'T WANT TO HANG OUT WITH YOU, BECAUSE THEY'RE A BUNCH OF LOSERS!
THAT MAY BE TRUE, BUT...
...THEY MAKE ME FEEL LIKE THEY WISH I WASN'T EVEN ALIVE!
LISTEN,
THEY'RE THE ONES WHO DON'T DESERVE TO LIVE, NOT YOU.

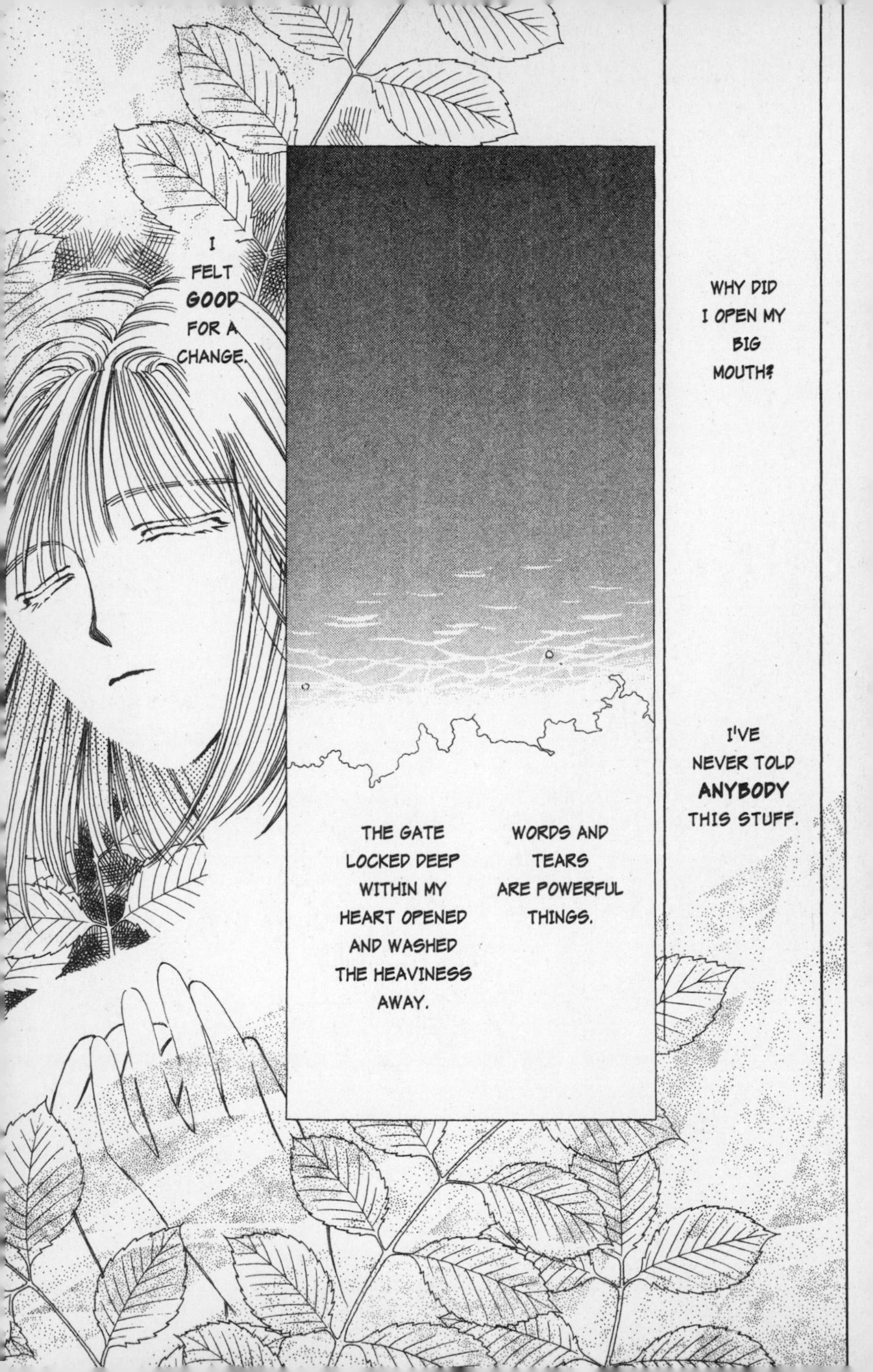
WHY DID I OPEN MY BIG MOUTH?
I'VE NEVER TOLD ANYBODY THIS STUFF.
I FELT GOOD FOR A CHANGE.
THE GATE LOCKED DEEP WITHIN MY HEART OPENED AND WASHED THE HEAVINESS AWAY.
WORDS AND TEARS ARE POWERFUL THINGS.

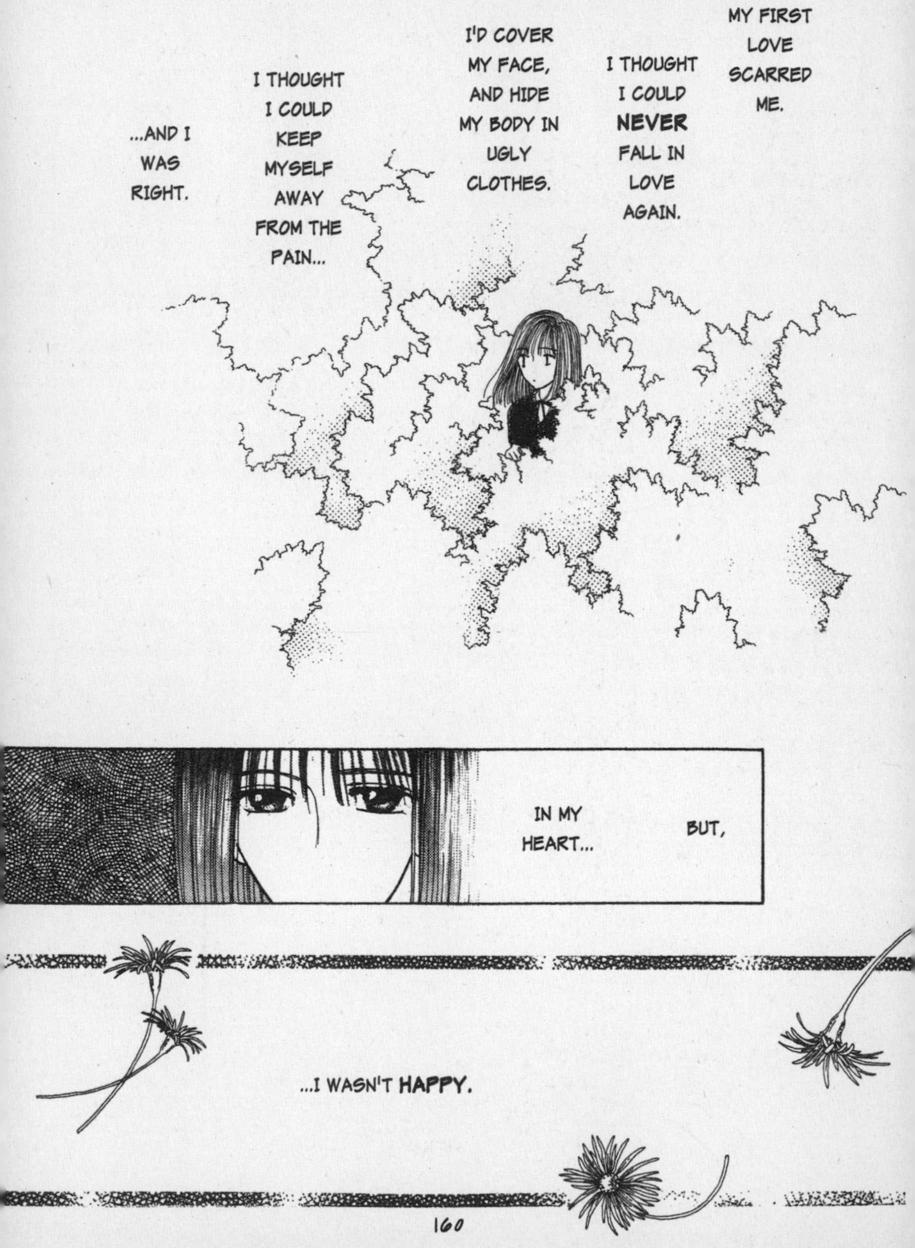
MY FIRST LOVE SCARRED ME.
I THOUGHT I COULD **NEVER** FALL IN LOVE AGAIN.
I'D COVER MY FACE, AND HIDE MY BODY IN UGLY CLOTHES.
I THOUGHT I COULD KEEP MYSELF AWAY FROM THE PAIN...
...AND I WAS RIGHT.
BUT,
IN MY HEART...
...I WASN'T **HAPPY**.

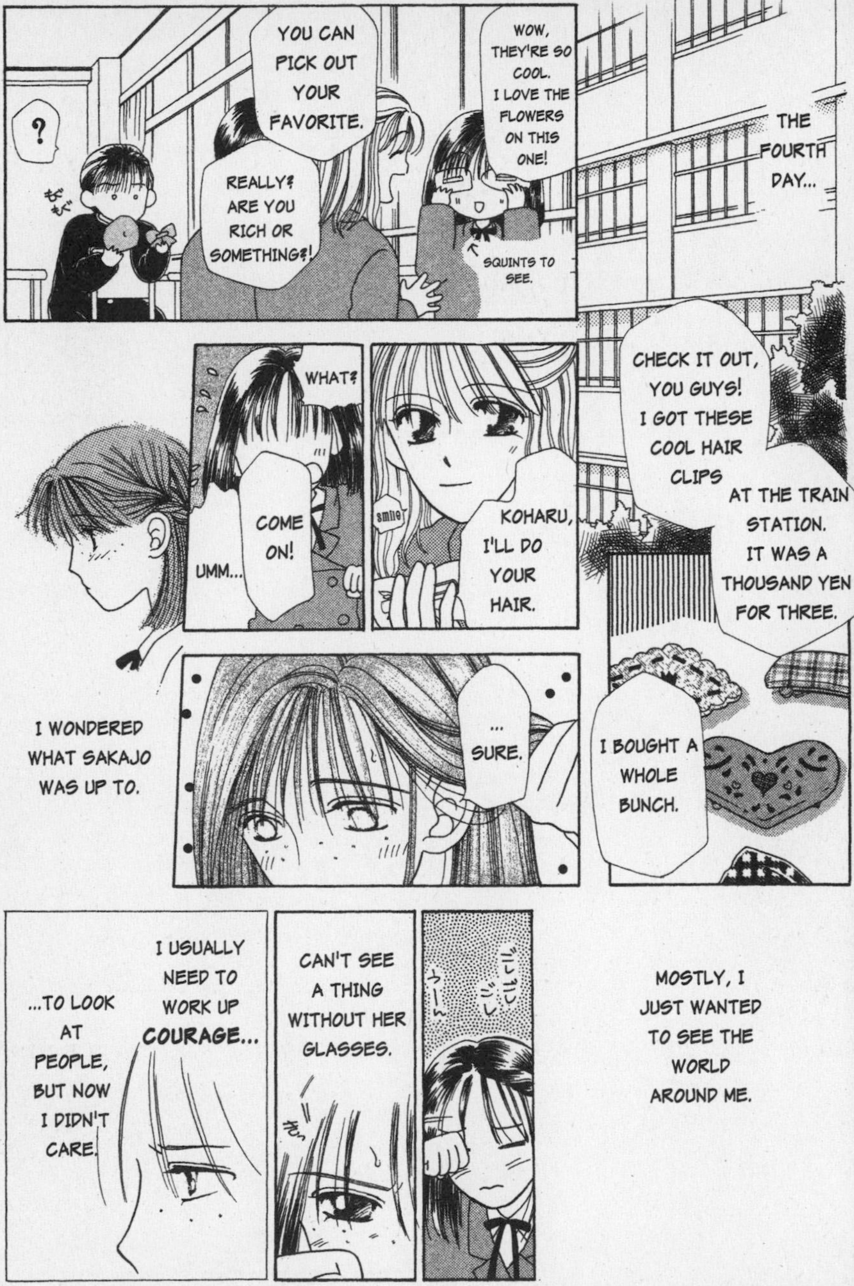
THE FOURTH DAY...
CHECK IT OUT, YOU GUYS! I GOT THESE COOL HAIR CLIPS
AT THE TRAIN STATION. IT WAS A THOUSAND YEN FOR THREE.
I BOUGHT A WHOLE BUNCH.
WOW, THEY'RE SO COOL. I LOVE THE FLOWERS ON THIS ONE!
SQUINTS TO SEE.
YOU CAN PICK OUT YOUR FAVORITE.
REALLY? ARE YOU RICH OR SOMETHING?!
?
もぐもぐ
KOHARU, I'LL DO YOUR HAIR.
smile
WHAT?
COME ON!
UMM...
I WONDERED WHAT SAKAJO WAS UP TO.
... SURE.
MOSTLY, I JUST WANTED TO SEE THE WORLD AROUND ME.
ごしごし
うーん
CAN'T SEE A THING WITHOUT HER GLASSES.
I USUALLY NEED TO WORK UP COURAGE...
...TO LOOK AT PEOPLE, BUT NOW I DIDN'T CARE.

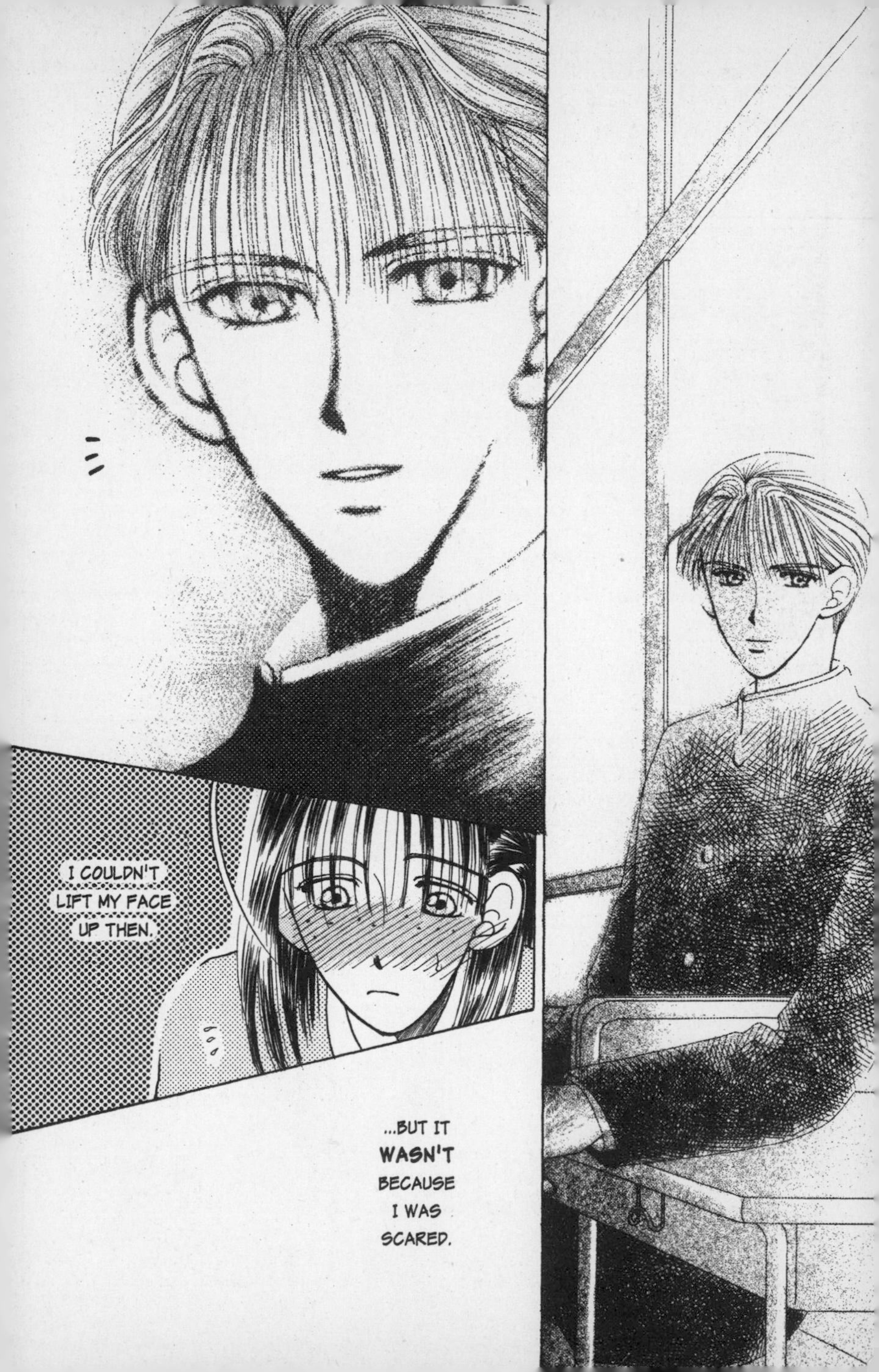
I COULDN'T LIFT MY FACE UP THEN.
...BUT IT WASN'T BECAUSE I WAS SCARED.

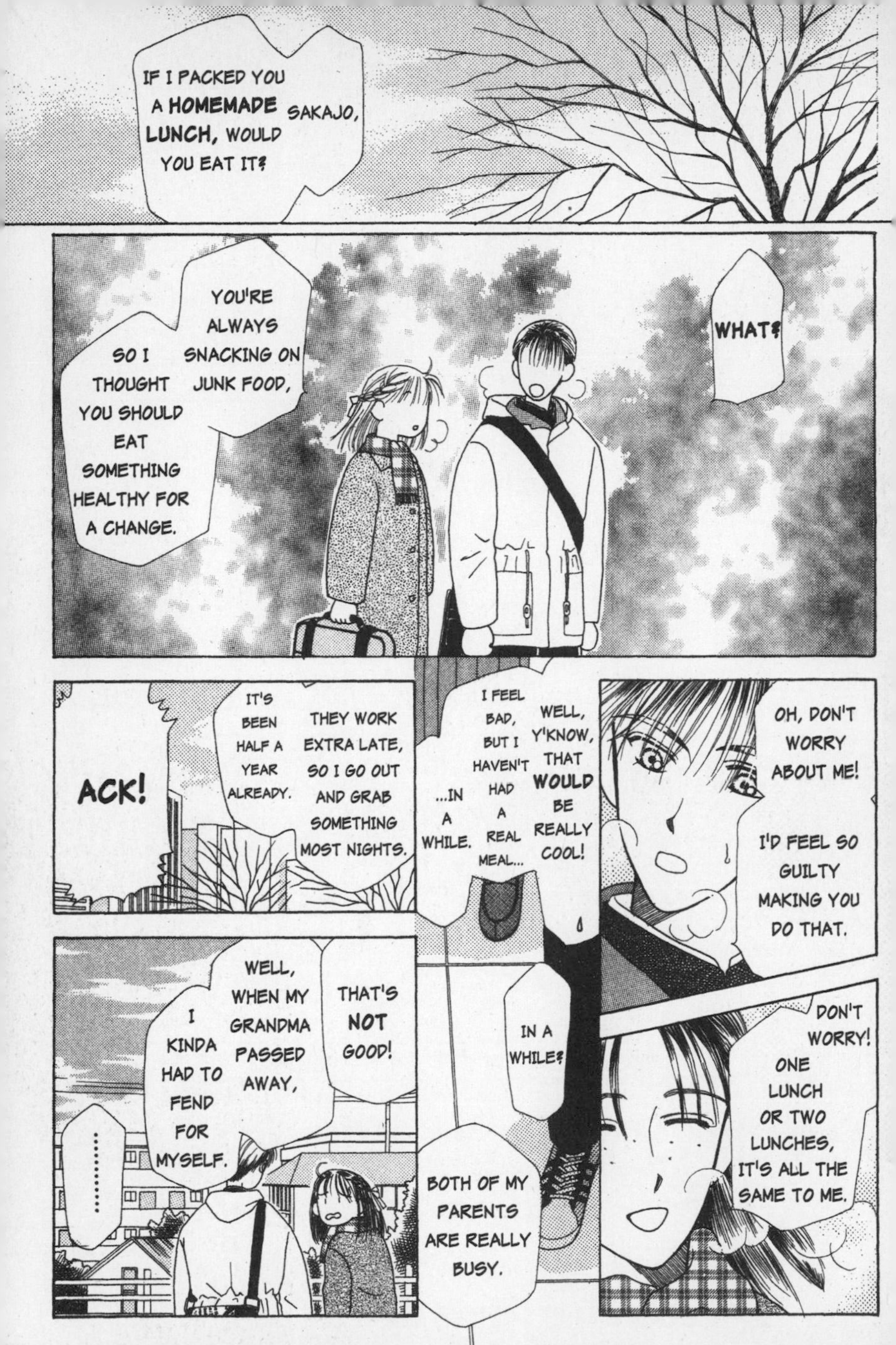
SAKAJO, IF I PACKED YOU A **HOMEMADE LUNCH**, WOULD YOU EAT IT?
WHAT?
YOU'RE ALWAYS SNACKING ON JUNK FOOD,
SO I THOUGHT YOU SHOULD EAT SOMETHING HEALTHY FOR A CHANGE.
OH, DON'T WORRY ABOUT ME!
I'D FEEL SO GUILTY MAKING YOU DO THAT.
DON'T WORRY!
ONE LUNCH OR TWO LUNCHES, IT'S ALL THE SAME TO ME.
WELL, Y'KNOW, THAT **WOULD** BE REALLY COOL!
I FEEL BAD, BUT I HAVEN'T HAD A REAL MEAL...
...IN A WHILE.
IN A WHILE?
BOTH OF MY PARENTS ARE REALLY BUSY.
THEY WORK EXTRA LATE, SO I GO OUT AND GRAB SOMETHING MOST NIGHTS.
IT'S BEEN HALF A YEAR ALREADY.
ACK!
THAT'S **NOT** GOOD!
WELL, WHEN MY GRANDMA PASSED AWAY,
I KINDA HAD TO FEND FOR MYSELF.
......

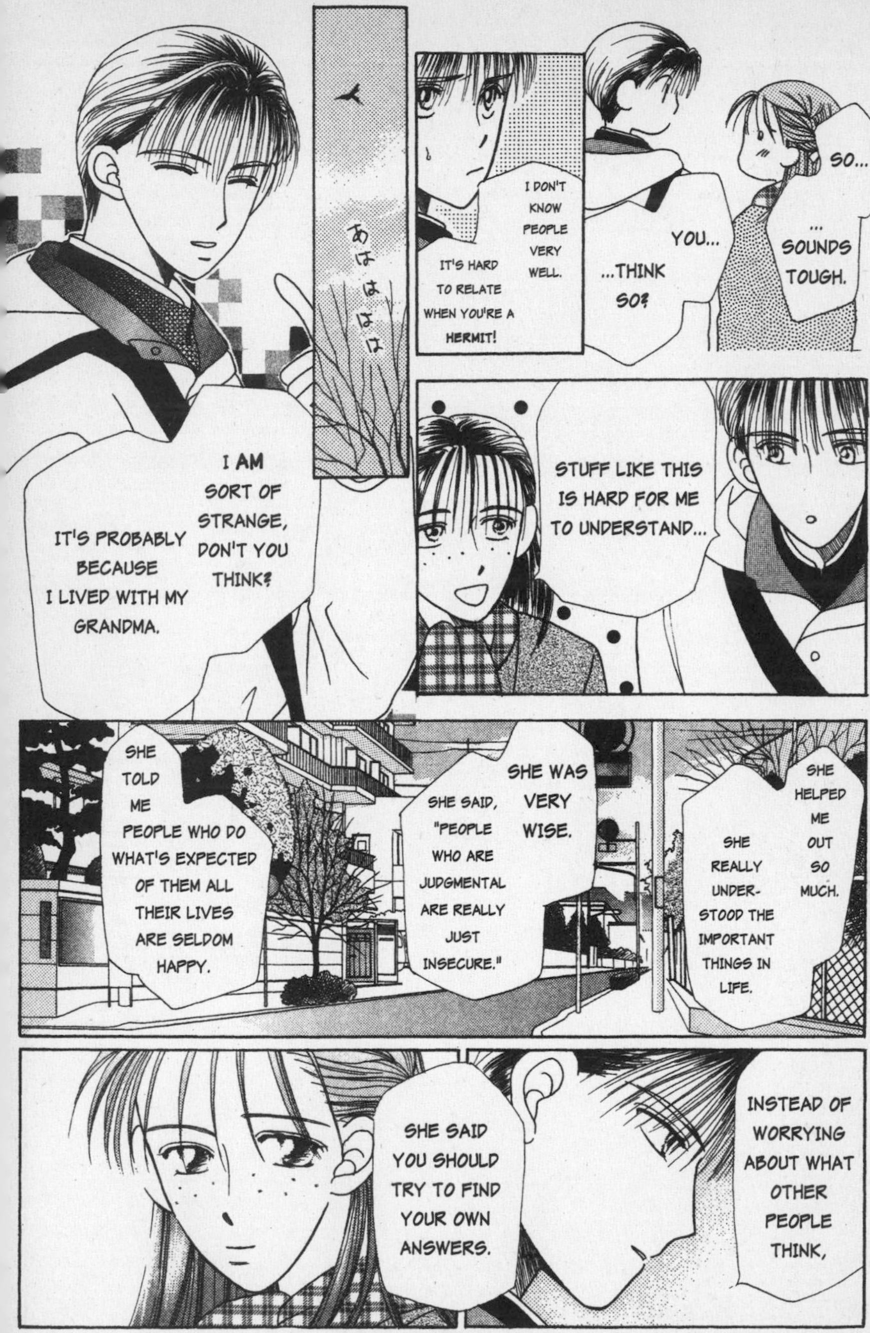
SO... ...SOUNDS TOUGH.
YOU... ...THINK SO?
I DON'T KNOW PEOPLE VERY WELL.
IT'S HARD TO RELATE WHEN YOU'RE A HERMIT!
あははは
STUFF LIKE THIS IS HARD FOR ME TO UNDERSTAND...
I AM SORT OF STRANGE, DON'T YOU THINK?
IT'S PROBABLY BECAUSE I LIVED WITH MY GRANDMA.
SHE HELPED ME OUT SO MUCH.
SHE REALLY UNDER-STOOD THE IMPORTANT THINGS IN LIFE.
SHE WAS VERY WISE.
SHE SAID, "PEOPLE WHO ARE JUDGMENTAL ARE REALLY JUST INSECURE."
SHE TOLD ME PEOPLE WHO DO WHAT'S EXPECTED OF THEM ALL THEIR LIVES ARE SELDOM HAPPY.
INSTEAD OF WORRYING ABOUT WHAT OTHER PEOPLE THINK,
SHE SAID YOU SHOULD TRY TO FIND YOUR OWN ANSWERS.

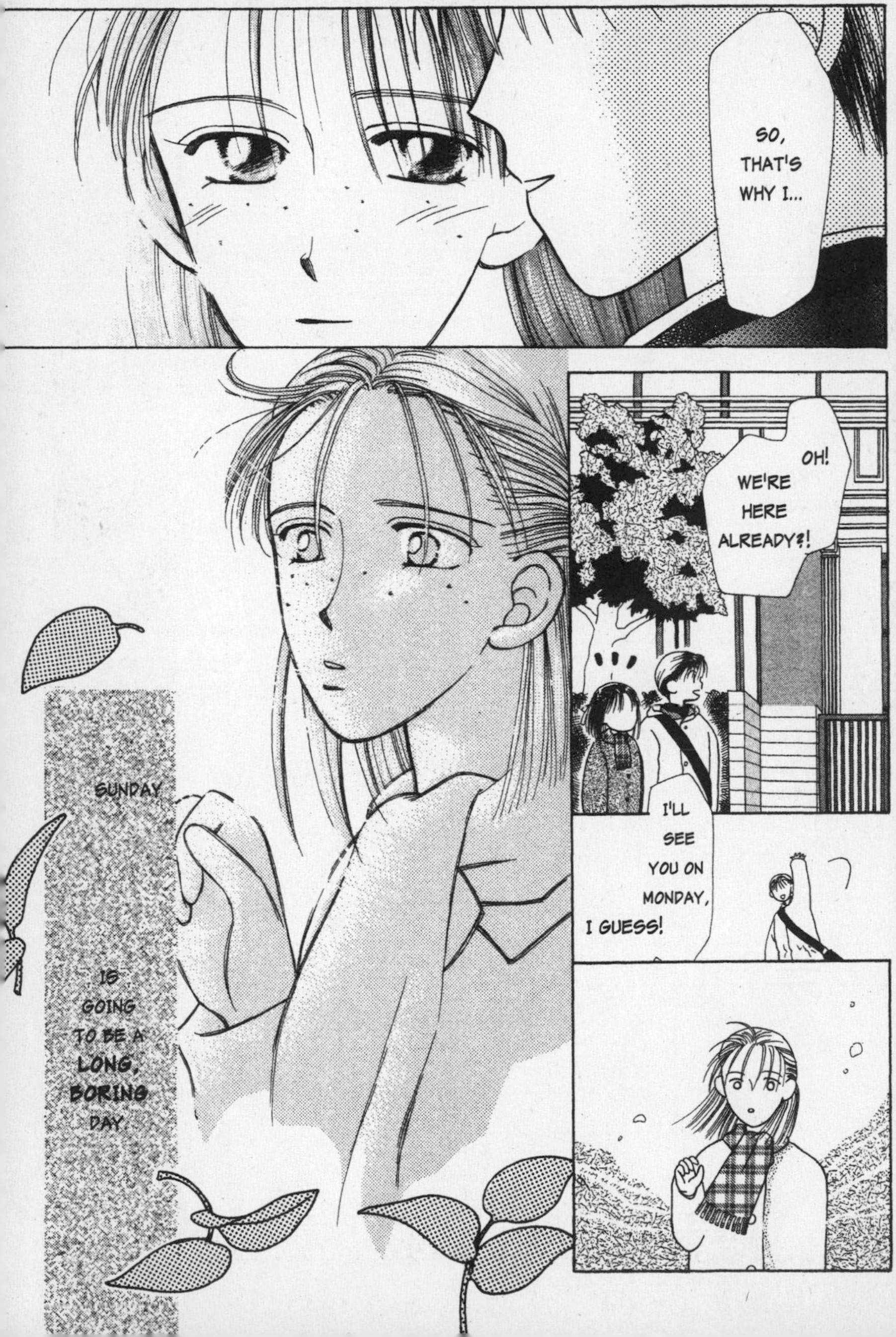
SO, THAT'S WHY I...
OH! WE'RE HERE ALREADY?!
I'LL SEE YOU ON MONDAY, I GUESS!
SUNDAY
IS GOING TO BE A LONG, BORING DAY.

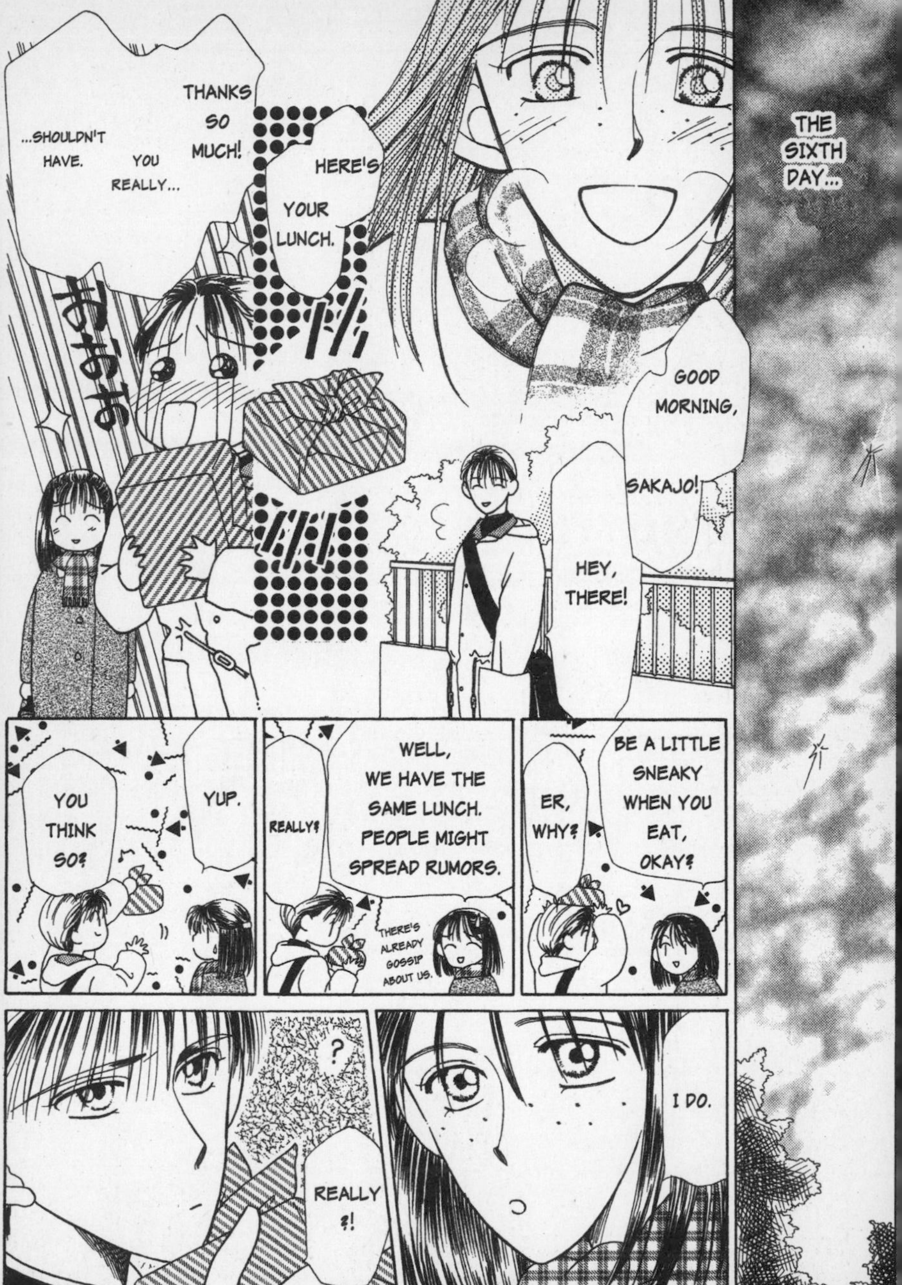
THE SIXTH DAY...
GOOD MORNING, SAKAJO!
HEY, THERE!
HERE'S YOUR LUNCH.
THANKS SO MUCH!
YOU REALLY... ...SHOULDN'T HAVE.
おおお
BE A LITTLE SNEAKY WHEN YOU EAT, OKAY?
ER, WHY?
WELL, WE HAVE THE SAME LUNCH. PEOPLE MIGHT SPREAD RUMORS.
REALLY?
THERE'S ALREADY GOSSIP ABOUT US.
YUP.
YOU THINK SO?
I DO.
?
REALLY?!

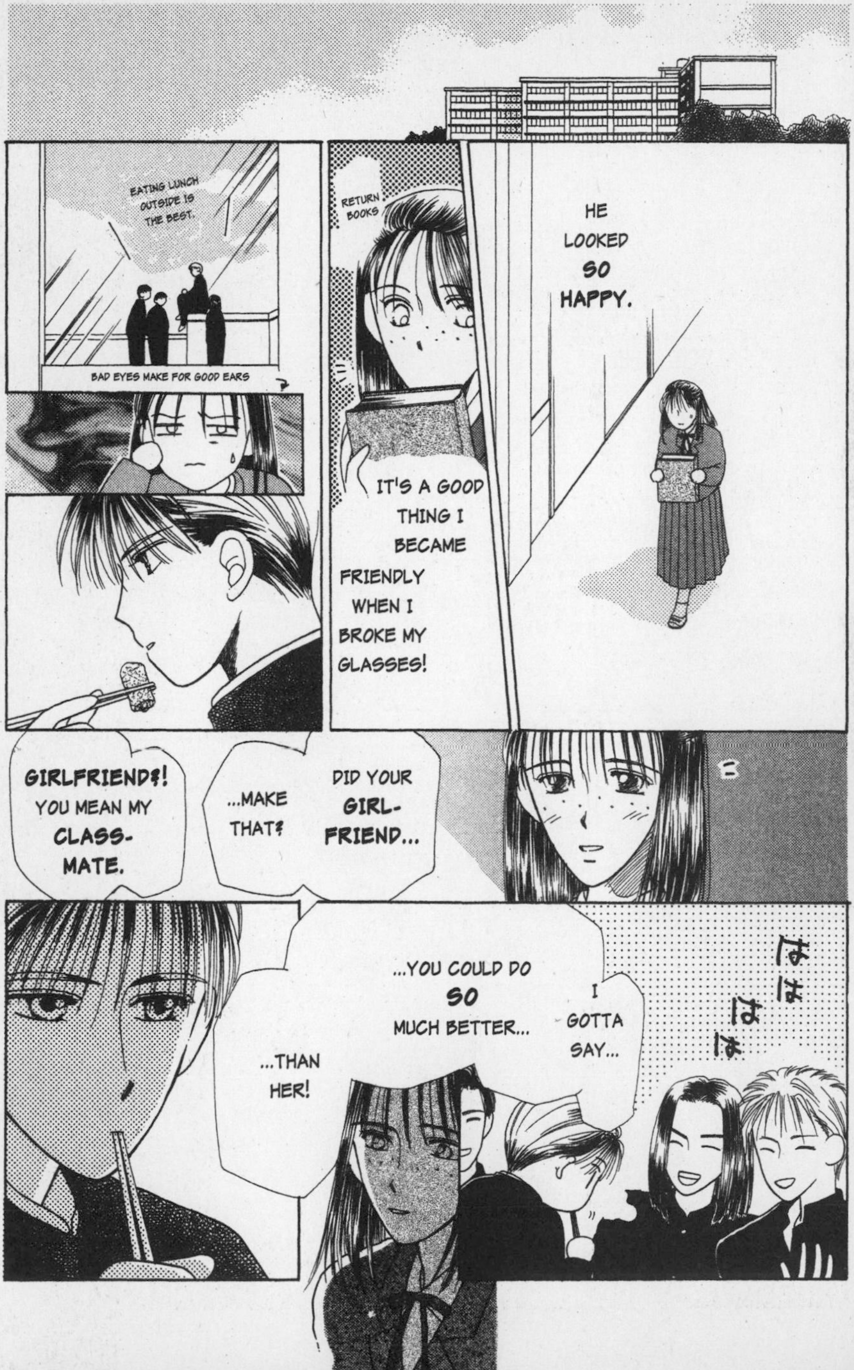
HE LOOKED SO HAPPY.
RETURN BOOKS
IT'S A GOOD THING I BECAME FRIENDLY WHEN I BROKE MY GLASSES!
EATING LUNCH OUTSIDE IS THE BEST.
BAD EYES MAKE FOR GOOD EARS
DID YOUR GIRL-FRIEND...
...MAKE THAT?
GIRLFRIEND?! YOU MEAN MY CLASS-MATE.
ははははは
I GOTTA SAY...
...YOU COULD DO SO MUCH BETTER...
...THAN HER!

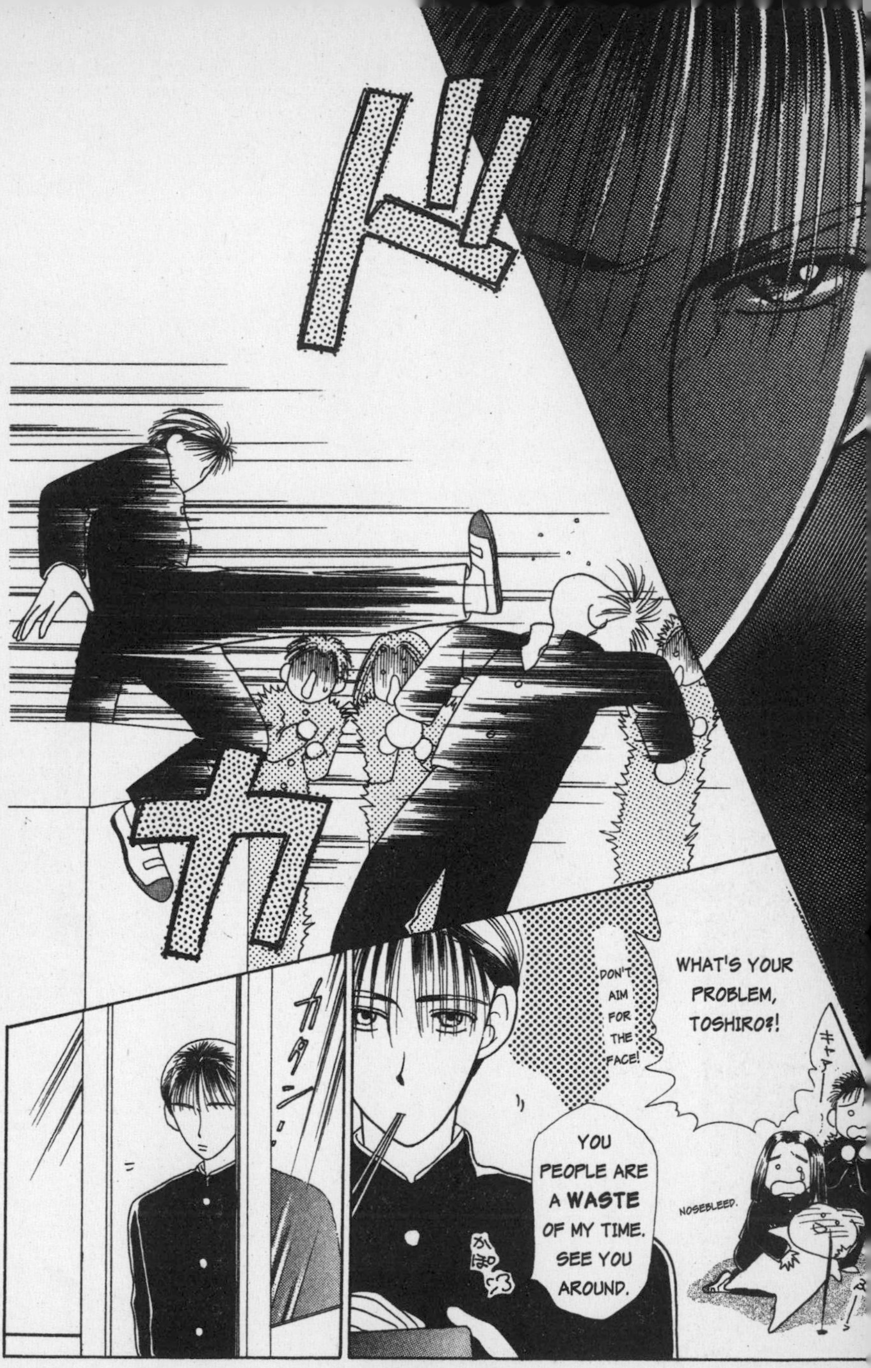
WHAT'S YOUR PROBLEM, TOSHIRO?!
DON'T AIM FOR THE FACE!
NOSEBLEED.
YOU PEOPLE ARE A WASTE OF MY TIME. SEE YOU AROUND.

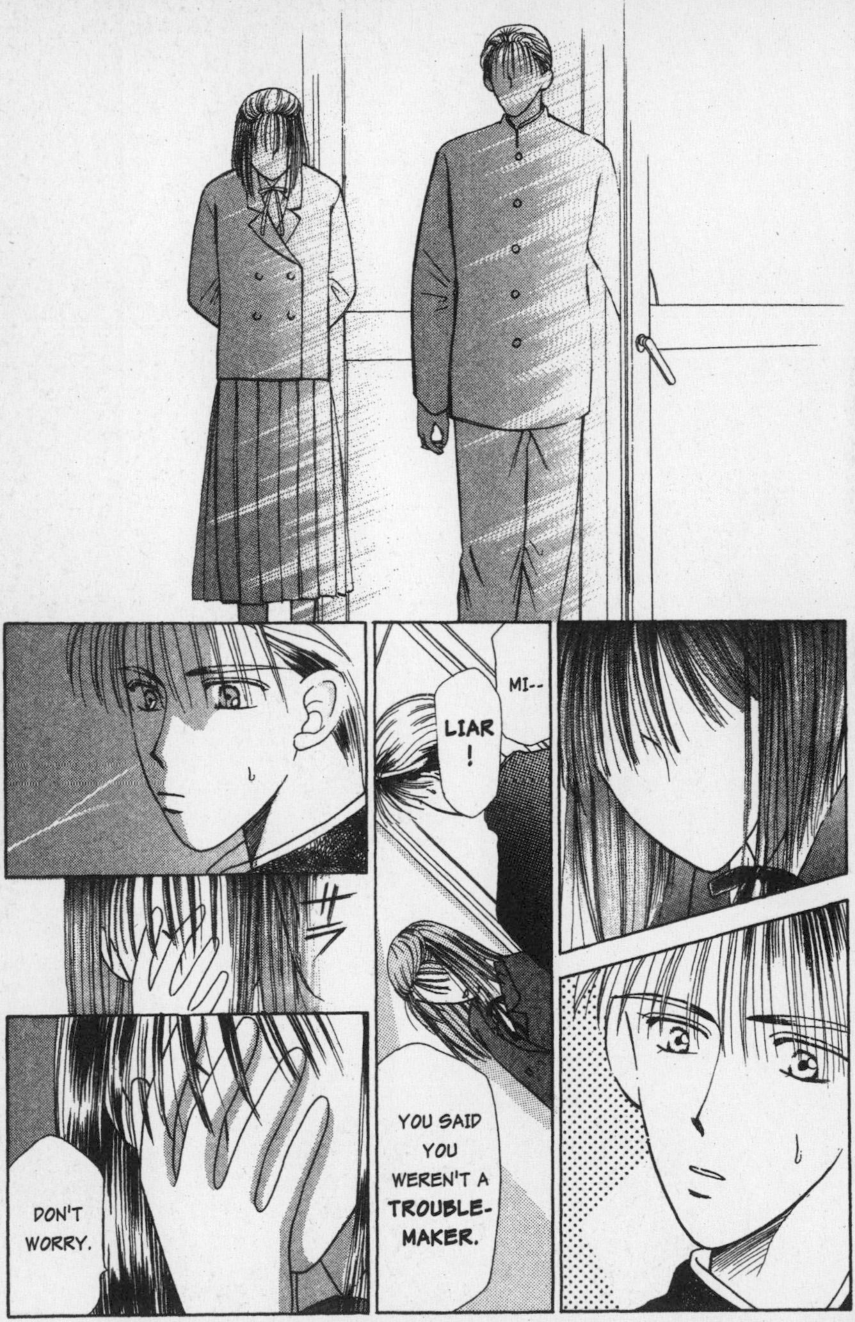
MI--
LIAR!
YOU SAID YOU WEREN'T A TROUBLE-MAKER.
DON'T WORRY.

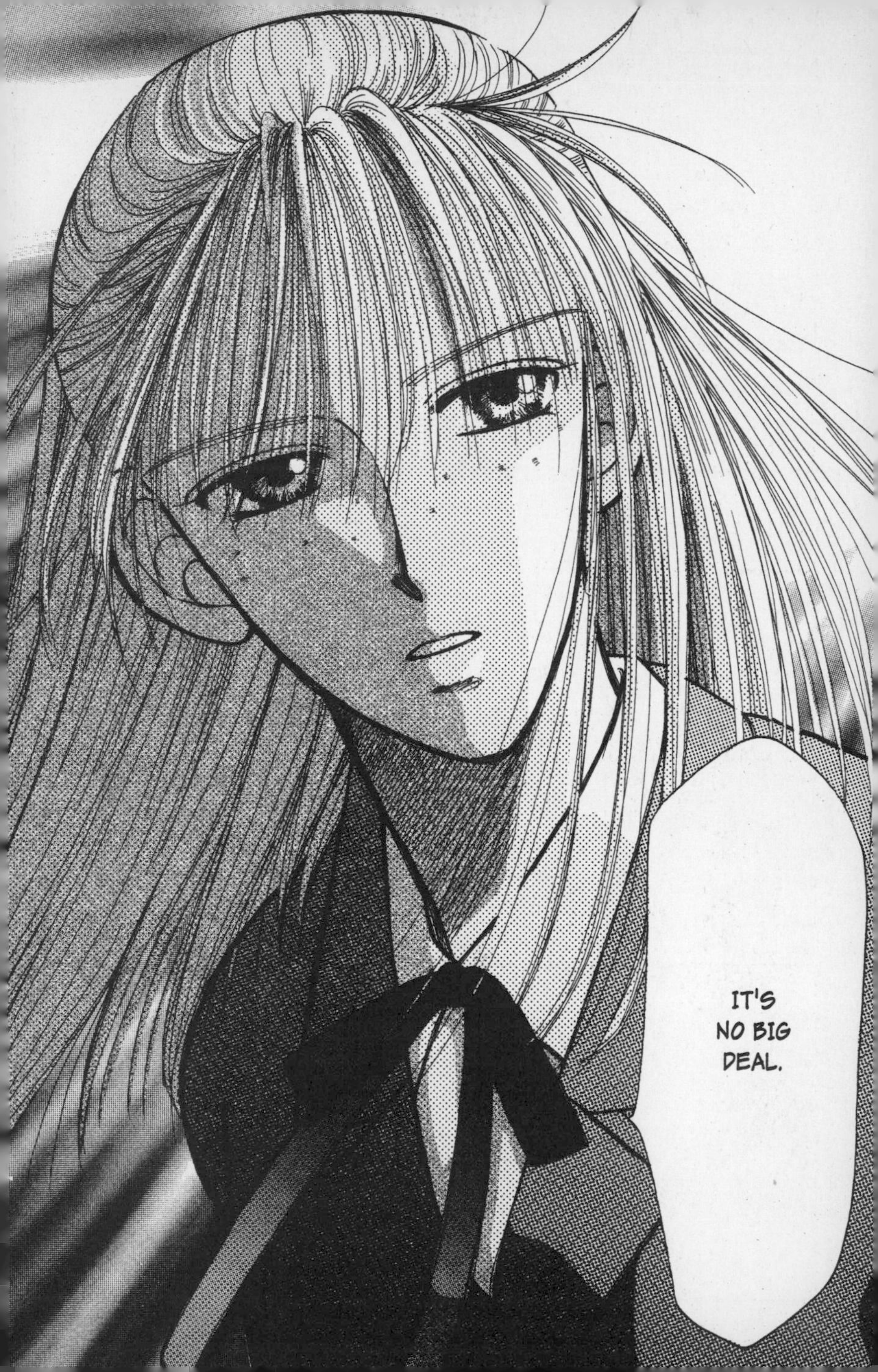
IT'S NO BIG DEAL.

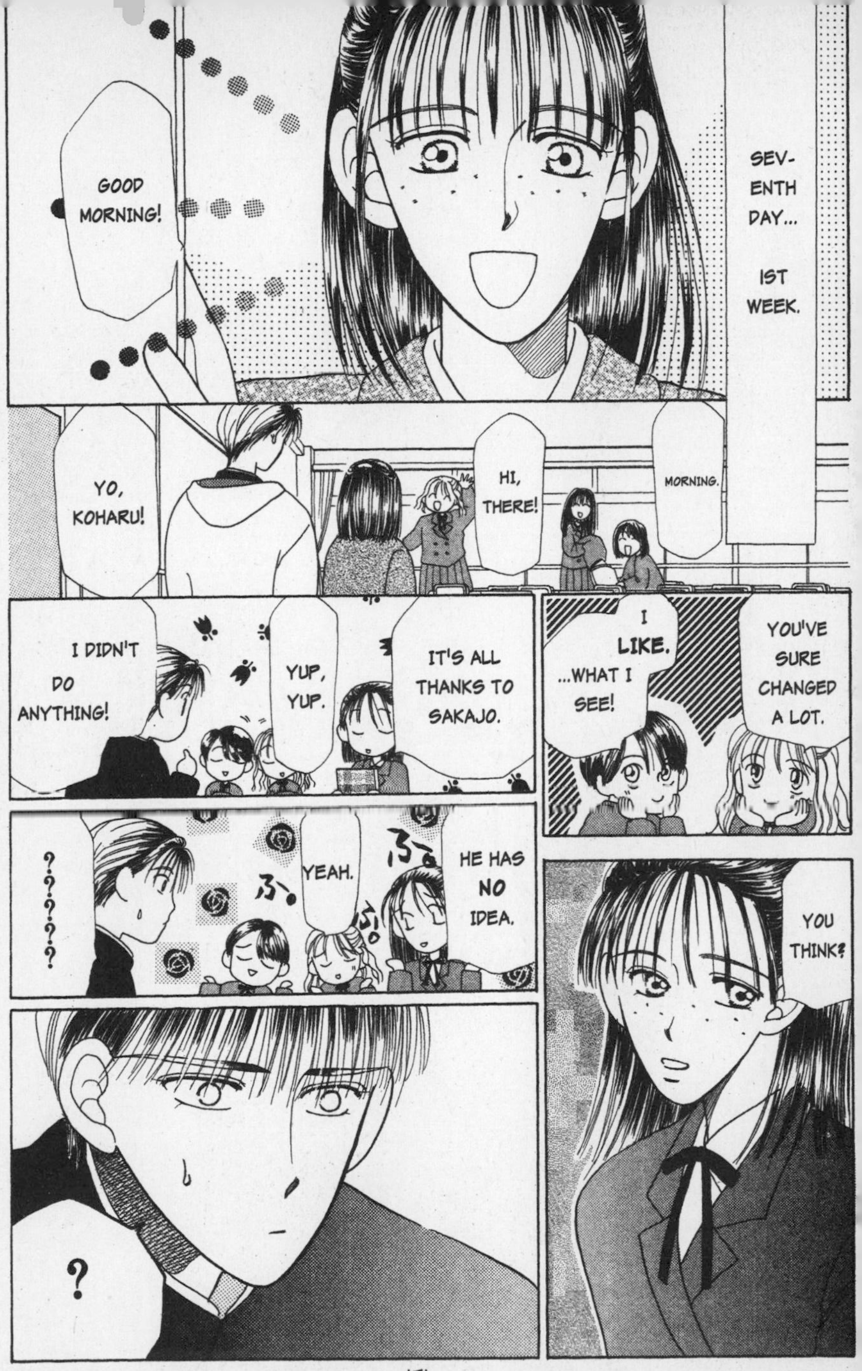
SEVENTH DAY...
1ST WEEK.
GOOD MORNING!
MORNING.
HI, THERE!
YO, KOHARU!
YOU'VE SURE CHANGED A LOT.
I LIKE... WHAT I SEE!
IT'S ALL THANKS TO SAKAJO.
YUP, YUP.
I DIDN'T DO ANYTHING!
YOU THINK?
HE HAS NO IDEA.
ふふ
YEAH.
ふ
ふ
?????
?

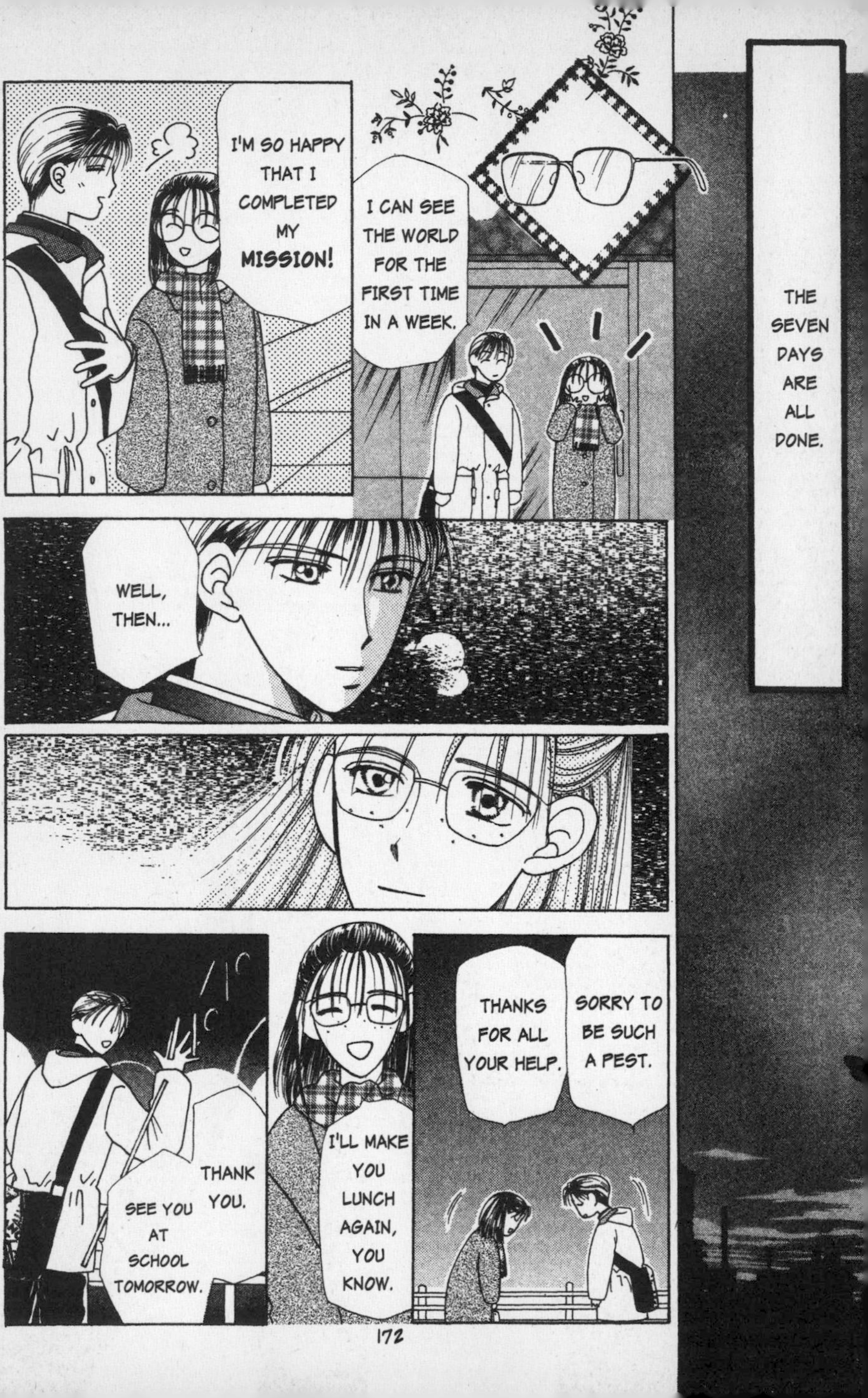
THE SEVEN DAYS ARE ALL DONE.
I CAN SEE THE WORLD FOR THE FIRST TIME IN A WEEK.
I'M SO HAPPY THAT I COMPLETED MY **MISSION!**
WELL, THEN...
SORRY TO BE SUCH A PEST.
THANKS FOR ALL YOUR HELP.
I'LL MAKE YOU LUNCH AGAIN, YOU KNOW.
THANK YOU.
SEE YOU AT SCHOOL TOMORROW.

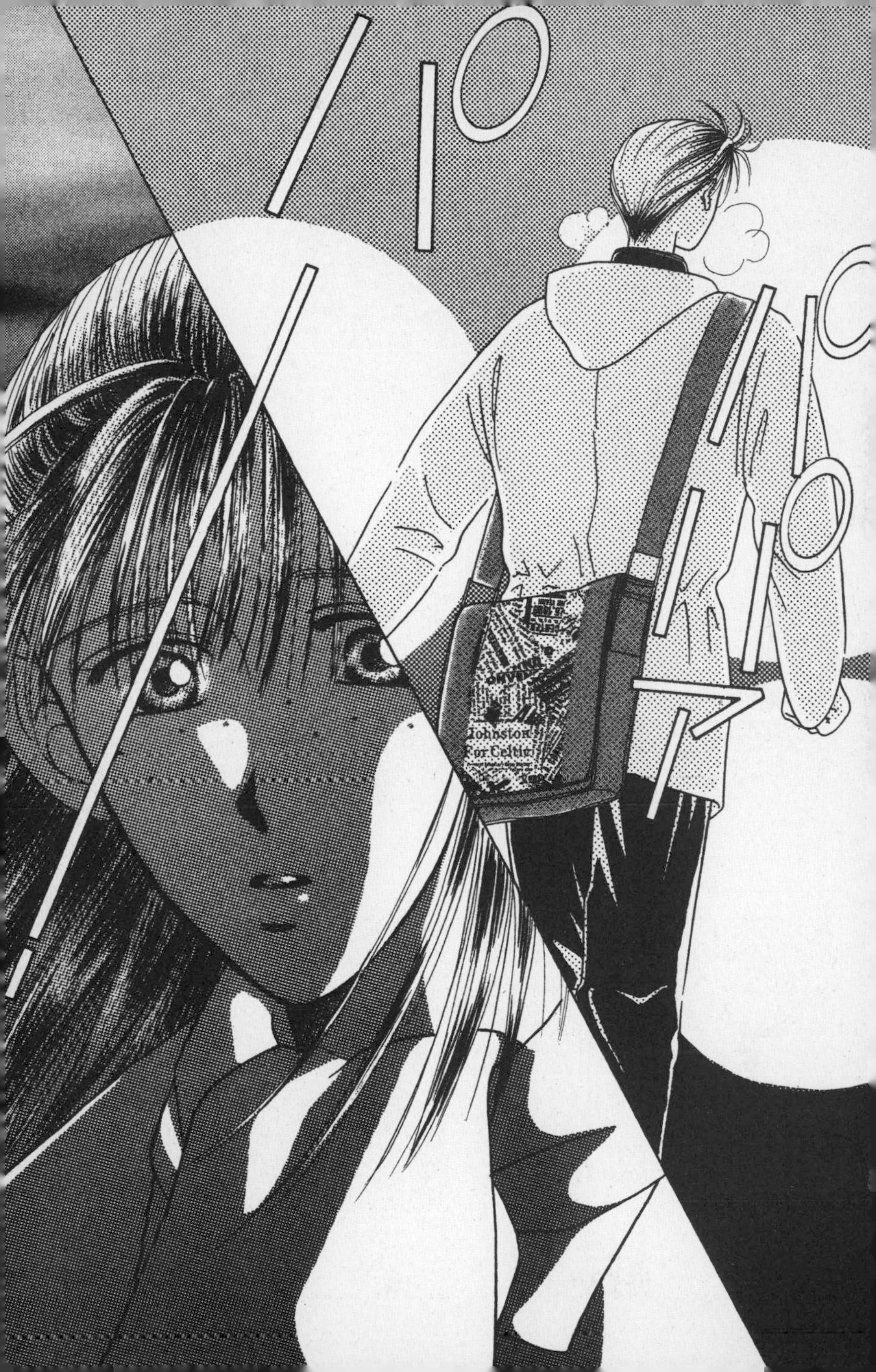
Johnston
For Celtic

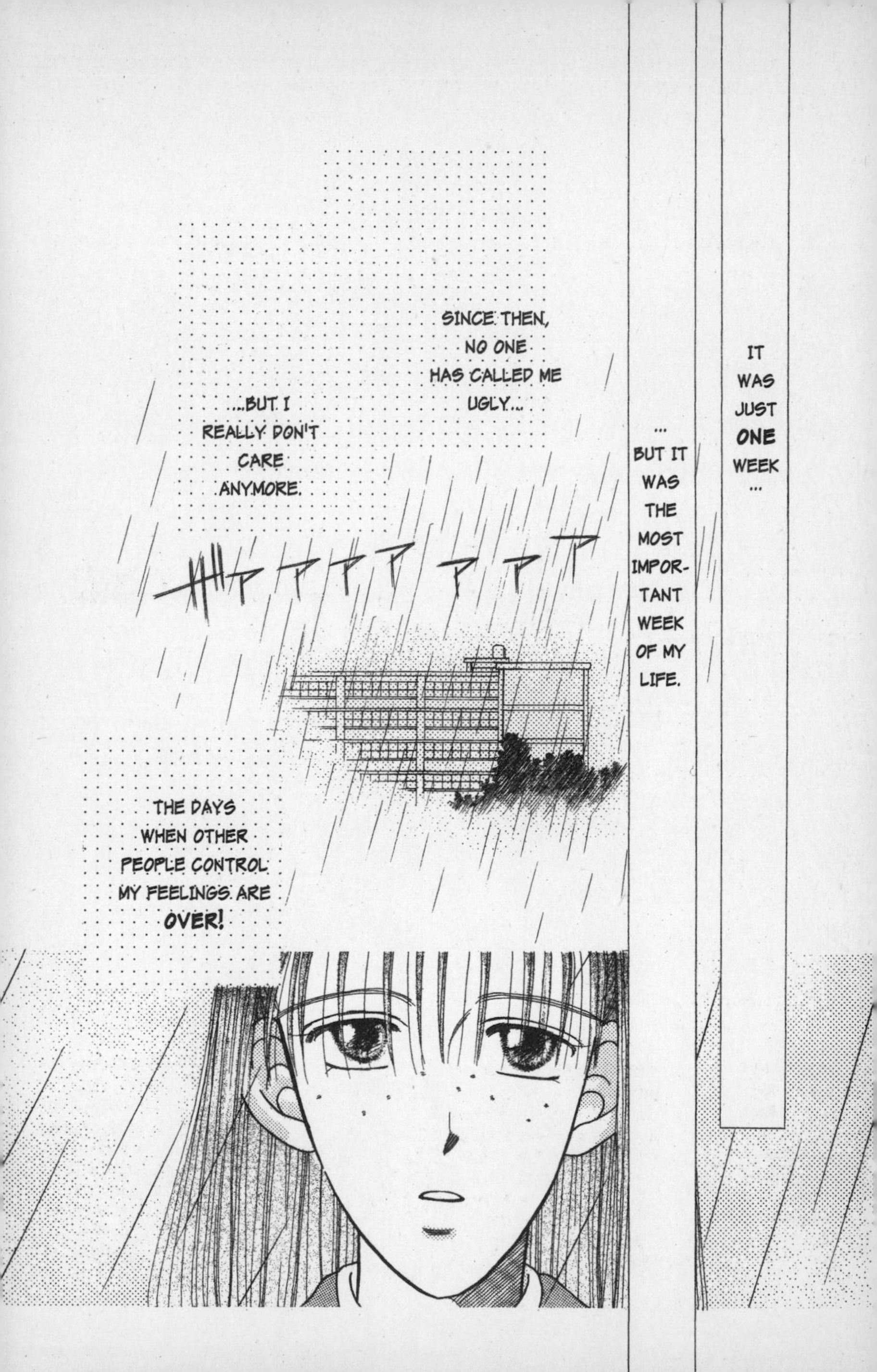
IT WAS JUST ONE WEEK ...
... BUT IT WAS THE MOST IMPOR-TANT WEEK OF MY LIFE.
SINCE THEN, NO ONE HAS CALLED ME UGLY...
...BUT I REALLY DON'T CARE ANYMORE.
THE DAYS WHEN OTHER PEOPLE CONTROL MY FEELINGS ARE OVER!

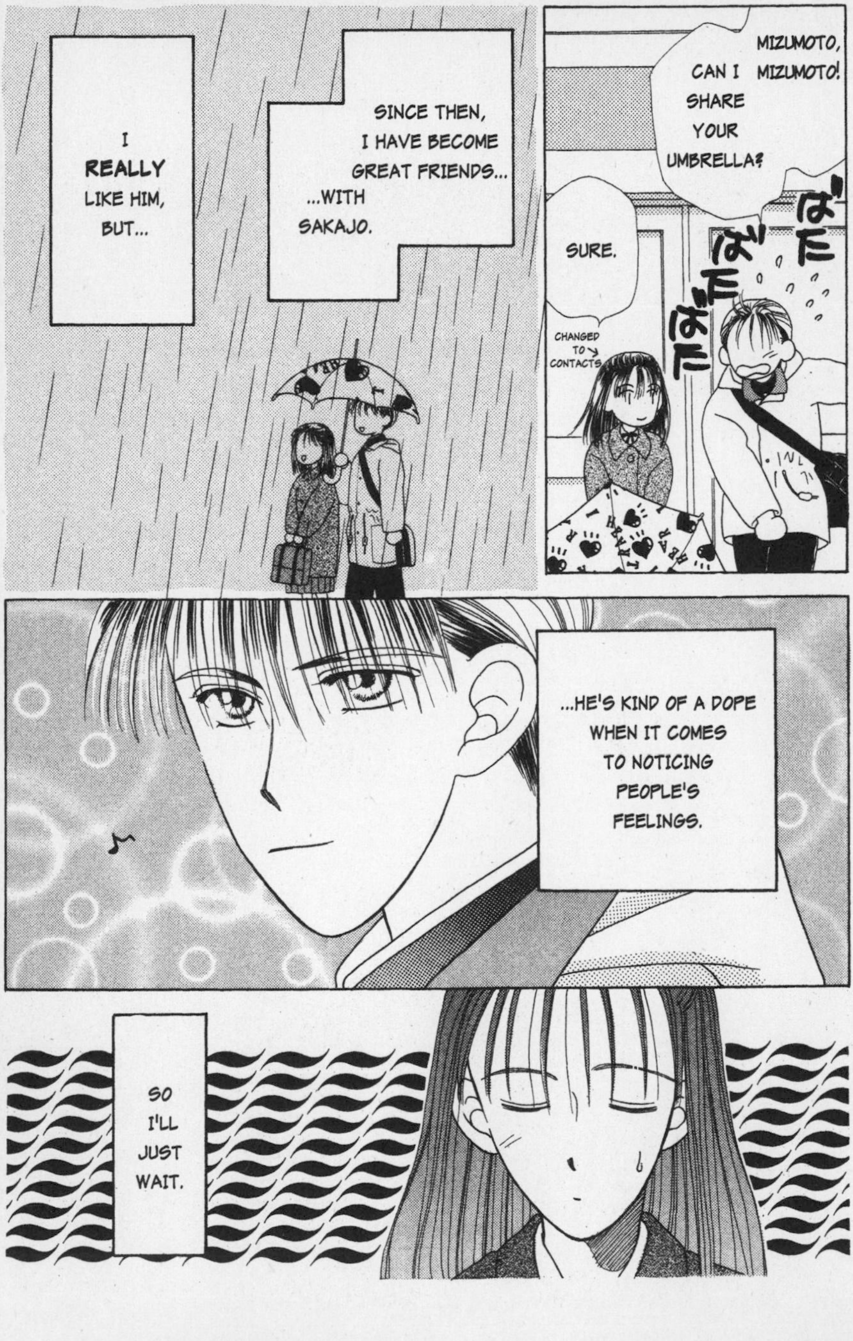
MIZUMOTO, MIZUMOTO!
CAN I SHARE YOUR UMBRELLA?
ばた ばた ばた
SURE.
CHANGED TO CONTACTS
SINCE THEN, I HAVE BECOME GREAT FRIENDS... ...WITH SAKAJO.
I REALLY LIKE HIM, BUT...
...HE'S KIND OF A DOPE WHEN IT COMES TO NOTICING PEOPLE'S FEELINGS.
SO I'LL JUST WAIT.

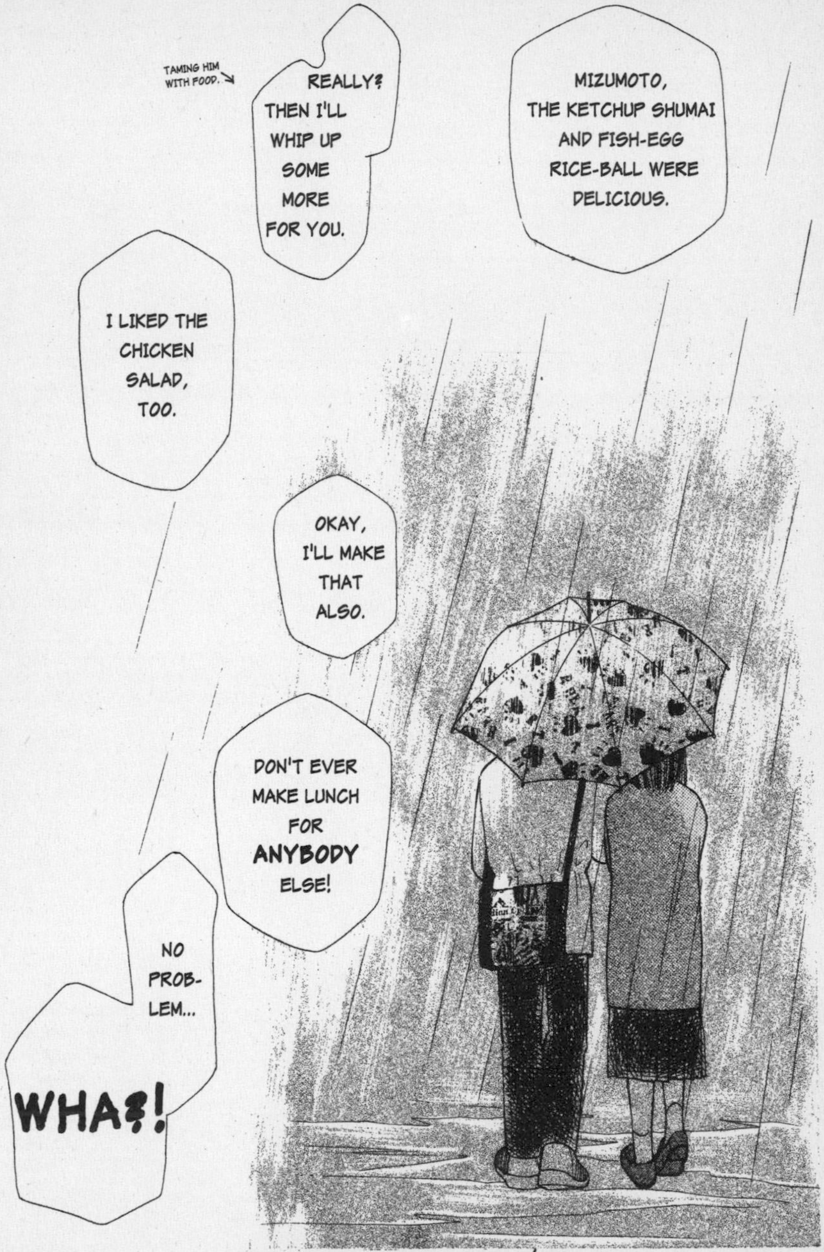
MIZUMOTO, THE KETCHUP SHUMAI AND FISH-EGG RICE-BALL WERE DELICIOUS.
TAMING HIM WITH FOOD.
REALLY? THEN I'LL WHIP UP SOME MORE FOR YOU.
I LIKED THE CHICKEN SALAD, TOO.
OKAY, I'LL MAKE THAT ALSO.
DON'T EVER MAKE LUNCH FOR ANYBODY ELSE!
NO PROB-LEM...
WHA?!

THE TIGER AND THE CHAMELEON / THE END

TSUDA DIARY

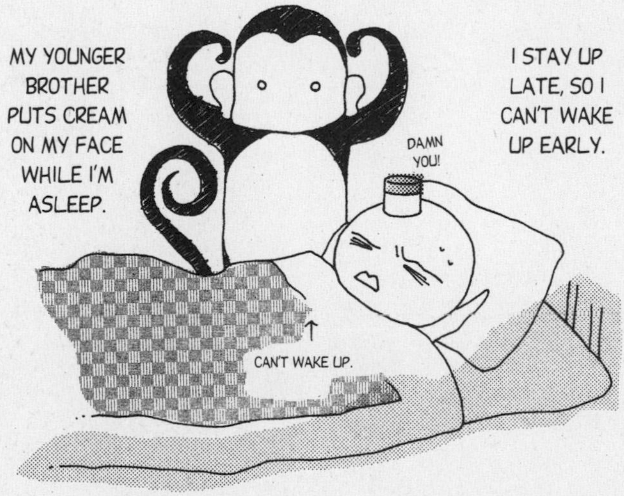

I STAY UP LATE, SO I CAN'T WAKE UP EARLY.
MY YOUNGER BROTHER PUTS CREAM ON MY FACE WHILE I'M ASLEEP.
DAMN YOU!
CAN'T WAKE UP.

WHAT THE ASSISTANTS LEARN FROM ME:

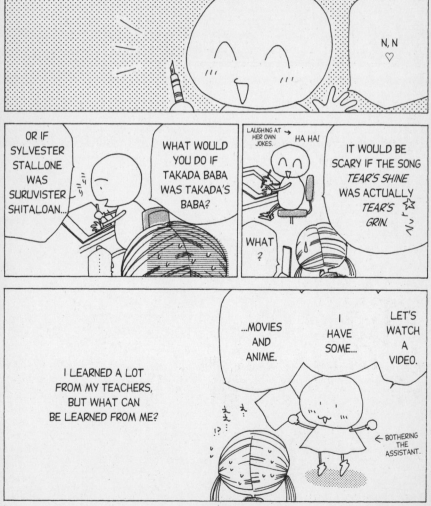

N, N ♡
IT WOULD BE SCARY IF THE SONG *TEAR'S SHINE* WAS ACTUALLY *TEAR'S GRIN.*
HA HA!
LAUGHING AT HER OWN JOKES.
WHAT?
WHAT WOULD YOU DO IF TAKADA BABA WAS TAKADA'S BABA?
OR IF SYLVESTER STALLONE WAS SURUVISTER SHITALOAN...
LET'S WATCH A VIDEO.
I HAVE SOME...
...MOVIES AND ANIME.
BOTHERING THE ASSISTANT.
I LEARNED A LOT FROM MY TEACHERS, BUT WHAT CAN BE LEARNED FROM ME?

THE MANAGER AND THE ARTIST... THESE TWO WILL GO TO GREAT LENGTHS TO CREATE A FABULOUS ARTICLE.

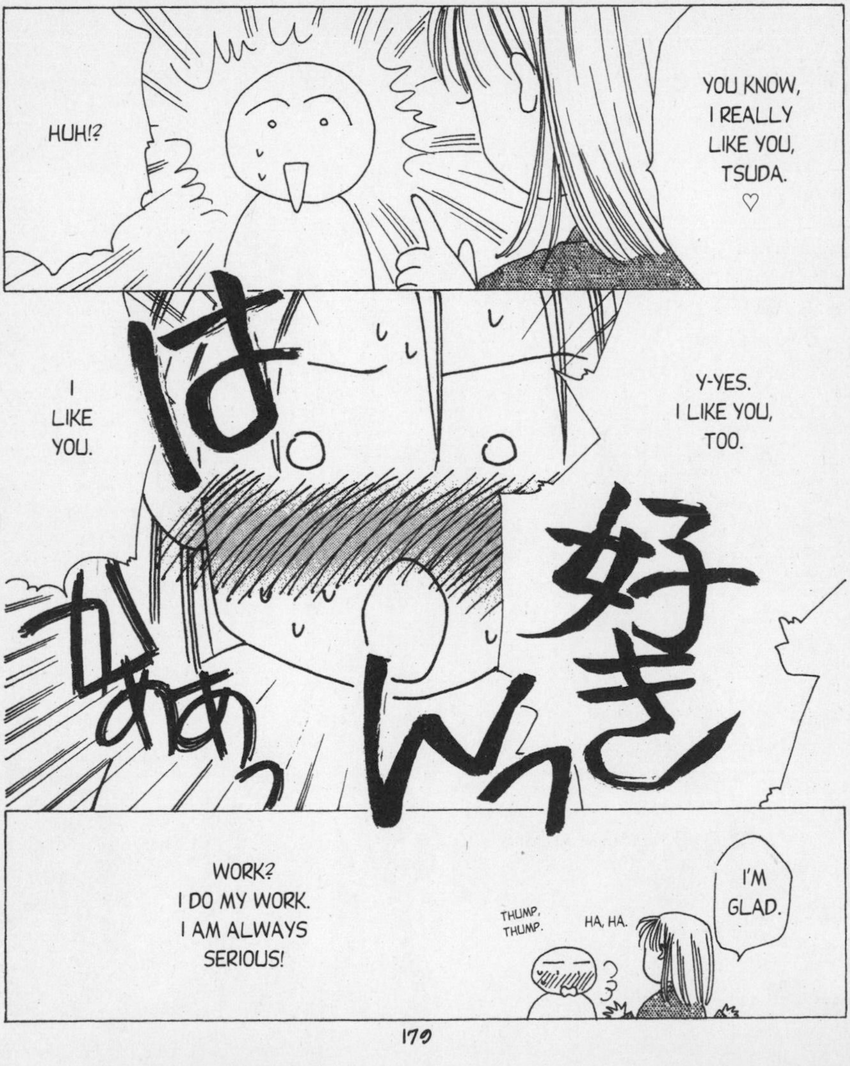
YOU KNOW, I REALLY LIKE YOU, TSUDA. ♡
HUH!?
Y-YES. I LIKE YOU, TOO.
I LIKE YOU.
好きぃっ
I'M GLAD.
HA, HA.
THUMP, THUMP.
WORK? I DO MY WORK. I AM ALWAYS SERIOUS!

DID YOU KNOW THAT A DAY IS REALLY 23 HOURS, 56 MINUTES, AND 4 SECONDS?

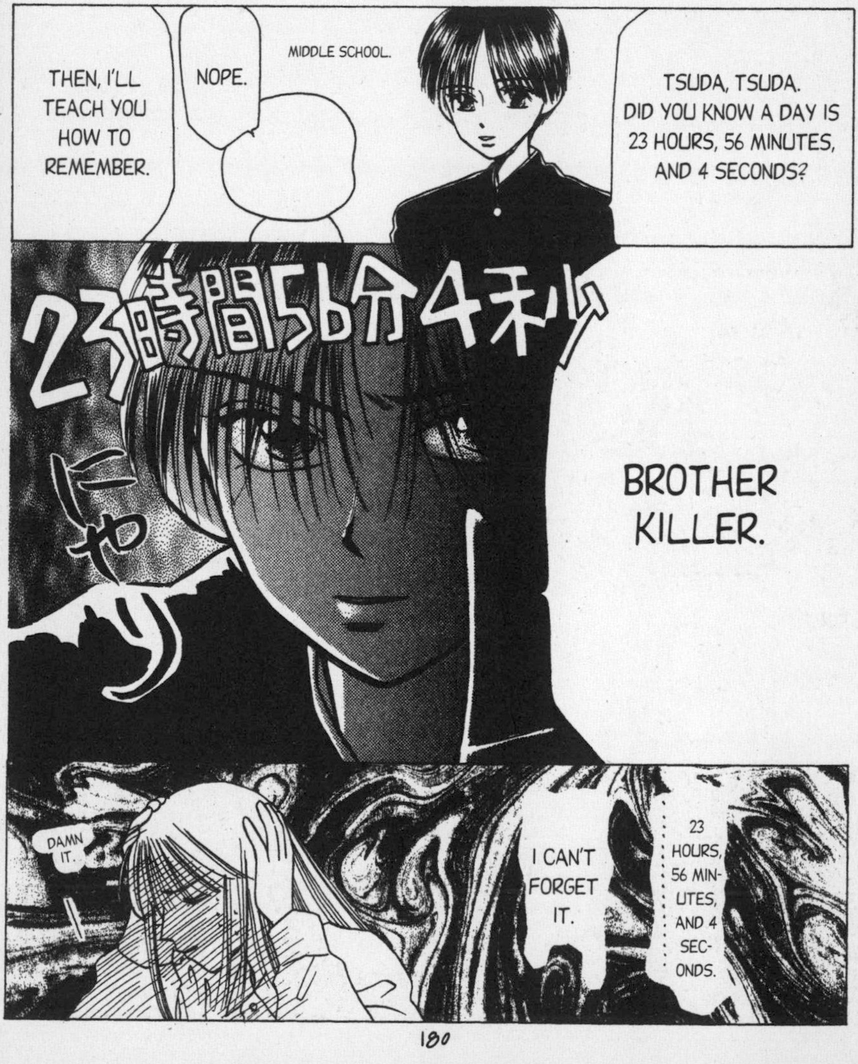
TSUDA, TSUDA. DID YOU KNOW A DAY IS 23 HOURS, 56 MINUTES, AND 4 SECONDS?
MIDDLE SCHOOL.
NOPE.
THEN, I'LL TEACH YOU HOW TO REMEMBER.
23時間56分4秒
BROTHER KILLER.
にやり
23 HOURS, 56 MIN-UTES, AND 4 SEC-ONDS.
I CAN'T FORGET IT.
DAMN IT.

DUNGEON OF MEMORIES 1...

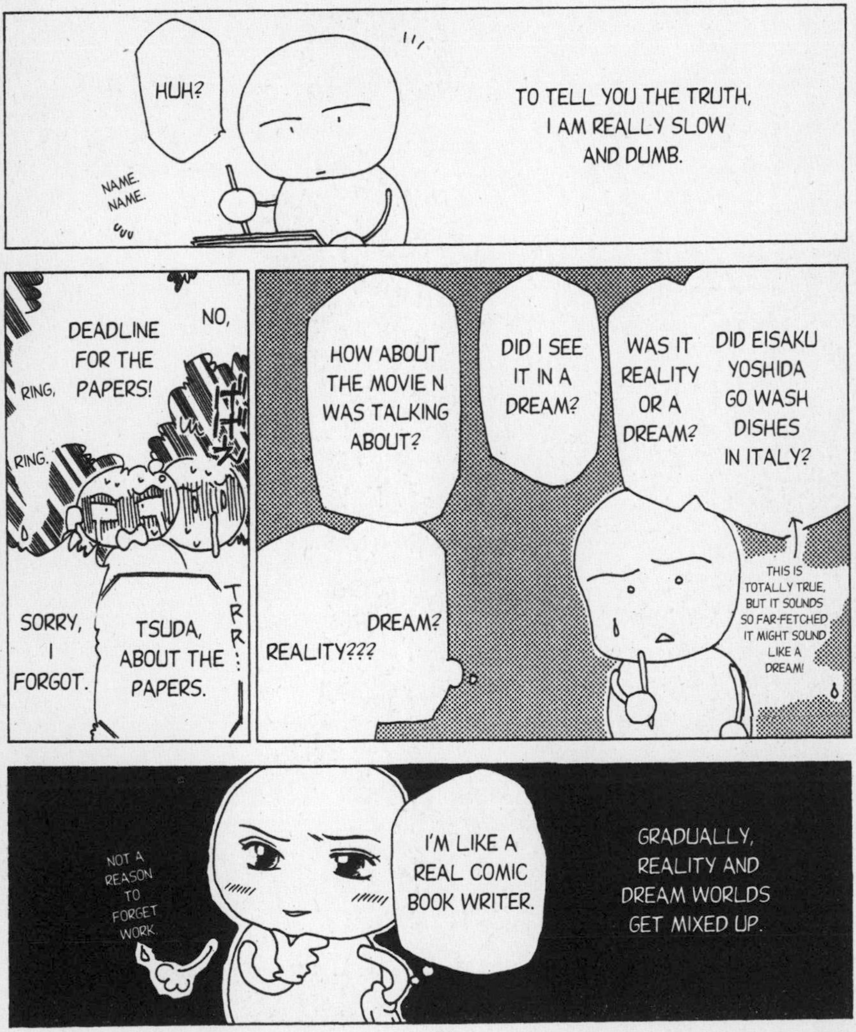
TO TELL YOU THE TRUTH, I AM REALLY SLOW AND DUMB.
HUH?
NAME. NAME.
DID EISAKU YOSHIDA GO WASH DISHES IN ITALY?
WAS IT REALITY OR A DREAM?
DID I SEE IT IN A DREAM?
HOW ABOUT THE MOVIE N WAS TALKING ABOUT?
THIS IS TOTALLY TRUE, BUT IT SOUNDS SO FAR-FETCHED IT MIGHT SOUND LIKE A DREAM!
DREAM?
REALITY???
NO,
DEADLINE FOR THE PAPERS!
RING, RING.
TRR...
TSUDA, ABOUT THE PAPERS.
SORRY, I FORGOT.
GRADUALLY, REALITY AND DREAM WORLDS GET MIXED UP.
I'M LIKE A REAL COMIC BOOK WRITER.
NOT A REASON TO FORGET WORK.

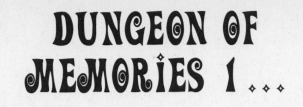

DUNGEON OF MEMORIES 2...

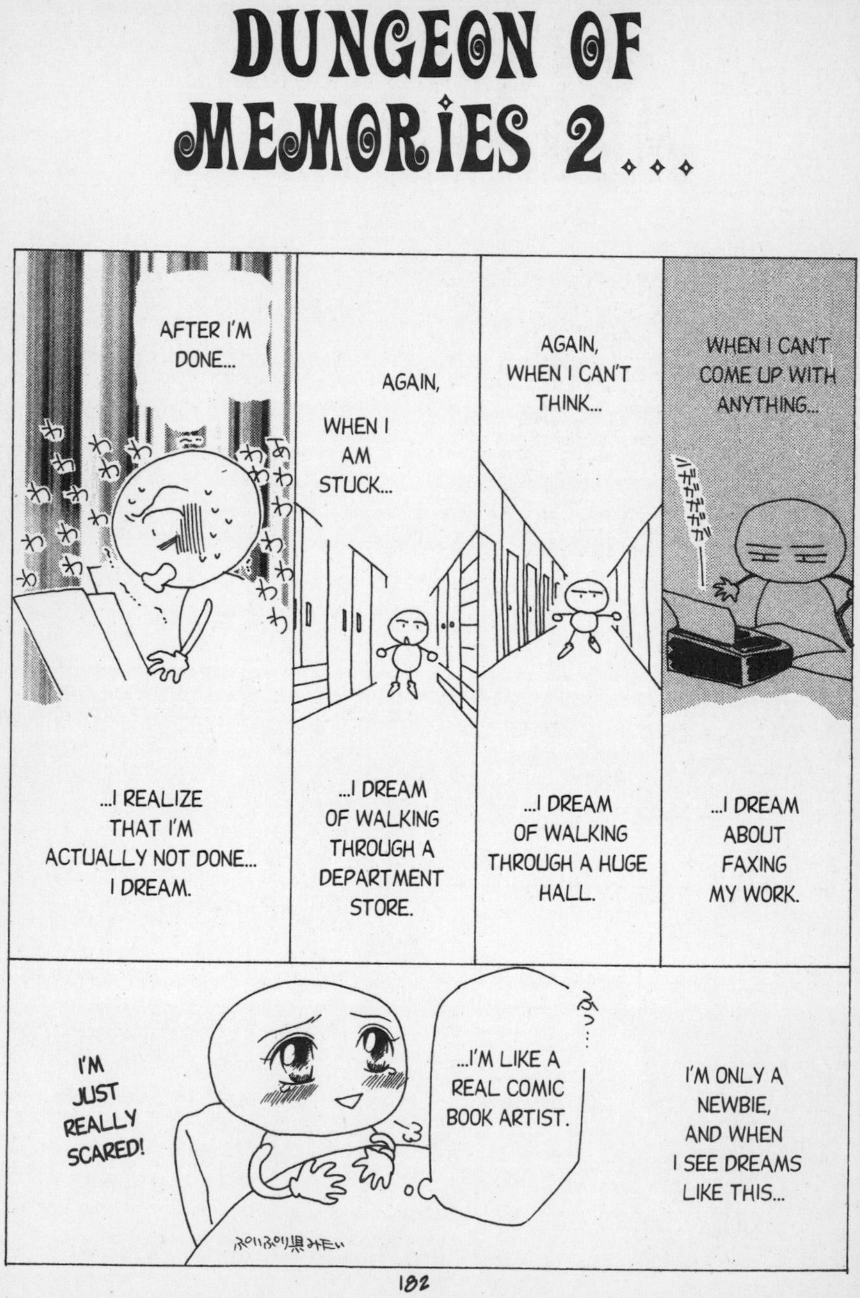

WHEN I CAN'T COME UP WITH ANYTHING...
...I DREAM ABOUT FAXING MY WORK.
AGAIN, WHEN I CAN'T THINK...
...I DREAM OF WALKING THROUGH A HUGE HALL.
AGAIN,
WHEN I AM STUCK...
...I DREAM OF WALKING THROUGH A DEPARTMENT STORE.
AFTER I'M DONE...
...I REALIZE THAT I'M ACTUALLY NOT DONE... I DREAM.
I'M ONLY A NEWBIE, AND WHEN I SEE DREAMS LIKE THIS...
...I'M LIKE A REAL COMIC BOOK ARTIST.
I'M JUST REALLY SCARED!

DUNGEON OF MEMORIES 3...

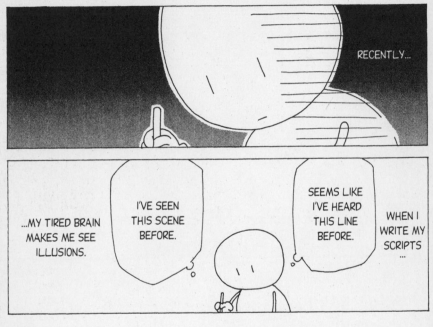

RECENTLY...

WHEN I WRITE MY SCRIPTS ...
SEEMS LIKE I'VE HEARD THIS LINE BEFORE.
I'VE SEEN THIS SCENE BEFORE.
...MY TIRED BRAIN MAKES ME SEE ILLUSIONS.

I MIGHT REALLY BE WRITING IT, THOUGH.

WHEN I SEE THOSE ILLUSIONS...

...I DON'T MIND WRITING ABOUT THEM.

SINCE THERE ARE READERS OUT THERE.

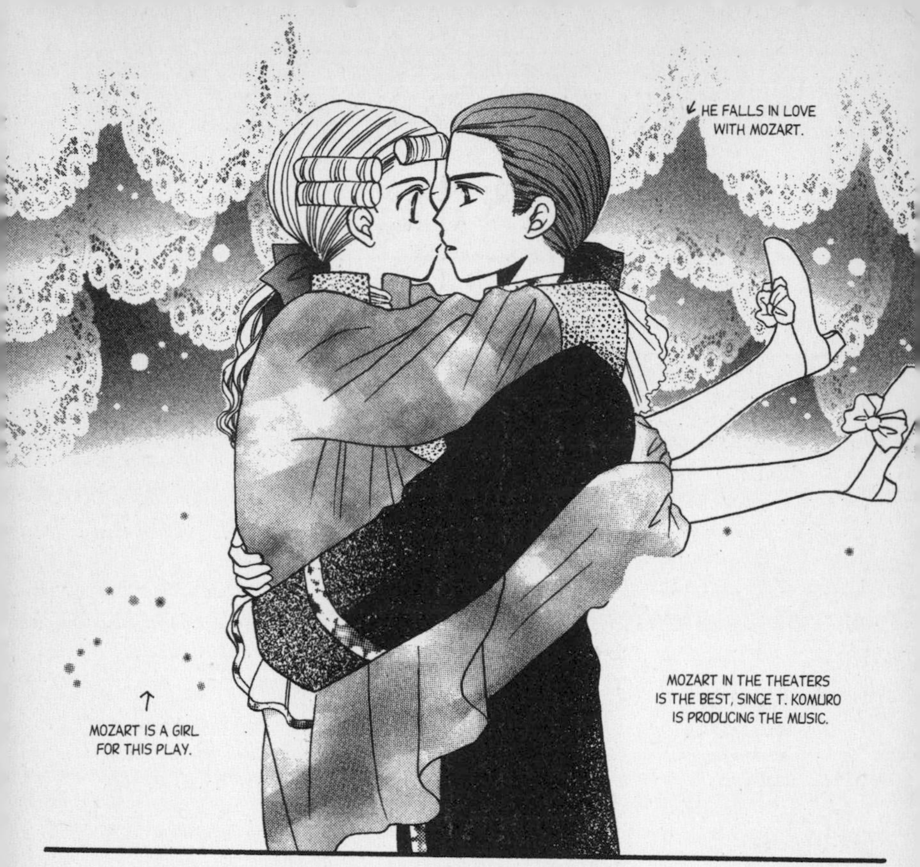
HE FALLS IN LOVE WITH MOZART.
MOZART IN THE THEATERS IS THE BEST, SINCE T. KOMURO IS PRODUCING THE MUSIC.
MOZART IS A GIRL FOR THIS PLAY.

I think opera and musicals are one of the best ways to express a story's feelings and emotions. This is because opera and musicals have dramatic stories, music, acting, and singing all together. I wish I had the ability to sing and dance. Nowadays, I'm really interested in actors and actresses. Their work is tough because they must become their characters at any time.

THANK YOU FOR THE LETTERS!

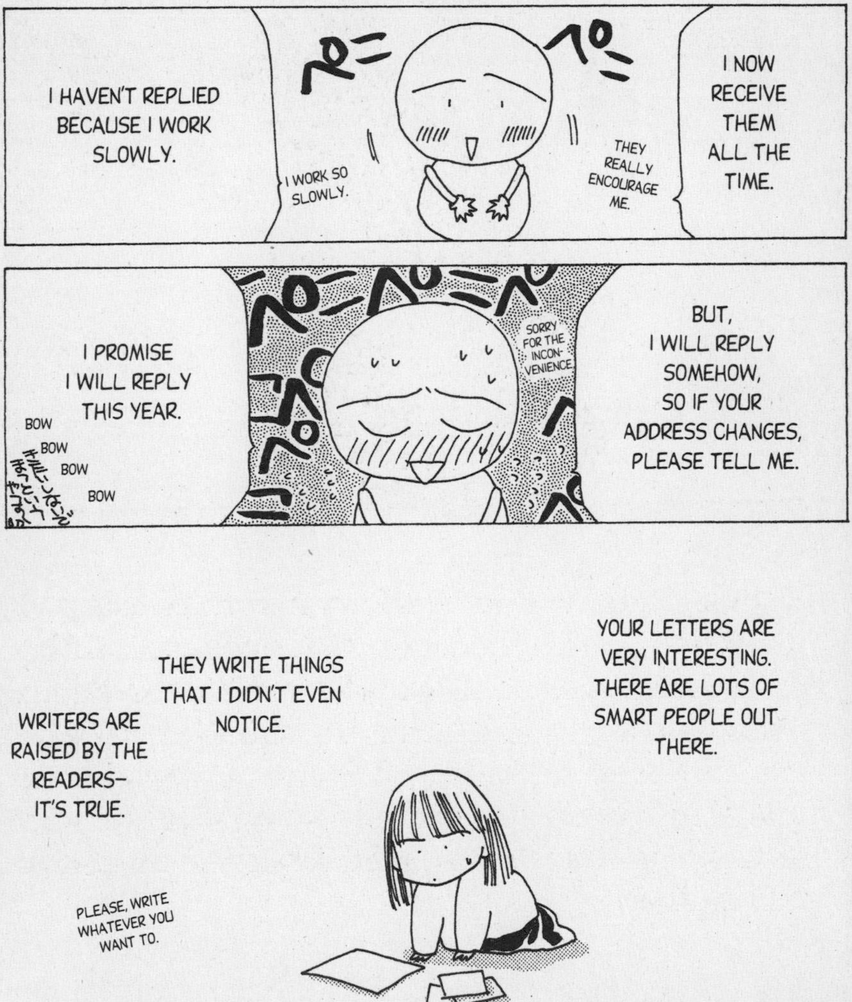
I NOW RECEIVE THEM ALL THE TIME.
THEY REALLY ENCOURAGE ME.
I WORK SO SLOWLY.
I HAVEN'T REPLIED BECAUSE I WORK SLOWLY.
BUT, I WILL REPLY SOMEHOW, SO IF YOUR ADDRESS CHANGES, PLEASE TELL ME.
SORRY FOR THE INCON-VENIENCE.
I PROMISE I WILL REPLY THIS YEAR.
BOW
BOW
BOW
BOW
YOUR LETTERS ARE VERY INTERESTING. THERE ARE LOTS OF SMART PEOPLE OUT THERE.
THEY WRITE THINGS THAT I DIDN'T EVEN NOTICE.
WRITERS ARE RAISED BY THE READERS— IT'S TRUE.
PLEASE, WRITE WHATEVER YOU WANT TO.

READER'S COMMENTS:

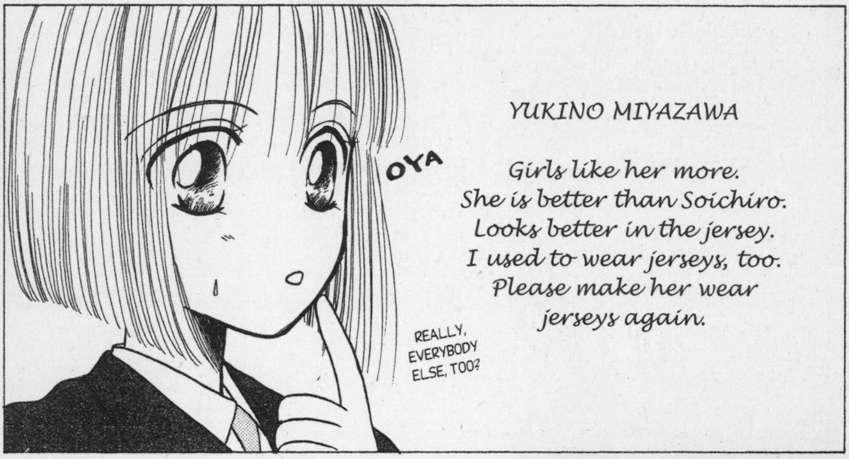
YUKINO MIYAZAWA
Girls like her more.
She is better than Soichiro.
Looks better in the jersey.
I used to wear jerseys, too.
Please make her wear jerseys again.
OYA
REALLY, EVERYBODY ELSE, TOO?

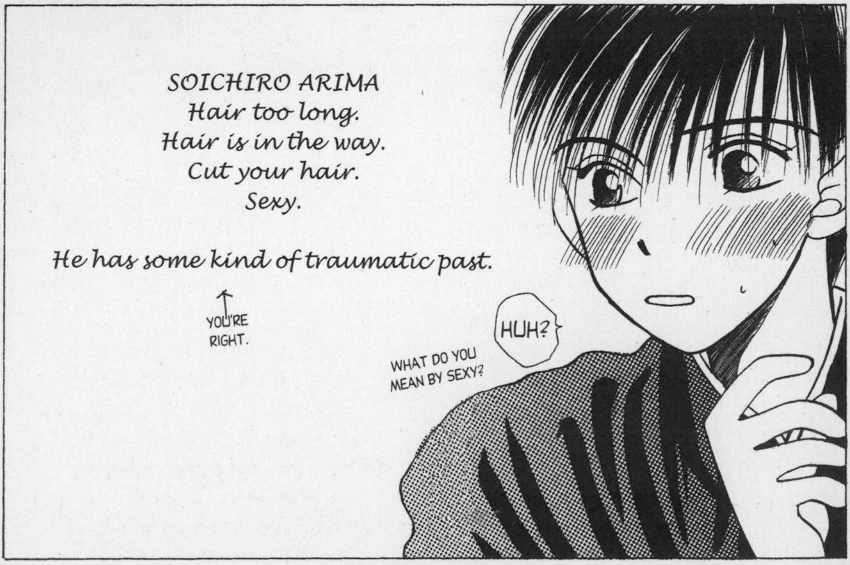
SOICHIRO ARIMA
Hair too long.
Hair is in the way.
Cut your hair.
Sexy.
He has some kind of traumatic past.
YOU'RE RIGHT.
HUH?
WHAT DO YOU MEAN BY SEXY?

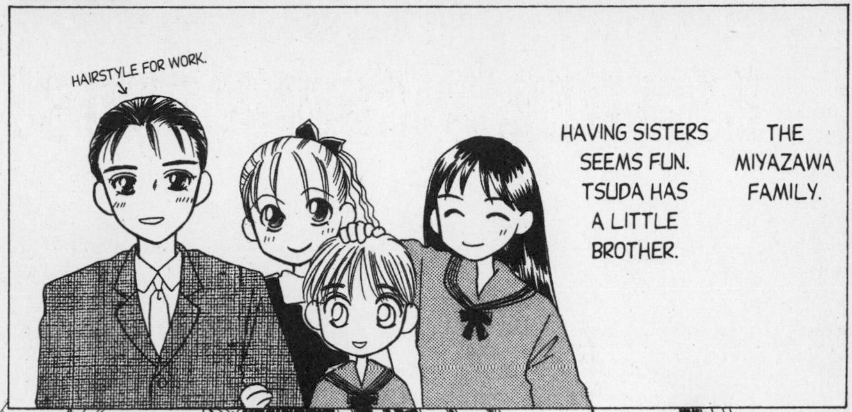
THE MIYAZAWA FAMILY.
HAVING SISTERS SEEMS FUN. TSUDA HAS A LITTLE BROTHER.
HAIRSTYLE FOR WORK.

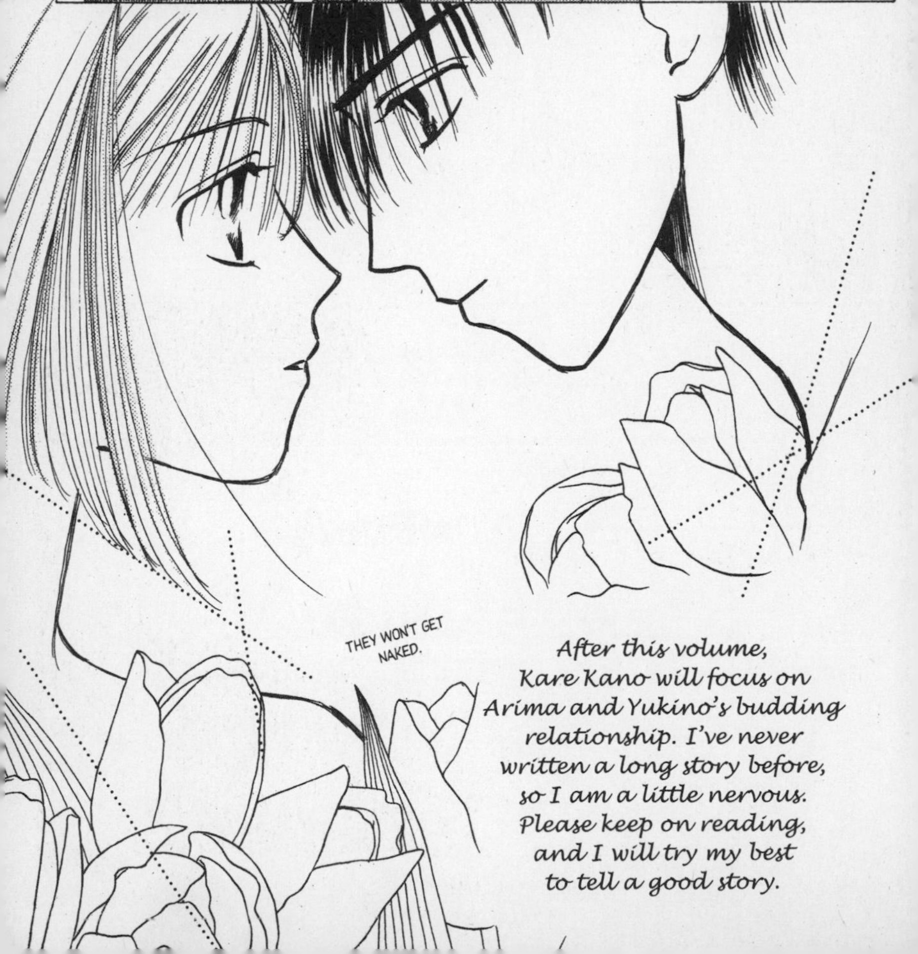
THEY WON'T GET NAKED.

After this volume, Kare Kano will focus on Arima and Yukino's budding relationship. I've never written a long story before, so I am a little nervous. Please keep on reading, and I will try my best to tell a good story.

I GUESS I'LL WRITE MORE COMICS.

Thank you and see you soon.

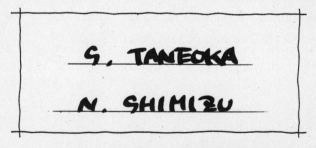

SPECIAL THANKS TO -

G. TANEOKA

N. SHIMIZU

THANK YOU SO MUCH. ♥

TSUDA DIARY / THE END

coming soon

kare kano

his and her circumstances

volume two

You know that couple who was obviously meant for each other, and everybody knew it, except them? That's Yukino and Soichiro, the two top students in school, who are capable of anything other than a normal relationship. Still, despite all they've been through, it seems they could finally be getting together. But now, the school's token pretty boy, Hideaki, is intent on wedging himself between them, for reasons they can't begin to imagine.

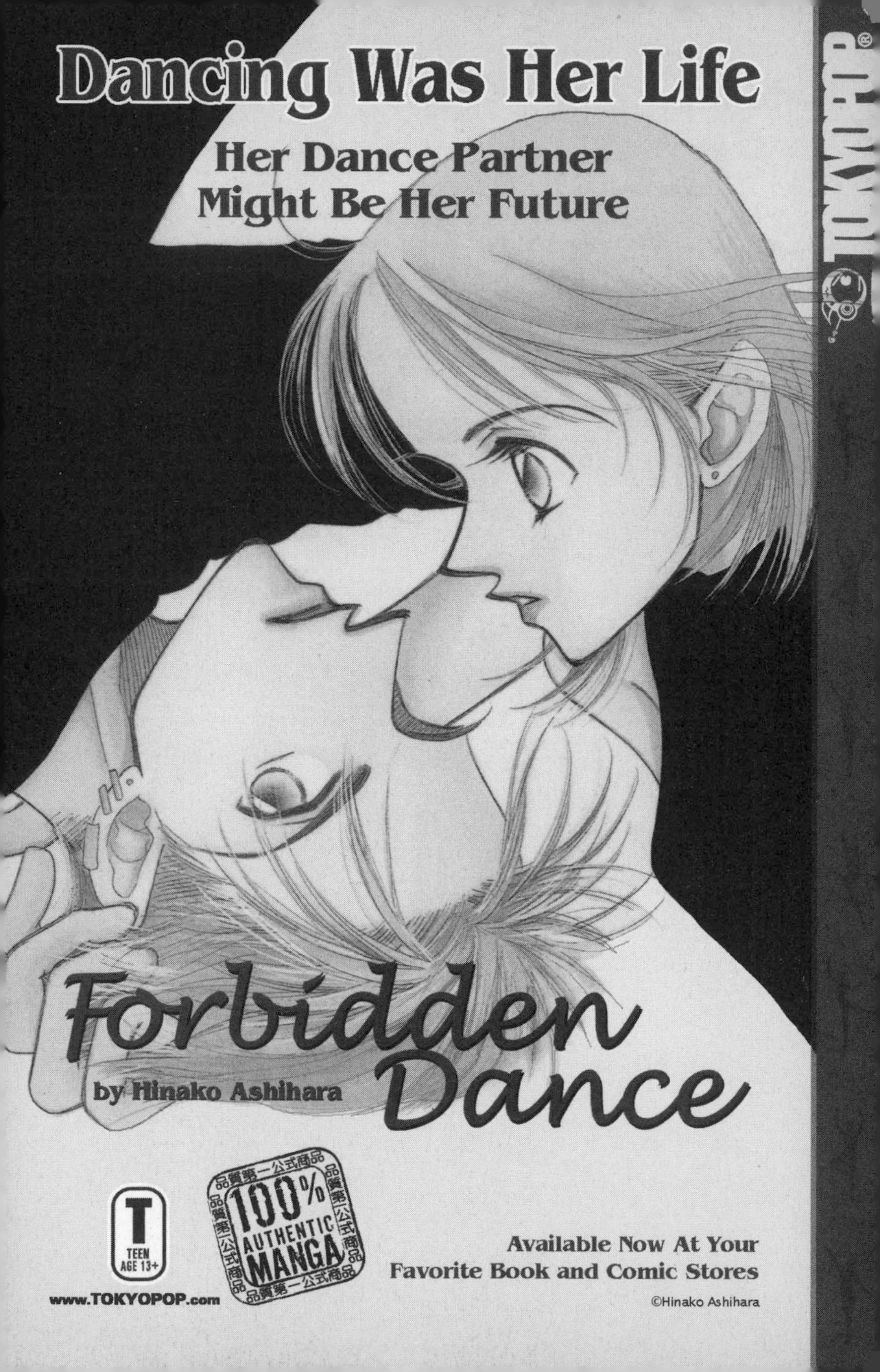
Dancing Was Her Life
Her Dance Partner Might Be Her Future
TOKYOPOP
Forbidden Dance
by Hinako Ashihara
T TEEN AGE 13+
100% AUTHENTIC MANGA
品質第一公式商品
Available Now At Your Favorite Book and Comic Stores
www.TOKYOPOP.com
©Hinako Ashihara

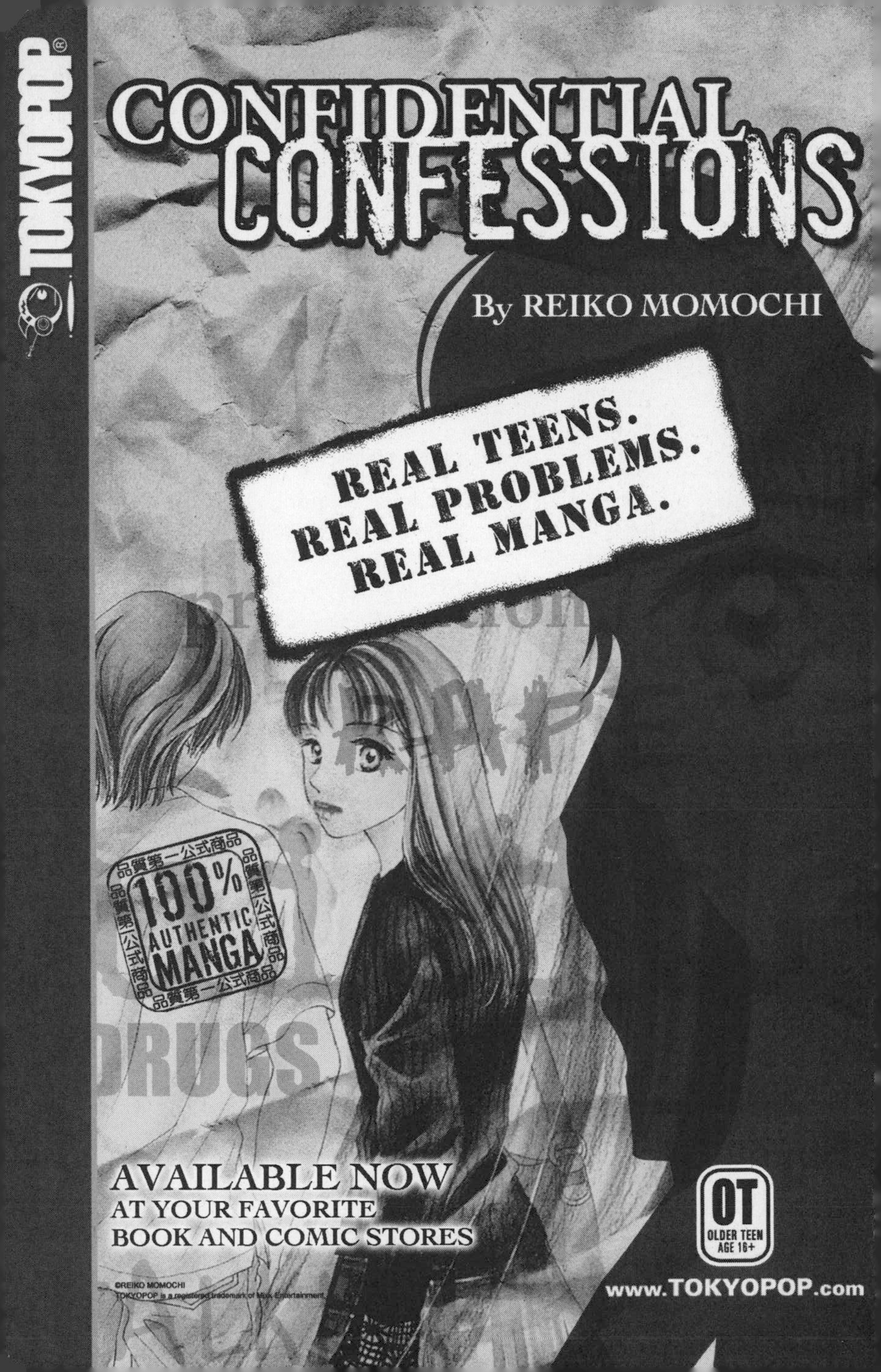
TOKYOPOP®
CONFIDENTIAL CONFESSIONS
By REIKO MOMOCHI
REAL TEENS.
REAL PROBLEMS.
REAL MANGA.
100% AUTHENTIC MANGA
品質第一公式商品
DRUGS
AVAILABLE NOW
AT YOUR FAVORITE
BOOK AND COMIC STORES
OT
OLDER TEEN
AGE 16+
©REIKO MOMOCHI
TOKYOPOP is a registered trademark of Mixx Entertainment
www.TOKYOPOP.com

STOP!

This is the back of the book.
You wouldn't want to spoil a great ending!

This book is printed "manga-style," in the authentic Japanese right-to-left format. Since none of the artwork has been flipped or altered, readers get to experience the story just as the creator intended. You've been asking for it, so TOKYOPOP® delivered: authentic, hot-off-the-press, and far more fun!

DIRECTIONS

If this is your first time reading manga-style, here's a quick guide to help you understand how it works.

It's easy... just start in the top right panel and follow the numbers. Have fun, and look for more 100% authentic manga from TOKYOPOP®!